INSTRUCTOR'S RESOURCE MANUAL
Dale N. Shook
Saratoga Center for Education and Development

MARKETING MANAGEMENT
Eleventh Edition

Philip Kotler

Pearson
Education

Upper Saddle River, New Jersey 07458

Acquisitions editor: Wendy Craven
Assistant editor: Melissa Pellerano
Production editor: Wanda Rockwell
Manufacturer: Courier (Bookmart Press, Inc.)

ISBN 0-13-009437-4

10 9 8 7 6 5 4 3 2

Instructor's Resource Manual

Dale N. Shook

To Accompany Philip Kotler, *Marketing Management*, 11th Edition, Prentice Hall, 2002

TABLE OF CONTENTS

PREFACE 1

TEACHING OPTIONS 2

Philosophy 2

Organization 2

Teaching Materials 3

Putting it all Together 3

SUGGESTED COURSE ORGANIZATION AND SYLLABI: 4

1. Course Background and Syllabus for a Project-oriented Course 4
2. Course Background and Syllabus for a Case/Lecture-oriented Course 10
3. Course Background and Syllabus for an Applications-oriented Course 30

COMPLETE TEXT AND IRM OUTLINE 36

CHAPTER-BY-CHAPTER INSTRUCTIONAL MATERIAL 41

Part I–Understanding Marketing Management

Chapter 1: Defining Marketing for the Twenty-first Century 42

Chapter 2: Adapting Marketing to the New Economy 60

Chapter 3: Building Customer Satisfaction, Value, and Retention 73

Part II–Analyzing Marketing Opportunities

Chapter 4: Winning Markets Through Market-Oriented Strategic Planning 84

Chapter 5: Gathering Information and Measuring Market Demand 98

Chapter 6: Scanning the Marketing Environment 111

Chapter 7: Analyzing Consumer Markets and Buyer Behavior 129

Chapter 8: Analyzing Business Markets and Business Buying Behavior 141

Chapter 9: Dealing with the Competition 154

Chapter 10: Identifying Market Segments and Selecting Target Markets 169

Part III–Developing Market Strategies

Chapter 11: Positioning and Differentiating the Market Offering Through the Product Life Cycle 180

Chapter 12: Developing New Market Offerings 196

Chapter 13: Designing Global Market Offerings 209

Part IV–Shaping the Market Offering

Chapter 14: Setting the Product and Branding Strategy 225

Chapter 15: Designing and Managing Services 245

Chapter 16: Developing Price Strategies and Programs 255

Part V–Managing and Delivering Marketing Programs

Chapter 17: Designing and Managing Value Networks and Marketing Channels 273

Chapter 18: Managing Retailing, Wholesaling, and Market Logistics 284

Chapter 19: Managing Integrated Marketing Communications 300

Chapter 20: Managing Advertising, Sales Promotion, Public Relations, and Direct Marketing 310

Chapter 21: Managing the Sales Force 332

Chapter 22: Managing the Total Marketing Effort 343

Preface

The Instructor's Resource Manual (IRM) for Philip Kotler, *Marketing Management*, 11th edition, interacts with the text to provide various resource modules for the instructor and the student. Beginning with this edition, the IRM integrates all of the teaching materials, based on teaching approach and on a chapter-by-chapter basis. The result is that the instructor has everything needed for daily operation of the course, all in one convenient location, utilizing a *daily planner* approach. There is no more scrambling between different course materials to put together the next class meeting. All the IRM materials match sequentially with the text and the teaching approach to minimize organization for the course and maximize the time available to concentrate on course content.

As you may have noticed in the Kotler text, there are various integrated analytical and application materials available to enhance student critical thinking and the ability to evaluate and apply marketing strategies and tools. The teaching tools available in the package include: *Chapter Overviews, Learning and Teaching Objectives, Chapter Outlines, Marketing and Advertising, Online Marketing Today, You're the Marketer: Sonic PDA Marketing Plan, Marketing Spotlight,* and *Application Exercises,* along with complete *Suggested Lectures* for every chapter. All these materials incorporate and apply the concepts and content of the text. You will find it easy to experiment with these tools to identify the most appropriate teaching methods and materials.

The IRM "daily planner" approach also enables advance course planning, including a complete outline of the course, a complete course syllabus, along with answers for all the applications activities and exercises. The broad range of options available will provide you and the students with a wide selection of teaching and learning options, from general to highly focused.

As noted above, the material for each chapter is organized as follows:

- *Chapter Overview*: A summarization of the major points emphasized in the corresponding Kotler text chapter.
- *Learning/Teaching Objectives*: Objectives that blend with and complement the Kotler text learning objectives.
- *Chapter Outline*: A detailed topic/sentence outline to provide an overall framework to determine when and how to utilize the suggested lectures and/or other support materials.
- *Suggested Lectures*: Complete lectures that can also serve as a starting point for the instructor's own personal lecture material. The suggested lectures can also provide structure for a class discussion around key issues.
- *Marketing and Advertising*: Contemporary advertising examples, with discussion and analysis in an applications context. BONUS examples provided—Ads on Website only.
- *Online Marketing Today*: A focus on firms in the Internet marketing environment, evaluating the present and future of this important new area of marketing.
- *You're the Marketer: Sonic PDA Marketing Plan*: Development of a strategic marketing plan for a firm. Brings the course material together in a decision-oriented package and creates the basis for preparation of student marketing plans.
- *Marketing Spotlight*: Short company case analyses that provide themes and specific content to augment the text and other course materials.
- *Application Exercises*: A computer-based blend of theory, concepts and applications, utilizing applied technical marketing research tools.

The Kotler text and the IRM provide an unprecedented set of tools for teaching marketing management. They can be applied to a wide variety of classroom situations. The text and IRM can effectively support graduate marketing management and strategy courses, upper division undergraduate courses or an executive/management marketing seminar. No matter whether the course or seminar is taught on a quarter, semester or year-long basis, the Kotler text and the IRM will provide you with the tools necessary to augment your own knowledge of the important and growing field of marketing management.

Teaching Options

Philosophy

The marketing management course can be taught effectively in many ways, helping to spark interest in those students who will make marketing their career as well as providing essential fundamentals for those students with other nonmarketing interests. In developing your course, you should consider the kind of orientation with which you are most comfortable, whether more academic or more applied, along with various means for bringing students to a better understanding of the material in each chapter. We have tried to make the IRM both complete and flexible, providing enough materials to make the course one where you may focus on a minimal number of chapters in the text, every chapter, or something in between. Our intention is to provide an array of resources so that your options are virtually unlimited.

In actually setting up your course, you must decide how to best use the Kotler text and all the possible supplements to meet your teaching goals with students. A large number of different possible course configurations could be chosen. Perhaps your most important decisions involve: 1) what students should do outside the classroom versus inside the classroom; 2) how much work students should do individually versus in groups; and 3) how much of the text is used versus how many (and what kinds of) supplementary materials are used. The challenge is how to utilize your interests and abilities throughout the term so that you can best engage your students to maximize the learning opportunities that you provide and are afforded by the extensive Kotler materials.

Organization

In terms of course organization, marketing management is typically run as a project course, a lecture/case course, a lecture/exercise course, or as some combination of the three. Each of the three major course structures are reviewed below, followed by a discussion of the teaching materials available to you and a sample syllabus for each of the course organization options:

1.	A *project course* uses a major project to focus learning. For example, a project course could be based on honing skills to create and critique marketing plans, e.g., by employing the Marketing PlanPro software. With this type of project course, some aspects of each class could at least touch upon how the particular topics from that section of the text applied to marketing plans, culminating with a final marketing plan produced at the end of the term. Other possible projects could involve conducting a marketing audit or running a company as part of the Brandmaps simulation game. Project courses typically involve group work among students and written and/or oral presentations.

2.	A *lecture/case course* could use the Harvard Business School cases suggested in this manual or cases from other sources. Students could be made responsible for write-ups—in groups or individually—as well as short in-class presentations. Cases could alternate with lectures each week.

3.	A *lecture/exercise course* could use the Application Exercises for Marketing Management where students could again work individually or in groups and be responsible for written and/or oral presentations (student materials and spreadsheets can be found on the Kotler Web site). Class discussion could focus on the text and different sequences of the applications materials provided at the end of each chapter (discussed below).

Regardless of which basic structure is employed, class sessions may build off either the text and/or the other available supplements in various ways to stimulate student learning and cover other topics. The course can be built almost entirely around the text—the IRM provides you with that capability. Each session can be devoted to a particular chapter or set of chapters. The next section reviews the possible teaching materials that could be brought into those class discussions.

Teaching Materials

The IRM provides you with substantial additional descriptive and conceptual material bearing on each chapter. The Kotler text includes much end-of-chapter material. In terms of using the book, in addition to assigned readings, students could be made responsible to prepare written analysis for the end-of-chapter application exercises (answers to the exercises in the text are provided in the IRM).

For a project course, students could follow the Sonic marketing plan exercises all the way through the book. Developing a marketing plan is a key marketing skill that such a project scheme would facilitate. For more lecture/case or lecture/exercise course material, students could analyze the marketing and advertising and/or the online marketing today exercises. Given their topical nature, these two series lend themselves particularly well to group work, as students would have the opportunity to debate among themselves. In this case, all groups could prepare short write-ups and one or perhaps several groups could present their analysis to the entire class and respond to critiques. This feature could be formalized at the beginning or end of each class as a "marketing application exercise."

A key element of virtually any course is media, and the Kotler package offers a comprehensive set of videos as well as a video guide that explains how they can be used to provide a rich multimedia experience for students. A set of recently-filmed custom videos on seven key companies provides valuable contemporary perspectives.

To provide even more application to the course, you could go beyond the Kotler package and provide various assignments and exercises that could include trips to company marketing departments or advertising agencies, marketing research projects, student marketing ventures, guest speakers, etc. In this context, the text provides the unifying element behind the diversity of assignments. The students can be held responsible for reading the text, raising questions and responding in depth. In this setting, the text remains the focal point of the course, but it also provides grist for many applied activities that will reduce the student transition from classroom to the challenging world of professional marketing.

Transparency masters and/or PowerPoint presentations also exist to facilitate the integration of text material into the class sessions. Exam questions provide a convenient means of testing student comprehension of course material. For instructors desiring to emphasize more academic content, a number of popular readings from books and magazine/journal articles are listed below and with each chapter. These readings allow students to explore various topics in depth and observe how marketing experts and commentators analyze marketing problems.

Putting It All Together

The myriad teaching materials offered with the Kotler text ensures that your students will receive state-of-the-art learning both in terms of concepts and methods. You should mix and match the various pieces to make sure that students gain the breadth and depth of knowledge you desire. The Kotler text provides a firm foundation for essential concepts and examples. The supplements help to "bring the text to life" through stimulating assignments. You can set up your course in terms of lectures, projects, cases, and exercises as you see fit and capitalize on the wealth of supplementary material available to develop a rich, engaging, and challenging course.

To start this process, you will find complete a syllabus and support materials below for each of the teaching approaches outlined above (project, case, and application). Following the syllabi, there is a complete outline of the materials available to teach the course. The outline includes both the text materials as well as those in the IRM, so that you can readily identify everything available to you, on a day-to-day basis.

Suggested Course Organization and Syllabi

1. *Course Background and Syllabus for a Project-oriented Course*

Background: Project/Company/Product Analysis Assignments

The project-oriented activity in the course can bring more active involvement with the local business community and/or better understanding of various marketing concepts in a business setting. Each student and/or team will select a company and one of the firm's products. The students then become the class experts on the product, the company, and the industry in which it operates. Student should be encouraged to look up articles about that company and industry in *Business Week, Forbes, Fortune, The Wall Street Journal, Marketing Communications, Media-Scope* and/or *Advertising Age*. If possible, the students should visit or correspond with the company, contact distributors or agents, and discuss the product with actual or potential users. The students can use the text-based "You're the Marketer: Sonic PDA Marketing Plan" and the "Systematic Marketing Audit" in the Kotler text as guides for the project. The audit and the Sonic PDA Marketing Plan will provide the basis for either presentations and/or a paper that analyzes and evaluates the marketing program of the chosen company and product. You could grade the effort based on the following criteria:

- Use of analytical marketing concepts to analyze the company and its products
- Degree to which information was sought and attained
- Quality of critique of company's marketing program
- Quality of suggestions for future marketing
- Quality of writing

Sample Course Syllabus—Project-oriented Course

Syllabus
Marketing Management
Xxx Semester, 200x

Course Materials:
Text: Philip Kotler, *Marketing Management*, 11ᵗʰ ed., Prentice Hall, 2002,
    Marketing Applications Exercises (Kotler Website)
Recommended: *Fortune, The Wall Street Journal,* and *Business Week*

Course Description: (university bulletin)
The characteristics and management of markets are described in topics that include the marketing environment, components of the marketing mix, market segmentation, and planning. Prerequisite: (university/college/school/department regulations).

Course Perspectives:
The course focuses on formulating and implementing marketing management strategies and policies, a task undertaken in most companies at the strategic business unit level. The marketing management process is important at all levels of the organization, regardless of the title applied to the activity. Typically, it is called corporate marketing, strategic marketing, or marketing management. For our purposes they all involve essentially the same process, even though the actors and activities may differ. The course will provide you with a systematic framework for understanding marketing management and strategy. Accordingly, the course emphasizes the following:

- Primary and changing perspectives on marketing management in the New Economy

- The impact of interactive media on marketing management

- Applied marketing management and strategy, domestic, and global

- An international focus in developing marketing management and strategy

The course is intended for:
- Marketing concentration students who wish to deepen their understanding of marketing management in a strategy-planning context
- Nonmarketing concentration students who desire a course in marketing strategy, with a management and planning orientation

Course Objectives/Goals/Learning Objectives/Format:

Course Objectives: This course is concerned with the development, evaluation, and implementation of marketing management in complex environments. The course deals primarily with an in-depth analysis of a variety of concepts, theories, facts, analytical procedures, techniques, and models. The course addresses strategic issues such as: What business should we be in? What are our long-term objectives? What is our sustainable marketing competitive advantage? Should we diversify? How? How should marketing resources be allocated? What marketing opportunities and threats do we face? What are our marketing organizational strengths and weaknesses? What are our marketing strategic alternatives?

Course Goals: To further develop knowledge and skills in the essential aspects of marketing management, marketing strategy, and emerging New Economy marketing applications, with a focus on the development and execution of programs, audits, and plans.

Learning Objectives:
- To become familiar with the range of decisions implicit in strategic marketing management and planning, and to develop skill in using a variety of analytical frameworks for making such decisions
- To develop an understanding of how markets contrast in terms of:

- Their "enduring characteristics"
- Their stage of development and how the nature of competition in such markets is impacted

- To develop skills in planning a variety of marketing management tools, ranging from new product entry strategy to international market product life cycle management and strategy

- To develop skill in organizing for effective strategic marketing and in implementing the market planning process

Course Format: The course is highly interactive between the class and the instructor. Through case studies/presentations, problems, and specific company client activities, students will have the opportunity to use the concepts, ideas, and strategies presented in class. Problem-solving sessions occur in both individual (primarily) and team (occasionally) settings.

Grading/Evaluation Criteria

Overview: The final grade will be based on the following: a team-prepared company/organization marketing audit, two exams, and an individually-based five-year strategic product marketing plan.

Activity	Percent
Exams	40
Marketing Audit	20
Marketing Plan	30
Participation	10
Total	100

- ***Exams:*** Comprehensive—Each exam will be in essay form and will cover all assigned readings and class discussions.

- ***Projects:*** To implement the project theme areas and the projects, all students must submit detailed resumes within three (3) days from the time you receive this syllabus. This is required and will be the basis for team assignments and project choices. The grades on these project activities will be based on both content and writing ability. In addition, you will be evaluated on meeting the learning objectives of the course. The instructor reserves the right to reject and/or modify any project selection. All project choices must exhibit "new" thinking and application.

  - ***Project 1— Marketing Audit (Team)*** The marketing audit is a team activity for an existing product or service of a multi-business and multi-product firm. The follow-up to the audit is a written strategic marketing management analysis of the same company that will indicate product acceptance by the target market segments and the promotional efforts necessary to stimulate the various segments to buy the concept and/or product.

  - ***Project 2—Five Year Marketing Plan (Individual)*** Develop a written five year strategic marketing management plan focused on one business unit of the same company. The plan will cover all critical areas for a five-year marketing plan, with marketing management the focal point. Specific theme topic areas (each student selects one) will apply to the product and company but provide a broader perspective as well:

    - Product/Service "Positioning" in an era of hyper change

    - Marketing management analysis and plan for a product(s) in specific stages of the PLC

    - Marketing management and strategic market forecasting on a shoestring

6

- Market forecasting: science or art? (could draw on the course Applications Exercises)
- Market(ing) and marketing management changes for the next decade
- Role of various political and economic organizations (domestic and global) impacting the marketing process in coming years

- *Class Participation*—There will be case, reading discussions, and analyses. You will be expected to respond orally to questions. Responses will be graded on a five (5) point scale, ranging from highly analytical (from a content perspective) to clear lack of knowledge of the material.

Course Outline

- Project Emphasis
- 12–15 week format

Week

PART I—UNDERSTANDING MARKETING MANAGEMENT

1   CHAPTER 1—DEFINING MARKETING FOR THE TWENTY-FIRST CENTURY

Lecture: "Marketing Enters the Twenty-first Century"
Marketing and Advertising—T.J. Maxx, Nexen, People Soft (BONUS)
Marketing Spotlight—GE
Application Exercise— Index Numbers

2   CHAPTER 2—ADAPTING MARKETING TO THE NEW ECONOMY
Lecture: E-Marketing and the Airlines
Online Marketing Today—Hewlett-Packard
CHAPTER 3—BUILDING CUSTOMER SATISFACTION, VALUE, AND RETENTION
Lecture: "Creating Customer Relationships That Last"
Marketing Spotlight—Charles Schwab
Application Exercise—Buying Power Index (BPI)

PART II—ANALYZING MARKET OPPORTUNITIES

3   CHAPTER 4—WINNING MARKETS THROUGH MARKET-ORIENTED STRATEGIC PLANNING
Lecture: "Establishing a Winning Strategic Planning Formula"
Online Marketing Today—Procter & Gamble
You're the Marketer: Sonic PDA Marketing Plan
Application Exercise—Brand/Category Development Index (BDI/CDI) Numbers
CHAPTER 6—SCANNING THE MARKETING ENVIRONMENT
Lecture: "The Marketing Environment Takes a Turn—An Older Turn"
You're the Marketer: Sonic PDA Marketing Plan
Marketing Spotlight—Mattel

4   CHAPTER 5—GATHERING INFORMATION AND MEASURING MARKET DEMAND
Lecture: "Marketing Research and Measurement at the Millennium"
You're the MarketerSonic PDA Marketing Plan
Application Exercise—Buying Power Index (BPI)

5   CHAPTER 7—ANALYZING CONSUMER MARKETS AND BUYING BEHAVIOR
Lecture: "Consumer Concerns"
Marketing and Advertising—Quaker, BlackBerry
You're the Marketer: Sonic PDA Marketing Plan
Marketing Spotlight—Nike
CHAPTER 8—ANALYZING BUSINESS MARKETS AND BUSINESS BUYING BEHAVIOR
Lecture—"Business Marketing in a Changing Global Environment"
Online Marketing Today—Bayer
You're the Marketer: Sonic PDA Marketing Plan
Marketing Spotlight—Branding Energy

6   CHAPTER 9—DEALING WITH THE COMPETITION
        Lecture: "Competitive Intelligence"
        Marketing and Advertising—Surf, Listerine
        Marketing Spotlight—Microsoft
        Application Exercise—Specialized Buying Power Indexes
        CHAPTER 10—IDENTIFYING MARKET SEGMENTS AND SELECTING MARKET
        TARGETS
        Lecture: "Understanding Market Segments"
        You're the Marketer: Sonic PDA Marketing Plan
        Marketing Spotlight—Marriott International
        PART III—DEVELOPING MARKETING STRATEGIES
7   CHAPTER 11—POSITIONING THE MARKET OFFERING THROUGH THE PLC
        Lecture: "Product Positioning in the New Economy"
        Online Marketing Today—eBay
        You're the Marketer: Sonic PDA Marketing Plan
        Marketing Spotlight—Monsanto Company
        CHAPTER 12—DEVELOPING NEW MARKET OFFERINGS
        Lecture: "Developing New Products: When and How?"
        Online Marketing Today—Intuit
        You're the Marketer: Sonic PDA Marketing Plan
8   CHAPTER 13—DESIGNING AND MANAGING GLOBAL MARKETING
        STRATEGIES
        Lecture: "Making Decisions in a Complicated International Marketplace"
        Online Marketing Today—Reebok
        You're the Marketer: Sonic PDA Marketing Plan
        Marketing Spotlight—Coca-Cola
        PART IV—SHAPING THE MARKET OFFERING
        CHAPTER 15—DESIGNING AND MANAGING SERVICES
        Lecture: "Services Marketing in the Twenty-first Century"
        You're the Marketer: Sonic PDA Marketing Plan
        Marketing Spotlight—Merrill Lynch
9   CHAPTER 14—SETTING THE PRODUCT AND BRANDING STRATEGY
        Lecture: "Reinventing Products and Companies"
        You're the Marketer: Sonic PDA Marketing Plan
        Marketing Spotlight—Anheuser-Busch
        CHAPTER 16—DESIGNING PRICING STRATEGIES AND PROGRAMS
        Lecture: "Measuring the Impact of Price—How Important Is the Pricing Variable"
        Online Marketing Today—Priceline.com
        You're the Marketer: Sonic PDA Marketing Plan
        Marketing Spotlight: Louis Vuitton Moet Hennessey (LVMH)
        PART V—MANAGING AND DELIVERING MARKETING PROGRAMS
10   CHAPTER 17—DESIGNING AND MANAGING VALUE NETWORKS AND
        MARKETING CHANNELS
        Lecture: "Measuring Channel Performance"
        You're the Marketer: Sonic PDA Marketing Plan
        CHAPTER 18—MANAGING RETAILING, WHOLESALING, MARKET LOGISTICS
        Lecture: "Retailing versus E-tailing"
        You're the Marketer: Sonic PDA Marketing Plan
        Marketing Spotlight—Wal-Mart
11   CHAPTER 19—DESIGNING AND MANAGING INTEGRATED MARKETING
        COMMUNICATIONS
        Lecture: "Marketing Communications: Key Tool in an Uncontrollable Environment"
        You're the Marketer: Sonic PDA Marketing Plan
        Marketing Spotlight—Mountain Dew Code Red
        CHAPTER 20—MANAGING ADVERTISING, SALES PROMOTION, PR AND
        DIRECT MARKETING
        Lecture: "Advertising in the New Economy"
        You're the Marketer: Sonic PDA Marketing Plan

12   CHAPTER 21—MANAGING THE SALES FORCE
      Lecture: "The Death and Rebirth of the Salesperson"
      You're the Marketer: Sonic PDA Marketing Plan
      Marketing Spotlight—Oracle
      CHAPTER 22—MANAGING THE TOTAL MARKETING EFFORT
      Lecture: "Reorganizing Marketing Management—Media Neutrality"
      You're the Marketer: Sonic PDA Marketing Plan

2.___ *Course Background and Syllabus for a Case/Lecture-oriented Course*

Background: Case Analysis and Case Selection

If you choose to focus on cases and lectures in the course, selecting the appropriate case(s) is important. Recency, popularity, relevance to the topic, availability of teaching notes, as well as other supplements such as video and computer software aids, should be considered. Appropriately chosen, cases not only stimulate the mind but also create an in-depth feel for the application of the course material. The Kotler text will create sensitivity and awareness for what is critical and important in the case, and the case will reinforce concepts presented in the text. Cases call for a decision and very often with less than perfect information concerning the problem, the environment, the actors, and the consequences of various actions. As such, the case nurtures management skills although the text and the other application-oriented tools discussed above can diffuse perspective and technical knowledge. There are a number of articles that discuss methods for using the case study approach. The following are suggested:

1. "Because Wisdom Can't Be Told," (Harvard Note 9-451-005). This article argues for the beneficial effect the case method has on both teachers and students and suggests the proper role of the instructor as a leader of the group.

2. "Learning by the Case Method," (Harvard Note 9-376-241). This article, prepared for executive education, identifies the issues to be confronted in the course of reaching a decision. It also provides useful guidelines for individual analysis of a case method teaching generally.

3. "Teaching and the Case Method," (9-387-001), by Roland Christensen. . A very useful textbook and instructor's guide (5-387-010), available through the Harvard Business School. This book includes text, cases, and readings for classes and seminars.

The Harvard Business School Publishing (HBSP) Website (www.hbsp.com) will provide you with listings of current marketing and marketing management cases, and related materials. HBSP also can package the selected cases to accompany the text.

Sample Case Analysis

An example of a case analysis follows, that can be utilized early in the course to provide a basis for written cases and class case discussions, if you choose to use cases in the course:

O'Hanlon Candy Company is a medium-size candy company located in the Midwest. In the past two years, its sales and profits have barely held their own. Top management feels that the trouble lies with the sales force because that they don't "work hard or smart enough." To correct the problem, management plans to introduce a new incentive-compensation system and hire a trainer to educate the sales force in modern merchandising and selling techniques. Before doing this, however, they decide to hire a marketing consultant to carry out a marketing audit. The auditor interviews managers, customers, sales representatives and dealers, and examines various sets of data. The auditor's findings are as follows:

- The company's product line consists primarily of 18 products, mostly candy bars. Its two leading brands are mature and account for 76 percent of the company's total sales. The company has looked at the fast-developing markets of chocolate snacks but has not made any moves yet.

- The company recently researched its customer profile. Its products appeal especially to lower-income and older people. Respondents who were asked to assess O'Brien's chocolate products in relation to competitors' products described them as "average quality and old-fashioned."

- O'Brien sells its products to candy jobbers and large supermarkets. Its sales force calls on many of the small retailers reached by the candy jobbers, to fortify displays and provide ideas; its sales force also calls on many small retailers not covered by jobbers. O'Brien enjoys good penetration of small retailing, though not in all segments, such as the fast-growing restaurant areas. Its major approach to intermediaries is a "sell-in" strategy discounts, exclusive contracts, and stock financing. At the same time, O'Brien has not adequately penetrated the mass-merchandise chains. Its competitors rely more heavily on mass-consumer advertising and in-store merchandising and are more successful with the mass merchandisers.
- O'Brien's marketing budget is set at 15 percent of its total sales, compared with competitors' budgets of close to 20 percent. Most of the marketing budget supports the sales force, and the remainder supports advertising. Consumer promotions are very limited. The advertising budget is spent primarily in reminder advertising for the company's two leading products. New products are not developed often, and when they are, they are introduced to retailers via a push strategy.
- The marketing organization is headed by a sales vice-president. Reporting to the sales VP is the sales manager, the market research manager, and the advertising manager. Having come up from the ranks, the sales VP is partial to sales-force activities and pays less attention to the other marketing functions. The sales force is assigned to territories headed by area managers.

The marketing auditor concluded that O'Brien's problems would not be solved by actions taken to improve its sales force. If you were the auditor, what short-term and long-term recommendations would you make to O'Brien's top management?

Short-term recommendations:

- Examine the current product line and weed out marginal performers with limited growth potential
- Shift some marketing expenditures from supporting mature products to supporting new products
- Shift the marketing-mix emphasis from direct selling to national advertising, especially for new products
- Conduct a market-profile study of the fastest growing segments of the candy market and develop a plan to break into these areas
- Instruct the sales force to drop some of the smaller outlets and not to take orders for under 20 items. Also, cut out the duplication efforts of sales reps and jobbers calling on the same accounts
- Initiate sales-training programs and an improved compensation plan

Medium to long-term recommendations.

- Hire an experienced marketing VP from the outside
- Set formal and operational marketing objectives
- Introduce the product manager concept into the organization
- Initiate effective new-product development programs
- Develop strong brand names
- Find ways to market its brands to the chain stores more effectively
- Increase the level of marketing expenditures to 20 percent of sales.
- Reorganize the selling function by specializing sales reps by distribution channels
- Set sales objectives and base sales compensation on gross profit performance

11

Note: This analysis is designed to help students recognize some of the marketing and sales management relationships that can occur in case and applied situations. If students apply the type of thinking utilized in this example, they should be able to improve their approaches to this and other marketing cases and related contemporary business analysis settings.

You might suggest that prior to each class students should take a few moments to think about the topics covered in each related chapter, using an approach similar to that utilized in this case. Based on this, they can spend 10 to 15 minutes writing down how the case concepts, theories, and applications integrate and complement what she/he has learned. Ask them to be as specific as possible with their analytical notes, bring those notes to class and be prepared to discuss how they have integrated the specific ideas covered in the text, lectures and discussions, based on the O'Hanlon case and the auditor's comments.

In addition, this case and the apparent questions bring up an important point because it may appear that the questions and issues are somewhat vague and lack focus. This is intentional, because that is the way things operate in the real world. In previous cases and case work, students likely focused on a specific topic. Here, however, it is up to them to choose a specific focus, reflect on it, show how it relates to what they have already learned or experienced, and examine how they can apply it in the future.

MBA students tend to value this exercise. It gives them a chance to discover relationships between what they read and hear and what they experience at work or in internships. After a few weeks of using this approach, they should be able to identify with the course material and begin to comment on how "good the text is," that they are actually reading the text, and that there is a reason why this and other courses are in the business program. Sometimes, the hardest part of the instructor's job is to cut off the opening class discussion and move on to new material.

This exercise is more difficult for undergraduates because they have had little practical business experience. This activity, however, can still be valuable if you ask the students to apply the concepts to their part-time work experiences, campus clubs, or other applied experiences.

Note to Instructor: It would be useful to bring this case and/or the analysis back into the course occasionally. For example, if students deal with this question occasionally it provides an effective way for them to recall and review prior material, filter it, and discover new applications.

Case Options for Kotler, Marketing Management, 11th ed., Prentice-Hall [1]

Case Title	Source, Number, Length, Teaching Note	Geographical and Industry Setting, Company Size, Timeframe	Case Decision Issue
PART I: UNDERSTANDING MARKETING MANAGEMENT			
Chapter 1: Defining Marketing for the Twenty-first Century			
CBS Evening News	HBSP #898-086, 32p	New York, television, 1,000 employees, 1998	The CBS Evening News looks for options to grow its franchise.
Sendwine.com	HBSP #800-211 23p TN #801-198	Massachusetts, internet retailing, 46 employees, 1999	How should Sendwine.com spend the venture capital money it attracted? Should the company consolidate its niche position in wine gift-giving? Or should it aggressively expand into new gift-giving categories

[1] Source: Harvard Business School Publishing, www.hbsp.edu

			under the "Send.com" name?
Intuit QuickBooks	HBSP #501-054 15p	California, software, 1999	Intuit QuickBooks, a successful product with a strong brand and an 85 percent share of retail sales, faces market growth expectations in a mature, slowing market segment. Providing value-added online services to complement the desktop software was an attractive solution, but should the firm build them in-house or acquire them through partnerships? This case explores the issues related to capturing value.
Chapter 2: Adapting Marketing to the New Economy			
BizRate.com	HBSP #501-024 22p TN #501-026	California, Internet, 200 employees, 2000	BizRate.com is a market research firm that collects point-of-purchase customer feedback data from retailing merchants. It then makes its findings available to consumers in the form of "BizRate star ratings" on its Web site. In 1999, the company also introduced several highly successful e-commerce initiatives. The case allows students to explore concepts of consumer trust and merchant credibility; to examine the roles an information intermediary can play in building customer relationships; and to consider the potential of database marketing in the new economy.
Arrow Electronics	HBSP #598-022 21p TN #500-111	North America, electronic parts, 8,000 employees, 1997	Deals with the issue of cross-selling and managing a portfolio of products and services in business markets. Management must decide whether to pursue an opportunity to sell its products through a new e-commerce site, which could threaten the viability of its overall business model.
Alloy.com: Marketing to Generation Y	HBSP #500-048 14p TN #501-043	New York, clothing and retailing, 100 employees, 1999	Alloy.com retails clothing to teens by catalog; it uses a Web site to convert prospects and build community. As a result, the firm has the economics of a direct marketer and the market capitalization of an Internet start-up. Top management must decide whether to partner with AOL or continue with the current mix of customer acquisition methods.
The Peppers and Rogers Group	HBSP #500-096 20p	United States, consulting, 160 employees, 2000	Can two successful authors build a scalable consulting practice based on their unique view of customer relationship management? The case introduces the concept of customer relationship management and the technologies that enable it.
Chapter 3: Building Customer Satisfaction, Value, and Retention			
A Measure of Delight: The Pursuit of Quality at AT&T Universal Card Services (A)	HBSP #694-047 23p TN #696-073	Jacksonville, FL, credit cards, 2,700 employees, 1989	Dedicated to improving service quality and customer satisfaction, Chief Quality Officer Rob Davis and his Quality Team have designed and put into place an unusual measurement and compensation system based on more than 100 performance measures monitored and communicated daily.
Alloy.com: Marketing to Generation Y	HBSP #500-048 14p TN #501-043	New York, clothing/retailing, 100 employees, 1999	Alloy.com retails clothing to teens by catalog; it uses a Web site to convert prospects and build community. As a result, the firm has the economics of a direct marketer and the market capitalization of an Internet start-up. Top management must decide whether to partner with AOL or continue with the current mix of customer acquisition methods.
Citibank: Launching the Credit Card in Asia Pacific (A)	HBSP #595-026 25p TN #595-104	Singapore, banking, 1989	Citibank's Asia Pacific Consumer Bank is considering launching a credit card in the Asia Pacific region. Students must make a decision, and if a "go" decision is made, they must work out a comprehensive launch plan. The case introduces the concepts of acquisition cost and

			lifetime value of a customer.
Hilton Honors Worldwide: Loyalty Wars	HBSP #501-010 19p TN #501-059	California, lodging/hotels, 1999	Hilton Hotels regards the frequent guest program as the industry's most important marketing tool, directing marketing efforts at the heavy user. What should Hilton do when a competitor ups the ante? The case illustrates the economics of loyalty marketing.
PART II: ANALYZING MARKET OPPORTUNITIES			
Chapter 4: Winning Markets through Market-Oriented Strategic Planning			
Matching Dell	HBSP #799-158 31p TN #700-084	Global, personal computers, Fortune 500, 1998	This case describes the evolution of the personal computer industry, Dell's "Direct Model" for computer manufacturing, marketing and distribution, and efforts by competitors to match its strategy. Students must formulate strategic plans of action for Dell and its various rivals.
Edmunds.com	HBSP #701-025 22p	Los Angeles, CA, auto, 2000	Edmund's began in 1966 as a publisher of new and used vehicle guides and grew into one of the leading third-party automotive Web sites. This case explores how Edmunds.com gained a competitive edge using strategic partnerships and alliances, as well as careful product positioning and strategy implementation.
ScreamingMedia, Inc.	HBSP #801-371 26p	New York, NY, computer-related services, 236 employees, 2000	ScreamingMedia, a provider of content syndication and services, must shift its customer base away from Internet start-ups toward more established firms to ensure future profitability. Students must develop a new market strategy and action plan for the firm, outlining steps necessary to achieve strategic goals: sales retraining, development of new products and services, and changing the organizational structure.
Hurricane Island Outward Bound School	HBSP #588-019 19p TN #589-049	Maine, education, 1986	Hurricane Island Outward Bound is a small, nonprofit school that helped pioneer experiential education in the United States. Students take the role of the school's new marketing manager, who is preparing his first marketing plan for the organization. Faced with a tight marketing budget, students must choose among several marketing programs by evaluating their past performance and further potential.
Oscar Mayer: Strategic Marketing Planning	HBSP #597-051 14p TN #597-052	United States, food, 1995	The marketing director of Oscar Mayer faces a series of strategic marketing options regarding established and new products, including budget and capacity allocation decisions.
Chapter 5: Gathering Information and Measuring Market Demand			
Juice Guys (A)	HBSP #800-122 27p	United States, food and beverage, 10 employees, 1999	Asks, who are the customers for a new beverage product, what are their desires as customers for this product, and what are their desires when ordering this product from a local specialty store location?
The Coop: Market Research	HBSP #599-113 14p	United States, quick service restaurant, 1995	Daryl Buckmeister, CEO of The Chicken Coop, must decide whether to invest in market research, how much money to spend, and which programs to fund.
Talbots: A Classic	HBSP #500-082 23p	Massachusetts, retailing, 1997–1999	Talbots has recently recovered from a disastrous 1997 that saw earnings fall from $1.91 per share to $0.18 per share after the company tried to attract a younger customer segment. This case traces why the $1 billion women's clothing retailer decided to attract younger customers, what went wrong, and the actions taken to recover. By the end of 1999, the company has reestablished itself and faces several growth opportunities and must decide on the best course of action. Illustrates the challenges of repositioning a store

			concept.
Omnitel Pronto Italia	HBSP #501-002 24p	Italy, telecommunication, 572 employees, 1996	Describes the situation faced by Omnitel soon after launching its mobile telecommunication services in Italy in December 1995. Omnitel has to decide whether to attack a new segment with a new service plan to improve on past performance.
Optical Distortion, Inc. (A)	HBSP #575-072 10p TN #577-161	California-Oregon, 1974	Classic case about a startup offering contact lenses for chickens in the egg production industry. The marketing vice president must make certain decisions to complete his marketing plan.
Chapter 6: Scanning the Marketing Environment			
Global Climate Change and BP Amoco	HBSP #700-106 24p	Global, energy, 1997-2000	BP Amoco is the world's third-largest oil firm. Its CEO, Sir John Browne, broke with industry colleagues in 1997 when he publicly declared that global climate change was a serious problem and pledged BP to play a significant role in the search for solutions.
Ciba Consumer Pharmaceuticals' Acutrim: Challenges and Opportunities in Today's Diet Industry	HBSP #795-043 20p	United States, OTC drugs, 1994	Ciba Geigy has to decide what to do with its Acutrim appetite suppressant in view of the changing market for such products.
Royal Dutch/Shell in Transition (A)	HBSP #300-039 31p	London, England, oil, 100,000 employees, 1997	The company is considering whether, as part of its transformation effort, to begin public reporting on its environmental and social as well as financial performance.
AES Global Values	HBSP #399-136 21p	India, power, 1994	Members of the development team for the AES Corp.'s power plant project in India must decide what plant technology to specify in their application for techno-economic clearance from the government of India's Central Electric Authority.
CHAPTER 7: ANALYZING CONSUMER MARKETS AND BUYER BEHAVIOR			
Clust.com: Dream More and Pay Less	HBSP #501-047 16p	Paris, France, Internet, 40 employees, 2000	The company has to decide whether to focus on group-buying and good deals versus consumer creation and exclusives.
TiVo	HBSP #501-038 16p TN #501-057	San Jose, CA, TV services, 181 employees, 2000	TiVo is a digital video recorder that allows viewers to watch what they want, when they want to watch it. Fourteen months into the launch, sales are very disappointing. Brodie Keast, VP of marketing and sales, wants to combine a catchy communications campaign, product bundling with satellite television receivers, aggressive pricing, and sales support, in order to boost demand for the new category. One important goal is to position TiVo as a strong brand before the entry of big player Microsoft. TiVo is confronted with the difficulty of selling a new and complex electronics product that is meant to change consumer habits radically. The case can be used to explore issues such as marketing a radically new product; changing consumer habits, privacy, consumer control, and permission-based advertising; relevance of targeting early adopters; creative communications strategy for a small first-mover; integrated marketing plan; and television and the advertising industry.
Microsoft CarPoint	HBSP #898-280 31p	Seattle, WA, computers, 1998	CarPoint.com was Microsoft's Web-based entry into on-line automobile retailing. Although CarPoint could not "sell" or deliver any cars, it could shift much of

			consumer search, comparison, and decision-making, including pricing, from the physical platform of the traditional car dealer to the virtual world of the Web. This shift in buying behavior from marketplace to marketspace was significant in its implications for consumers and dealers; it gave consumers a wealth of information that they previously did not have, although it challenged dealers to change their approaches to these newly empowered and better informed consumers. CarPoint, however, was a late entrant, and it faced competition from category first-movers AutoByTel.com, AutoWeb.com, and AutoVantage.com. As a result, the case deals with larger issues of channel and consumer behavior change as well as tactical issues pertaining to competitive positioning in a competitive market both on-line and off-line.
Heineken N.V.: Global Branding and Advertising	HBSP #596-015 13p TN #598-080	Amsterdam/ Netherlands, beer, 1994	Heineken managers are evaluating the results of the research projects designed to identify the values of the Heineken brand and to translate these into effective advertising messages.
Ciba Consumer Pharmaceuticals' Acutrim: Challenges and Opportunities in Today's Diet Industry	HBSP #795-043 20p	United States, OTC drugs, 1994	Ciba Geigy has to decide what to do with its Acutrim appetite suppressant in view of the changing market for such products.
Chapter 8: Analyzing Business Markets and Business Buying Behavior			
VerticalNet	HBSP #500-041 25p TN #501-060	United States, Internet, 7,300 employees, 1999	VerticalNet, a leading creator of targeted business-to-business vertical trade communities on the Internet, is trying to expand its model to facilitate e-commerce as well. CEO Mark Walsh must decide how far he can extend the firm's business model without adversely affecting his current franchise.
Arrow Electronics	HBSP #598-022 21p TN #500-111	North America, electronic parts, 8,000 employees, 1997	Deals with the issue of cross-selling and managing a portfolio of products and services in business markets. Management must decide whether to pursue an opportunity to sell its products through a new e-commerce site, which could threaten the viability of its overall business model.
Becton Dickinson & Company: VACUTAINER Systems Division (Condensed)	HBSP #592-037 17p TN #595-084	United States, pharmaceuticals, 500 employees, 1985	Becton Dickinson, a phenomenally successful company with an 80 percent market share in the blood collection needles and syringes market, faces a change in the customer-buying environment (cost containment pressures at hospitals).
Optical Distortion, Inc. (A)	HBSP #575-072 10p TN #577-161	California-Oregon, 1974	Classic case about a startup offering contact lenses for chickens in the egg production industry. The marketing vice president must make certain decisions to complete his marketing plan.
Chapter 9: Dealing with the Competition			
eBay, Inc.	HBSP #700-007 27p	San Jose, CA, e-commerce, 300 employees, 1999	eBay was the world's largest and most popular person-to-person trading community on the Internet. In early 1999, however, Amazon.com announced that it was entering the online auction arena. What should eBay do in light of the entry of its most recent and serious competitor to date?
Robert Mondavi: Competitive	HBSP #799-125 23p	Global, wine, 1,100 employees, 1999	Describes the competitive situation facing Robert Mondavi, the leading premium California winery.

Strategy			Mondavi has to cope with growing domestic competition as well as market share growth by wineries from Chile and Australia.
Matching Dell	HBSP #799-158 31p TN #700-084	Global, personal computers, Fortune 500, 1998	This case describes the evolution of the personal computer industry, Dell's "Direct Model" for computer manufacturing, marketing and distribution, and efforts by competitors to match its strategy. Students must formulate strategic plans of action for Dell and its various rivals.
Skil Corp.	HBSP #389-005 20p TN #389-021	United States, power tools, 1979	This classic case focuses on the Skil Corp., the third largest U.S. competitor, in 1979, in the U.S. portable electric power tool market. Skil, acquired by Emerson Electric in 1979, faced intense competition from Black & Decker and emerging foreign competitors.
Chapter 10: Identifying Market Segments and Selecting Market Targets			
Granny's Goodies, Inc.	HBSP #500-049 21p	Marketing promotional material, 1999	The young entrepreneurs of Granny's Goodies, Inc., a corporate gift package specialist, face the challenge of finding ways to create consistent revenue streams and reduce sales costs. Outside of a few long-term contracts, the two founders have had to work very hard for each sale. Using extensive customer information that the firm has diligently collected over the previous two years, students need to develop a plan that covers market selection, product policy, and relationship management strategy for the firm. Enables students to use customer data to segment markets, design appropriate products to meet the needs of each segment, and design go-to-market strategies for each segment.
Vistakon: 1 Day Acuvue Disposable Contact Lenses	HBSP #596-087 26p	United States, healthcare, 2,500 employees, 1994	Gary Kunkle, president of Vistakon, was presented with the test market results for an addition to the firm's product line, 1 Day Acuvue, the world's first daily disposable contact lens. Kunkle must evaluate the risks associated with commencing an immediate launch with an unproven strategy as opposed to extending the test market.
Eastman Kodak Co.: Funtime Film	HBSP #594-111 5p TN #597-080	United States, photography, Fortune 500, 1994	Eastman Kodak has suffered significant declines in film market share at the hands of lower-priced branded producers and private label products. The case presents Kodak's proposal to launch a new, economy brand of film to combat these rivals.
Dell Computer Corporation	HBSP #596-058 23p TN #596-098	Global, personal computers, 1994	Dell is faced with a set of decisions on the product markets it needs to serve in order to sustain its growth profitably into the future.
PART III: DEVELOPING MARKETING STRATEGIES			
Chapter 11: Positioning the Market Offering Through the Product Life Cycle			
BET.com	HBSP #800-283 26p TN #801-196	Washington, DC, Internet, 1999-2000	Black Entertainment Television, a leading cable programmer, is launching BET.com, an Internet portal targeted toward African-Americans. This case examines the challenges facing BET management as it defines its service offerings and target customer segments in a fast-moving, highly competitive environment. BET.com faces two decisions: 1) whether to bundle Internet access service with its ethnic portal; and 2) whether to strictly target African-Americans or also pursue the "urban market," a young, cross-racial segment that is part of the core audience for BET's cable programming.
Autobytel.com	HBSP #500-015 21p TN	Irvine, CA, internet,	Autobytel enjoys first-mover advantage in the Internet new car buying space. According to a number of metrics,

	#500-076	automotive, 200 employees, 1999	it is the online leader in this category. A number of competitors have emerged, however, raising questions about the long-term viability of Autobytel's purchase referral model. In addition, Autobytel is struggling to accelerate revenue growth.
Juice Guys (A)	HBSP #800-122 27p	United States, food and beverage, 10 employees, 1999	Asks, who are the customers for a new beverage product, what are their desires as customers for this product, and what are their desires when ordering this product from a local specialty store location?
The Brita Products Co.	HBSP #500-024 18p TN #501-067	United States, packaged goods, 1989–1999	Clorox's Brita skillfully exploited a tide of water safety concerns, growing a home water filtration business from inception to a 15 percent U.S. household penetration in 10 years. As the period of increasing returns seems to be drawing to a close, management must use its legacy, an installed base, and strong brand equity to take the business forward into a less friendly environment.
MedSim	HBSP #599-020 22p	Global, medical, 25 employees, 1998	An Israeli high-tech start-up has developed an innovative simulator that makes possible nonpatient training in medical ultrasound. It now must choose a strategy for growth.
Microsoft CarPoint	HBSP #898-280 31p	Seattle, WA, computers, 1998	CarPoint.com was Microsoft's Web-based entry into on-line automobile retailing. The case deals with larger issues of channel and consumer behavior change as well as tactical issues pertaining to competitive positioning in a competitive market both on-line and off-line.
Sears, Roebuck and Co.	HBSP (Graduate School of Business, Stanford University) #M278 24p	United States, retail, 335,000 employees, 1993	Arthur Martinez, the new CEO of Sears Merchandise Group, must decide how to turn around Sears' slumping retail sales performance. After decades of dominance, Sears had lost its top retailing position to Wal-Mart. Martinez must determine whether Sears should expand its most successful product lines, switch to higher-margin lines, or tout its strength as the last true one-stop-shopping department store.
Sharp Corp.: Technology Strategy	HBSP #793-064 26p TN #794-025	Japan, consumer electronics, large company, 41,800 employees, 1992	Teaches the evolution of the corporate strategy of Sharp Corp., Japan. Sharp Corp., a second-tier assembler of TV sets and home appliances, gradually and consistently improved performance by developing expertise in electronic device technologies such as specialized ICs and LCDs and used these technologies to develop innovative end products.
Chapter 12: Developing New Market Offerings			
Abgenix and the XenoMouse	HBSP #501-061 14p	California, biotechnology, 150 employees, 2000	In early 2000, Abgenix's cancer drug has performed well in animal testing and is moving to early-stage human testing. The firm must decide whether to sell the product development program to a large pharmaceutical company or to enter into a joint venture to push the product ahead.
Pepcid AC (A): Racing to the OTC Market	HBSP #500-073 15p	Pennsylvania, pharmaceuticals, Fortune 500, 1995	Pepcid management must decide whether to risk all in a race to be first in the over-the-counter market with a new heartburn remedy.
Oscar Mayer: Strategic Marketing Planning	HBSP #597-051 14p TN #597-052	United States, food, 1995	The marketing director of Oscar Mayer faces a series of strategic marketing options regarding established and new products, including budget and capacity allocation decisions.
Vistakon: 1 Day Acuvue Disposable Contact Lenses	HBSP #596-087 26p	United States, healthcare, 2,500 employees, 1994	Gary Kunkle, president of Vistakon, was presented with the test market results for an addition to the firm's product line, 1 Day Acuvue, the world's first daily disposable contact lens. Kunkle must evaluate the risks associated with commencing an immediate launch with

			an unproven strategy as opposed to extending the test market.
Colgate-Palmolive Company: The Precision Toothbrush	HBSP #593-064 24p TN #595-025	United States, consumer products, 1992	Brand manager Susan Steinberg has to develop a marketing mix and pro forma profit-and-loss in preparation for the launch of a new and superior toothbrush.

Chapter 13: Designing and Managing Global Marketing Strategies

Hewlett-Packard's Home Products Division in Europe—1996–2000	HBSP #501-053 –17p	Europe, computers, 2000	By the end of 2000, Hewlett-Packard's Home Products Division (HPD) Products Division in Europe had been selling its Pavilion line of PCs in Europe for almost five years. During that time, HPD had entered and exited Germany, struggled in France and the United Kingdom, and significantly reorganized its European operations twice. Students must evaluate how well the firm is prepared by 2001 to compete in the European home PC market.
Supermercados Disco: Regional Strategy	HBSP #599-127 24p TN #501-008	South America, retailing, 1998	The Disco supermarket chain has pursued a successful local niche strategy in Argentina to compete with multinational chains. Now, Disco considers options for expanding its regional strength.
Vietnam: Market Entry Decisions	HBSP #597-020 13p TN #598-081	Vietnam, adhesives and athletic footwear/toys, 1996	Three U.S. multinationals must decide whether to enter the Vietnam market and, if so, how.
Gillette Indonesia	HBSP #597-009 15p TN #598-086	Indonesia, consumer products, 1996	The country manager of Gillette Indonesia is reviewing his 1996 marketing plan and considering whether the pace of market development and mix of product sales can be impacted by the level and type of Gillette expenditures in the market.
Mary Kay Cosmetics: Asian Market Entry	HBSP #594-023 35p TN #595-073	Japan/China, cosmetics, 1993	Executives at Mary Kay Cosmetics are evaluating opportunities to enter the Japanese and/or Chinese markets. The comparative opportunities must be assessed and guidelines for entry strategies must be determined.

PART IV: SHAPING THE MARKET OFFERING

Chapter 14: Setting the Product and Branding Strategy

Monster.com	HBSP #801-145 26p	Maynard, MA, online job site, 2000	Jeff Taylor, founder and CEO of Monster.com, ponders how his online site, the leading career site on the Web, can continue its dominance (60 percent share in 1999) and growth on the Internet. Monster.com had just launched a nationwide branding campaign on television and entered a four-year deal with AOL.
Abgenix and the XenoMouse	HBSP #501-061 14p	California, biotechnology, 150 employees, 2000	In early 2000, Abgenix's cancer drug has performed well in animal testing and is moving to early-stage human testing. The firm must decide whether to sell the product development program to a large pharmaceutical company or to enter into a joint venture to push the product ahead. This case introduces students to produce line planning in largely uncertain environments.
Net.Genesis, Inc.	HBSP #500-009 18p TN #501-062	United States, internet software, 70 employees, 1999	Net.Genesis needs to plan a strategy for the developing Internet market. In particular, it is creating the category of e-business intelligence and striving to be the brand leader in it.
Snapple	HBSP #599-126 17p TN #500-033	New York, beverages, 500 employees, 1972–1997	Tells the story of Snapple's rise and fall and poses the question, "Can it recover?" Snapple went from local to national success and was poised to go international when the founders sold out to Quaker. The brand proved harder

			to manage than Quaker anticipated, and in 1997 was sold for a fraction of its acquisition price. The case presents factors accounting for the growth and decline and provides a qualitative study of the brand.
Aladdin Knowledge Systems	HBSP #598-018 19p TN #598-071	Israel, Germany, United States, software piracy, 80, 1996	Following an acquisition, the management team has to determine whether and how to integrate the worldwide marketing, sales, and distribution of the firm's two overlapping software security product lines.

Chapter 15: Designing and Managing Services

Gateway: Moving Beyond the Box	HBSP #601-038 18p	San Diego, CA, computers, 21,000 employees, 2000	Gateway must balance the cost efficiencies of its direct channels with its increased ability to sell in its physical channels. This challenge occurs although Gateway is trying to move away from dependence on PC revenue streams to the PC solutions revenue stream, which includes Internet access, computer training, content, financing, and other related activities.
Four Seasons Hotels and Resorts	HBSP #800-385 26p TN #801-048	Canada, hotels and resorts, 2,000 employees, 2000	This case explores how a leading service firm delivers high tech/high touch, including its progressive human resource strategy.
RadioShack	HBSP #500-081 24p TN #500-106	United States, consumer electronics retailing, 2000	Outlines the transformation of RadioShack from a parts and accessories business to a provider of high bandwidth Internet access.
First USA and Internet Marketing	HBSP #500-043 20p	Delaware, financial services, 10,000 employees, 1999	Is this new retail strategy viable Explores First USA's decision to use the Internet for acquiring customers. The case highlights issues related to marketing on the Internet and trade-offs involved in allocating resources in online versus off-line marketing options.
Xerox Corp.: The Customer Satisfaction Program	HBSP #591-055 23p TN #593-027	United States, copiers/office equipment, Fortune 500, 1990	This classic case focuses on analyzing the strategic role of Xerox's customer satisfaction program. To increase customer satisfaction, top management believes that the firm should offer a service guarantee. What type of guarantee would work best?
LifeSpan Inc.: Abbott Northwestern Hospital	HBSP #587-104 20p TN #589-047	Minnesota, healthcare, midsize company, 1986	Abbott Northwestern, LifeSpan's premier hospital, adopted a very market-oriented approach to increase its share of a business that was both shrinking in size and becoming increasingly competitive. The marketing group wanted to nearly double the advertising budget; the board of directors wanted some evidence that advertising, phone calls, inquiries, and other programs lead to filled beds and increased business.

Chapter 16: Designing Pricing Strategies and Programs

InPart	HBSP #898-213 24p	Silicon Valley, CA, CAD software, 30 employees, 1997-1998	The case examines issues involving the organization of the sales force and the pricing of the product.
Omnitel Pronto Italia	HBSP #501-002 24p	Italy, telecommunication, 572 employees, 1996	Describes the situation faced by Omnitel soon after launching its mobile telecommunication services in Italy in December 1995. Omnitel has to decide whether to attack a new segment with a new service plan to improve on past performance.
Vistakon: 1 Day Acuvue Disposable Contact Lenses	HBSP #596-087 26p	United States, healthcare, 2,500 employees, 1994	Gary Kunkle, president of Vistakon, was presented with the test market results for an addition to the firm's product line, 1 Day Acuvue, the world's first daily disposable contact lens. Kunkle must evaluate the risks associated with commencing an immediate launch with an unproven strategy as opposed to extending the test market.

Becton Dickinson & Company: VACUTAINER Systems Division (Condensed)	HBSP #592-037 17p TN #595-084	United States, pharmaceuticals, 500 employees, 1985	Becton Dickinson, a phenomenally successful company with an 80 percent market share in the blood collection needles and syringes market, faces a change in the customer-buying environment (cost containment pressures at hospitals).
Cumberland Metal Industries: Engineered Products Division—1980	HBSP #580-104 16p TN #585-115	United States, construction equipment, 1980	The classic case on value pricing. Cumberland Metal Industries has developed a new product to help contractors drive piles faster, and must decide how to price it.

PART V: MANAGING AND DELIVERING MARKETING PROGRAMS

Chapter 17: Designing and Managing Value Networks and Marketing Channels

CVS: The Web Strategy	HBSP #500-008 16p TN #501-064	New England, drug retailing	How should America's second-largest pharmacy chain respond to the challenge from online drugstores? What threat does the Web pose to bricks-and-mortar distribution of prescription drugs and the other items that make up 50 percent of a drugstore's sales? This case describes the purchase of Soma.com by CVS and its integration into the corporation.
MedSim	HBSP #599-020 22p	Global, medical, 25 employees, 1998	An Israeli high-tech start-up has developed an innovative simulator that makes possible nonpatient training in medical ultrasound. It now must choose a strategy for growth.
Arrow Electronics	HBSP #598022 21p TN #500-111	North America, electronic parts, 8,000 employees, 1997	Deals with the issue of cross-selling and managing a portfolio of products and services in business markets. Management must decide whether to pursue an opportunity to sell its products through a new e-commerce site, which could threaten the viability of its overall business model.
Goodyear: The Aquatred Launch (Condensed)	HBSP #500-039 13p TN #500-044	Akron, OH, tires, Fortune 500 company, 1992	Goodyear is planning to launch an innovative new tire in a price-sensitive and highly competitive category. The case deals with channel conflicts and management issues arising in mature product categories.
MathSoft, Inc. (A)	HBSP #593-094 25p	United States, software, small company, 1989	CEO David Blohm had to decide how to allocate its marketing and sales resources to different channels in the face of a sales decline that threatened the company's viability.
Becton Dickinson & Company: VACUTAINER Systems Division (Condensed)	HBSP #592-037 17p TN #595-084	United States, pharmaceuticals, 500 employees, 1985	Becton Dickinson, a phenomenally successful company with an 80 percent market share in the blood collection needles and syringes market, faces a change in the customer-buying environment (cost containment pressures at hospitals).

Chapter 18: Managing Retailing, Wholesaling, and Market Logistics

RadioShack	HBSP #500-081 24p TN #500-106	United States, consumer electronics retailing, 2000	Outlines the transformation of RadioShack from a parts and accessories business to a provider of high bandwidth Internet access. Is this new retail strategy viable?
Staples.com	HBSP #800-305 10p TN #800-412	Massachusetts, office supplies retailing, 46,000 employees, 2000	Staples.com, the online unit of the U.S. office supplies retailing chain Staples, faces a range of strategic and organizational issues as it accelerates its growth. Should it pursue only existing Staples customers, or consumers who do not shop in Staples stores? How quickly should it add services to its product offering? Which operating functions should be shared between the online units and the core business?
Eddie Bauer, Inc.	HBSP #500-034 15p TN	Washington State, apparel, 1999	Eddie Bauer has decided to coordinate its merchandising strategy (price, selection) across stores and catalog. But

	#500-077		now with e-commerce, is this still sensible?
Costco Companies, Inc.	HBSP #599-041 21p TN #599-088	United States, retail/membership clubs, 55,000 employees, 1998	Costco Companies, a major player in the wholesale club industry, has developed a new class of membership that offers discounted services in exchange for a higher annual fee. How should the new membership be marketed, to whom, and how much should be spent on the effort? What are the potential risks and benefits for Costco?
Wal-Mart Stores, Inc.	HBSP #794-024 21p TN #395-225	United States, retail, 444,000 employees, 1994	This classic case focuses on the evolution of Wal-Mart's remarkably successful discount operations and the company's attempts to diversify into other businesses. Wal-Mart has advantages over its competitors in areas such as distribution, information technology, and merchandising. How sustainable are these advantages? What are the threats to Wal-Mart's continued success?
Body Shop International	HBSP #392-032 19p TN #395-148	United Kingdom, retailing, 2,000 employees, 1991	This classic case describes the start-up and rapid growth of Body Shop International. After profiling founder Anita Roddick, the case describes her antimainstream approach to building her highly successful business (no advertising, simple packaging, nontraditional R&D). Can the business survive as Roddick steps back?
Chapter 19: Designing and Managing Integrated Marketing Communications			
yesmail.com	HBSP #500-092 15p TN #501-028	Chicago, IL, Internet/advertising 71 employees, 1999	Yesmail.com sends clients' promotional e-mail messages to targeted consumers who said "yes" when asked whether they wished to receive promotional offers in certain categories of interest. The company's CEO must decide how best to build a large membership base quickly. The case highlights trends in marketing communications, with a focus on permission marketing.
Bronner Slosberg Humphrey	HBSP #598-136 22p TN #598-141	United States, direct marketing and advertising, 700 employees, 1998	Bronner Slosberg Humphrey has succeeded by providing integrated direct marketing solutions for major service companies such as AT&T, American Express, and FedEx. A new CEO takes over from the company's founder and is wondering how to grow the company. Options include selling individual services and/or opening global offices.
Hunter Business Group: TeamTBA	HBSP #500-030 16p	Milwaukee, direct marketing, 30 employees, 1994	The Hunter Business Group (HBG) is a direct marketing consulting firm specializing in reorganizing the sales and marketing efforts of industrial firms. The firm uses integrated customer contact technologies (e.g., field sales, telephone, and mail), and believes that a seller's communications provide genuine value to a customer. This case highlights HBG's implementation of its approach for Star Oil's tire, battery, and accessory (TBA) business that has been facing declining market share and profitability in the face of ever-increasing competition.
Heineken N.V.: Global Branding and Advertising	HBSP #596-015 13p TN #598-080	Amsterdam/ Netherlands, beer, 1994	Heineken managers are evaluating the results of the research projects designed to identify the values of the Heineken brand and to translate these into effective advertising messages.
Cunard Line Ltd.: Managing Integrated Marketing Communications	HBSP #594-046 25p TN #595-028	United States, cruise lines, 1992	Cunard, the world's oldest luxury line company, is confronted with several key issues involving its marketing and marketing communications strategy. One concerns the balance between image/positioning advertising and short-term promotional advertising/ communications on behalf of each Cunard ship (i.e., pull versus push communications). Related to this is the overall mix of marketing communications tools used by

			Cunard—media advertising, direct marketing, etc.
Chapter 20: Managing Advertising, Sales Promotion, Public Relations, Direct Marketing			
Cofidis	HBSP #501-055 19p TN #501-084	France, consumer credit, 1,452 employees, 2000	An offspring of French catalog marketer 3 Suisses, and a popular sponsor of Tour de France, Cofidis sells consumer credit over the phone, defying conventional banking with a product policy and a communication strategy that perfectly fits the company's comparative (dis)advantages. This case describes: 1) Cofidis' product and value proposition; 2) the evolving competitive context and cultural complexity of the European credit market; 3) the adaptive marketing strategy of the company, which evolved from bundling with the 3 Suisse catalog, to direct mail, to print advertising in TV guides, to bicycling sponsorship; 4) the results of the strategy; and 5) the challenge and opportunities posed by the Internet. Based on the lessons of the past, can we advise Michel Guillois, CEO of Cofidis, on the best way for him to preserve Cofidis' competitive edge?
Edmund's—www.edmunds.com	HBSP #397-016 14p	Los Angeles, CA, auto, 30 employees, 1996	Edmund's publishes automobile price guides in books and over the Internet. In the marketplace, it makes money by selling books; in the marketspace, it makes money on referrals. The case shows how a trusted intermediary can reconfigure the demand patterns of individual shoppers, and also examines the potential price and channel pressure this new type of intermediary may have on the auto industry.
Autobytel.com	HBSP #500-015 21p TN #500-076	Irvine, CA, Internet, automotive, 200 employees, 1999	Autobytel enjoys first-mover advantage in the Internet new car buying space. According to a number of metrics, it is the online leader in this category. A number of competitors have emerged, however, raising questions about the long-term viability of Autobytel's purchase referral model. In addition, Autobytel is struggling to accelerate revenue growth.
Bronner Slosberg Humphrey	HBSP #598-136 22p TN #598-141	United States, direct marketing and advertising, 700 employees, 1998	Bronner Slosberg Humphrey has succeeded by providing integrated direct marketing solutions for major service companies such as AT&T, American Express, and FedEx. A new CEO takes over from the company's founder and is wondering how to grow the company. Options include selling individual services and/or opening global offices.
Dewar's (A): Brand Repositioning in the 1990s	HBSP #596-076 29p	United States, distilled spirits, 400 employees, 1993–1995	Dewar's, the U.S. leader in the Scotch category with a 15 percent market share, faced a declining market among traditional consumers of distilled spirits. Given the growing societal, legal, and regulatory opposition to drinking in the United States, the marketing options were limited. In addition, drinking preferences had shifted away from distilled spirits to lighter, lower alcohol beverages like wine, wine coolers, and beer. In early 1993, Dewar's U.S. importer, Schieffelin and Somerset, in cooperation with the brand's longstanding advertising agency, Leo Burnett, began to explore the opportunities for repositioning Dewar's to younger adults. Repositioning Dewar's was a necessity for the brand to remain viable in the long term. The brand manager faces the decision of planning the strategy for a repositioning or "recruitment" campaign for the brand.
Intel's Pentium: When the Chips	HBSP #595-058 3p TN	United States, computer chips,	Intel, the largest-selling manufacturer of microprocessor computer chips, finds itself in a brand-threatening

are Down (A)	#595-089	1994	situation when a flaw is revealed in its top-of-the-line Pentium chip. The story is front page news for weeks. The company invested tens of millions of dollars in advertising its branded Pentium chip as a high-quality component via the campaign slogan "Intel Inside." Issues include salience of the problem, when Intel knew of the problem, how it was revealed, and what actions should be undertaken.
Heineken N.V.: Global Branding and Advertising	HBSP #596-015 13p TN #598-080	Amsterdam/ Netherlands, beer, 1994	Heineken managers are evaluating the results of the research projects designed to identify the values of the Heineken brand and to translate these into effective advertising messages.
Vistakon: 1 Day Acuvue Disposable Contact Lenses	HBSP #596-087 26p	United States, healthcare, 2,500 employees, 1994	Gary Kunkle, president of Vistakon, was presented with the test market results for an addition to the firm's product line, 1 Day Acuvue, the world's first daily disposable contact lens. Kunkle must evaluate the risks associated with commencing an immediate launch with an unproven strategy as opposed to extending the test market.
Hunter Business Group: TeamTBA	HBSP #500-030 16p	Milwaukee, WI, direct marketing, 30 employees, 1994	The Hunter Business Group (HBG) is a direct marketing consulting firm specializing in reorganizing the sales and marketing efforts of industrial firms. The firm uses integrated customer contact technologies (e.g., field sales, telephone, and mail), and believes that a seller's communications provide genuine value to a customer. This case highlights HBG's implementation of its approach for Star Oil's tire, battery, and accessory (TBA) business that has been facing declining market share and profitability in the face of ever-increasing competition.
Calyx and Corolla	HBSP #592-035 31p TN #596-116	United States, new firm, mail order flowers, 1991	Calyx and Corolla has successfully penetrated the retail flower industry, shipping cut flowers via FedEx directly from growers to consumers. Now it has to decide how to grow.
Warner-Lambert Ireland: Niconil	HBSP #593-008 16p TN #594-062	Ireland, pharmaceuticals, 1989	The company's launch of "the patch" was impending. Declan Dixon must decide on a sales forecast, pricing, and an advertising strategy for the launch.
Chapter 21: Managing the Sales Force			
InPart	HBSP #898-213 24p	Silicon Valley, CA, CAD software, 30 employees, 1997–1998	The case examines issues involving the organization of the salesforce and the pricing of the product.
Howard, Shea & Chan Asset Management (A)	HBSP #597-021 13p	United States, investment management, midsize company, 28 employees, 1996	A medium-sized investment management firm is attempting to decide whether to try to grow, and if so, how. The case focuses on the development of a growth strategy and a sales strategy for the firm.
Hewlett-Packard— Computer Systems Organization: Selling to Enterprise Customers	HBSP #500-064 23p	Computers, high-technology, Fortune 500, 1996	HP's current customer management approach, though successful, involved structural changes that forced a deep-rooted overhaul of HP's traditional regional sales approach. The new recommendations would necessitate another round of drastic changes in the way HP manages relationships with its large enterprise customers.

Hunter Business Group: TeamTBA	HBSP #500-030 16p	Milwaukee, WI, direct marketing, 30 employees, 1994	The Hunter Business Group (HBG) is a direct marketing consulting firm specializing in reorganizing the sales and marketing efforts of industrial firms. The firm uses integrated customer contact technologies (e.g., field sales, telephone, and mail), and believes that a seller's communications provide genuine value to a customer. This case highlights HBG's implementation of its approach for Star Oil's tire, battery, and accessory (TBA) business that has been facing declining market share and profitability in the face of ever-increasing competition.
Chapter 22: Managing the Total Marketing Effort			
WingspanBank. com (A)	HBSP #600-035 21p	Wilmington, DE, financial services, 1999	Describes the new product development process for WingspanBank.com, an Internet-only financial services infomediary created by a team from Bank One's First USA division.
Wells Fargo Online Financial Services (A)	HBSP #198-146 18p TN #199-058	California, banking, 1997	Describes how Wells Fargo, the industry leader in electronic banking, implemented a Balanced Scorecard in its online financial services group (OFS) to track and measure performance.
Jeanne Lewis at Staples, Inc. (A) (Abridged)	HBSP #400-065 14p	Boston, MA, office supplies, 30,000 employees, 1997	Staples' new senior vice president of marketing, Jeanne Lewis, must determine how the marketing department can most effectively and efficiently help the company maintain its competitive edge in an increasingly competitive and complex market.
Cunard Line Ltd.: Managing Integrated Marketing Communications	HBSP #594-046 25p TN #595-028	United States, cruise lines, 1992	Cunard, the world's oldest luxury-line company, is confronted with several key issues involving its marketing and marketing communications strategy. One concerns the balance between image/positioning advertising and short-term promotional advertising/communications on behalf of each Cunard ship (i.e., pull versus push communications). Related to this is the overall mix of marketing communications tools used by Cunard—media advertising, direct marketing, etc.

Syllabus
Marketing Management
Xxx Semester, 200x

Course Materials:

Text: Philip Kotler, *Marketing Management*, 11th ed., Prentice Hall, 2002,
    Selected Harvard Business School Cases

Recommended: *Fortune, The Wall Street Journal,* and *Business Week*

Course Description: (university bulletin)

The characteristics and management of markets are described in topics that include the marketing environment, components of the marketing mix, market segmentation, and planning. Prerequisite: (university/college/school/department regulations).

Course Perspectives:

The course focuses on formulating and implementing marketing management strategies and policies, a task undertaken in most companies at the strategic business unit level. The marketing management process is important at all levels of the organization, regardless of the title applied to the activity. Typically, it is called corporate marketing, strategic marketing, or marketing management. For our purposes they all involve essentially the same process, even though the actors and activities may differ. The course will provide you with a systematic framework for understanding marketing management and strategy. Accordingly, the course emphasizes the following:

- Primary and changing perspectives on marketing management in the New Economy

- The impact of interactive media on marketing management

- Applied marketing management and strategy, domestic and global

- An international focus in developing marketing management and strategy

The course is intended for:

- Marketing concentration students who wish to deepen their understanding of marketing management in a strategy-planning context

- Nonmarketing concentration students who desire a course in marketing strategy, with a management, and planning orientation

Course Objectives/Goals/Learning Objectives/Format:

Course Objectives: This course is concerned with the development, evaluation, and implementation of marketing management in complex environments. The course deals primarily with an in-depth analysis of a variety of concepts, theories, facts, analytical procedures, techniques, and models. The course addresses strategic issues such as: What business should we be in? What are our long-term objectives? What is our sustainable marketing competitive advantage? Should we diversify? How? How should marketing resources be allocated? What marketing opportunities and threats do we face? What are our marketing organizational strengths and weaknesses? What are our marketing strategic alternatives?

Course Goals: To further develop knowledge and skills in the essential aspects of marketing management, marketing strategy, and emerging New Economy marketing applications, with a focus on the development and execution of programs, audits, and plans.

Learning Objectives:

- To become familiar with the range of decisions implicit in strategic marketing management and planning, and to develop skill in using a variety of analytical frameworks for making such decisions.

- To develop an understanding of how markets contrast in terms of:

    - Their "enduring characteristics"

    - Their stage of development and how the nature of competition in such markets is impacted

- To develop skills in planning a variety of marketing management tools, ranging from new product entry strategy to international market product life cycle management and strategy

- To develop skill in organizing for effective strategic marketing and in implementing the market planning process

Course Format: The course is highly interactive between the class and the instructor. Through case studies/presentations, problems, and specific company client activities, students will have the opportunity to use the concepts, ideas, and strategies presented in class. Problem-solving sessions occur in both individual (primarily) and team (occasionally) settings.

Grading/Evaluation Criteria:

Overview: The final grade will be based on the following: Four (4) individual case analyses, three (3) team-prepared case analysis, two exams and participation:

Activity	Percent
Cases	60
Exams	30
Participation	10
Total	**100**

- *Case Write-ups:* Due via e-mail 24 hours before the case is to be discussed in class. Write-ups not submitted on time will not be evaluated and will result in a zero grade. Format information is on the course Web site.

- *Exams:* Comprehensive—Each exam will be essay and will cover all assigned readings and class discussions.

- *Class Participation*: There will be case and reading discussions and analyses. You will be expected to respond orally to questions. Responses will be graded on a five (5) point scale, ranging from highly analytical (from a content perspective) to clear lack of knowledge of the material).

Course Outline

Week

- **Case and Lecture Emphasis**
- **12–15 week format**

PART I—UNDERSTANDING MARKETING MANAGEMENT

1   CHAPTER 1—DEFINING MARKETING FOR THE TWENTY-FIRST CENTURY
Lecture: "Marketing Enters the Twenty-first Century"
Marketing and Advertising—T.J. Maxx, Nexen, People Soft (BONUS)
Marketing Spotlight—GE
Case Analysis Concepts—read CBS Evening News

2   CHAPTER 2—ADAPTING MARKETING TO THE NEW ECONOMY
Lecture: E-Marketing and the Airlines
Online Marketing Today—Hewlett-Packard
Case discussion: Alloy.com: Marketing to Generation Y/The Peppers and Rogers Group
CHAPTER 3—BUILDING CUSTOMER SATISFACTION, VALUE AND RETENTION

Lecture: "Creating Customer Relationships That Last"
Marketing Spotlight—Charles Schwab
Case discussion: Citibank: Launching the Credit Card in Asia Pacific (A)
PART II—ANALYZING MARKET OPPORTUNITIES
3   CHAPTER 4—WINNING MARKETS THROUGH MARKET-ORIENTED STRATEGIC PLANNING
Lecture: "Establishing a Winning Strategic Planning Formula"
Online Marketing Today—Procter & Gamble
Case discussion: Matching Dell
CHAPTER 6—SCANNING THE MARKETING ENVIRONMENT
Lecture: "The Marketing Environment Takes a Turn—An Older Turn"
Marketing Spotlight—Mattel
Case discussion: Global Climate Change and BP Amoco
4   CHAPTER 5—GATHERING INFORMATION AND MEASURING MARKET DEMAND
Lecture: "Marketing Research and Measurement at the Millennium"
Case discussion: Juice Guys (A)
5   CHAPTER 7—ANALYZING CONSUMER MARKETS AND BUYING BEHAVIOR
Lecture: "Consumer Concerns"
Marketing and Advertising—Quaker, BlackBerry
Case discussion: TiVo
Marketing Spotlight—Nike
CHAPTER 8—ANALYZING BUSINESS MARKETS AND BUSINESS BUYING BEHAVIOR
Lecture—"Business Marketing in a Changing Global Environment"
Online Marketing Today—Bayer
Case discussion: Arrow Electronics
Marketing Spotlight—Branding Energy
6   CHAPTER 9—DEALING WITH THE COMPETITION
Lecture: "Competitive Intelligence"
Marketing and Advertising—Surf, Listerine
Marketing Spotlight—Microsoft
Case discussion: Skil Corp.
CHAPTER 10—IDENTIFYING MARKET SEGMENTS AND SELECTING MARKET TARGETS
Lecture: "Understanding Market Segments"
Case discussion: Dell Computer Corporation
Marketing Spotlight—Marriott International
PART III—DEVELOPING MARKETING STRATEGIES
7   CHAPTER 11—POSITIONING THE MARKET OFFERING THROUGH THE PLC
Lecture: "Product Positioning in the New Economy"
Online Marketing Today—eBay
Marketing Spotlight—Monsanto Company
Case discussion: BET.com
CHAPTER 12—DEVELOPING NEW MARKET OFFERINGS
Lecture: "Developing New Products: When and How?"
Online Marketing Today—Intuit
Case discussion: Abgenix and the XenoMouse
8   CHAPTER 13—DESIGNING AND MANAGING GLOBAL MARKETING STRATEGIES
Lecture: "Making Decisions in a Complicated International Marketplace"
Online Marketing Today—Reebok
You're the Marketer: Sonic PDA Marketing Plan
Marketing Spotlight—Coca-Cola
PART IV—SHAPING THE MARKET OFFERING
CHAPTER 15—DESIGNING AND MANAGING SERVICES
Lecture: "Services Marketing In the Twenty-first Century"
Case discussion: Four Seasons Hotels and Resorts
Marketing Spotlight—Merrill Lynch
9   CHAPTER 14—SETTING THE PRODUCT AND BRANDING STRATEGY
Lecture: "Reinventing Products and Companies"
Case discussion: Monster.com

Marketing Spotlight—Anheuser-Busch
CHAPTER 16—DESIGNING PRICING STRATEGIES AND PROGRAMS
Lecture: "Measuring the Impact of Price—How Important Is the Pricing Variable"
Online Marketing Today—Priceline.com
Marketing Spotlight: Louis Vuitton Moet Hennessey (LVMH)
Case discussion: Cumberland Metal Industries
PART V—MANAGING AND DELIVERING MARKETING PROGRAMS

10 CHAPTER 17—DESIGNING AND MANAGING VALUE NETWORKS AND MARKETINGG CHANNELS
Lecture: "Measuring Channel Performance"
Marketing Spotlight:
Case discussion: CVS: The Web Strategy
CHAPTER 18—MANAGING RETAILING, WHOLESALING, MARKET LOGISTICS
Lecture: "Retailing versus E-tailing"
Marketing Spotlight—Wal-Mart
Case discussion: Wal-Mart Stores, Inc.

11 CHAPTER 19—DESIGNING AND MANAGING INTEGRATED MARKETING COMMUNICATIONS
Lecture: "Marketing Communications: Key Tool in an Uncontrollable Environment"
Marketing Spotlight—Mountain Dew Code Red
Case discussion: Cunard Line Ltd.
CHAPTER 20—MANAGING ADVERTISING, SALES PROMOTION, PR AND DIRECT MARKETING
Lecture: "Advertising in the New Economy"
Case discussion: Cofidis
Marketing Spotlight: Volkswagen

12 CHAPTER 21—MANAGING THE SALES FORCE
Lecture: "The Death and Rebirth of the Salesperson"
Case discussion: Hunter Business Group
Marketing Spotlight—Oracle
CHAPTER 22—MANAGING THE TOTAL MARKETING EFFORT
Lecture: "Reorganizing Marketing Management—Media Neutrality"
Marketing Spotlight: Socially Conscious Marketers
Case Discussion: Jeanne Lewis at Staples (A) (Abridged)

3. Course Background and Syllabus for an Applications-oriented Course

Background: Application Exercises

This section, available on the Kotler Website, provides a Student Guide and computerized workbook, based on a number of applied marketing applications. There are explanations of the applications and/or database tools, along with the methodology to solve the exercises. Once the students understand the concept and the uses, the accompanying interactive spreadsheets enable them to apply the concepts in many other settings.

The Application Exercises provide students with examples of the types of applied problems and syndicated research materials that marketing professionals work with daily. In addition, the Exercises will assist students who may wish to better understand marketing concepts discussed in the Kotler text, enabling them not only to understand the technique but also to work on other methods for evaluating marketing information, thus moving beyond the subject matter to find methods to improve the marketing management process.

The Application Exercises can assist you in the teaching and learning process as follows:

- You could utilize the material for lecture demonstrations and class discussions. The answers for all the exercises are in the IRM.

- Periodic use of the Application Exercises can maintain and increase student awareness of the analytical aspects of the marketing profession and provide marketing and nonmarketing concentration students with evidence of the potential analytical depth and breadth of various marketing activities.

- Students could utilize the spreadsheets to analyze data utilized in various research activities, team projects or company assistance projects.

- You could provide various modifications of the examples as the basis for quizzes, exams, term projects, extra credit, etc.

The Application Exercises relate to various materials discussed in the Kotler text. Accordingly, you may utilize the Exercises to relate directly to the material in the text, providing you with a number of lecture/discussion options. In addition, you could pose questions to the students such as:

- Are there better ways of solving such problems?

- What type of research information would provide better results?

- How has the New Economy (from the Kotler text) changed the application of marketing concepts and techniques?

This approach can help enable students to think beyond textual materials and learn about how to adjust to the New Economy as it applies to marketing.

Introduction to the Student Guide for the Applications Exercises
(Source: Kotler Text Website)

The purpose of the Application Exercises material is to enable students to better understand and apply various significant marketing management concepts discussed in the Kotler text. The material also provides students with an opportunity to experience and work with some of the analytical marketing tools available to professional marketers. The accompanying interactive worksheets provide "active" or "live" spreadsheet templates for each of the analytical tools.

The complete Application Exercises package has two (2) major components:

1. The Student Guide includes descriptions of the Applications Exercises, along with explanations of techniques and the methodology for learning and applying the concepts and solving the Exercises.

2. The spreadsheets for the Application Exercises (downloaded from the Kotler text Website) contain interactive ("live") spreadsheets for the Exercises discussed in the Student Handout. Each spreadsheet contains instructions for proceeding with the exercise and solution. The "formula" cells are protected (locked) to prevent accidental elimination of the formulas.

The primary purposes of Applications Exercises are to:

- Provide examples of the different types of analyses and problems that marketing professionals work with and thus show students some of the meaningful and dynamic aspects of marketing management.

- Introduce students to some of the syndicated research materials available to marketers. Many issues and problems discussed in the Kotler text can be more effectively understood with the use of these materials.

- Encourage students to analyze and question the processes and techniques involved in the Exercises and thereby move beyond the immediate subject matter to develop the means to improve marketing management capabilities in the future.

Sample Course Syllabus: Applications Emphasis

Syllabus
Marketing Management
Xxx Semester, 200x

Course Materials:

Text: Philip Kotler, *Marketing Management*, 11th ed., Prentice Hall, 2002, and *Student Guide to Marketing Applications*, Kotler Website

Recommended: *Fortune, The Wall Street Journal,* and *Business Week*

Course Description: (university bulletin)

The characteristics and management of markets are described in topics that include the marketing environment, components of the marketing mix, market segmentation, and planning. Prerequisite: (university/college/school/department regulations).

Course Perspectives:

The course focuses on formulating and implementing marketing management strategies and policies, a task undertaken in most companies at the strategic business unit level. The marketing management process is important at all levels of the organization, regardless of the title applied to the activity. Typically, it is called corporate marketing, strategic marketing, or marketing management. For our purposes they all involve essentially the same process, even though the actors and activities may differ. The course will provide you with a systematic framework for understanding marketing management and strategy. Accordingly, the course emphasizes the following:

- Primary and changing perspectives on marketing management in the New Economy

- The impact of interactive media on marketing management

- Applied marketing management and strategy, domestic and global

- An international focus in developing marketing management and strategy

The course is intended for:

- Marketing concentration students who wish to deepen their understanding of marketing management in a strategy-planning context.

- Nonmarketing concentration students who desire a course in marketing strategy, with a management and planning orientation

Course Objectives/Goals/Learning Objectives/Format:

Course Objectives: This course is concerned with the development, evaluation, and implementation of marketing management in complex environments. The course deals primarily with an in-depth analysis of a variety of concepts, theories, facts, analytical procedures, techniques, and models. The course addresses strategic issues such as: What business should we be in? What are our long-term objectives? What is our sustainable marketing competitive advantage? Should we diversify? How? How should marketing resources be allocated? What marketing opportunities and threats do we face? What are our marketing organizational strengths and weaknesses? What are our marketing strategic alternatives?

Course Goals: To further develop knowledge and skills in the essential aspects of marketing management, marketing strategy, and emerging New Economy marketing applications, with a focus on the development and execution of programs, audits, and plans.

Learning Objectives:

- To become familiar with the range of decisions implicit in strategic marketing management and planning, and to develop skill in using a variety of analytical frameworks for making such decisions.

- To develop an understanding of how markets contrast in terms of:

  - Their "enduring characteristics"

  - Their stage of development and how the nature of competition in such markets is impacted

- To develop skills in planning a variety of marketing management tools, ranging from new product entry strategy to international market product life cycle management and strategy

- To develop skill in organizing for effective strategic marketing and in implementing the market planning process

Course Format: The course is highly interactive between the class and the instructor. Through case studies/presentations, problems, and specific company client activities, students will have the opportunity to use the concepts, ideas, and strategies presented in class. Problem-solving sessions occur in both individual (primarily) and team (occasionally) settings.

Grading/Evaluation Criteria:

Overview: The final grade will be based on the following: two exams, an individually-based marketing applications analysis, a team-prepared marketing applications problems strategy analysis and participation,

Activity	Percent
Exams	30
Applications analysis papers/presentations	30
Applications strategy papers/presentations	30
Participation	10
Total	**100**

- *Exams:* Comprehensive—Each exam will be in essay form and will cover all assigned readings and class discussions.

- *Applications Activities:* The grade on these reports/projects will be based on both content and writing ability. In addition, you will be evaluated on meeting the learning objectives of the course. The instructor reserves the right to reject and/or modify any applications project selection. All project choices must exhibit "new" thinking and application.

  - *Individual Applications Analysis:* This activity will involve an existing product or service of a multi-business and multi-product firm. The analysis will include development of data related to market segmentation and/or the promotional efforts necessary to stimulate the various segments to buy the concept and/or product. The strategic analysis also presents an estimate of market potential, sales analysis and appropriate research, and financial data.

  - *Team Applications Presentation:* Develop a written five-year strategic marketing concepts applications plan focused on an entire business unit of a firm or organization. The plan will cover all critical areas for a marketing data analysis, with marketing decision-making the focal point. Specific theme topic areas (each student or team selects one) will apply to the product and company but provide a broader perspective as well, considering such areas as:

    - Product/Service "Positioning" in an era of hyper change

- Marketing management analysis and plan for a product(s) in specific stages of the PLC
- Marketing management and strategic market forecasting on a shoestring
- Market forecasting: science or art? (draw on the course Applications Exercises)
- Market(ing) and marketing applications changes for the next decade

- *Class Participation:* There will be case and reading discussions and analyses. You will be expected to respond orally to questions. Responses will be graded on a five (5) point scale, ranging from highly analytical (from a content perspective) to clear lack of knowledge of the material).

Course Outline

Week

- **Applications Emphasis**
- **12–15 week format**

PART I—UNDERSTANDING MARKETING MANAGEMENT

1 CHAPTER 1—DEFINING MARKETING FOR THE TWENTY-FIRST CENTURY
Lecture: "Marketing Enters the Twenty-first Century"
Marketing and Advertising—T.J. Maxx, Nexen, People Soft (BONUS)
Marketing Spotlight—GE
Application Exercise—Index Numbers

2 CHAPTER 2—ADAPTING MARKETING TO THE NEW ECONOMY
Lecture: E-Marketing and the Airlines
Online Marketing Today—Hewlett-Packard
CHAPTER 3—BUILDING CUSTOMER SATISFACTION, VALUE AND RETENTION
Lecture: "Creating Customer Relationships that Last"
Marketing Spotlight—Charles Schwab
Application Exercise—Buying Power Index (BPI)
PART II—ANALYZING MARKET OPPORTUNITIES

3 CHAPTER 4—WINNING MARKETS THROUGH MARKETORIENTED STRATEGIC PLANNING
Lecture: "Establishing a Winning Strategic Planning Formula"
Online Marketing Today—Procter & Gamble
Application Exercise—Brand/Category Development Index (BDI/CDI) Numbers
CHAPTER 6—SCANNING THE MARKETING ENVIRONMENT
Lecture: "The Marketing Environment Takes a Turn—An Older Turn"
Marketing Spotlight—Mattel

4 CHAPTER 5—GATHERING INFORMATION AND MEASURING MARKET DEMAND
Lecture: "Marketing Research and Measurement at the Millennium"
Marketing Spotlight:
Application Exercise—Buying Power Index (BPI)

5 CHAPTER 7— ANALYZING CONSUMER MARKETS AND BUYING BEHAVIOR
Lecture: "Consumer Concerns"
Marketing and Advertising—Quaker, BlackBerry
Marketing Spotlight—Nike
CHAPTER 8—ANALYZING BUSINESS MARKETS AND BUSINESS BUYING BEHAVIOR
Lecture—"Business Marketing in a Changing Global Environment"
Online Marketing Today— Bayer
Marketing Spotlight—Branding Energy

6 CHAPTER 9—DEALING WITH THE COMPETITION
Lecture: "Competitive Intelligence"
Marketing and Advertising—Surf, Listerine
Marketing Spotlight—Microsoft
Application Exercise—Specialized Buying Power Indexes
CHAPTER 10—IDENTIFYING MARKET SEGMENTS AND SELECTING MARKET TARGETS
Lecture: "Understanding Market Segments"

Marketing Spotlight—Marriott International
PART III—DEVELOPING MARKETING STRATEGIES
7   CHAPTER 11—POSITIONING THE MARKET OFFERING THROUGH THE PLC
Lecture: "Product Positioning in the New Economy"
Online Marketing Today—eBay
Marketing Spotlight—Monsanto Company
Application Exercise—Market Segmentation
Class Application Analysis Presentations
CHAPTER 12—DEVELOPING NEW MARKET OFFERINGS
Lecture: "Developing New Products: When and How?"
Online Marketing Today—Intuit
Marketing Spotlight:
Application Exercise—New Product Planning
Class Application Analysis Presentations
8   CHAPTER 13—DESIGNING AND MANAGING GLOBAL MARKETING STRATEGIES
Lecture: "Making Decisions in a Complicated International Marketplace"
Online Marketing Today—Reebok
Marketing Spotlight—Coca-Cola
PART IV—SHAPING THE MARKET OFFERING
CHAPTER 15—DESIGNING AND MANAGING SERVICES
Lecture: "Services Marketing In the Twenty-first Century"
Marketing Spotlight—Merrill Lynch
9   CHAPTER 14—SETTING THE PRODUCT AND BRANDING STRATEGY
Lecture: "Reinventing Products and Companies"
Marketing Spotlight—Anheuser-Busch
Application Exercise—Positioning a Brand in a Category
CHAPTER 16—DESIGNING PRICING STRATEGIES AND PROGRAMS
Lecture: "Measuring the Impact of Price—How Important Is the Pricing Variable"
Online Marketing Today—Priceline.com
Marketing Spotlight: Louis Vuitton Moet Hennessey (LVMH)
Application Exercise—Using Costs in Setting Prices
PART V—MANAGING AND DELIVERING MARKETING PROGRAMS
10   CHAPTER 17—DESIGNING AND MANAGING VALUE NETWORKS AND MARKETING CHANNELS
Lecture: "Measuring Channel Performance"
Application Exercise—New Product Planning
CHAPTER 18—MANAGING RETAILING, WHOLESALING, MARKET LOGISTICS
Lecture: "Retailing versus E-tailing"
Marketing Spotlight—Wal-Mart
Application Exercise—Nielsen Television Audience Analysis
11   CHAPTER 19—DESIGNING AND MANAGING INTEGRATED MARKETING COMMUNICATIONS
Lecture: "Marketing Communications: Key Tool in an Uncontrollable Environment"
Class Applications Presentations
Marketing Spotlight—Mountain Dew Code Red
CHAPTER 20—MANAGING ADVERTISING, SALES PROMOTION, PR AND DIRECT MARKETING
Lecture: "Advertising in the New Economy"
Class Applications Presentations
Application Exercise—Advertising Weight Decisions
12   CHAPTER 21—MANAGING THE SALES FORCE
Lecture: "The Death and Rebirth of the Salesperson"
Class Applications Presentations
Marketing Spotlight—Oracle
CHAPTER 22—MANAGING THE TOTAL MARKETING EFFORT
Lecture: "Reorganizing Marketing Management—Media Neutrality"
Final Exam

Complete Text and IRM Outline

PART I—UNDERSTANDING MARKETING MANAGEMENT
CHAPTER 1—DEFINING MARKETING FOR THE TWENTY-FIRST CENTURY
Lecture # 1: "Marketing Enters the Twenty-first Century"
Lecture # 2: "The Changing Image of Marketing"
Marketing and Advertising—T.J. Maxx, Nexen, People Soft (BONUS)
Online Marketing Today—Tesco
Marketing Spotlight—GE
Application Exercise—Index Numbers
CHAPTER 2—ADAPTING MARKETING TO THE NEW ECONOMY
Lecture: E-Marketing and the Airlines
Marketing and Advertising—ePad, Garmin
Online Marketing Today—Hewlett-Packard
Marketing Spotlight—Yahoo!
CHAPTER 3—BUILDING CUSTOMER SATISFACTION, VALUE AND RETENTION
Lecture: "Creating Customer Relationships That Last"
Marketing and Advertising—Doubletree Hotels, Blue Martini
Online Marketing Today—Verisign
Marketing Spotlight—Charles Schwab
Application Exercise—Buying Power Index (BPI)
PART II—ANALYZING MARKET OPPORTUNITIES
CHAPTER 4—WINNING MARKETS THROUGH MARKET-ORIENTED STRATEGIC
PLANNING
Lecture: "Establishing a Winning Strategic Planning Formula"
Marketing and Advertising—Aero Mexico, Ernst & Young, Gillette (BONUS)
Online Marketing Today—Procter & Gamble
You're the Marketer: Sonic PDA Marketing Plan
Marketing Spotlight—Sara Lee
Application Exercise—Brand and Category Development Index (BDI/CDI) Numbers
CHAPTER 5—GATHERING INFORMATION AND MEASURING MARKET
DEMAND
Lecture: "Marketing Research and Measurement at the Millennium"
Marketing and Advertising—Beef Producers, Mutual of America
Online Marketing Today—Northwest Airlines
You're the Marketer: Sonic PDA Marketing Plan
Marketing Spotlight—Knowledge Networks
Application Exercise—Buying Power Index (BPI)
CHAPTER 6—SCANNING THE MARKETING ENVIRONMENT
Lecture # 1: "Demographic Data Analysis"
Lecture # 2: "The Marketing Environment Takes a Turn—An Older Turn"
Marketing and Advertising—Coppertone, Colorado, Morton (BONUS), Shell (BONUS)
Online Marketing Today—Peapod
You're the Marketer: Sonic PDA Marketing Plan
Marketing Spotlight—Mattel
CHAPTER 7—ANALYZING CONSUMER MARKETS AND BUYING BEHAVIOR
Lecture: "Consumer Concerns"

Marketing and Advertising—Quaker, BlackBerry
Online Marketing Today—Premier Pet Insurance
You're the Marketer: Sonic PDA Marketing Plan
Marketing Spotlight—Nike
CHAPTER 8—ANALYZING BUSINESS MARKETS AND BUSINESS BUYING BEHAVIOR
Lecture—"Business Marketing in a Changing Global Environment"
Marketing and Advertising—Ford Credit, Cessna
Online Marketing Today—Bayer
You're the Marketer: Sonic PDA Marketing Plan
Marketing Spotlight—Branding Energy
CHAPTER 9—DEALING WITH THE COMPETITION
Lecture # 1—"Competitive Intelligence"
Lecture # 2—"Does Preemptive Marketing Work?"
Marketing and Advertising—Surf, Listerine
Online Marketing Today—NetFlix
Marketing Spotlight—Microsoft
Application Exercise—Specialized Buying Power Indexes
CHAPTER 10—IDENTIFYING MARKET SEGMENTS AND SELECTING MARKET TARGETS
Lecture: "Understanding Market Segments"
Marketing and Advertising—Bahlsen, Hertz
Online Marketing Today—Levi Strauss
You're the Marketer: Sonic PDA Marketing Plan
Marketing Spotlight—Marriott International
PART III—DEVELOPING MARKETING STRATEGIES
CHAPTER 11—POSITIONING THE MARKET OFFERING THROUGH THE PRODUCT LIFE CYCLE
Lecture: "Product Positioning in the New Economy"
Marketing and Advertising—T-Fal, USPS, Snyder's (BONUS), Hefty (BONUS)
Online Marketing Today—eBay
You're the Marketer: Sonic PDA Marketing Plan
Marketing Spotlight—Monsanto Company
Application Exercise—Market Segmentation
CHAPTER 12—DEVELOPING NEW MARKET OFFERINGS
Lecture: "Developing New Products: When and How?"
Marketing and Advertising—Mrs. Dash, Steelcase, Hoover
Online Marketing Today—Intuit
You're the Marketer: Sonic PDA Marketing Plan
Marketing Spotlight—3M
Application Exercise—New Product Planning
CHAPTER 13—DESIGNING AND MANAGING GLOBAL MARKETING STRATEGIES
Lecture # 1: "Winning in the Global Consumer Marketplace"
Lecture # 2: "Making Decisions in a Complicated International Marketplace"
Marketing and Advertising—Kellogg's, HSBC
Online Marketing Today—Reebok
You're the Marketer: Sonic PDA Marketing Plan

Marketing Spotlight—Coca-Cola

PART IV—SHAPING THE MARKET OFFERING

CHAPTER 14—SETTING THE PRODUCT AND BRANDING STRATEGY

Lecture # 1—"Reinventing Products and Companies"

Lecture # 2—"Brands: Are They Dead?" and "A New Look at Packaging"

Marketing and Advertising—Pepperidge Farm, Crayola

Online Marketing Today—Virgin

You're the Marketer: Sonic PDA Marketing Plan

Marketing Spotlight—Anheuser-Busch

Application Exercise—Positioning a Brand in a Category

CHAPTER 15—DESIGNING AND MANAGING SERVICES

Lecture: "Services Marketing In the Twenty-first Century"

Marketing and Advertising—CIGNA, Concierge.com

Online Marketing Today—Schwab.com

You're the Marketer: Sonic PDA Marketing Plan

Marketing Spotlight—Merrill Lynch

CHAPTER 16—DESIGNING PRICING STRATEGIES AND PROGRAMS

Lecture: "Measuring the Impact of Price—How Important Is the Pricing Variable"

Marketing and Advertising—1-800-Contacts, eBay, Baymont (BONUS)

Online Marketing Today—Priceline.com

You're the Marketer: Sonic PDA Marketing Plan

Marketing Spotlight: Louis Vuitton Moet Hennessey (LVMH)

Application Exercise—Using Costs in Setting Prices

PART V—MANAGING AND DELIVERING MARKETING PROGRAMS

CHAPTER 17—DESIGNING AND MANAGING VALUE NETWORKS AND MARKETING CHANNELS

Lecture: "Measuring Channel Performance"

Marketing and Advertising—Ford

Online Marketing Today—Peoples Bank

You're the Marketer: Sonic PDA Marketing Plan

Marketing Spotlight—Disney Licensed Products

Application Exercise—New Product Planning

CHAPTER 18—MANAGING RETAILING, WHOLESALING, AND MARKET LOGISTICS

Lecture: #1: "Retailing versus E-tailing"

Lecture # 2: "International Retailing—Business Without Borders"

Marketing and Advertising—Mayor's Jewelry, UPS

You're the Marketer: Sonic PDA Marketing Plan

Marketing Spotlight—Wal-Mart

Application Exercise—Nielsen Television Audience Analysis

CHAPTER 19—DESIGNING AND MANAGING INTEGRATED MARKETING COMMUNICATIONS

Lecture: "Marketing Communications: Key Tool in an Uncontrollable Marketing Environment"

Marketing and Advertising—UpWords, Sharp

Online Marketing Today—VF

You're the Marketer: Sonic PDA Marketing Plan

Marketing Spotlight—Mountain Dew Code Red

CHAPTER 20—MANAGING ADVERTISING, SALES PROMOTION, PUBLIC RELATIONS, DIRECT MARKETING
Lecture: "Advertising in the New Economy"
Lecture: "Marketing On the Information Superhighway: Are We There Yet?"
Marketing and Advertising—Absolut, Ask Jeeves, Reckitt Benckiser (BONUS), Toyota (BONUS)
Online Marketing Today—StartSampling.com
You're the Marketer: Sonic PDA Marketing Plan
Marketing Spotlight—Volkswagen
Application Exercise—Advertising Weight Decisions
CHAPTER 21—MANAGING THE SALES FORCE
Lecture: "The Death and Rebirth of the Salesperson"
Marketing and Advertising—Saab, Anthro, Dassault (BONUS), Ericsson (BONUS)
Online Marketing Today—Siebel Systems
You're the Marketer: Sonic PDA Marketing Plan
Marketing Spotlight—Oracle
CHAPTER 22—MANAGING THE TOTAL MARKETING EFFORT
Lecture: "Reorganizing Marketing Management—Media Neutrality"
Marketing and Advertising—Bumble Bee, Iomega, Eggbeaters (BONUS)
Online Marketing Today—BrightHouse
You're the Marketer: Sonic PDA Marketing Plan
Marketing Spotlight—Socially Conscious Marketers (Avon, British Airways, Tesco)

Chapter-by-Chapter
Instructional Material

Part I—UNDERSTANDING MARKETING MANAGEMENT

Chapter 1—Defining Marketing for the Twenty-first Century

Overview

Marketing is the organization function charged with defining customer targets and the best way to satisfy their needs and wants competitively and profitably. Because consumers and business buyers face an abundance of suppliers seeking to satisfy their every need, companies and not-for-profit organizations cannot survive today by simply doing a good job. They must do an excellent job if they are to remain in the increasingly competitive global marketplace. Many studies have demonstrated that the key to profitable performance is knowing and satisfying target customers with competitively superior offers. This process takes place today in an increasingly global, technical, and competitive environment.

Marketing has its origins in the fact that humans have needs and wants. Needs and wants create a state of discomfort in people, relieved through acquiring products to satisfy these needs and wants. Because many products can satisfy a given need, product choice is guided by the concepts of value, cost, and satisfaction. These products are obtainable in several ways: self-production, coercion, begging, and exchange. Most modern societies work on the principle of exchange, which means that people specialize in producing particular products and trade them for the other things they need. They engage in transactions and relationship building. A market is a group of people who share a similar need. Marketing encompasses those activities that represent working with markets and attempting to actualize potential exchanges.

Marketing management is the conscious effort to achieve desired exchange outcomes with target markets. The marketer's basic skill lies in influencing the level, timing, and composition of demand for a product, service, organization, place, person, idea or some form of information.

There are five alternative philosophies that can guide organizations in their efforts to carry out their marketing goal(s). The production concept holds that consumers will favor products that are affordable and available, and therefore management's major task is to improve production and distribution efficiency and bring down prices. The product concept holds that consumers favor quality products that are reasonably priced, and therefore little promotional effort is required. The selling concept holds that consumers will not buy enough of the company's products unless they are stimulated through a substantial selling and promotion effort.

The marketing concept moves toward a more enlightened view of the role of marketing. The marketing concept holds that the main task of the company is to determine the needs, wants, and preferences of a target group of customers and to deliver the desired satisfactions. The four principles of the marketing concept are: target market, customer needs, integrated marketing, and profitability. The marketing concept places primary focus on the needs and wants of customers who comprise the target market for a particular product.

Rather than coax customers into purchasing a product they may not find satisfying, the emphasis is on determining the types of markets to be satisfied and creating the product that achieves this satisfaction objective. Choosing target markets and identifying customer needs is no small task; a marketer must dig beyond a customer's stated needs. Once this is accomplished, a marketer can offer for sale the products that will lead to the highest satisfaction. This encourages customer retention and profit, which is best achieved when all areas/departments of a company become "customer-focused."

Beyond the marketing concept, the societal marketing concept holds that the main task of the company is to generate customer satisfaction and long-run consumer and societal well-being as the keys to satisfying organizational goals and responsibilities.

Interest in marketing is intensifying as more organizations in the business sector, the nonprofit sector, and the global sector recognize how marketing contributes to improved performance in the marketplace. The result is that marketers are re-evaluating various marketing concepts and tools that focus on relationships, databases, communications, and channels of distribution, as well as marketing outside and inside the organization.

Learning Objectives

After reading this chapter students should:

- Know why marketing is important to contemporary organizations
- Understand the core concepts of marketing
- Know the basic tasks performed by marketing organizations and managers
- Understand the differences between the various orientations to the marketplace
- Know the components of the marketing concept and why they are critical to successful marketing practice
- Know why marketing has been found to be critical to different types of organizations and in different environments

Chapter Outline

I.   Introduction

    A.   New economy

        1.   Focus on the digital revolution (Internet and related) and the impact on businesses and consumers in terms of capabilities

            a)   For consumers: multiple new capabilities related to increases in buying power, variety of goods and services available, information, interactivity and product comparability

            b)   For companies: enhanced marketing reach, direct connectivity, information on all of its stakeholders and competitors, communications (internal and external), customized services and products, enhanced logistics, enhanced training

    B.   Information age versus industrial age

        1.   Management has recognized the potential quickly

        2.   Marketing: meeting needs profitably

        3.   "Change or die" (Welch)

II.   Marketing tasks

    A.   Radical marketing

        1.   Firms moving closer to the customer versus expensive research and mass marketing

2. Note the 10 rules of "radical marketing"—including CEO direct involvement, close to the customer, rethinking the marketing mix, and focus on brand integrity (others in text)

3. Stages of marketing practice: entrepreneurial, formulated marketing, intrepreneurial marketing

4. Kotler focus on formulated marketing versus creative marketing

B. Scope of marketing, which involves a broadened view of marketing (including goods, services, and ideas)

1. Products—anything offered for sale or exchange that satisfies a need or want

2. Products can be goods, services, ideas

3. Scope of marketing—includes people, places, activities, organizations, and information

C. Broadened view of marketing tasks—decisions marketers make

1. Focus on demand states and marketing tasks, along with the questions that marketers ask to remain aware and focused

2. Consumer markets and business markets—each requires new tools and capabilities to better understand and respond to the customer

3. Global markets, nonprofit and governmental markets—becoming more sophisticated in recognizing and dealing with marketing challenges and decisions

III. Marketing concepts and tools

A. Defining marketing

1. Marketing defined—a social and managerial process by which individuals and groups obtain what they need and want through creating, offering, and exchanging products of value with others

B. Core marketing concepts

1. Target markets and segmentation

a) Every product or service contains features that a marketer must translate into benefits for a target market

b) The consumer perceives these benefits to be available in a product and directly impacts the perceived ability to meet the consumer need(s) or want(s)

2. Marketers and prospects

a) A marketer is someone actively seeking one or more prospects for an exchange of values

b) A prospect has been identified as willing and able to engage in the exchange

3. Needs, wants, and demands

a) To need is to be in a state of felt deprivation of some basic satisfaction

b) Wants are desires for specific satisfiers of needs

c) Demands are wants for specific products that are backed by an ability and willingness to buy them

4. Product or offering

    a)   Anything offered for sale that satisfies a need or want.

    b)   Products consist of three primary components: goods, services and ideas

    c)   The physical product provides the desired service or action.

5.   Value and satisfaction

    a)   Value is the consumer's estimate of the product's overall capacity to satisfy his or her needs

    b)   Needs are determined according to the lowest possible cost of acquisition, ownership and use

6.   Exchange and transactions—exchange means obtaining a desired product by offering something desirable in return

    a)   Five conditions must be satisfied (see text)

    b)   A transaction is the trade of values (involves several dimensions)

7.   Relationships and networks

    a)   Relationship marketing seeks long-term, "win-win" transactions between marketers and key parties (suppliers, customers, distributors)

    b)   The ultimate outcome of relationship marketing is a unique company asset called a marketing network of mutually profitable business relationships

8.   Marketing channels

    a)   Reaching the target market is critical

    b)   To do this the marketer can use two-way communication channels (media including newspapers and the Internet), versus more traditional means

    c)   The marketer also must decide on the distribution channel, trade channels, and selling channels (to effect transactions)

9.   Supply chain

    a)   The long channel process that reaches from the raw materials and components to the final product/buyers

    b)   Perceived as a value delivery system

10.   Competition

    a)   Includes actual and potential rival offerings and substitutes

    b)   A broad view of competition assists the marketer to recognize the levels of competition, based on substitutability: brand, industry, form, and generic

11.   Marketing environment

    a)   The task (immediate actors in the production, distribution, and promotional environments)

    b)   The broad environments (demographic, economic, natural, technological, political/legal, and social/cultural)

12.   Marketing mix

    a)   The set of marketing tools the firm uses to pursue marketing objectives with the target market

| | | b) | Involves recognition and use of the four Ps and the four Cs in the short run and the long run |

IV. Company orientations toward the marketplace

    A.   Production concept—assumes consumers will favor those products that are widely available and low in cost

    B.   Product concept—assumes consumers will favor those products that offer the best combination of quality, performance, or innovative features

    C.   Selling concept—assumes organizations must undertake aggressive selling and promotion efforts to enact exchanges with otherwise passive consumers

    D.   Marketing concept—assumes

         1.   The key to achieving organizational goals consists of being more effective than competitors in integrating marketing activities toward determining and satisfying the needs and wants of target markets

         2.   Target market—no company can operate in every market and satisfy every need

         3.   Customer needs—it's not enough to just find the market; marketers must also understand their customer's needs and wants. This is not a simple task

         4.   Integrated marketing—all of a company's departments must work together to serve the customer's interests. This begins among the various marketing functions and carries into other departments

         5.   Profitability—the ultimate purpose of marketing is to help organizations achieve profitability goals

         6.   Hurdles to adopting the marketing concept

             a)   Organized resistance—some departments see marketing as a threat to their power in the organization

             b)   Slow learning—despite efforts by management, learning comes slow

             c)   Fast forgetting—there is a strong tendency to forget marketing principles

         7.   Profitability

    E.   Societal marketing concept

         1.   The organization's task is to determine the needs, wants, and interests of target markets

         2.   To deliver the desired satisfactions more effectively and efficiently than competitors in a way that preserves or enhances the consumer's and the society's well-being

V. How business and marketing are changing

    A.   Major new forces changing the way business markets

         1.   Customers expect more and better, rising brand competition, and store-based retailers suffering

         2.   Company responses and adjustments—new focal points

             a)   Re-engineering the firm—more multidiscipline teaming

             b)   Outsourcing goods and services—decapitalizing

　　c)　　E-commerce—everything from the consumer buyer to the purchasing operations

　　d)　　Benchmarking—best practices

　　e)　　Alliances (networking), partner-suppliers—versus winning alone

　　f)　　Market-centered (versus product-centered)—by market segment

　　g)　　Local and global marketing (versus only local)—"glocal"

　　h)　　Decentralization to encourage innovative thinking and marketing (more intrepreneurial)

B.　　Marketer responses and adjustments

　　1.　　Focus on relationship marketing (versus transactional marketing)

　　2.　　Creation of customer lifetime value orientation

　　3.　　Focus on customer share marketing versus only market share

　　4.　　Target marketing (versus mass marketing)

　　5.　　Individualization of marketing messages and offerings

　　6.　　Customer databases for data-mining

　　7.　　Integrated marketing communications for consistent images

　　8.　　Consideration of channel members as partners

　　9.　　Recognition of every employee as a marketer

　　10.　　Model and fact-based decision making versus intuition alone

VI.　　Summary

Lecture 1—Marketing Enters the Twenty-first Century

This lecture is intended for use with Chapter 1, "Marketing in the Twenty-first Century." The focus is on the increasingly important role of the marketing process in the ever-changing domestic and global business environment.

Teaching Objectives

- To explain the concepts related to understanding the role and potential of marketing in the larger business environment.

- To provide students a new and possibly different perspective on the role of marketing in business and society.

- To indicate areas where the marketing process and concept will be useful to the student in assessing business developments.

Discussion

Introduction

Many observers argue that all new or important directions in management thought and practice are marketing-oriented. Marketing is no longer something done when a company has extra revenue to invest. It must be implemented for a business to survive.

The marketing concept has changed dramatically over the last several decades, and recently the focus has increasingly moved to customers (versus products and selling) marketing globally and the various technology issues that impact the market. In addition, there is renewed emphasis in marketing on creating and innovating with new and better products and services rather than just competing against other firms and following the marketing patterns established by competitors.

The marketing concept is a matter of increased marketing activity, but it also implies better marketing programs and implementation efforts. In addition, the internal market in every company, marketing your company and products to and with the employees of the company, has become as challenging as the external marketplace due to diversity and many other social/cultural issues.

Changes in Consumer Behavior

There have been many major marketing shifts during the last few decades of marketing change that have shaped marketing in the twenty-first century. There is a view among professional marketers that there is no longer the substantial product loyalty that existed over the last few decades. Product and brand loyalty, many argue, has been replaced by something more akin to a consumer decision that is based on the absence of a better product or service. In addition, there are major changes in the way customers look at market offerings. During the 1980s customers were optimistic, and in the early 1990s they were pessimistic. Later in the 1990s, consumers appeared rather optimistic, but still cautious at times. The following chart demonstrates some of the major shifts that have occurred to the present:

1980s	1990s	2002
Conspicuous consumer	Frugal consumer, becoming more well-off	Suspicious but generally well-off consumer
Image-driven	Value- and quality-driven	Highly eclectic
Trusting	Skeptical and cynical	A "prove it" attitude
Brand loyal	Does not exhibit loyalty	Believes that there is always something better
Emotional buyer	Informed buyer	Highly informed and specialized buyer
Dreamers	Escapists	Focused on personal needs
Overindulgent	Health- and wellness-conscious	Health, wellness, and some overindulgence, without expectation of costs or consequences
Overworked	Burned out, stressed out, and placing tremendous value on convenience and time	Reliant on technology and telecommunications to save time in making purchasing decisions
Industrious Baby Boomer	Responsible Baby Boomer	Unconvinced Generation Xer

It is increasingly clear that although the four Ps (product, price, promotion and place) have value for the consumer, the marketing strategies of the 21st century will use the four Cs as added critical marketing variables:

Care: It has replaced service in importance. Marketers must really care about the way they treat customers, meaning that customers are really everything.

Choice: Marketers need to reassess the diversity and breadth of their offerings into a manageable good-better-best selection.

Community: Even national marketers must be affiliated, attached to neighborhoods wherever they operate stores.

Challenge: That is the task of dealing with the ongoing reality of demographic change.

End of the Mass Market

During the late 1990s, we witnessed the death of the concept of the mass market. Regardless, some marketers continue to argue that database marketing will never replace mass marketing for most products. The view is that communicating with users by e-mail, Web site, mail, phone, or fax will never become cost-efficient enough to justify the return. However, the success of the Internet provides considerable evidence that one-to-one marketing is and will be appropriate for many packaged goods and other high- and low-involvement products that in the past sold almost exclusively with brand advertising.

Through the 1970s, only high-end retailers and personal-service firms could afford to practice one-to-one marketing. For the most part, they did it the old-fashioned way—with personal selling and index-card files. In the 1980s, as the mainframe computer became more practical, airlines got into the act with a proliferation of frequent flyer programs. Frequency marketing programs such as these relied on monthly statement mailings and large, batch-processed databases of customer records.

Later in the 1990s, bookstore chains, supermarkets, warehouse clubs, and even restaurants began to track individual purchase transactions to build their "share of the customer." Many of these programs now run on PC platforms or workstation environments much more powerful than the most capable mainframes of the 1970s. It is possible today to track 5 or 6 million customers for the same real cost as tracking a single customer in 1950. With Internet-based databases and remote access, this capability has literally exploded in the last few years.

The situation will become even more interesting as one-to-one marketing becomes increasingly more pervasive. With an increasingly powerful array of much more efficient, individually interactive vehicles, the options are virtually unlimited, including on-site interactivity, Web site connections, fax-response, e-mail, and interactive television.

Most households today either have direct Internet access or TV sets that provide real-time interactivity through the Internet. We are closing rapidly on the time when individuals will interact with their television or computer simply by speaking to it. Via the Internet dot-coms, we are able to remember transactions and preferences, getting smarter and smarter about finding just the right entertainment, information, products, and services. Likewise, online capabilities enable providers to anticipate what a consumer might want today or in the future. Unfortunately, the system has been slower to protect consumers from commercial intrusions that they may not find relevant or interesting.

The increasing level of market definition and refinement (and resulting opportunities for marketers) is possible through the massive social, economic, and technological changes of the past three decades. There is no longer a U.S. mass market because lifestyles have changed so dramatically. Some of the important demographic shifts have been:

- *Increasing diversity of the population:* The United States has always been an immigrant nation. However, large numbers of immigrants from Latin America and Asia have increased the proportion of minorities in the country to one in three, up from one in five in 1980. This diversity is even more noticeable in the younger market.

- *Changing family and living patterns:* There has been a substantial rise in the divorce rate, cohabitation, nonmarital births, and increased female participation in the labor force. In addition, married couples with one earner make up only 15 percent of all households. Dual-earner households have become much more common—the additional income is often necessary for the family to pay their bills. Thus, the stereotypical family of the 1950s has been replaced by two older, more harried working parents with much less time available.

- *Emergence of a new children's market:* Minorities are overrepresented in the younger age brackets due to the higher fertility and the younger population structure of many recent immigrants. The result is that one in three children in the United States is black, Hispanic, or Asian. In addition, nearly all of today's children grow up in a world of divorce and working mothers. Many are doing the family shopping and have tremendous influence over household purchases. In addition, they may simply know more than their elders about products involving new technology, such as computers.

- *Income and education increases:* These are the two other important demographic factors impacting the marketing management arena. Generally, income increases with age, as people are promoted and reach their peak earning years, and the level of education generally has increased over the last few decades. Family units today often have higher incomes because they may have two earners. Accordingly, there is an increased need for products and services because they likely have children and are homeowners.

In sum, the need for market analysis and marketing decision making, and managers to perform those tasks, has never been greater. But, as the course will demonstrate, the complexities of, and analytical tools required for, these activities have never been greater. Be prepared for a challenging experience.

Lecture 2—The Changing Image of Marketing

This discussion is intended for use with Chapter 1, "Marketing in the Twenty-first Century." The focus is on the changing perceptions of marketing in the contemporary business environment.

Teaching Objectives

- To explain the concepts related to understanding the role and potential of marketing in the larger business environment.

- To provide students a new and possibly different perspective on the role of marketing in business and society.

- To indicate areas where the marketing process and concept will be useful to the student in assessing business developments.

Discussion

Introduction

What image comes to mind when you hear the word *marketing?* Some people think of advertisements or brochures, while others think of public relations (for instance, arranging for clients to appear on TV talk shows). The truth is, all of these—and many more things—make up the field of marketing. The *Knowledge Exchange Business Encyclopedia* defines marketing as "planning and executing the strategy involved in moving a good or service from producer to consumer."

With this definition in mind, it's apparent that marketing and many other business activities are related in some ways. In simplified terms, marketers and others help move goods and services through the creation and production process; at that point, marketers help move the goods and services to consumers. But the connection goes even further: Marketing can have a significant impact on all areas of the business and vice versa.

Marketing Basics

In your introductory marketing class, you learned some basics—first the four Ps, and then the six Ps:

- Product: What are you selling? (It might be a product or a service.)

- Price: What is your pricing strategy?

- Place or distribution: How are you distributing your product to get it into the marketplace?

- Promotion: How are you telling consumers in your target group about your product?

- Positioning: What place do you want your product to hold in the consumer's mind?

- Personal relationships: How are you building relationships with your target consumers?

The sum of the above is called the marketing mix. It is important to have as varied a mix as possible in marketing efforts, because each piece plays a vital role and boosts the overall impact.

Let's take a closer look at the basic Ps of marketing and particularly at how they might affect what you do in business.

- Product

Marketers identify a consumer need and then provide the product or service to fill that need. The marketer's job is to pinpoint and understand existing needs, expand upon them, and identify new ones. For example, because there are more single people and small families these days than in years past, marketers might see a need for products to be sold in smaller quantities and offered in smaller packages.

How can this impact other professionals in the business/marketing process? Let's say your company has developed a new product that generates enormous consumer demand. Your marketing department may ask you to find a way to speed up the workflow in order to crank out more products faster. A year after the product is introduced, however, the market might be flooded with cheap imitations. Because one marketing strategy is to keep products price-competitive, a marketer may then ask you to find a way to make the product less expensively.

This relationship works both ways. There may be production and industrial engineers who may see a way to change the work process that would create additional options for consumers. Those engineers will also be instrumental in design and development of products for which human factors and ergonomics are important considerations. Maybe there's room to add another product line—so that product X is still blue but new product Y is red. You can suggest this to your marketing department; it, in turn, would do research to gauge potential consumer demand for the new line.

- Price

Ideally, a marketer wants to be proactive in setting price rather than simply reacting to the marketplace. To that end, the marketer researches the market and competition and plots possible price points, looking for gaps that indicate opportunities. When introducing a new product, the marketer needs to be sure that the price is competitive with that of similar products or, if the price is higher, that the consumers perceive they're getting more value for their money.

Various other technical professionals can have an important impact on marketers' pricing decisions. Again, you may be asked to determine if productivity can be enhanced so that the product can be manufactured and then sold for a lower price.

- Place or distribution

What good is a product if you can't get it to people who want to purchase it? When marketers tackle this issue, they try to figure out what the optimum distribution channels would be. For example, should the company sell the product to distributors who then wholesale it to retailers or should the company have its own direct sales force?

Marketers also look at where the product is placed geographically. Is it sold regionally, nationally, or internationally? Will the product be sold only in high-end stores or strictly to discounters? The answers to all of these questions also help shape how a product can be distributed in the best way.

Such distribution questions are potentially of great significance to many professionals, including industrial and other types of engineers in a company. For instance, whether a product will be marketed regionally or internationally can have enormous implications for package design as well as obvious areas of the supply chain: logistics, transportation, distribution, and warehousing.

- Promotion

Promotion encompasses the various ways marketers get the word out about a product—most notably through sales promotions, advertising, and public relations.

Sales promotions are special offers designed to entice people to purchase a product. These can include coupons, rebate offers, two-for-one deals, free samples, and contests.

Advertising encompasses paid messages that are intended to get people to notice a product. This can include magazine ads, billboards, TV and radio commercials, Web site ads, and so forth. Perhaps the most important factor in advertising success is repetition. We're all bombarded with an enormous number of media messages every day, so the first few times a prospective customer sees an ad, it usually barely makes a dent. Seeing the ad over and over is what burns the message into people's minds. That's why it's good to run ads as frequently as possible.

Public relations refers to any nonpaid communication designed to plant a positive image of a company or product in consumers' minds. One way to accomplish this is by getting the company or product name in the news. This is known as media relations, and it's an important aspect of public relations.

As with price, changes in demand created by promotions can have a direct impact on the work of many other professionals.

- Positioning

By employing market research techniques and competitive analysis, the marketer identifies how the product should be positioned in the consumer's mind. As a luxury, high-end item? A bargain item that clearly provides value? A fun product? Is there a strong brand name that supports how the image is fixed in the consumer's mind? Once the marketer answers these kinds of questions, he or she develops, through a host of vehicles, the right image to establish the desired position.

This, too, can affect the work you do. If an upscale image is wanted, the materials used in the product and packaging are likely to be different from those used in a bargain product—a fact that could make the workflow significantly more complex. On the other hand, with your engineering knowledge, you may be able to suggest alternative materials that would preserve the desired image but be easier or less expensive to use.

▪ Personal Relationships

In recent years, personal relationships have come to the forefront of marketing programs. Now even the largest companies want their customers to feel that they have a personal relationship with the company. Companies do this in two ways: They tailor their products as much as possible to individual specifications, and they measure customer satisfaction.

Your contribution can significantly impact the area of personal relationships. If the work processes you create can't meet consumers' time frames, the relationship will be damaged. If you develop manufacturing lines that cannot be tailored to fit customers' individual needs, it will be difficult for the company to give consumers the perception of personal commitment. If salespeople promise delivery by a certain date but the product cannot be produced on schedule, consumers will not be happy.

Marketing, engineering and many other professional areas are interrelated and interdependent disciplines. By understanding the role that marketers play in moving a good or service to consumers, others can operate more effectively, for the present and the future.

Marketing and Advertising

1. The T. K. Maxx ad shown in Figure 1 stresses the money-saving aspect of shopping for brand-name merchandise at the chain's stores in the United Kingdom. T. J. Maxx in the United States, operated by the same corporate parent, also attracts shoppers by promoting low prices on well-known brands.

   a. How is the combination of brand-name products at low prices likely to affect the customer's perception of value at T. K. Maxx?

   b. What else is T. K. Maxx stressing in its advertising to affect customers' perceptions of value?

   c. How might T. K. Maxx use the other aspects of its four Ps (product, place, price, promotion) to enhance customers' perceptions of the value of its total offer?

Answer

   a. Customers generally see brand-name apparel as more desirable than nonbranded apparel, so this part of the offering is likely to increase the perceived benefits and increase the offer's overall value. At the same time, low price reduces the perceived cost of the offering. The combination should make the perceived value of T. K. Maxx's offering seem even higher.

   b. T. K. Maxx is stressing a number of benefits to increase the benefit part of the equation, including the high number of products per store and the range of merchandise for sale. The tag line "The Smarter Way to Shop" reinforces the emotional benefit of saving money by purchasing at T. K. Maxx. The store is also stressing discounts of "up to 60 percent off" to show how the store lowers monetary costs in the value equation.

   c. Students can be creative in answering this question. Evaluate their responses on the basis of how well the four Ps have been applied to either enhance/showcase customer benefits or minimize customer costs. One sample response: T. K. Maxx might use sales promotion to minimize customer costs by including a 10 percent discount coupon in selected ads. This additional discount would lower the overall cost of the offering, thereby boosting the perceived value.

2.   Canada-based Nexen focuses on exploration and production of natural gas and crude oil in locations around the world. Its success depends on a complex network of customers, employees, suppliers, distributors, investors, and other stakeholders. Yet the ad shown in Figure 2 focuses on Nexen's commitment to social responsibility.

   a.   Why would Nexen advertise its socially responsible activities in a business magazine?

   b.   What effect does the company expect this ad to have on its relationships with various stakeholders?

   c.   How can Nexen build on strong stakeholder relationships to compete more effectively in the energy industry?

Answer

   a.   Nexen is demonstrating its commitment to the societal marketing concept and explaining how its social responsibility "creates stability, which ensures long-term profits," according to the ad copy. Business magazines reach current and potential customers and suppliers as well as current and potential investors, members of the media, and public policy officials, all of whom play an important role in Nexen's strategies and performance.

   b.   Nexen may want to impress and influence government officials in countries where it does business and hopes to do business. It may also want to stimulate media coverage of its societal marketing activities and performance. In addition, the company may expect socially conscious customers, suppliers, and investors who see this ad to buy Nexen products, seek out Nexen as a customer, or buy Nexen stock.

   a.   Nexen certainly needs the goodwill of customers and regulators to compete in the energy industry. If these stakeholders have a positive image of Nexen and believe it is acting responsibly, they will be more inclined to buy from it (customers) and work closely with it to resolve any regulatory issues (regulators). Also, Nexen needs a network of loyal, committed suppliers who can be counted on to respond to the company's needs. Ads like this make suppliers feel good about doing business with a socially responsible customer, which in turn may reinforce their loyalty and commitment and enable them to work more closely with Nexen to build competitive advantage. Students may suggest additional ideas.

3.   ****BONUS AD--See Companion Web site!** PeopleSoft makes software to help companies conduct business more effectively and efficiently, on and off the Internet. This ad showcases a software product that companies can use to manage relationships with both suppliers and customers.

   a.   Which characteristics of the New Economy does PeopleSoft touch on in this ad?

   b.   What type of product entity is the software highlighted in this ad, and for which type of market is it intended?

   c.   To support its brand image, what associations does PeopleSoft want to create with this ad?

Answer

   a.   Among the New Economy characteristics in this ad are: wording about customers being demanding, which alludes to their power in the New Economy; wording about 24/7 order capture, which alludes to greater ease in placing and receiving orders; wording about relationship management wrapped in Internet technology, which alludes to two-way communication with customers and improved logistics; and wording about insightful sales and marketing and customers collaborating on forecasts, which alludes to fuller and richer information. Students may cite additional characteristics.

b. The PeopleSoft software highlighted in this ad is a tangible good ("PeopleSoft Supply Chain Management in a Box") if it is purchased on CDs. In turn, this product enables businesses to gather and analyze information (which is itself intangible). However, when a business customer downloads the software, it is accessing the software in an intangible form, as information. PeopleSoft is targeting business buyers who need help orchestrating supplies, customer ordering and deliveries, and sales forecasts.

c. With this ad, PeopleSoft wants to create a brand image of innovation through words such as *ingenious* and *innovative, pure-Internet technology*. It is also creating a brand image of competence through wording that suggests PeopleSoft products can be used "right out of the box." Students may offer other responses, as well.

Online Marketing Today

Tesco, the largest supermarket chain in Great Britain, is also the world's most successful online grocery retailer. Tesco rings up $32 billion in annual sales through 900 stores in the United Kingdom, Eastern Europe, and Southeast Asia, and through its profitable Tesco.com Web site (www.tesco.com), which processes 70,000 orders every week. From appliances to apples, garbage bags to gifts, Tesco.com will deliver whatever its one million customers order, adding a per-order fee of $7. Tesco is now bringing its proven online system to the United States through a partnership with the Safeway chain and Dallas-based GroceryWorks.com (www.groceryworks.com). Visit both sites to see what they offer. What benefits might customers perceive in ordering groceries from Tesco.com or GroceryWorks.com? What costs might customers perceive? How might the value equation differ for a customer shopping in a local Safeway store?

Answer

Among the benefits customers may perceive when ordering from these sites are: the range of products available for purchase, the convenience of ordering from home, and the assurance that food items are fresh-picked from local stores. Among the costs are the delivery fee and the prices charged for individual items. Students may note additional benefits and costs for each site. The value equation for a local Safeway shopper will differ because store customers may perceive less benefit from home delivery, may prefer to personally select items, and may enjoy the shopping experience. These customers may also see the online delivery fee as tilting the value equation too much in the direction of cost, which lowers the perceived value of the online grocery offering.

Marketing Spotlight—GE

GE was established in 1892 when Edison General Electric merged with Thomson-Houston. The company produced light bulbs, elevators, motors, and appliances. Early success came as a result of J. P. Morgan's financial backing and a focus on research and development. Over the next century, GE evolved into one of the world's biggest companies, with a diverse portfolio of products and businesses. It is among the largest U.S. companies in terms of revenues and offers an incredible variety of products, from consumer electronics and industrial power to financial services and television broadcasting. Other operating segments include plastics, aircraft engines, and technical products and services for medicine and science. Under the leadership of Jack Welch, who became GE's CEO in 1981, the company enjoyed two decades of unprecedented growth and prosperity.

Welch is widely praised as a visionary business leader due to his performance at GE. He restructured the industrial giant by decentralizing the company's operations. He also sought to expand GE's business with highly profitable ventures and worked to shed low-performing businesses, such as air-conditioning and housewares. This massive restructuring came at a significant cost to GE's workforce: Between 1981 and 1985, the company cut 100,000 jobs.

Once the restructuring was completed, Welch pursued an aggressive acquisition strategy. Some of the major acquisitions included GE's purchases of NBC Television in 1986 and Kidder, Peabody investment bank in 1990 (which it later sold to Paine Webber). In the 1990s, Welch greatly expanded the historically small GE Capital Services with bank and insurance company acquisitions. GE Capital now operates a diverse range of 27 business, including real estate, insurance, finance, and heavy equipment leasing, and provides more than 40 percent of the company's revenues. The pace increased between 1997 and 2000, during which time GE averaged more than 100 acquisitions per year. In 1999, GE acquired 134 companies worth $17 billion. In 2000, Welch oversaw the company's biggest acquisition during his tenure, the $45 billion purchase of manufacturing titan Honeywell International.

Today, GE has 49 strategic business units operating under the larger master brand. Despite its size, the company is able to react to the fast pace of the New Economy. In 2000, the company reorganized GE Information Systems into an e-commerce unit called GE Global Exchange Services and a support unit named GE Systems Services. These two units manage the world's largest electronic trading community comprised of more than 100,000 trading partners. Additionally, at Welch's urging, GE employees saved billions of dollars for the company by finding ways to involve the Web in their jobs. The company developed an online network to monitor its manufacturing practices, put its human resources reviews online, and established a 24/7 service center for its plants. Welch sees GE as well positioned to take advantage of the Internet because he thinks content is the easy part of e-commerce while "infrastructure is the hard part, and we have the infrastructure to capitalize on" (McGinn, Daniel, "Jack Welch Goes Surfing," *Newsweek,* December 25, 2000).

In the 20 years Jack Welch was at GE's helm, the company prospered tremendously. GE stock rose 3,098 percent between April 1981 and February 2001, compared with 896 percent growth for the S&P 500 during that same period. Once Welch named his successor—Jeffrey Immelt, head of GE's medical imaging business—in November 2000, analysts wondered what effect the change would have on the company. Immelt, like Welch, has professed a dedication to the Internet. He describes it as "a transformational technology that is right in our sweet spot" (Useem, Jerry, "Meet 'Da Man," *Fortune,* January 8, 2001). What remains to be seen, though, is whether Immelt will conduct GE through a period of prosperity the way Welch has.

Questions

1. Marketing would appear to be an important part of what Welch did with GE. Where and how did Welch apply some of the marketing concepts discussed in the text?

2. If Welch were to return to the company in 2002, after September 11, 2001, and the Enron debacle, what changes do you think he might make in the GE marketing strategy?

Suggested Responses

1. Welch was the right man for the times at GE. He understood the core value concepts, both for the firm and the markets it intended to pursue. Welch knew that with products similar to what many other firms offered he would have to provide more value for the customer and the channel. His dedication to the value of the Internet for GE and the marketplace demonstrate this point very well.

2. Welch probably would look much more carefully at the way in which the firm's advertisers apply the concepts of trust that Welch and GE built up over the years. He would also review carefully the advertising and marketing processes and applications that oversell goods and services that companies and consumers now are beginning to look at with much more suspicion than in the past.

Analytical Tools for Marketing Management— Index Numbers

Note that the Student Guide for these materials, and the accompanying spreadsheet exercises, are integral for complete understanding of this analytical tool.

Index number development is an important basic marketing tool. As a result, it is important for students to understand what they mean, how to develop them, and know how they are used.

The Index Number Concept

Index numbers are statistics used for comparing things. They enable marketers to make many comparisons quickly and easily. However, index numbers are used in different ways in marketing, and it is necessary to understand the basics of their use.

Using Index Numbers for Selecting Demographics

One of the most frequent uses for index numbers is to compare consumer product usage with a population base, to see if there is a high ratio between the two. These index numbers are used to select demographic targets for advertising or other marketing purposes. However, there are so many demographic segments to choose from that marketers require a means to make quick comparisons between the alternatives. Index numbers are quite useful for any demographic segment that is above 100. An index number above 100 suggests that there is a potentially greater degree of usage in that demographic segment than in other possible segments and thus is a prospect for marketing attention and activity. Following are two demographic segments from a Simmons Research Bureau consumer research study of the household product decision makers who use frozen pizza products that illustrates how index numbers may be used:

Ages	Number of homemakers, in the age group, in the U.S. (000)	Percent	Number of product users (000)	Percent of all users as a percent of the total user base	Index
35–44	12,512	16.7*	8,132	21.5**	129
55–64	10,905	14.5*	4,780	12.6	87

*Base = 74,975 (in thousands)
**Base = 37,791 (in thousands)

The formula used for calculating index numbers:

1. Pizza index number for age group 35–44

    a. Number of homemakers aged 35–44, divided by the household product decision maker population aged 35–44—12,512 / 74,975 = 16.7%

    b. Number of frozen pizza users aged 35–44, divided by the total number of users—8,132 / 37,791 = 21.5%

    c. Pizza index = Percent of homemakers aged 35–44, divided by the percent of population 35–44 who have indicated in surveys that they purchase/use the product

        1. 21.5% / 16.7% = 129 (index number)

        2. The indication is that homemakers 35–44 consume more of the product than their percentage share of the total homemaker population

2. Pizza index number for age group 55–64

    a. Use the same procedure as above for the 55–64 age group—Index number = 87

    b. Indication is that 55–64 group consumes less than their percent share of the homemaker population

An interpretation of these index numbers is that the 35–44 group is a better marketing target than the 55–64 age group. Although this can be observed by studying the raw data alone, it is much easier to see the difference when the two segments are compared on a basis of 100. (One group is 29 points higher than 100, while the other group is 13 points below 100.) It is obvious now that the 35–44 group is a much better target because that group has a propensity to consume more and is a larger-size market.

Index numbers used in this manner resemble an average. The average is of the population base and the user base. Therefore, an index number of 100 would represent an average sales potential segment and anything over 100 generally represents good sales potential. Another way to perceive the index number for the 35–44 group is to think of it as 1 percent of the population that consumes 1.29 percent of the product, or, consumption is at a 1:1.29 ratio. That represents good sales potential.

Conversely, when an index number is far below 100, it likely does not represent as much sales potential. For example, the 55–64 age group had only an 87 index number, suggesting that this group would probably not be a good target market. There may be niche marketing products and situations where low index numbers would not deter the marketing effort, but these activities require thorough research and planning

Thus, marketing index numbers generally are indicators of sales potential. Usually, the larger the number, the better the sales potential. However, one must be careful in situations where a segment with a large index number has a small population base or has a small number of users. Accordingly, it likely would not be wise to select that segment as a target market. The following example, taken from actual frozen pizza market, demonstrates this point:

Homemakers with presence of children of various ages	Number in United States (000)	Percent in United States	Number users with children at "x" age (000)	Percent of all users	Index
Under 2 years	5,834	7.8	3,277	8.7	111
2–years	10,955	14.6	6,246	16.5	113

It is logical to think that families with children younger than two years old would have relatively equal sales potential as those with children from two to five because there is such a small difference between the two index numbers. However, the population of the under-two group is about half those with children aged two to five, suggesting that the under-two-year-old group might not be a good target market.

Chapter 2—Adapting Marketing to the New Economy

Overview

The New Economy presents many new challenges and opportunities for the marketer. The most important point is that the New Economy assuredly places the customer more firmly in the driver's seat for decisions on her/his product and service choices (customization and customerization). In addition, there have been and will be many changes in business and marketing practices as both consumers and businesses have virtual and real-time access to literally millions of products, offers, options, prices, people, competitors, and sources of information that did not exist until recent years. As a result, the marketing mix will change as marketers and firms identify new uses for intangible assets and effective customer relationship management that is more than a marketing term. We can assume that this increasingly rapid growth and rate of change will continue, and despite the dot-com bust, recession, and other major social, political, and economic adjustments, the Internet and the New Economy have changed marketers and marketing for the long-term future.

Many specific areas of marketing also will feel the sting of change. Marketing channels are becoming increasingly direct, as customers control the time and place of contact. International marketing is becoming more localized as the marketing images from one region can quickly be identified and utilized in other regions. Information dissemination capability, despite virtual overload, is bringing massive changes to advertisers, competitors, suppliers, and other stakeholders, with only the most customer-aware and market-aware players surviving. Marketers who take for granted their past images, market positions, and channel positions can and often do find themselves on the outside looking in rather than the inside looking out.

Database marketing continues to be an important element in the New Economy marketing process, placing even more responsibility on marketers to ensure that data is accurate, up-to-date, and nonintrusive. Marketers have higher levels of responsibility for abuses that have occurred in direct marketing over the last few years. Despite the potential for online and direct marketing, the controversy associated with direct marketing continues. There are issues of concern regarding irritation, unfairness, deception, and fraud, and increasingly the invasion of privacy. Internal monitoring between marketers is all that stands between unfettered growth of the Internet, e-marketing, direct marketing, and eventual government control of the Internet.

As band-width (broadband) capabilities increase, the level of marketing detail and quality adds the potential for "remote marketing" that brings the world closer to true 24/7 marketing, limited only by the creativity and integrity of marketers. The job/career options for marketers will likely reach new levels in coming years, but it is important not to ignore the basics of marketing and constantly to observe the consumer and changing consumer lifestyle directions and patterns from a global perspective.

Learning Objectives

After reading the chapter the student should understand:

- The major forces driving the New Economy

- How business and marketing practices change as a result of the New Economy

- How marketers use the Internet, customer databases, and customer relationship management in the New Economy

Chapter Outline

I.   Introduction

        A.   Hybrid nature of forces in the new economy

        B.   Subcontracting and outsourcing, retain core, benchmarking, partnering, interdepartment teaming, develop new advantages, market intangibles, information, customer grouping versus products

        C.   Old economy marketing around, but more on relationships and information in new economy marketing

II.   Major drivers of the new economy

        A.   Generally, technology, globalization, and market deregulation

        B.   Specific drivers that underpin the new economy:

                1.   Digitalization and connectivity

                2.   Disintermediation and reintermediation

                3.   Customization and customerization

                4.   Industry convergence

                5.   Industry boundaries are blurring rapidly

                6.   Examples include Kodak (chemicals to electronics), Shiseido (cosmetics to dermatology drugs), Disney (cartoons and theme parks to major films, licensing, retail stores, hotels, cruise ships, and educational facilities)

                7.   Recognition that new opportunities may be at the intersection of two or more industries

III.   How business practices are changing

        A.   Old economy business beliefs

                1.   Organize by product units, focus on profitable transactions, focus on shareholders, only marketing does the marketing, build brands through advertising

                2.   Focus on customer acquisition, no customer satisfaction measurement, overpromise, underdeliver

        B.   New economy business beliefs

                1.   Marketing should build brands through behavior that

                      a)   Focuses on customer retention and growth

                      b)   Measures customer satisfaction and retention rates

                      c)   Organizes by customer segments

                      d)   Focuses on customer lifetime value

                      e)   Focuses on marketing scorecard (along with financial scorecard)

                      f)   Focuses on stakeholders

                      g)   Underpromises

                      h)   Overdelivers

                      i)   Moves from no customer satisfaction measurement to in-depth customer satisfaction measurement

C.   New hybrid

    1.   Most companies are a hybrid of the old and the new economies. They retain skills and competencies that worked in the past but add new understandings and competencies

    2.   The marketplace today is made up of traditional consumers (who don't buy online), cyberconsumers (who mostly buy online), and hybrid consumers (who do both)

IV.   How marketing practices are changing: e-business

A.   Definitions: e-business, e-commerce, e-purchasing, e-marketing

B.   E-Business and e-vcommerce take place over four major internet domains: B2C (business to consumer), B2B (business to business), C2C (consumers to consumers), and C2B (consumers to businesses).

    1.   B2C (business to consumer)

        a)   Target the right customers

        b)   Own the customer's total experience

        c)   Streamline business processes that impact the customer

        d)   Provide a 360-degree view of the customer relationship

        e)   Let customers help themselves

        f)   Help customers do their jobs

        g)   Deliver personalized service

        h)   Foster community.

        i)   Internet is less useful for products that must be touched or examined in advance.

        j)   *Note: cluetrain manifesto—companies are too bureaucratic, too artificial, too manipulative, too given to one-way rhetoric. Companies that don't recognize that today's markets are conversations are destined to flounde.*

    2.   B2B (business to business)

        a)   10–15 times the volume of B2C

        b)   Auction sites, spot exchanges, online product catalogs, barter sites, and so on

        c)   Lowering invoice costs from $100 to $20

        d)   Buying alliances

        e)   Efficiencies based on use of supplier Web sites, infomediaries, market makers, and customer communities, with the result that pricing is much more transparent

C.   C2C (consumer to consumer)

    1.   Share information (word of web) growing

    2.   eBay, Agriculture.com, WebMD

D.   C2B (consumer to business)

    1.   Offering call-in, customer service

    2.   Need for faster, better response

    3.   Newsletters, special promotions (based on purchasing history), other reminders

4.   Pure-click versus brick-and-click companies

5.   Pure-click companies

6.   Web site without prior experience as a firm

7.   Search engines, ISPs, commerce, transaction, content and enabler sites

E.   Dot-coms failed for a variety of reasons

    1.   Rushed to market without proper research or planning, poorly designed Web sites, complexity, poor navigation, and downtime

    2.   Lacked adequate infrastructures for shipping on time and for answering customer inquiries. Believed that first company entering a category would win category leadership

    3.   Wanted to exploit network economics—the value of a network to each of its members is proportional to the number of other users (Metcalfe's Law)

    4.   Some rushed to the market in the hope of launching an initial public offering (IPO) while the market was hot

    5.   But, many pure-click dot-coms are surviving and even prospering

    6.   Others are showing losses today, but their business plans are fundamentally good. Consider Earthlink.com.

V.   How marketing practices are changing: setting up web sites

A.   Companies need to Move into E-marketing and E-purchasing

    1.   How can we use marketing to spread word-of-mouth?

    2.   How can we convert visitors into repeaters?

    3.   How do we make our Web site more experiential and real?

    4.   How can we build a strong relationship with our customers?

    5.   How can we build a customer community?

    6.   How can we capture and exploit customer data for up-selling and cross-selling?

    7.   How much should we spend on building and marketing our Web site?

    8.   How do we choose the right sites for placing our ads or sponsorship?

    9.   How can we coordinate our online commerce and store sales and service?

    10.   How much will our retail operations be hurt by our online sales and by other e-tailers?

    11.   Should the site be set up inside or outside of the company?

    12.   How do we get management buy-in and funding?

    13.   How can we fight price pressure and price transparency on the Internet?

VI.   Designing an attractive web site

A.   Attractive on first viewing; interesting enough to encourage repeat visits

B.   Early text-based web sites replaced by sophisticated sites that provide text, sound, and animation. examples:

- Context: layout and design
- Content: text, pictures, sound, and video the Web site contains
- Community: how the site enables user-to-user communication

- Customization: site's ability to tailor itself to different users or to allow users to personalize the web site
- Communication: how the site enables site-to-user, user-to-site, or two-way communication
- Commerce: site's capabilities to enable commercial transactions
- Context factors
- Content factors
- Getting feedback
- Placing ads and promotion online
- Banner ads and small boxes containing text and perhaps a picture are the most basis
- Building a revenue and profit model. The company's revenue stream may come from several sources:
  - Advertising income
  - Sponsorship income
  - Alliance income
  - Membership and subscription income
  - Profile income
  - Product and service sales income
  - Transaction commissions and fees
  - Market research/information
  - Referral income

VII. How marketing practices are changing: customer relationship marketing

    A. Customer relationship marketing and database marketing (CRM)

        1. Enable companies to provide excellent real-time customer service by developing a relationship with each valued customer through the effective use of individual account information

        2. Based on customer attributes, companies can customize market offerings, services, programs, messages, and media

        3. Reduces the rate of customer defection

        4. Increases the longevity of the customer relationship

        5. Enhances the growth potential of each customer through "share of wallet," cross-selling, and up-selling

        6. Makes low-profit customers more profitable or terminates them

        7. Focuses disproportionate effort on high value customers

    B. Note differences in mass marketing versus one-to-one marketing

Mass Marketing	One-to-One Marketing
Average customer	Individual customer
Customer anonymity	Customer profile
Standard product	Customized market offering
Mass production	Customized production
Mass distribution	Individualized distribution

Mass advertising	Individualized message
Mass promotion	Individualized incentives
One-way message	Two-way messages
Economies of scale	Economies of scope
Share of market	Share of customer
All customers	Profitable customers
Customer attraction	Customer retention
	Other considerations:
	Interact with individual customers to improve knowledge of their individual needs and to build stronger relationships
	Customize products, services, and messages to each customer
	Customer databases and database marketing

VIII. Data warehouses and datamining

    A. Capturing information every time a customer comes into contact with any of its departments

        1. The touch points include a customer purchase, a customer-requested service call, an online query, or a mail-in rebate card. These data are collected by the company's contact center and organized into a data warehouse. Company personnel can capture, query, and analyze the data

        2. Inferences can be drawn about an individual customer's needs and responses

        3. Telemarketers can respond to customer inquiries based on a total picture of the customer relationship

    B. Companies can use their databases in five ways

        1. Identify prospects

        2. Decide which customers should receive a particular offer

        3. To deepen customer loyalty

        4. To reactivate customer purchases

        5. To avoid serious customer mistakes

IX. Downside of database marketing

    A. Good and bad sides—three problems can deter a firm from effectively using CRM:

        1. Requires a large investment in computer hardware, database software, analytical programs, communication links, and skilled personnel. Building a customer database not be worthwhile

            a) When the product is a once in a-lifetime purchase (e.g., a grand piano)

            b) When customers show little loyalty to a brand (e.g., there is lots of customer churn)

            c) When the unit sale is very small (e.g., a candy bar)

        d)   When the cost of gathering information is too high

    2.   The second problem is the difficulty of getting everyone in the company to be customer-oriented and to use the available information. It's easier to carry on traditional transaction marketing

    3.   The third problem is that not all customers want a relationship with the company and resent collected utilization of personal information

  B.   Marketers must be concerned about customer attitudes toward privacy and security

    1.   European countries in particular do not look favorably upon database marketing.

    2.   Database marketing is not for everyone

        a)   Most frequently used by business marketers and service providers (hotels, banks, and airlines) that normally and easily collect a lot of customer data.

        b)   It is used less often by packaged-goods retailers and consumer-packaged-goods companies, though some companies (Kraft, Quaker Oats, Ralston Purina, and Nabisco) have built databases for certain brands

        c)   70 percent of firms found little or no improvement through CRM implementation

    3.   All this points to the need for each company to determine how much to invest in building and using database marketing to conduct its customer relationships

    4.   The growth and benefits of direct marketing—direct marketing is an interactive building process (direct relationship marketing).

Lecture—E-Marketing and the Airlines [1]

Introduction

Following the dismal earnings during the last four months of 2001, U.S. airlines scrambled to fill their seats, and many relied on e-marketing to drum up business, improve customer service, and keep a lid on costs.

The crisis of September 11 and after, forced airlines to obtain the greatest possible value out of their information technology and e-marketing systems. These systems were never pushed to perform like they were after September 11. As the president of Continental Airlines noted: "We're living on our systems and our people right now." As consumers postponed flights and businesses restricted travel, the airlines attempted to enhance scheduling and revenue-management systems to control costs and maximize revenue. At the same time, the airlines also accelerated planned e-marketing, Web-site, and customer-service initiatives to keep profitable customers happy and recruit new ones.

Background

The nine largest airlines in the United States collectively reported net losses of $2.43 billion for the third quarter of 2001 and operating losses of $3.65 billion for the same period. Before September 11, industry analysts were forecasting that U.S. airlines would have about $2 billion in losses, but after September 11 they predicted losses for the fourth quarter alone of $3 to 4 billion.

---

[1] *Information Week,* November 12, 2001.

Boeing planned to deliver as many as 520 new aircraft during 2002, and that number dropped to around 400. Southwest Airlines said it filled only 63.7 percent of its seats in October 2001, compared with 70 percent in October 2000. Northwest Airlines's load factor fell to 66.3 percent from 75.2 percent, and United Airlines's was down 7.7 percent to 63.4 percent.

United reported the worst results in its history, with $542 million in net losses, after taking in half of the government's $5 billion bailout for the third quarter. Air Canada announced it may sell its very successful regional aircraft manufacturing division to erase some of its $6.3 billion debt. Lastly, America West announced it was losing about $2 million a day.

The steep losses forced carriers to rethink some long-planned initiatives. Southwest had for months been planning to start service to Virginia's Norfolk International Airport on October 7, and had ordered aircraft from Boeing to support the new route. However, after the September 11 attacks Southwest deferred its shipment from Boeing and instead redirected some of its existing planes to Norfolk.

Post September 11, 2001, Marketing

Soon after the attacks, Southwest executives spent a weekend analyzing data in the airline's scheduling and logistics systems to figure out where pilots, crew, and aircraft had ended up after the mandatory grounding. Then they repositioned them as new flight trends emerged. Accordingly, they had to make various marketing decisions that the interactive marketing system enabled them to accomplish quickly.

Meanwhile, as schedules changed, airlines relied on revenue-management systems to analyze timetables, capacity, and passenger demand to determine ticket prices that maximize revenue. In boom times, if certain flights lost money, profitable flights could make up the difference. Now, every dollar on every flight counted.

Before September 11, air traffic was predictable, and airlines typically stored three years' worth of data to project future business. But the attacks have made it all but impossible to estimate how many ticketed passengers would show up. "Yield management basically went out the window," an airline executive said.

In the weeks after the attacks, revenue-management analysts adjusted the predictive models to assume that customers who bought tickets after September 11 would fly; those who purchased tickets before September 11 were less likely. That let airlines sell more tickets without fear of overbooking.

At Frontier Airlines Inc., the terrorist attacks hurt demand for flights in and out of Boston, New York, and Washington, D.C., worse than those in the western United States. Frontier adjusted its system in the east to use different models to predict demand and no-shows for each flight. For many airlines, revenue-management systems were the lifeline that determined whether they would stay in business.

Thirty-five airlines use Sabre's AirMax revenue-management system, which combines data on fares that all airlines offer with a particular flight schedule to calculate ticket prices. After September 11, Sabre reprogrammed the system to reflect fluctuating demand and the fact that business travel rebounded faster than leisure travel.

Earlier in 2001, Continental Airlines rolled out marketing and financial applications packages that interacted with the other IT systems to provide key details about overall performance. Airline managers were able to analyze the profit of any flight on any given day. Before the attacks, Continental was shifting from monthly to weekly financial reviews. Following September 11, however, executives began to review the data daily to spot trends and change schedules more quickly to maximize revenue.

Many airlines also ramped up customer service and e-marketing projects. For example:

- Alaska Airlines worked around the clock to launch an automated phone system on September 19, two months ahead of schedule. They utilized PAR3 Communications software to automatically call passengers to inform them of schedule changes and ask whether they intend to keep their reservations. Alaska Airlines sent more than 100,000 alerts to customers, freeing reservations staff to book new flights.

- Southwest Airlines began targeting its frequent flyers with an e-marketing campaign. They receive "featured destination" e-mails that highlight certain cities and include hotel and car rental rates, along with a list of places to visit. The goal was simple: Get people back in the air.

- United Airlines focused on frequent fliers. In the past, when a top-tier mileage member called to book a seat on a sold-out flight, he or she was turned away. Now, United reservations agents can view revenue-management data to see what percentage of people are expected to show up and decide whether to sell the important customer a ticket.

To tie together the airline marketing information with that in other industries, consider what else has happened since September 11, 2001. Source: *InformationWeek,* November 5, 2001.

The Internet now offers an alternative to direct-mail marketing. Anthrax worries have sent companies scrambling to come up with electronic marketing options:

- Electronic marketing providers are offering Web-based alternatives to businesses concerned about the anthrax scare's effect on their direct-mail marketing campaigns. However, given the immaturity of e-marketing software and services, some observers questioned whether the Internet has the same reach and impact as direct mail.

- An Oklahoma-based media company (PennWell Corporation of Tulsa, Oklahoma) uses direct marketing to reach magazine subscribers. The publisher expected a 10 percent drop in subscriber responses due to concerns about the safety of postal mail. Many in the online-marketing arena have been vocal in promoting the Internet as a safe alternative to snail mail. The company is advising companies with direct-mail programs to turn to the relative safety and cost-efficiency of the Internet.

- To help move businesses online, BigFoot Interactive, which sells e-mail marketing systems, put out guidelines for e-marketers while encouraging them to integrate e-mail into their campaigns.

- In an effort to make marketers feel more secure, e-mail list-management software-maker L-Soft International made available free virus-checking tools from F-Secure Corporation as part of its software.

- A direct marketer (Brann Baltimore) that used both online and direct-mail marketing noted that many of its customers began thinking about the impact of the anthrax scare on their marketing efforts. Interestingly, however, none of the firm's clients eliminated direct mail or made drastic changes in their overall marketing plans. The primary reason was that the reach of e-mail was not yet close to the level of direct mail. As a company executive put it: "There are hundreds of millions of postal addresses, but only 20 to 22 million e-mail addresses."

To summarize: Marketers that have not yet built up a database of customers who opt to receive electronic messages must buy those e-mail names and then send out unsolicited mail to unqualified prospects. Marketers will say that's no different from sending unsolicited paper mail, says an industry analyst from Forrester Research. As a result, companies could be perceived as spammers, and this makes it not yet a viable long-term solution.

Marketing and Advertising

1. The ePad ad in Figure 1, targeted to consumers, highlights one aspect of the boom in electronic payment: the legality of electronic signatures for completing a variety of sales transactions. Interlink Electronics is positioning the ePad as a simple yet technologically advanced method of securely and permanently documenting a consumer's signature on a paperless real estate contract or any other electronic transaction.

    a. How does Interlink Electronics build on the major drivers of the New Economy in marketing the ePad?

    b. If Interlink wanted to expand from this B2C ad to a B2B ad, who might the company target and with what benefits?

    c. How might Interlink Electronics enhance its revenue stream by targeting business buyers for ePad purchases?

Answer

    a. This ad stresses digitalization of a customer's signature; digitalization is one of the New Economy's drivers. It also stresses customerization because it captures the customer's unique signature. Students may mention other aspects of the new Economy, such as convergence.

    b. For a B2B ad, Interlink might target businesses that require signatures to complete transactions, such as major banks, insurance companies, and securities brokerage firms. It might also target businesses such as Western Union, which can use signatures to verify identities of people sending or receiving money in remote locations. Interlink could stress such B2B benefits as being able to complete a transaction without the customer's physical presence, and the convenience and cost-efficiency of completing transactions across miles rather than having to travel to a single location. Students may cite additional benefits as well.

    a. To enhance its revenue stream, Interlink might offer to sell ePads in volume (at a reduced price) to Western Union (for its money transfer service), Wells Fargo (for its banking and real estate loan businesses), Charles Schwab (for its brokerage business), and other financial services firms that could provide the ePads to consumers or business owners for use in completing transactions. It might also investigate the need for ePads to complete online purchases of products that are financed, such as cars, in order to target B2B marketing toward car-makers and their dealers.

2. Ad number 2: This ad for the Garmin StreetPilot in-vehicle satellite navigation system focuses on New Economy connectivity. At the same time, it suggests access to the burgeoning world of m-commerce, in which customers will be able to locate and buy goods and services in the vast virtual marketspace, not just the marketplace.

    a. Which core marketing concepts are reflected in the text of this ad?

    b. If Garmin collected data about customer use of the StreetPilot, how might it use this information for relationship marketing?

c.   What concerns might customers have if Garmin decided to track their use of the StreetPilot? How could Garmin respond to such concerns?

Answer

a.   The ad reflects several core marketing concepts: target markets (addressing drivers, specifically those who are interested in in-car navigation devices); needs, wants, and demands (customers want to be able to find hotels and other destinations listed in the ad); product or offering (described as an "in-car satellite navigation system"); value and satisfaction (the product is described as "affordable," relating to its costs, and is also described as being "portable" and offering "peace of mind," relating to its benefits); marketing channels (the ad includes communication channels such as Garmin's phone number and Web address).

b.   Knowing how customers use the StreetPilot would help Garmin better understand its customers' needs and wants. In turn, this deeper understanding would enable Garmin to proactively offer improved product uses or new products that are likely to interest its customers. By satisfying customers on an ongoing basis, Garmin increases their loyalty and strengthens the relationship over time.

a.   If Garmin tracked usage of the StreetPilot, customers might be concerned about invasion of privacy and commercial use of the information. Garmin could respond to such concerns and reassure customers by developing and communicating a detailed privacy policy covering any release of customer information, opportunities for opt-out, and customer review of information in company records. This question is a good way to initiate classroom discussion about balancing privacy concerns with legitimate business needs.

Online Marketing Today

Although some resellers fear that pure click e-tailers will steal their customers, they also worry about losing business to big suppliers who can afford to establish flashy e-commerce sites. For their part, suppliers want to ensure proper attention and emphasis from resellers who handle a variety of brands and products. With these issues in mind, Hewlett-Packard set up the AisleOnline e-commerce framework, complete with ordering, inventory, and fulfillment functions—as a free service for resellers of its DesignJet printers. Smaller HP resellers simply post a link to the main AisleOnline e-commerce site; larger resellers get their own customized versions, complete with logos and pricing. Visit the site of Laser-Life Technologies (www.laser-life.com) and follow the HP DesignJet link to see a customized AisleOnline site. How does AisleOnline help HP build supply-chain relationships and deliver value to final buyers? Which of the New Economy practices is HP applying with the AisleOnline program?

Answer

AisleOnline is designed to support its resellers' efforts to market HP printers online. Many resellers lack the necessary technical expertise and financial ability to build proprietary Web sites; by linking to AisleOnline, these resellers can serve their buyers without having to establish a separate Web site. Small and large resellers are a vital part of Hewlett-Packard's supply chain because their marketing and service-support efforts reach customers that the company might otherwise not attract. Final buyers benefit because they can easily point and click to buy the printer they want. The AisleOnline program shows the New Economy practices of connectivity, reintermediation, and customization in action.

Marketing Spotlight—Yahoo!

In the second half of the 1990s, Yahoo! grew from a tiny upstart surrounded by Silicon Valley heavyweights to a major contender in Internet media. David Filo and Jerry Yang, two computer science Ph.D. students at Stanford University, created the Yahoo! search engine in 1994. Using a homemade filing system, the pair catalogued various Web sites and published the directory for free on the Internet. The original version was called Jerry and David's Guide to the World Wide Web. It was renamed Yahoo! once Filo and Yang left their studies to devote their attention to the business. The company's search engine was unique because in addition to the standard word search features, Yahoo! offered its users a massive searchable index. Surfers could search for sites in generic categories like Business and Economy, Arts and Humanities, and Entertainment, organize the results by country or region, and look at results from within just one category. Because Yahoo! was among the first searchable Internet guides, the site attracted hundreds of thousands of Web surfers within a year of its introduction. This early attention attracted investors, and in April 1995 founders Filo and Yang raised $1 million in first-round venture capital.

From its start, Yahoo! sought to convey an irreverent attitude to Internet users and potential users. This attitude originated at the top of the corporate ladder, in the personalities of founders Filo and Yang. The two had conceived of Yahoo! while housed "in trailers full of pizza boxes," and each of their business cards bore the title "Chief Yahoo!" The acronym the pair invented to serve as the company name also contained a promise of fun and excitement. Yahoo!'s marketing reflected the company's heritage as well. Each ad closed with the tagline "Do You Yahoo!?" and the signature "Yahoo! yodel," an audio cue designed to reinforce customer recall of the brand.

Yahoo! executives realized early on that the key to long-term success in the rapidly developing portal market was to transform the site from a portal to a destination where Web surfers lingered and perhaps stayed. The key to retaining an audience was developing a "sticky" site with appealing content that kept consumer eyeballs glued to the site's page. Jerry Yang said, "Most of our users today approach Yahoo and type in a keyword and go from there. They do not stop at our other sites"("As quoted in "Yahoo! Still Searching for Profits on the Internet," *Fortune,* December 9, 1996). This behavior did not sit well with Yahoo!'s advertising clients, who naturally wanted their ads to be seen. Yahoo! executives looked to boost the time spent at the site per user in a variety of ways. This required the addition of homegrown content and vastly expanded onsite offerings, such as Yahoo! Finance, Yahoo! Travel, or the Yahooligans kids directory, which would attract new users and keep them and existing users on Yahoo! pages. In the last half of the decade, Yahoo! added all manner of special features and specialized content, from an online shopping mall to content for wireless applications, which increased traffic and lengthened the average time spent at Yahoo! sites.

By 2000, what began as a mere search engine had become a global media giant, with a meteoric stock to match its new economy renown. As the dot-com crash worsened throughout that year, however, its adverse affects finally reached Yahoo! Analysts who considered Yahoo!'s stock overvalued saw their suspicions confirmed as the price fell 80 percent in the year. Because Yahoo! derived more than 80 percent of its revenue from online advertising sales, and the bulk of its advertisers were Internet companies, their collective struggles affected Yahoo!'s revenues. Click-through rates for banner ads plummeted from 2 percent in 1999 to below 1 percent, lower than the response rate for junk mail. Because Yahoo! was the last major portal to remain independent, after Excite merged with the @Home Network, Snap.com with NBC, Lycos with CMGI, Infoseek with Disney, and AOL with Time Warner, speculation about a possible takeover increased as its stock price plunged. Analysts figured a major global media company, such as Viacom, would be the most likely to pursue Yahoo!.

Questions

1. If "point of destination" placed Yahoo! on the Internet map, what marketing miscue caused Yahoo!'s "point of departure" from the scene? Discuss.

2. If Yahoo! was caught in the web of overconfidence with the dot-coms in 2000, can you suggest marketing management strategies that would help it avoid this situation in 2002 and after? Is a merger the only answer?

3. What changes would you suggest for Yahoo! to give their marketing strategy a longer range marketing perspective?

Suggested Responses

1. There could be class discussion that Yahoo! sought to become a Web destination. Like cities, hotels, and so forth that strive to become physical destination points, Yahoo! became a "virtual" destination and a place where the Internet traveler can home in to for her/his Internet needs. The problem was that there was too much content on the Internet and a failure to provide enough non-Internet marketing to draw people to the site for specific buying purposes.

2. In order to avoid the same fate as other dot.coms, Yahoo! has gone after fee-based business, with only modest success. If students are not aware of this, you might suggest that such actions, even if the site is considered a destination, can be dangerous when there are so many good and competing Internet choices that it is difficult to differentiate with less than spectacular marketing efforts.

3. In the Text, Kotler notes that there are many things a firm in this type of situation can do to improve overall marketing strategy. For example:

    a. Use of traditional marketing to spread word-of-mouth
    b. Develop programs to convert visitors into repeaters
    c. Make the site more experiential and real
    d. Create and build a strong relationship with customers
    e. Build a customer community
    f. Capture and exploit customer data for up-selling and cross-selling

    These and many other suggestions for more effective Web marketing could be of great value for Yahoo to consider in their long-range marketing strategy.

Chapter 3—Building Customer Satisfaction, Value, and Retention

Overview

Today's customers face a growing range of choices in the products and services they can buy. They are making their choice on the basis of their perceptions of quality, service, and value. Companies need to understand the determinants of customer value and satisfaction. Customer delivered value is the difference between total customer value and total customer cost. Customers will normally choose the offer that maximizes the delivered value.

Customer satisfaction is the outcome felt by buyers who have experienced a company performance that has fulfilled expectations. Customers are satisfied when their expectations are met and delighted when their expectations are exceeded. Satisfied customers remain loyal longer, buy more, are less price sensitive, and talk favorably about the company.

A major challenge for high-performance companies is that of building and maintaining viable businesses in a rapidly changing marketplace. They must recognize the core elements of the business and how to maintain a viable fit between their stakeholders, processes, resources, and organization capabilities and culture. Typically, high-performing businesses develop and emphasize cross-functional skills rather than functional skills (overall project management and results versus functional strengths (best engineers, and so on.). They also build their resources into core capabilities that become core competencies, distinctive abilities, and competitive advantages. This along with a corporate culture of shared experiences, stories, beliefs, and norms unique to the organization are the keys to their success.

To create customer satisfaction, companies must manage their value chain as well as the whole value delivery system in a customer-centered way. The company's goal is not only to get customers, but even more importantly to retain customers. Customer relationship marketing provides the key to retaining customers and involves providing financial and social benefits as well as structural ties to the customers. Companies must decide how much relationship marketing to invest in different market segments and individual customers, from such levels as basic, reactive, accountable, proactive, and full partnership. Much depends on estimating customer lifetime value against the cost stream required to attract and retain these customers.

Total quality marketing is seen today as a major approach to providing customer satisfaction and company profitability. Companies must understand how their customers perceive quality and how much quality they expect. Companies must then strive to offer relatively higher quality than their competitors. This involves total management and employee commitment as well as measurement and reward systems. Marketers play an especially critical role in their company's drive toward higher quality.

Learning Objectives

After reading this chapter students should:

- Know what constitutes customer value and satisfaction
- Know how leading companies organize to produce and deliver high customer value and satisfaction
- Know how companies can retain customers as well as attract customers
- Know how companies can determine customer profitability
- Know how companies can practice a total quality marketing strategy

Chapter Outline

I.   Introduction

     A.   Chapter focus

          1.   How companies can win customers

          2.   How companies can outperform competitors

     B.   Marketing starts with good products that meet a need

          1.   Marketing can happen only when the firm has a competitively superior customer value-delivery system

          2.   A customer-focused firm with a value marketing orientation is essential

II.   Defining customer value and satisfaction

     A.   Customer perceived value

          1.   Customer delivered value

               a)   Difference between total customer value and total customer cost or "profit" to the customer

               b)   Total customer value is the expected bundle of benefits

          2.   Total customer cost

               a)   Bundle of costs consumers expect to incur in evaluating, obtaining, and using the product or service

          3.   Customer value assessment—weighing the value against all of the costs

     B.   Total customer satisfaction

          1.   Perceived performance and expectations, and how they contribute to overall satisfaction

          2.   Methods of tracking and measuring customer satisfaction (includes customer satisfaction surveys, ghost shopping, and lost customer analysis)

III.   Nature of high-performance businesses

     A.   Stakeholders

          1.   Customers, employees, suppliers, distributors

     B.   Processes

          1.   Work flows through an organization to achieve cross functional skills

     C.   Resources

          1.   Labor, power, materials, machines, information, energy, and so on, to achieve core competence, distinctive ability(ies), and competitive advantage

     D.   Organization and organizational culture

          1.   Structures and policies. Corporate Culture is the shared experiences, stories, beliefs, and norms that characterize an organization

IV.   Delivering customer value and satisfaction

     A.   Value chain

          1.   Used as a tool for identifying ways to create more value, includes the nine value-creating activities

     B.   Value-delivery network

1. To be successful a firm has to look for competitive advantages beyond its own operations

2. Building a better network can be a highly successful differentiation tactic that leads to greater customer satisfaction

V. Attracting and retaining customers

   A. Attracting customers

      1. Becoming harder to please, smarter, more demanding, and less forgiving

   B. Computing the cost of lost customers

      1. Compute customer defection rate (4-step process) and steps to reduce the defection rate

   C. Need for customer retention

      1. Cost of attracting a new customer is five times that of retaining a satisfied current customer

   D. Measuring customer lifetime value

      1. Details developed in the text

   E. Customer relationship management (crm): the key—lifetime customer equity

      1. The main drivers of customer equity

         a) Value equity

         b) Brand equity

         c) Relationship equity

      2. The result is an integration of value management, brand management, and relationship management

      3. The levels of investment in CRM building move from basic marketing (sell) to partnership marketing

   F. Forming strong customer bonds: the basics

      1. Adding financial benefits—frequency marketing programs and club marketing programs

      2. Adding social benefits—individualize and personalize customer relationships

      3. Adding structural ties—help customers manage themselves

VI. Customer profitability, company profitability, and total quality management

   A. Measuring profitability

      1. The ultimate test of a profitable customer is

         a) A person, household, or company that over time yields a revenue stream that exceeds by an acceptable amount the company's cost stream of attracting, selling, and servicing the customer

         b) A company should not attempt to pursue and satisfy all customers

   B. Increasing company profitability

      1. Based on sustainable competitive advantage (Porter)

      2. However, at best it may be leverageable advantage

VII. Implementing total quality management

   A. Total Quality Marketing (TQM)—quality is the key to everything else

1. Most customers will no longer accept or tolerate average quality performance
2. There is an intimate connection among product and service quality, customer satisfaction, and company profitability

B. Role of marketing now is
   1. Extended beyond external marketing activities
   2. Includes internal marketing roles to act as the customer's watchdog within the organization

VIII. Summary

Lecture—Creating Customer Relationships that Last

This lecture is intended for use with Chapter 3, "Building Customer Satisfaction, Value, and Retention." The focus is on the increasingly powerful role of customers in the marketing process and the need for marketers to provide value that exceeds customer expectations. The concept of relationship marketing is also presented for further discussion, providing a link with other areas of the text.

Teaching Objectives

- Help students to better understand the changing role of the customer in today's marketplace

- To explain the concepts of product and service quality as they contribute to perceived value for the customer

- To present specific methods whereby marketers can engage in value-creating activities

Discussion

Introduction

In the contemporary marketplace, it is hard to believe there was ever a time when customers were not treated as an integral part of the exchange process. Prior chapters consider some of the many shifts taking place in today's marketing environment. Competition in the marketplace, along with advancing technology, affords customers the ability to learn significantly more about the products they will consider purchasing.

The same factors also have created both the need and the opportunity for marketers to know their customers on a more personal level. Ever-increasing competition has forced marketers to seek out the information necessary to provide customers with the products and services they truly desire. Technology, when used to create a customer database, is one way marketers are answering to this new trend. Product development will be discussed in a later chapter; for now, we will focus on building satisfaction through customer relationship development activities.

The concept of perceived value is based on Kotler's explanation of customer delivered value. Customers, like marketers, seek to profit from an exchange. Perceived value is aptly named because it supports the notion that the customer and not the marketer determine value. The marketer's responsibility is to create value, in both product and service quality, that lead to increased satisfaction and encourage a high perceived value.

For example, service excellence is determined by customer perceptions and motivated by customer needs. Ken Blanchard, author of *The One Minute Manager,* says that the secret to competing successfully in today's environment is to provide customers with service that is so far above their expectations that it is perceived to be legendary.

Marketers, with both large and small organizations, can engage in activities that exceed expectations and lead to customer delivered value. Marketers with large organizations have the ability to tap into a sophisticated database, utilizing past purchase data to customize marketing programs. These marketers also can become experts at "guerrilla marketing," or the implementation of local promotions for the purpose of getting closer to customers. Furthermore, large organization marketers also have the ability to create Web site and store-specific marketing programs that create retailer loyalty, build differentiation, and increase sales in desired market areas.

Small business marketers, however, also have many opportunities to create strong customer relationships. By placing extra focus on what might generally be considered a commodity product, these marketers can stimulate demand and compete with large rivals in the same industry. If a company is small enough, its top executives can serve as the communication link for the company and various external publics, such as customers and retailers. Even internal publics, such as the sales staff, should be encouraged to make suggestions to top management. Finally, database programs are becoming more and more affordable, making direct-mail programs a viable option even for smaller firms. This leads to a discussion of an evolving direction for relationship marketing.

Relationship Marketing Expanded

Even though it is becoming increasingly possible, why would any rational customer actually want a "relationship" with the company that makes his or her razor blades, or dishwasher soap, or toilet paper? The answer is that the consumer probably would not necessarily desire a "relationship" with these companies, but the customer will want more spare time. Accordingly, he or she might like to have routine or repeat purchases for soap, paper towels, grocery staples, and so forth automated.

What if you could turn on your personal computer or your interactive television set, call up a list of last week's grocery purchases, make a few changes, and then simply order them delivered to your door? And what if, when you did this, the computer reminded you to order certain items such as toothpaste and paper towels because you might be running low on those items? What if, to help choose the groceries you wanted for your family, you asked the computer for a week's worth of dinner menus, specifying recipes and ingredients?

In many product categories, you don't really care what brand the computer selects, but in some product categories you have a list of "approved" brands, as well as brands you never want to see again. The computer automatically seeks out the least expensive basket of products that meet these criteria. Once you confirm it, your order is paid for via credit card or direct debit. The elapsed time for all this shopping was just seven minutes.

Now, from the marketer's side of the equation, consider the immense business opportunity in serving your customers more thoroughly. Delivering grocery staples is one thing. But what about pharmaceuticals? Dry cleaning and laundry? Ready-made meals? FedEx and other pickups and deliveries? The companies become, in essence, share-of-customer marketers.

A marketer's primary task in the one-to-one future is not to find customers for the marketer's products but rather to find more products and services for its customers. Consider that most retail chains have not really tried to figure out how to offer such conveniences as home delivery, because they don't want to consider this for various internal reasons. They want customers to need to come in to the store (or into the virtual store) because they like to have customers walking up and down the aisles (or virtual aisles), making last-minute impulse purchases. For a large part of their business, today's retailers depend on inconveniencing customers by requiring them to drive to their store (or virtual store) location to do their shopping.

However, consider that marketers today jam twice as many products in the average supermarket as there were just over a decade ago (30,000 products now, compared with 15,000 in 1985). Furthermore, commercial messages abound for these products, the overwhelming majority of which do not now appeal to any particular consumer. Instead, we must all fight our way through the increasing number of advertising messages to pick out the information we need, just as we must struggle through the proliferating barrage of products in or out of stores just to select the ones we want to buy. Every shopping trip becomes an increasingly difficult attempt to accomplish the same basic task, thus adding to the increasing use of the Internet.

Having an ability to buy these products more conveniently doesn't mean people will completely stop going into stores, nor does it mean advertising will cease to exist. But if getting your regularly consumed products could be made nearly as convenient as "pushing a button," wouldn't you go into the store less frequently? Wouldn't you, for the most part, prefer not having to shop for routine things? You could always choose to go out if you wanted to—after all, shopping is often a social experience, as well as a necessity.

As with stores and other enterprises that cater to the interests of the interactive consumer (including information and entertainment providers), the manufacturer will be able to succeed competitively only by relying on individual feedback. For the manufacturer, success in the one-to-one marketing environment will mean soliciting information from consumers, individually, and then using that feedback to customize an offering to each individual customer, one at a time. This is the essence of one-to-one marketing.

Marketing and Advertising

1. Doubletree targets both vacationers and business travelers for its hotels and resort accommodations. The ad in Figure 1 shows how this hotel chain seeks to build relationships with business travelers by adding value in a variety of ways.

    a. What types of benefits are being emphasized in Doubletree's relationship-building efforts with business travelers? Why are these appropriate for the target market?

    b. Which of the customer value and customer cost factors are being addressed in this ad? How do they affect the customer's determination of delivered value?

    c. How else does Doubletree use this ad to stress benefits that appeal to customers as value-maximizers?

Answer

    a. The Doubletree ad emphasizes both financial benefits (the Hilton HHonors and airline frequency marketing programs) and social benefits (friendlier service by Doubletree employees). Both types of benefits are valued by business travelers. These customers have many hotel choices when they travel, so they would be more inclined to return to chains that offer rewards such as free hotel stays. In addition, because travelers have so many choices, they can make their decision on the basis of staff service and attitude as well as hotel location and room rate.

    b. The value of Doubletree's services and personnel are highlighted in this ad. Doubletree wants customers to put a higher value on its services (because of nice touches such as fresh-baked cookies at check-in) and its personnel (as evidenced by wording such as "honest, eager staff" and "people who are genuinely interested in making your stay more comfortable"). On the cost side, Doubletree's inclusion of the Hilton HHonors reward program encourages business travelers to see the monetary cost as lower because (1) they can earn free hotel stays and (2) they do not need to tip hotel employees all the time. Doubletree also wants to minimize the psychic cost by emphasizing that its employees really care about guests and are "not just going through the motions." Students may offer additional ideas.

c. Students may suggest a variety of responses. For example, the photo suggests that business travelers who choose Doubletree can relax and enjoy themselves after the business day is over, a benefit that is valued by the target market.

2. Blue Martini in Figure 2 makes software that enables people in different locations to move through a Web site at the same time, shopping or chatting as they progress through the pages. By facilitating collaboration between individuals or groups, Blue Martini enhances users' online experience, according to this ad. How does this help customer satisfaction?

a. If a company using Blue Martini software allowed two sisters to simultaneously browse the same retailing Web site, how would this be likely to affect the sisters' perception of value?

b. Would Blue Martini be part of the primary or support activities of a business customer's value chain?

c. What else might Blue Martini do in its advertising to stress the value of its software to its customers' customers?

Answer

a. The sisters are likely to perceive more benefit from a retailing Web site that allows them to shop online together and consult with each other before one or both makes a purchase. They are also more likely to perceive a lower cost because the process takes less time and costs less than if the sisters had to search the site separately, call or write one another to discuss specific products, and log on again to make their purchases.

b. Blue Martini would be part of the primary activities of marketing (which covers marketing and sales) and service. It enables businesses to facilitate online sales by allowing two customers or a customer and a salesperson or technical representative to examine the same Web page at the same time. It also enhances service capabilities by allowing a company representative to guide a customer through the use of a particular online process or page or provide other assistance while the customer is visiting the same Web page.

c. Students may have a number of ideas for ways in which Blue Martini can use advertising to stress the value of its software to its customers' customers. One sample response: With the permission of one of its business customers, Blue Martini could include a testimonial or a case study showing how that business used Blue Martini software to solve its customers' problems or boost its customers' satisfaction. This would make the benefits more concrete and provide prospects with ideas about putting Blue Martini to best use.

Online Marketing Today

Any time a company registers a Web site ending in .com or .net, Verisign makes money as the administrator of these U.S. Internet domain names. Verisign also manages electronic payments for Bank of America as well as signature security—allowing legal documents to be signed and exchanged over the Internet—for Ford, Microsoft, and 3,000 other corporations. Quality is therefore very important to the satisfaction of Verisign's business customers, who value both security and accuracy. Visit Verisign's Web site (www.verisign.com), follow the link to its products page, and read about the SSL Certificates or Web Site Trust Services. What are the benefits of this bundle of services? Would customers who buy this set of services be seeking conformance or performance quality? How does this set of services contribute to Verisign's competitive advantage?

Answer

The main benefit of Verisign's Web Site Trust Services is to reassure visitors that the company's Web site is genuine and the data they transmit is secure (so customers will feel safer and not worry about any personal information or payment data they send). Some of the services in this bundle relate specifically to payment services, while others relate to network security. As a bundle, this set of services is designed to give the Web site a more trustworthy image. Customers who buy this set of services—businesses that operate Web sites—want both performance and conformance quality. Not only do they want the product to meet the performance specifications promised by Verisign, but they also want every one of the products to deliver the same high level of quality. Verisign's security experience and expertise is one of its core competences; this set of services contributes to competitive advantage because it promises and delivers site security as one of its valued customer benefits.

Marketing Spotlight—Charles Schwab

Charles Schwab founded the discount brokerage named for him in 1974. The company's no-frills investment offerings were predicated on Charles Schwab's distaste for traditional brokers, who he labeled "hucksters of inside information, always trying to get me to buy this product or investment." Until 1993, Schwab's brokers were instructed not to offer investment advice, but rather to refer curious customers to publicly available research from Standard & Poor's or Morningstar.

Schwab benefited from the online trading boom. Long before any of the traditional brokerage houses considered an e-commerce move, in 1997 Schwab was one of the first discount brokerages to offer online trading. It offered online trades at $29.95 for the first 1,000 shares, compared with the per-trade fees that exceeded $100. Starting at zero in 1995, online trades accounted for 85 percent of all trades executed by Schwab by 2001. The company's retail assets grew threefold to almost $1 trillion during the same time period, putting it in league with the biggest brokerages in America. Between 1997 and 2000, daily trades rose 183 percent, while profits increased 112 percent during that time frame.

Schwab's marketing activities helped the company become a household name synonymous with online trading. Early ads used real Schwab customers and employees in testimonial advertisements. In 1999, the company enlisted celebrity spokespersons to advertise its full-service online investing offerings. The humorous ads featured sports stars such as football player Shannon Sharpe and tennis star Anna Kournikova in cameo roles as Schwab customers who surprised competitors with their knowledge of investing principles. The tagline served to reinforce Schwab's difference from online-only brokerages: "We've created a smarter kind of investing. We've created a smarter kind of investor." These ads were part of Schwab's $200 million marketing budget for 1999.

In 2001, as online trading slowed in the wake of the dot-com crash, Schwab sought to expand its business by providing its customers with a greater number of services. Rather than rely on a high volume of low-cost trades to drive revenues, Schwab began focusing on providing investment advice to its clients. In new brokerage offices, Schwab placed financial advisers from whom clients could seek investment tips and other services for a fee. Schwab also considered offering proprietary stock research for its customers. Industry experts expected these new services would recast Schwab in a role more similar to traditional brokerage houses. A former Schwab executive predicted, "Schwab will be a lot closer to Merrill Lynch than it is to the Schwab of yesterday."

(Sources: John Gorman, "Charles Schwab, Version 4.0," *Forbes*, January 8, 2001, pp. 89–95. Charles Gasparino and Ken Brown, "Schwab's Own Stock Suffers from Move into Online Trading," *Wall Street Journal*, June 19, 2001, p. A1. Rebecca Buckman and Kathryn Kranhold, "Schwab Serves Up Sports-Themed Ads," *Wall Street Journal*, August 30, 1999, p. B9.)

Questions

1.   What changes in the marketing environment does the Schwab marketing effort reflect? How has Schwab effectively anticipated the needs of the market?

2.   Draw on recent economic developments to anticipate where the next changes likely will be for Schwab. Consider what past and future events might have a substantial impact on the way it operates in the future.

Suggested Responses

1.   Schwab recognized the needs of a more egotistical and self-confident generation of Baby Boomers and Generation Xers who wanted more control and wanted it faster. This fits with much of what Kotler talks about as the key variables for successful marketers today. Although there will always be room for Merrill Lynch and other full service brokers, it is also likely that with ups and downs in the market there will always be those who feel they have the ability to do their own investment planning and action and will turn to Schwab. Schwab provides superior online research and other investor services at a modest price and with only as much live involvement as the customer desires.

2.   It is clear that various issues occur to affect the economic and investment environment. For Schwab, this could mean that investors will think about the safety of their investments and the quality of corporate management, but Schwab and other investment professionals know that current concerns will pass, replaced by human action to trust and find a better way.

      Schwab should remain flexible and evaluate the long-term strategy to pursue more upscale target markets, such as the Merrill Lynch higher discretionary income market, which desires more services. The events of the first years of the twenty-first century may prove beneficial, for Schwab, if it remains flexible in its marketing activities, because the Schwab target market tends not to follow blindly the market, no matter whether the economic environment is good or bad. There is considerable marketing data to indicate that even the more affluent investor has become more interested in online trading as a way to maintain control and knowledge and less interested in merely handing over his/her investments to someone who may or may not have greater investing insight.

Analytical Tools for Marketing Management—Buying Power Index (BPI)

Note: Suggest that students study the "Survey of Buying Power," published in Sales & Marketing Management *because it has much to offer in providing the means to better understand the key demographic variables in the marketplace. This section covers only a small portion of the Survey's full potential.*

Answers to Questions

1. Students only have to subtract the 1996 BPI figures from the 2000 BPI figures for each market and then select the top five (5) markets. They also can calculate percent of change. Here are the answers:

		1998 BPI	2002 BPI	Difference	Percent increase
(1)	San Diego	.8483	.9333	.0850	+10.0
(2)	Orlando	.3170	.3584	.0414	+13.1
(3)	Phoenix	.6762	.7551	.0789	+11.7
(4)	Grand Rapids	.2593	.2894	.0301	+11.6
(5)	Salt Lake City	.3802	.4149	.0347	+9.1

Some students may note that many people living in the north have moved to the sunbelt, and these figures to some extent reflect that change. Salt Lake City and Grand Rapids, however, are exceptions. There are other variables at work in these locations.

2. To allocate a $500,000 budget to the these five markets, one should add the Year 2002 BPIs, calculate percentages, and project the percentages to the $500,000 base as follows:

2000 BPI rank		BPIs	Percents	Budget
(1)	San Diego	.9333	33.9%	$169,500
(2)	Phoenix	.7551	27.5	137,500
(3)	Salt Lake City	.4149	15.1	75,500
(4)	Orlando	.3584	13.0	65,000
(5)	Grand Rapids	.2894	10.5	52,500
Totals		2.7511	100.0%	$500,000

Note: The five markets were ranked on the basis of BPIs rather than percent of change as they were in Question 1.

3. The danger of weighting markets is that the weights may distort the data. There are underlying assumptions about the weighting employed in the BPI that are not spelled out. For example, the Effective Buying Income (EBI) has been weighted 5x, assuming that it is more important in evaluating markets than either population (weighted 2x) or Retail Sales (weighted 3x). This may or may not be the case, but the analyst must always be aware of this process. For this reason, *Sales & Marketing Management* suggests that the general BPI probably is best for mass-consumed products selling at popular prices.

4. If we were selling relatively more expensive products, such as projection television systems, it may be better to weight the EBI more (perhaps 7x) because these products are more expensive and are usually purchased by consumers with higher income levels. However, we also would not use total retail sales as a factor. It would be much better to

use a specific factor such as sales of TV sets or sales of video cameras. The problem is that some of this data may not be available for every market in the United States.

Part II—ANALYZING MARKETING OPPORTUNITIES

Chapter 4—Winning Markets Through Market-Oriented Strategic Planning

Overview

A major challenge for marketing-oriented companies as they respond to the rapidly changing marketplace is to engage continuously in market-oriented strategic planning. They must learn how to develop and maintain a viable fit among their objectives, resources, skills, and opportunities. The strategic planning process is carried out at the corporate level, business level, and product level. The objectives developed at the corporate level move down to lower levels where business strategic plans and marketing plans are prepared to guide the company's activities. Strategic planning involves repeated cycles of planning, implementation, and control.

Corporate strategic planning involves four planning activities. The first is to develop a clear sense of the company's mission in terms of its industry scope, products and applications scope, competence scope, market segment scope, vertical scope, and geographical scope. A well-developed mission statement provides employees with a shared sense of purpose, direction, and opportunity.

The second activity calls for identifying the company's strategic business units (SBUs). A business is best defined by its customer groups, customer needs, and technologies. SBUs are business units that can benefit from separate planning, face specific competitors, and be managed as profit centers.

The third activity calls for allocating resources to the various SBUs based on their market attractiveness and business strength. Several portfolio models, including those developed by the Boston Consulting Group and General Electric, are available to help determine which SBUs should be built, maintained, harvested, or divested.

The fourth activity calls for expanding present businesses and developing new products to fill the strategic planning gap. The company can identify opportunities by considering intensive growth (market penetration, market development, and product development), integrative growth (backward, forward, and horizontal), and diversification growth (concentric, horizontal, and conglomerate).

Each SBU conducts its own business strategic planning that consists of eight steps: defining the business's mission, analyzing the external environment, analyzing the internal environment, choosing business objectives and goals, developing business strategies, preparing programs, implementing programs, and gathering feedback and exercising control. All of these steps keep the SBU close to its environment and alert to new opportunities and problems. Furthermore, the SBU strategic plan provides the context for preparing market plans for specific products and services.

Marketing plans focus on a product/market and consist of the detailed marketing strategies and programs for achieving the product's objectives in a target market. Marketing plans are the central instrument for directing and coordinating the marketing effort. The distinction between the strategic and tactical marketing plans and efforts is very important, because if the firm and its marketing organization fail to recognize the interdependent yet separate activities involved in the strategic and tactical marketing efforts, the results will be less than expected. Without effective value development in the strategy planning, which come from the firm's research and analysis programs, the tactical marketing activities likely will not be as successful as when the coordination effort starts from the beginning.

The marketing planning process consists of five steps: analyzing market opportunities; researching and selecting target markets; designing market strategies; planning marketing programs; and organizing, implementing, and controlling the marketing effort.

Marketing planning results in a marketing plan document that consists of the following sections: executive summary, current market situation, opportunity and issue analysis, objectives, marketing strategy, action programs, projected profit and loss statement, and controls.

To plan effectively, marketing managers must understand the key relationship between types of marketing-mix expenditures and their sales and profit consequences.

Learning Objectives

After reading this chapter students should:

- Know the characteristics of high performance business

- Understand what is meant by "strategic" planning

- Know the major steps in strategic planning and their contribution to development of a successful strategy

- Understand the strengths and weaknesses of the business portfolio techniques

- Understand the difference between strategic and business unit planning

- Understand the contribution of the steps of business unit planning to the development of a successful business strategy

- Know what is meant by the "marketing management process" and its various steps

- Understand the contents of a marketing plan

Chapter Outline

I.   Introduction: strategic planning: three key areas and four organizational levels

      1.   Definition of market-oriented strategic planning—managerial process of developing and maintaining a viable fit between the organization's objectives, skills, and resources and its changing market opportunities in order to yield target profits and growth

      2.   Managing the firm's business as an investment portfolio

      3.   Assessment based on market growth and the firm's competitive position

      4.   Establishing a strategy

      5.   Four organizational levels of corporate, division, business unit, and product

      6.   The marketing plan (strategic and tactical)

II.   Corporate and division strategic planning

    A.   Defining the corporate mission

      1.   What is our business? Who is the customer? What is of value to the customer? What will our business be? What should our business be?

      2.   Mission statements, based on limited goals, stress major policies and values and define the major competitive scopes for the firm

    B.   Establishing strategic business units

        1.   The organization should be seen as a satsifier of needs rather than a producer of goods

        2.   Large companies manage different businesses, each requiring its own strategy

        3.   Business units can be defined in terms of customer groups served, customer needs, and technology. Also, they are defined by unique business, competitor, and profit performance variables

C.   Boston consulting group approach—question marks, stars, cash cows, dogs

        1.   SBU strategies for each of the categories

        2.   SUB life cycle and changing strategies over time

D.   General Electric model

        1.   Matrix approach—market attractiveness

        2.   Business strength

E.   Critique of portfolio models

        1.   The Arthur D. Little model and the shell directional-policy model have improved portfolio model capabilities but still must be used with caution

F.   Planning new businesses or downsizing older businesses

        1.   Intensive growth (Ansoff matrix)

           a)   Market penetration strategy—current products to current markets

           b)   Market development strategy—current products to new markets

           c)   Product development strategy—new products to current markets

        2.   Integrative growth—backward, forward, or horizontal integration

        3.   Diversification growth—new products to new markets. Three types are possible: concentric, horizontal, and conglomerate

        4.   Downsizing older businesses—to pursue growth companies must not only develop new businesses but also carefully divest tired old businesses

III.   Business unit strategic planning

A.   Business mission—each business unit must define its specific mission

B.   SWOT analysis

        1.   External environment analysis (opportunity and threat analysis)

           a)   Environmental scanning analysis—discerning new marketing opportunities

           b)   Marketing opportunities analysis—classified according to attractiveness and probability of success

        2.   Internal environment analysis (strengths and weakness analysis)

C.   Goal formulation—establish objectives that are specific with respect to magnitude and time

D.   Strategic formulation—game plan for achieving the stated objectives

        1.   Three generic types of strategic thinking

2. Porter's generic strategies: overall cost leadership, differentiation, and focus

3. Operational effectiveness and strategy—based on strategic groups to achieve distinctive market positions

4. Strategic alliances

    a) In the form of marketing alliances—product or service, promotional, logistical, pricing collaborations

    b) Partnership relationship management—to complement or leverage existing marketing capabilities and resources

E. Program formulation and implementation

1. Develop detailed programs to support the strategy

2. Implementation—McKinsey 7-S framework

F. Feedback and control—a firm must track the results of its strategy

IV. Marketing process

A. Value-delivery sequence

1. Steps in the planning process (see charts)

    a) Analyzing marketing opportunities

    b) Developing marketing strategies

    c) Planning marketing programs—the marketing mix

    d) Managing the marketing effort

V. Product planning: the nature and contents of a marketing plan

A. Contents of the marketing plan

1. Executive summary and table of contents

2. Current marketing situation

3. Opportunity and issue analysis (opportunities/threats analysis, strengths/weaknesses analysis, issues analysis)

4. Objectives (financial, marketing)

5. Marketing strategy

6. Action programs

7. Financial projections

8. Implementation controls

B. Sample marketing plan—sonic personal digital assistant

VI. Summary

Lecture—Establishing a Winning Strategic Planning Formula

This lecture is intended for use with Chapter 4, "Winning Markets: Market-Oriented Strategic Planning." The focus is on strategy in a market-oriented setting and specifically the role and value of selecting clear and effective approaches in the overall marketing process and strategy for the company or organization. The discussion begins by considering examples of particular strategies as a means of maintaining or increasing the firm's market position. This leads into a discussion of the implications for the introduction of related strategies for the firm and the industry.

Teaching Objectives

*   To stimulate students to think about the critical issues, pro and con, for a firm when it moves toward adoption of a market-oriented strategy

*   To consider and reinforce various points from the marketing environment before proceeding with specific strategy plans and programs

*   To describe and illustrate the processes and policies utilized in helping the firm achieve a balanced strategic position within the industry

Discussion

Introduction

In the years following the energy crises of the 1970s, our style of living has changed considerably. Most businesses today are forced to deal strategically with a global world in which markets experience little or no real growth. There have been attempts to find a way to "re-strategize," "restructure," and "downsize" in order to overcome this malaise. Unfortunately, virtually none of these approaches have worked, and many of the organizations that tried them are no longer around.

The firms that do well tend to employ simple strategies in which they identify real customers and give those customers what they want. These firms recognize that customers choose one product or service over another for a very simple reason: They believe it's a better value than they could expect to get from the alternatives. Among the more successful endeavors in this area are firms that recognize the consumer's desire for value and high-quality products and engage in marketing strategy and activity to raise the perception of their product from a commodity to a differentiated product. They also pursue a policy designed to offer a combination of "high-tech" and "high-touch," depending on the needs of the target market(s).

Obsolescence or Success?—Strategy, the Customer, and Competitive Advantage

In attempts to ensure that their product or service is a value leader, many firms have gone the way of the horse and buggy, setting themselves up for obsolescence. Although most firms profess to follow accepted accounting principles, with relatively uniform descriptions of financial goals and financial measurements, few firms have ever moved toward a similar acceptance of strategy development rules. If firms really believed in the concepts of customer value creation and incorporated them into their corporate philosophies, there would be far fewer business failures. There has been little agreement on how the components of competitive advantage should be pursued or how to measure progress. This has made it hard for people in organizations to work together to achieve competitive success.

The objective in effective strategic planning should be based on the recognition that companies succeed by providing superior customer value. Of course, value is simply quality, however the customer defines it, offered at the right price. This clear strategic principle is both simple and powerful because superior customer value is the best leading indicator of market share and competitiveness. And, market share and competitiveness in turn drive the achievement of long-term financial goals such as profitability, growth, and shareholder value.

Many corporations, including General Electric, AT&T, and others, have developed strategy-making programs to prove that these strategy considerations are valid. Technical improvement in the quality of products tends to be followed in three to six months by changes in the consumer perception of the quality of those products. Changes in perceived quality, on the other hand, are followed a mere two months afterward by changes in market share.

The first step toward achieving leadership in market-perceived quality and value is to understand what causes customers in the targeted market to make their decisions—to decide that one product offers better value than another. This understanding is the most important objective of a customer value analysis.

The factors that contribute to quality in the customer's mind are not mysteries. Customers can readily tell a researcher what the critical value factors are to him or her. A customer value analysis uses consumer value and purchasing information to show how consumers make decisions in the marketplace. With this information, managers should be able to understand what changes should be made to ensure that more of their customers would buy from the firm.

The simplest customer value analysis consists of two phases. First, the firm should create a customer value profile that compares their performance with that of one or more competitors. This customer value profile itself usually has two elements: a market-perceived quality profile and a market-perceived price profile. The former summarizes the aspects of the marketplace that are usually easiest to change to improve the business. In many markets, market-perceived price may be a greater driver of customer decisions than market-perceived quality; however, cutting prices won't usually improve the bottom line for the firm, despite some common misconceptions.

Developing a quality profile. The market-perceived quality profile. This chart does three things:

- It identifies what quality really means to customers in the marketplace.

- It tells which competitors are performing best on each aspect of quality.

- It provides overall quality performance measures based on the definition of quality that customers actually use in making their purchase decisions.

The process of creating a market-perceived quality profile is relatively simple. Here are the steps:

- Ask people in the targeted market, both the firm's customers and those of the competitors, to list the factors that are important in their purchase decisions. This can be done in focus groups or individually.

- Using either approach it is possible to establish how the various quality attributes are weighted in the customer's decision.

- Customers also may be asked directly how they weight the various factors.

- Also, customers may be able to rate, on a scale of 1 to 10, the performance of each business on each competing factor.

- Multiply each business's score on each factor by the weight of that factor and add the results to get an overall customer satisfaction score.

Customer Value Analysis

The second phase of the customer value analysis follows: Once the customer value profile has been established, it is possible to draw a customer value map (see Kotler text).

Very few companies have developed customer value analysis/profiles and fewer still have customer value maps, but executives often argue that most operating managers have an "implicit model" in their heads. Managers supposedly have a "feel" for who their competitors are, for what is important to purchases, and for how their company performs versus competitors.

Sometimes in organizations with exceptionally good leadership, these implicit models work well and are truly aligned to the real needs of customers. But marketers should check the situation in their organizations. This can be done via the Delphi technique by simply asking top-ranking members of the management team to produce, individually, a picture of the customer value profile for the business and its key competitors.

If it is determined that all top managers have similar opinions, there is a reasonable chance that the implicit models in their heads are accurate. This is particularly true if several members of the top-management team spend most of their time with customers. But the firm should check management perceptions carefully to ensure that the purchase-selection criteria, weights, and relative performance scores are appropriately aligned within the management group—and with customers in the targeted market.

Most organizations find that when they make this implicit model check there is much less alignment within the organization than was expected. Thus, if the managers can't agree among themselves about the purchase criteria and desires of the customers, it is unlikely they can achieve rapid progress toward fulfilling those needs.

Conclusion

A key implication is that firms that tend to base their business strategy more on the basis of accounting principles alone fundamentally hamstring their efforts. An income statement provides only a financial history. It tells much about the components of sales and costs and the amount of resulting profit, but the accounting data will not tell much about why sales are growing or shrinking.

By contrast, the customer value map shows where the firm ranks with the customer, compared to the competition. The customer value profile shows why customers rank one firm higher or lower than the competitors. Thus, the income statement looks at the past while customer value maps and customer value profiles look to the future.

Marketing and Advertising

1. Strategic alliances are extremely common in the airline industry. The ad in Figure 1, which appeared in a business magazine, promotes the North American alliance between AeroMexico and Delta Airlines. This alliance allows business travelers and vacationers to conveniently fly between many destinations in Mexico and the United States.

    a. In which of the four major categories does this strategic alliance fit?

    b. What benefits does this alliance offer the two partners? What benefits does it offer the partners' customers?

    c. What threats and opportunities might confront the partners in this alliance?

Answer

a. The alliance between AeroMexico and Delta is a service alliance, with the goal of encouraging travelers to use one of the airlines to connect to flights on the other. Their service areas are complementary, so the alliance will benefit the airlines as well as their customers. This is secondarily a promotional alliance, because the two airlines advertise jointly and travelers can choose to have frequent-flyer miles (a promotional device) credited and redeemed on either of the two airlines.

b. The two partners benefit from the increased patronage of customers who want a simple and convenient way to fly from the United States to Mexico or vice versa. They also benefit from lower costs because of shared promotional expenses and from the ability to reach a much larger audience through their joint marketing communications. The customers benefit because they can book more convenient flights from a location in one country to a location in the other. They also benefit from being able to earn and redeem frequent-flyer miles on either airline, offering more flexibility in choosing rewards for loyalty.

c. Two threats that the alliance of Delta and AeroMexico may have to confront include: lower demand for travel between the United States and Mexico and the possibility that one airline's problems (such as a crash) may affect customers' perceptions of the other partner. Two opportunities are: Changes in U.S. or Mexican immigration policies could stimulate higher demand for air travel between the two countries and rising income among Mexican families could encourage more people to travel to the United States to see friends and relatives. Again, students will have many ideas about threats and opportunities.

2. Ernst & Young's specialists are equipped to "more than just advise on the tax implications of doing international business," as the ad in Figure 2 explains. In today's global economy, more and more companies need professional help to be sure their accounting and financial activities comply with the regulations of every country where they do business.

a. Is the strategy being used by Ernst & Young one of cost leadership, differentiation, or focus? How does this ad support the company's strategy?

b. What feedback mechanisms might Ernst & Young use to learn about the effect of the campaign that includes this ad?

c. Which factors in the macroenvironment might exert the most influence on Ernst & Young's plans to market its foreign tax services?

Answer

a. Ernst & Young's strategy appears to be one of focus, here centering on the specific segment of businesses that need foreign tax advice. Ernst & Young is using differentiation in its focus strategy. This ad supports the company's strategy by graphically and verbally suggesting that Ernst & Young has many foreign tax specialists—who know more about global business and tax issues—key attributes that differentiate this firm from competitors.

b. Two feedback mechanisms Ernst & Young might use to learn about market reaction to this ad are (1) solicit customer/prospect comments on its Web site and

(2) conduct marketing research to gather feedback from businesses in the targeted segment. Students may suggest additional methods.

    c.   Two macroenvironmental forces that may particularly affect the firm's plans to market foreign tax services are economic forces (which influence sales, profits, and—often—cost-consciousness of prospects) and political-legal forces (because legal, regulatory, or political changes may prompt a prospective customer to consider using Ernst & Young rather than handling its own foreign tax reporting or using a different firm to do so. Students may make convincing cases for other macroenvironmental forces, as well.

3.   **BONUS AD--See Companion Web site!** Gillette keeps its competitive edge by investing in research and development to create new razors and blades launched with the support of massive marketing campaigns. The Mach3 featured in the ad in Figure 1 looks a bit different than most men's razors but promises the coveted benefit of a close shave.

    a.   Is this product an example of a market-penetration, product-development, market-development, or diversification strategy for growth?

    b.   What internal strengths has Gillette applied to develop and market this product?

    c.   What external threats might Gillette want to monitor in marketing this product?

Answer

    a.   This is an example of product-development strategy, because it is a new product for a current market (the market for men's shaving products).

    b.   Gillette is clearly applying its internal strengths in shaving technology, new product development, and marketing (including targeting and promotion). Students may suggest other strengths, as well.

    c.   Students may cite various threats, including competitive responses to this product introduction, changes in customer preferences and buying patterns, and distributors' reaction to carrying more inventory of this and other new products.

Online Marketing Today

Reflect.com, set up by Procter & Gamble (P&G), is applying customization to take advantage of a New Economy opportunity in beauty products. Instead of selling standard, branded products, Reflect.com invites customers to log on, get beauty advice, and then click to customize cosmetics and fragrances for their individual needs and tastes. The company even allows customers to personalize the packaging and choose from different logos. A P&G manufacturing plant in New York formulates products according to customer specifications, and a service center in Ohio handles customer inquiries. Visit Reflect.com (www.reflect.com) and follow the "About Us" link to read about the company's background and offerings. Also browse the other sections of the site. What environmental threats might influence Reflect.com's ability to fully exploit its market opportunity? What strengths can Reflect.com build on to overcome these threats? What weaknesses should Reflect.com bear in mind as it formulates its marketing strategy?

Answer

Reflect.com could have difficulty exploiting its market opportunity if more strong, well-established cosmetics firms follow its lead in offering products formulated to customer specifications. It could also have difficulty if styles change or cultural acceptance changes, resulting in fewer consumers being interested in cosmetics and related products. And slower growth or lack of growth among the targeted population could hamper Reflect.com's ability to reach ambitious sales goals. Ask students to consider how other areas of the marketing environment, such as economic elements and environmental issues, might affect Reflect.com. Among Reflect.com's strengths in coping with threats are: the financial stability of parent Procter & Gamble, the marketing and production savvy of Procter & Gamble, the company's ability to cross geographic borders to reach faster-growing markets by establishing local language versions of Reflect.com. However, P&G's large size and relative inflexibility could be a weakness in dealing with sudden threats and opportunities. Suggest that students use the Checklist for Performing Strengths/Weaknesses Analysis in Chapter 4 to prompt additional ideas about strengths and weaknesses.

You're the Marketer—Sonic PDA Marketing Plan

Every marketing plan must include the company's mission and financial and marketing objectives to guide the implementation of specific strategies and programs during the period covered by the plan. The marketing plan should also indicate the major competitive scopes within which the business will operate.

As shown in the sample marketing plan, Sonic is a start-up company that will soon introduce a new multifunction personal digital assistant (PDA) to compete with products made by Palm, Handspring, and others. As an assistant to Jane Melody, Sonic's chief marketing officer, you have been assigned to draft a mission statement for top management's review. You are also expected to suggest how Sonic should define its competitive scopes and recommend an appropriate generic competitive strategy for the business. Using your knowledge of marketing, the information you have about Sonic, and library or Internet resources, answer the following questions:

- What should Sonic's mission be?

- In what competitive scopes (industry, products and applications, competence, market-segment, vertical, and geographic) should Sonic operate?

- Which of Porter's generic competitive strategies would you recommend that Sonic follow in formulating overall strategy?

- How do the firm's marketing and financial objectives fit with your recommended mission and strategy?

As your instructor directs, enter Sonic's mission statement, overall strategy, and objectives in a written marketing plan or type them into the Your Company and Mission sections of the *Marketing Plan Pro* software. Also enter information on the competitive scope and generic strategy in the Executive Summary and Current Situation sections of the marketing plan.

Answer

Students should start this exercise by reviewing the chapter data about Sonic so they understand its competitive situation and its product. Students may offer differing definitions of Sonic's mission. One possibility: "Sonic is dedicated to producing and marketing high-quality, value-priced personal digital assistant products that enable U.S. consumers and business users to organize data and stay in touch whenever and wherever they choose."

Sonic's mission provides clues to the major competitive scopes in which it operates. One sample response:

- *Product:* Personal digital assistant products. According to the marketing plan excerpt in the chapter, Sonic's products include features (such as voice recognition) that are unique to this category plus other features found only in higher-priced models.

- *Industry:* The PDA market for hand-held computing devices covers both consumers (primarily professionals who buy for their own use) and businesses.

- *Competence:* Producing quality electronics with innovative features.

- *Market segments:* Among consumers, middle- to upper-income professionals who need one portable device to coordinate their busy schedules and communicate with family and colleagues. Among businesses, mid- to large-size corporations that want to help their workforce stay in touch and input or access critical data on the go.

- *Vertical scope:* Manufactures its own products for distribution through a network of select online and computer retailers in top 50 U.S. markets.

- *Geographic scope:* Nationwide across the United States.

Marketing Spotlight—Sara Lee

What do Hanes underwear, Coach leather goods, Ball Park hot dogs, and Wonder Bra have in common? They're all brands manufactured and sold by Sara Lee Corporation, a company most people associate with frozen cheesecake. The Sara Lee brand accounts for a paltry 25 percent of the company's $19.7 billion revenues, and it is the brand on which its namesake company has spent the least time, money, and focus. Yet, on September 29, 1997, Chicago-based Sara Lee Corporation stunned the business world by announcing an abrupt shift in strategy and focus; it would outsource its manufacturing operations and concentrate on building the Sara Lee brand and marketing its other name brands. Outsourcing will allow Sara Lee to lower its cost structure to make its brands price-competitive and release more funds for marketing.

Sara Lee's strategic change represents a nod to the future. Companies are increasingly focusing on their core competencies and leaving the dirty, less glamorous manufacturing operations to lower-cost manufacturers located overseas. "It's passe for us to be as vertically integrated as we were," says John Bryan, in his twenty-third year of being Sara Lee's CEO. The company even coined its own word for the new strategy: *de-verticalize*. Others call it *decapitalizing*—tying up much less fixed assets in the business. Those most surprised by Sara Lee's move are those in the heavily "verticalized" home textile industry, in which Sara Lee, with Hanes and its other brands, earns one-third of its revenues. The home textile industry is dominated by the giant mills. They are state-of-the-art, highly efficient, and extremely automated manufacturing operations. Yet, according to Sara Lee, they are edging toward obsolescence in the United States.

A more recent critique says that although Sara Lee succeeded in reducing its capital as a percentage of sales, its growth has been lackluster. Sara Lee runs some 200 operating companies, each with its own profit center. There are few economies of scale because each company is run independently. There is no united front in facing the giant supermarkets. Even payroll and computer systems are not centralized at Sara Lee. At issue is whether conglomerates can be profitable.

Sources: Based on "Sara Lee to Build Brand Through Outsourcing, Marketing," *Discount Store News,* October 20, 1997, p. A4. David Leonhardt, "Sara Lee: Playing with the Recipe," *Business Week,* April 27, 1998, p. 114. Rance Crain, "Sara Lee Uses Smart Alternative to Selling Some Valuable Brands," *Advertising Age,* September 22, 1997, p. 25. Warren Shoulberg, "Que Sara," *Home Textiles Today,* September 29, 1997, p. 70. and "Fashion Victim," *The Economist,* February 26, 2000, p. 73–74.

Questions

1. Although Sara Lee has recognized some key variables in the process of dealing with modern marketing, it could encounter problems as a pure marketing ("deverticalizing" or "decapitalizing") versus manufacturing and asset-based firm that also engages in considerable marketing strategy and application. What are the implications of this and the options for Sara Lee's future marketing strategy?

2. Based on the current direction for Sara Lee, where do you expect they will be in the next five to six years? Will they be successful or not? Why?

Suggested Responses

1. The point may be that if in the "deverticalizing/decapitalizing" process Sara Lee gives up the core strategy(ies) that made it successful in the past, it also may lose control of not only the economies of scale but the quality of its labels. This can be an interesting approach, but the downside could be equally interesting, especially when the conglomerate firm does not have centralized IT and marketing systems.

It is impossible to predict with any level of certainty where the company will be in the next five to six years, but if students draw on the information from the text and the case they might come up with perspectives that indicate the company could be headed for difficulties. There could be considerable discussion on the changing marketing environment, especially with what might happen in a recessionary economy when a firm spins off its operations to capitalize on its brand image and increase margins. When price becomes an issue, a "deverticalized" firm may find itself too far from the center point in consumer needs and expectations.

Analytical Tools for Marketing Management—Brand and Category Development Index (BDI / CDI) Numbers

Note: It could be useful to remind students that there are some considerations in the use of index numbers.

1. It is possible to be deceived by large index numbers when either the population or user bases are very small. It is tempting to make decisions entirely on the basis of a large index number, without ever checking population or user bases. When such bases are very small, it is wise to disregard the large index number.

2. Analysts should not make decisions on index numbers that are 1 to 9 points higher than some other index. The reason for this is that an index of 100 is not much better than an index of 109, even though it seems much larger. It should be remembered that there is only nine-tenths of one percent absolute difference.

Problems

1. Calculate index numbers from the data below and then select the best demographic target from among those listed. (calculate percentage first). Show work below.

Education of fruit drinkers	Population size	Number of users	Index
Attended college	13,238,000	1,659,000	
Graduated high school	24,295,000	2,587,000	
Did not graduate high school	23,798,000	1,946,000	

(Bases)	61,331,000	6,192,000

2. Calculate the BDIs and CDIs of the following two markets, and explain the implications of each index number for selling in each market.

	Population	Brand sales	Category sales
Seattle	2,841,000	$2,781,000	$21,680,000
Toledo	1,824,000	873,000	6,480,000
Total U.S.	231,000,000	$90,000,000	$800,000,000

	Percent of total U.S. population	Percent of Total U.S. Brand Sales	BDI	Percent of Total U.S. Category Sales	CDI
Seattle					
Toledo					

3. Shown below are the average prices of 30-second network television commercials. Calculate the index based on the 1996 prices and indicate the significance of these increases.

1996	$37,800,000
1997	49,400,000
1998	58,000,000
1999	62,600,000
2000	74,300,000

4. Is an index number of 1.23 acceptable for marketing work? Explain.

Answers to Questions

1. Calculate index numbers from the data below and then select the best demographic target from among those listed (calculate percentage first).

	Percent of total Population	Percent of total users	Index
Attended college	21.6	26.8	124
Graduated high school	39.6	41.8	106
Did not graduate high school	38.8	31.4	81
	Totals	100.0	

Calculations: 26.8 / 21.6 x 100 = 124

41.8 / 59.6 x 100 = 106

31.4 / 38.8 x 100 = 81

The best demographic target obviously is those who graduated from high school. Not only does that segment have the largest number, but it also has the largest population base.

2. Calculate the BDIs and CDIs for the following two markets and explain the implications of each index number for selling in each market.

	Percent of total US population	Percent of total U.S. Brand sales	BDI	Percent of total US Category Sales	CDI
Seattle	1.23	3.09	251	2.71	220
Toledo	.79	.97	123	123	103

Calculations:

3.09 / 1.23 x 100 = 252
2.71 / 1.23 x 100 = 220
.97 / .79 x 100 = 123
.81 / .79 x 100 = 103

Seattle has the largest CDI, and this tells us that the product category is selling very well in that market. Toledo is not nearly as good a category market as Seattle. Both BDIs are fairly high, but because Seattle's is much higher than Toledo's, it is likely that marketing investments, including advertising placed there, probably will do well. But Toledo is a different situation. The brand seems to be doing well, so perhaps some extra advertising expenditures would be appropriate in the Toledo market. But with a relatively low CDI, it may not be worthwhile to spending much there.

3. Using the average prices of off-peak 30-second network television commercials, calculate the index based on the 1996 prices and indicate the significance of these increases.

The indices are		Index	Calculations
1996	$37,800,000	100	
1997	49,400,000	131	494 / 378 = 131
1998	58,000,000	153	580 / 378 = 153
1999	62,600,000	166	626 / 378 = 166
2000 (est.)	74,300,000	197	743 / 378 = 197

Prices of off-peak network television commercials have increased since 1996, and they are almost 100 percent higher in 1999 (or almost double what they were in 1996). If the trend continues, it may be possible to predict fairly well what prices will be in the future.

4. Is an index number of 1.23 acceptable for marketing work? Explain.

An index of 1.23 should not be used in marketing, even though it may be correct. Marketers usually do not use decimal points in index numbers, so any communication using them may confuse rather than clarify a problem.

Chapter 5—Gathering Information and Measuring Market Demand

Overview

Marketing information is a critical element in effective marketing as a result of the trend toward global marketing, the transition from buyer needs to buyer wants, and the transition from price to nonprice competition. All firms operate some form of marketing information system, but the systems vary greatly in their sophistication. In too many cases, information is not available or comes too late or cannot be trusted. Too many companies are learning that they lack an appropriate information system, still do not have an information system, lack appropriate information, or they do not know what information they lack or need to know to compete effectively.

A well-designed market information system consists of four subsystems. The first is the internal records system, which provides current data on sales, costs, inventories, cash flows, and accounts receivable and payable. Many companies have developed advanced computer-based internal reports systems to allow for speedier and more comprehensive information.

The second market information subsystem is the marketing intelligence system, supplying marketing managers with everyday information about developments in the external marketing environment. Here a well-trained sales force, purchased data from syndicated sources, and an intelligence office can improve marketing intelligence available to company marketing managers.

The third subsystem, marketing research, involves collecting information that is relevant to specific marketing problems facing the company. The marketing research process consists of five steps: defining the problem and research objectives; developing the research plan; collecting information; analyzing the information; and presenting the findings. Good marketing research is characterized by the scientific method, creativity, multiple methodologies, model building, and cost/benefit measures of the value of information.

The fourth system is the Marketing Decision Support System (MDSS marketing system) that consists of statistical and decision tools to assist marketing managers in making better decisions. MDSS is a coordinated collection of data, systems, tools, and techniques with supporting software and hardware. Using MDSS software and decision models, the organization gathers and interprets relevant information from the business and the environment and turns it into a basis for marketing action. MDSS experts use descriptive or decision models, and verbal, graphical, or mathematical models, to perform analysis on a wide variety of marketing problems.

To carry out their responsibilities, marketing managers need estimates of current and future demand. Quantitative measurements are essential for market opportunity, planning marketing programs, and controlling the marketing effort. The firm prepares several types of demand estimates, depending in the level of product aggregation, the time dimension, and the space dimension.

A market consists of the set of actual and potential consumers of a market offer. The size of the market depends on how many people have interest, income, and access to the market offer. Marketers also must know how to distinguish between the potential market, available market, qualified available market, served market, and the penetrated market. Marketers must also distinguish between market demand and company demand, and within these, between potentials and forecasts. Market demand is a function, not a single number, and as such is highly dependent on the level of other variables.

A major marketing research task is to estimate current demand. Total demand can be estimated through the chain ratio method, which involves multiplying a base number by successive percentages. Area market demand is estimated by the market-buildup method (for business markets) and the multiple-factor index method (for consumer markets). In the latter case, geodemographic coding systems are proving a boon to marketers. Estimating industry sales requires identifying the relevant competitors and estimating their individual sales in order to judge their relative performance.

To estimate future demand, the company can use several major forecasting methods: expert opinion, market tests, time-series analysis, and statistical demand analysis. The appropriate method will vary with the purpose of the forecast, the type of product, and the availability and reliability of data.

Learning Objectives

After reading this chapter students should:

- Understand demand measurement terminology
- Know the methods of estimating current demand
- Know the methods of estimating future demand

Chapter Outline

I. Components of a modern marketing information system

    1. Expansion of detailed buyer wants, preferences, and behavior, but still many gaps

    2. Components of the system: people, equipment, and procedures to gather, sort, analyze, evaluate, and distribute needed, timely, and accurate information to marketing decision-makers

    3. Many questions must be answered before determining MIS configuration

II. Internal records system

    A. Order-to-payment cycle—the heart of the internal records system

    B. Sales Information Systems—technology has allowed sales reps to have immediate access to information about their prospects and customers

III. Marketing intelligence system

    A. A set of procedures for managers to obtain everyday information about pertinent developments in the marketing environment

    B. Internal records systems supplies "results" data, and the marketing intelligence system supplies "happenings" data

    C. Steps for improving marketing intelligence

        1. Train sales force

        2. Motivate intermediaries to share intelligence

        3. Purchase information from outside suppliers

        4. Establish an internal marketing information center to collect and circulate intelligence

IV. Marketing research system

    A. Marketing research—the systematic design, collection, analysis, and reporting of data and findings relevant to a specific marketing situation facing the company

B.   Suppliers of marketing research—can be achieved through an in-house department, an outside marketing research firm, or a variety of other cost-efficient ways. increasing amounts of information available via the internet

C.   Marketing research process

    1.   Define the problem and research objectives

    2.   Developing the research plan—decisions on data sources, research approaches, research instruments, sampling plan, and contact methods

    3.   Collect the information—phase most expensive and prone to error

    4.   Analyze the information—extract pertinent findings from the collected data

    5.   Present the findings—pertinent to the major marketing decisions facing management

D.   Overcoming barriers to the use of marketing research—details on requirements for good marketing research and reasons for failure in the research effort

V.   Marketing Decision Support System (MDSS)

A.   Coordinated collection of data, systems, tools and techniques with supporting software and hardware by which an organization gathers and interprets relevant information from business and environment and turns it into a basis for marketing action

B.   *Note:* The *Marketing News* lists of marketing research programs, including BRANDAID, CALLPLAN, DETAILER, GEOLINE, MEDIAC, PROMOTER, ADCAD, COVERSTORY

    1.   Quantitative tools used in MDSS systems: multiple regression, discriminant analysis, factor analysis, cluster analysis, conjoint analysis, mulitidimensional scaling

    2.   Models include Markov-process, queuing, and new-product pretest

    3.   Optimization routines: differential calculus, mathematical programming, statistical decision theory, game theory, heuristics

VI.   Forecasting and demand measurement

A.   Measures of market demand

B.   Which market to measure?—available market, qualified available market, target (served) market, or penetrated market?

C.   Vocabulary for demand measurement

    1.   Market demand

    2.   Market forecast

    3.   Market potential

    4.   Company demand

    5.   Company sales forecast

    6.   Company sales potential

D.   Estimating current demand

    1.   Total market potential

    2.   Area market potential

       a)   Market-buildup method

       b)   Multiple-factor index method

3.   Estimating industry sales and market shares
        a)   identifying competitors and
        b)   estimating their sales
   E.   Estimating future demand
      1.   Survey of buyers' intentions, including the purchase probability scale
      2.   Composite of sales-force opinion
      3.   Expert opinion
      4.   Past-sales analysis
      5.   Market test method

VII.   Summary

Lecture—Marketing Research and Measurement at the Millennium

This lecture is intended for use with Chapter 5, "Managing Marketing Information and Measuring Market Demand." It focuses on the development of information for marketing management. The discussion begins by considering examples of particular approaches in developing market research. This leads into a discussion of the implications for the introduction of other research opportunities to the firm and the industry. It is useful to keep the examples current so that students will be able to identify readily with this concept based on their general knowledge of the techniques, companies, and products involved in the discussion.

Teaching Objectives

- Introduce students to some of the more important concepts in contemporary marketing research

- Consider the role of marketing research and information systems in helping the firm achieve its overall marketing strategies

- Discuss specific marketing research considerations and principles

- Open a line of discussion related to several of the computer exercises in the IRM and the accompanying interactive spreadsheets

Discussion

Introduction

Marketing research and measurement long have been areas of great difficulty and opportunity for the marketer, not just because they provide more complex and precise responses, but also because the training, analytical, and communication requirements are substantial. Measurement in some areas has been much easier than in others. For example, it is much more difficult to measure directly the results of advertising expenditures than to learn about the attitudes of prospective buyers toward a product or service. Between an advertisement and the actual purchase of goods or services there are lag effects, multiple distribution channels, and other intervening variables. With the exception of direct marketing, it is very difficult to relate marketing efforts directly to sales.

However, the other side of the equation relates to what we are able to do with an area of marketing research where there is more certainty. Marketers increasingly utilize marketing research to improve product and service value to current customers and find new customers.

Marketing research is used in the contemporary environment to provide more information on the customer, the market, and the channels of distribution. Among the more important information is that which relates to the factors influencing sales. This can be done in many ways, ranging from population sampling to on-on-one personal interviews and a range of options in between.

Marketing Research with a Purpose

Note: Consider the possible tie of this material to some of the applications exercise discussions and applications materials (especially Simmons and Nielsen).

However, before we can do any of this we need to determine what we want to ask and why, and recognize that every marketing research tool has a different purpose. With all the new technologies available and some very sophisticated interpretation tools, the research and analysis process is much easier than it was just a few years ago. However, most managers still have difficulty in determining which tools are right for their needs, especially whether qualitative or quantitative information is most important and which type of research technique will provide the best value for the money.

Quantitative research deals with numbers and answers questions about how many, how much, or how often. Quantitative-oriented survey research generally relies on close-ended questions—questions that can be answered briefly, often with a yes, a no, or a number.

Qualitative research deals primarily with the feelings and attitudes that drive behaviors. Open-ended questions that cannot be answered in one word encourage respondents to describe their feelings, opinions, attitudes, and values.

In some situations a telephone survey may be the best way to talk to consumers about the product, but in other situations focus groups may provide a better result. One of the more important questions is whether the company can or should attempt to perform independent research projects or buy into a syndicated or omnibus study.

This choice is important because the cost in terms of time, money, and effort can throw the strategy and planning effort for the firm into the wrong gear or worse yet into the wrong direction. Further, if the firm is not entirely clear on the research needs and process, it must decide whether or not to use a professional researcher versus pay for information from existing sources.

One of the best methods for getting good quantitative research data is to use scanner information. This information has become much more flexible and usable. Effective use of tools such as Behavior Scan and InfoScan, both products of Information Resources, Inc. (IRI), has added substantial depth to efforts to understand the buying process.

This is not project information but rather it is available on a continuous weekly basis, usually contracted on a multiyear basis to provide sufficient information over a period of time. This powerful capability enables firms to micromarket effectively and plan down to the individual store level. Data on the factors influencing product sales, such as client and competitor advertising, and other promotional activities, can be effectively assessed. In addition, the capability now exists to obtain information on a specific store or all the stores in a system, enabling not only enhanced data-checking capabilities but also rapid and effective comparisons at various local, regional, and national levels.

Although such information by itself cannot provide predictions of the future, it can and does provide the means to evaluate various trends and make it possible to apply an expert system in the analysis process to forecast more precisely than in the past.

On the qualitative side of the equation, there are other methods such as the static panel, a sample of households in the United States. An example is Simmons Market Research Bureau (SMRB), which has a 13,000+ household panel that is representative of the national census in terms of the significant demographics. Conducted frequently over a year or more, the panel provides a means to measure relatively small changes in household purchases and product usage (see Analytical Tools for Marketing Management [Computer Exercises] for more information on Simmons research information).

Another method is the consumer diary. Diaries are especially appropriate for answering questions on brand penetration and loyalty. This approach indicates what factors influence purchasing behaviors, such as price and advertising, and where purchases are made—supermarkets, warehouse outlets, drugstores. This method appeals to a wide range of clients in packaged goods, apparel, home furnishings, financial services, travel, and entertainment.

An area of less measurement, advertising impact measurement, remains the activity where research efforts have been less successful. Until recent years the result is that most marketers of consumer products have developed mass marketing programs rather than target more narrowly. This has been by necessity. Without sufficient consumer purchase or usage information that could be tied directly to the advertising/promotion effort, they could not do otherwise. Because marketers have not been able to gauge the results of advertising and various other forms of marketing communication directly, they instead surveyed the psychological impact of the communications programs on customers and prospects.

Advertisers and agencies have been able to evaluate consumer attitudes toward the product, plus awareness and knowledge levels about their advertising and marketing communications program. Much of this research was based on testing the ability of the consumer to recall advertising messages or state how seeing or hearing advertising messages might, could, or in fact had changed their attitudes toward the product or their inclination to either buy or continue buying it.

Thus, mass marketing in the past has operated on the assumption that attitudes lead to behavior. That may be true, but it is just as likely true that behavior leads to attitudes. If you see an ad on TV, form a favorable impression of a product, try it out, and decide you hate it, then your new attitude is a result of your purchase behavior. So perhaps there is more going on in a purchase decision than the linear model suggests.

A more central difficulty with the mass marketing model is the measurable surrogates or substitutes that we have used to stand in for unmeasurable purchase behavior. Recall does not necessarily equal sales or even favorable recall: Does anyone really miss "Ring Around the Collar," or did "the Heartbeat of America" ever really cause someone to buy an automobile? Likewise, brand awareness does not guarantee success. The IBM brand is recognized by 90 percent of its potential customers around the world, yet the company still has some substantial marketing and sales problems.

There have been efforts to measure the effects of marketing communications on sales even less directly, for example, by looking at incremental units sold after a promotion. But by and large, incremental units have measured sales stolen from a competitor for a short period of time or that we have cannibalized from our own future business.

Database Marketing and the Future

Database marketing eliminates much of the need for surrogates. With cheap computing power and the ability to capture, store, and manipulate massive amounts of data, new methods of marketing communications and planning are possible. For example, with what is called single-source data, marketers can identify specific customers and users of products and services, measure their actual purchase behavior, and relate it to specific brand and product categories:

Up to now, database-centered advertising and marketing communications research for the most part has been conducted with consumers who shop in supermarkets, drugstore chains, and mass-merchandising outlets. This is because these retailer categories have been the pioneers in various forms of electronic data capture and storage. The technology is rapidly diffusing, and it is likely that during the early years of the next century almost all types of retail vendors will be able to gather, conduct, and evaluate this type of customer information. As a result of working with retailers and market research groups, increasing numbers of manufacturers, brand managers, and so on will be able to capture and use purchase data on their brand customers and prospects.

To a large extent, the contemporary database marketing approach makes obsolete the statistical research and analysis techniques in which marketers have traditionally been trained. In the past, researchers took a sample, projected it to the whole world, and hoped they had it right. An interesting aspect of the current techniques is that when the researcher deals with real-world data, he or she begins to understand that quite often traditional statistical techniques do not make any sense.

Normal curves are generally irrelevant in database-derived marketing because all the interesting things are happening at the tails of the distribution, not in the middle. And, with the ability to capture longitudinal data (collected on the same person over a period of time) on individual customers, you can actually look at your customer's behavior over time and thereby reach much more meaningful conclusions concerning attitudes and buying behavior.

The old linear model of consumer behavior was built on a one-way process, but the new direction is research built on two-way communication between marketer and customer. The marketer receives feedback from the customer, both explicitly (through survey responses, warranty cards, and so forth) and implicitly (through purchase behavior tracked in the database). The dialogue between marketer and customer is always evolving. While mass marketing treats every customer as a new prospect, integrated marketing creates individual dialogues and even changes its message as marketer and customer get to know each other. This provides the basis for the one-to-one marketing process that is at the center of contemporary consumer marketing activities.

Marketing and Advertising

1.   American beef producers sponsored the print ad in Figure 1 promoting the nutritional benefits of beef. The ad addresses misconceptions that U.S. consumers have about beef's nutritional value, as revealed in survey research conducted for the National Cattleman's Beef Promotion and Research Board.

    a.   When measuring market demand for beef, what space and product levels would the National Cattleman's Beef Promotion and Research Board be most interested in?

    b.   Is this ad seeking to increase primary or selective demand for beef? Why?

    c.   If the beef producer's group needed a relatively accurate measure of market response to this ad, would you recommend that it use a probability or a nonprobability sample?

Answer

    a.   As discussed in the text, demand can be measured for six different product levels, five different space levels, and three different time levels. The National Cattleman's Beef Promotion and Research Board would probably be most interested in U.S. nationwide market demand for beef. It would also be most interested in the product levels of industry sales. This is because the organization is trying to stimulate overall demand for beef.

b. The ad seeks to increase primary demand for beef as a product category, because the organization represents producers who will benefit whenever beef is sold, regardless of the particular company or product form.

c. For a relatively accurate measure of market response, the beef producers should use a probability sample so the researchers can calculate the confidence limits for sampling error.

2. As advertised in Figure 2, Mutual of America wants to help companies of all sizes and types handle their retirement and insurance needs. According to the copy, all business customers "receive the same quality service and care" and "the same freedom of choice" regardless of size.

a. Which research approaches would be most helpful in identifying any problems that customers might have experienced in working with Mutual of America consultants?

b. If company marketers decide to collect primary data, would you recommend they use closed-end or open-end questions? Why?

c. Draft a brief questionnaire that Mutual of America could use to identify additional needs that the company might try to satisfy with new financial services products or services.

Answer

a. Mutual of America might use focus-group research to get detailed customer comments about its consultants. It might also use customer surveys to ask users what they like and don't like about their consultants, check its internal records for information, and monitor complaint letters and e-mails.

b. Closed-end questions can be tallied more quickly and conveniently but open-end questions will allow customers more freedom to explain what their problems have been in some detail.

c. Evaluate students' questionnaires on the basis of whether the questions are unbiased, simple, direct, flow in logical order, and elicit the information about customer needs that Mutual of America could use in designing new offerings.

Online Marketing Today

Research conducted by Purdue University shows that up to 75 percent of consumers fail to complete their online purchases, primarily because of sluggish Web sites, poor site design, and related factors. Seeking to learn what online visitors do and don't do at its Web site, Northwest Airlines has added a new software tool to its online operations. "The success of our online business comes down to our customers and how satisfied they are with our products and services," says Northwest's manager of e-commerce. "This new tool," he says, "makes it very easy to determine where we should focus our efforts," by analyzing the online behavior of visitors, finding out which affiliates send the most visitors to the site, and tracking response to online promotions. With this information, the airline will be able to make the site function more efficiently and more effectively to increase sales and customer satisfaction.

Browse Northwest's home page (www.nwa.com) and then follow the link to the "Talk to Us" page. Sample several of the links on this page to see how customers can submit questions and feedback. Would such data be included as part of Northwest's marketing information system, marketing intelligence system, or marketing research system? Where would the airline store the primary data about online visitor behavior that its new software tool is collecting? What kind of research approach does this primary data represent? How else might Northwest use its Web site to gather primary data?

Answer

Feedback and questions from online customers would be included as part of Northwest's marketing intelligence system, because this information concerns developments in the marketing environment. The airline would store the primary data about online visitor behavior in its data warehouse, specifically in its customer database. This research represents an observational approach because it involves observing what customers do online.

Students may suggest numerous ways in which Northwest might use its Web site to gather primary data. One sample response: Northwest could use cookies to track how often customers visit the site, which pages they look at and for how long, how often their visits culminate in purchases, how many leave in the middle of a purchase but before finalizing the transaction, and other information.

You're the Marketer: Sonic PDA Marketing Plan

Marketing information systems, marketing intelligence systems, and marketing research systems are used to gather and analyze data for various parts of the marketing plan. These systems can help marketers examine changes and trends in markets, competition, consumer needs, product usage, and distribution channels, among other areas. They can also turn up evidence of important opportunities and threats that must be addressed.

You are continuing as Jane Melody's assistant at Sonic. She has collected a considerable amount of marketing intelligence about the market and the competitive situation, but you believe Sonic needs more data in preparation for launching the first product. Based on the marketing plan contents discussed in Chapter 4, answer the following questions about how you can use MIS and marketing research to support the development and implementation of Sonic's marketing plan for its new PDA:

- For which sections will you need secondary data? Primary data? Both? Why do you need the information for each section?

- Where can you find suitable secondary data? Identify two non-Internet sources and two Internet sources, describe what you plan to draw from each source, and indicate how you will use the data in your marketing planning.

- What surveys, focus groups, observation, behavioral data, or experiments will Sonic need to support its marketing strategy, including product management, pricing, distribution, and marketing communication? Be specific about the questions or issues that Sonic should seek to resolve using market research data.

Enter your answers about Sonic's use of marketing data and research in the appropriate sections of a written marketing plan or in the Marketing Research, Market Analysis, and Market Trends sections of the *Marketing Plan Pro* software.

Answer

Referring to Table 5.1, students will need secondary data as well as primary data as they examine Sonic's current marketing situation, the opportunity and issue analysis, and marketing strategy. This is because they need to collect primary data from external sources (such as consumer surveys to answer specific, immediate questions) and secondary data (such as competitive product specifications) as background for writing about the marketing situation, analyzing opportunities and issues facing Sonic, and developing a suitable marketing strategy.

Students will offer various ideas for sources of secondary data to support a marketing plan. Some sample ideas include: searching printed materials or Internet sites maintained by trade associations or technology analysis to learn about trends in PDA products that compete with Sonic's product line, and searching government publications and Web sites to learn about current and pending regulations that might affect Sonic's ability to buy parts from international suppliers.

Students will also provide a variety of ideas about surveys, focus groups, observation, behavioral data, or experiments Sonic needs to support its marketing strategy decisions. Evaluate their responses on the basis of how well the research they suggest will help Sonic answer specific questions and resolve specific issues that are important to the company's marketing planning process. As one example, the research should help Sonic better describe attractive, profitable market segments to be targeted.

Marketing Spotlight—Knowledge Networks

Marketing research firm Knowledge Networks was founded by two Stanford University professors in 1998. The company is one of the leaders in the emerging field of Internet research. It boasts an online panel of more than 100,000 consumers connected via WebTV interactive television boxes. In order to approximate a cross-section of the U.S. population, Knowledge Networks uses "random digit dialing" phone surveys—which give each household in the United States an equal probability of selection—to fill its panel. The WebTV survey system has the advantage of allowing panelists to respond at their convenience, as opposed to phone surveys. Interactive televisions operate with a remote control in exactly the same fashion as normal TVs, so Internet literacy is not required for participation in Knowledge Networks research. The WebTV sets also enable Knowledge Networks to test advertising for companies in a realistic setting, by simulating commercial television viewing. The network of panelists enables the company to pursue its mission: "To help companies transform their markets by providing valid, timely, and cost-efficient information about consumers."

Knowledge Networks sends Web surveys to its panel to determine their attitudes toward commercial products and their opinions on public issues. The company also monitors its panelists' in-home media intake and their purchase behaviors, which allows the company to track spending as it relates to marketing messages. For example, a company making computers could use the results of Knowledge Networks surveys to determine the ideal target audience for a new product. Knowledge Networks could tell the computer company what television shows and Web sites the target audience viewed most often, and the computer company could then buy advertising accordingly. Finally, Knowledge Networks would track if the target audience saw the advertising, and then correlate this with the purchase rate of the product among the target audience. In addition to product and advertising testing, Knowledge Networks conducts Web surveying. The company conducted numerous polls during the 2000 election season for CBS News and the *Washington Post,* and even did a lighthearted poll after the TV show *Survivor* finale.

Additionally, Knowledge Networks keeps consumer profiles with more than 1,000 data points updated weekly for all its panelists, which companies can access to learn about potential customers. The company seeks to become a one-stop marketing research company, performing television- and Internet-usage tracking studies, brand management diagnostics and tracking, product and advertising evaluations, and traditional survey applications. Knowledge Networks claims this comprehensive research coverage yields a "360-degree view of the consumer" by:

- Capturing and recording marketing inputs, such as advertising and environmental factors that affect consumers
- Observing and analyzing how consumers process these stimuli, and how, in turn, this shapes their thoughts, attitudes, and feelings
- Tracking what action consumers take in response to their experience of these stimuli

Sources: www.knowledgenetworks.com; Peter Sinton. "Polling Using the Internet Seeks to Improve Accuracy." *San Francisco Chronicle,* October 28, 2000, p. B1. Rebecca Buckman. "Pollster Aims at One-Stop Marketing Shop." *Wall Street Journal,* September 7, 2000, p. B6.

Questions

1. How is the Knowledge Networks different from Nielsen, Simmons, and other research capabilities?

2. Has the nature of consumer buying habits and demographic patterns changed to make this method more or less viable? Are there any possible drawbacks to this apparently revolutionary method of measuring advertising effectiveness and consumer response?

3. Just because Knowledge Networks may provide more information about consumer consumption patterns, are there other unknowns this system cannot predict? How do you overcome the "self-selection" syndrome in the Knowledge Networks system?

Suggested Responses

1. The description of the Knowledge Networks capabilities does not indicate that the end results achieved with older, less sophisticated, methods would be substantially different. Apparently, the major difference is in the frequency of evaluation and the technology, but that cannot ensure a more consistent or valid response.

2. Possibly the main positive difference is in the additional environmental input. If developed effectively to respond to local, regional, national, and global issues of concern to consumers, this could be a useful addition.

3. Consumer purchasing and consumer demographics today are much more diffused than even 10–15 years ago. The decline in brand franchise with some consumer groups, global competition, global fashion transparency, price transparency, the Internet, and many other dynamic variables make it difficult to understand how any one consumer-demand forecasting tool will provide better answers.

4. Since the 1970s and 1980s, consumer buying patterns have become much more eclectic and difficult to discern when consumers are faced with many alternative choices. It is likely that no system available at present can discern between all possible options/choices.

5. "Self-selection" of respondents to consumer surveys remains a problem with this system as with similar programs. With the increase in telemarketing intrusion, the rising invasion of privacy via the Internet, and so forth, many consumers who in the past might have responded to survey research efforts now will decline to participate. Accordingly, research firms (including Knowledge Networks) end up with those who have the time and inclination but not necessarily the purchasing power or knowledge to respond effectively. With much more marketing focus on the upscale buyers, it is important that firms raise the level of knowledge of the buying habits of this group. The jury remains out on the degree to which newer technology can penetrate the anonymity that upscale

buyers desire, especially during periods of complex and rapidly changing social and economic conditions.

Applications—Buying Power Index (BPI)

Suggest that students study the *Survey of Buying Power (in S&MM)* because it has so much to offer them. This assignment covers only a small portion of the Survey's full potential.

Answers

1. Students only have to subtract the 1996 BPI figures from the 2000 figures for each market and then select the top five (5) markets. They also may want to calculate percent of change. Here are the answers:

		1996 BPI	2000 BPI	Difference	Percent increase
(1)	San Diego	.8483	.9333	.0850	+10.0
(2)	Orlando	.3170	.3584	.0414	+13.1
(3)	Phoenix	.6762	.7551	.0789	+11.7
(4)	Grand Rapids	.2593	.2894	.0301	+11.6
(5)	Salt Lake City	.3802	.4149	.0347	+9.1

Some students may note that many people living in the north have moved to the sunbelt, and these figures, to some extent, reflect that change. Salt Lake City and Grand Rapids, however, are exceptions. There are other variables at work in these locations.

2. To allocate a $500,000 budget to these five markets, one should add the year 2000 BPIs, calculate percentages, and project the percentages to the $500,000 base as follows:

2000 BPI rank		BPIs	Percents	Budget
(1)	San Diego	.9333	33.9%	$169,500
(2)	Phoenix	.7551	27.5	137,500
(3)	Salt Lake City	.4149	15.1	75,500
(4)	Orlando	.3584	13.0	65,000
(5)	Grand Rapids	.2894	10.5	52,500
Totals		2.7511	100.0%	$500,000

Note: The five markets were ranked on the basis of BPIs rather than percent of change as they were in Question 1.

3. The danger of weighting markets is that the weights may distort the data. There are underlying assumptions about the weighting employed in the BPI that are not spelled out. For example, the Effective Buying Income (EBI) has been weighted 5x, assuming that it is more important in evaluating markets than either population (weighted 2x) or Retail Sales (weighted 3x). This may or may not be the case, but the BPI analyst must always be aware of this process. For this reason, *Sales & Marketing Management* suggests that the BPI probably is best for mass-consumed products selling at popular prices.

4. If we were selling videotape machines, it may be better to weight the EBI more (perhaps 7x) because these products are very expensive and are usually purchased by consumers

with higher income levels. However, we also would not use Total Retail Sales as a factor. (It would be much better to use a specific factor such as sales of TV sets, or even better, sales of videotape machines. The problem is that the latter data may not be available for every market in the United States.)

Chapter 6—Scanning the Marketing Environment

Overview

Change in the macroenvironment is the primary basis for market opportunity. Organizations/firms must start the search for opportunities and possible threats with their macroenvironment. The macroenvironment consists of all the actors and forces that affect the organization's operations and performance. They need to understand the trends and megatrends characterizing the current macroenvironment. This is critical to identify and respond to unmet needs and trends in the marketplace.

The macroenvironment consists of six major forces: demographic, economic, natural, technological, political/legal, and social/cultural. The demographic environment shows a worldwide explosive population growth; a changing age, ethnic, and educational mix; new types of households and geographical shifts in population; and the splintering of a mass market into micromarkets. The economic environment shows an emphasis on global income distribution issues, low savings and high debt, and changing consumer-expenditure patterns. The natural environment shows potential shortages of certain raw materials, unstable cost of energy, increased pollution levels, and the changing role of governments in environmental protection.

The technological environment exhibits accelerating technological change, unlimited opportunities for innovation, varying R&D budgets, and increased regulation of technological change. The political/legal environment shows substantial business regulation and the growth of special interest groups. The social/cultural environment shows individuals are changing their views of themselves, others, and the world around them. Despite this, there is a continuing trend toward self-fulfillment, immediate gratification, and secularism. Also of interest to marketers is the high persistence of core cultural values, the existence of subcultures, and rapidly changing secondary cultural values.

Learning Objectives

After reading this chapter students should:

- Understand some of the major forces impacting an organization or firm's macroenvironment
- Know the major trends influencing marketing decisions in the macroenvironment

Chapter Outline

I.   Introduction—successful companies take an outside-inside view of their business

II.   Analyzing needs and trends in the macroenvironment —successful companies recognize and respond profitably to unmet needs and trends in the macroenvironment

III.   Identifying and responding to the major macroenvironment forces—"noncontrollables" that require a response

      A.   Demographic environment

            1.   Worldwide population growth—although it brings with it inherent risk, it also presents opportunities

            2.   Population age mix—a strong determinant of needs

3. Ethnic markets—each population group has specific wants and buying habits

4. Educational groups—from illiterates to those with professional degrees

5. Household patterns—traditional household is no longer the dominant pattern

6. Geographical shifts in population—migration to safer countries and different types of areas

7. From a mass market to micromarkets—fragmentation is causing companies to abandon the "shotgun" approach

B. Economic environment

1. Income distribution—nations vary greatly in their level and distribution of income. It is related to industrial structure but is also affected by the political system

2. Savings, debt, credit availability—affects consumer expenditures

C. Natural environment

1. Shortage of raw materials—infinite, finite renewable, and finite nonrenewable

2. Increased cost of energy—oil is a finite nonrenewable resource

3. Increased levels of pollution—industrial activity will inevitably harm the environment

4. Changing role of governments—environmental concern varies by country

D. Technological Environment

1. Accelerating pace of technological change

1. Unlimited opportunities for innovation

2. Varying R&D budgets—United States leads the world in expenditures

3. Increased regulation of technological change—complex products cause safety concerns to arise

E. Political/Legal environment

1. Legislation regulating business—has three main purposes: to protect companies from unfair competition, to protect consumers from unfair business practices, and to protect the interests of society from unbridled business behavior

2. Growth of special interest groups—number and power have increased over the last three decades, putting more constraints on marketers

   a) Cause-related marketing a key marketing outcome

   b) Problems perceived that such efforts could backfire if consumers fail to see a link between the product and the cause

F. Social/Cultural environment—the society in which people grow up shapes their beliefs, values, and norms of interest to marketers

1. High persistence of core cultural values

2. Existence of subcultures—emerging from special life experiences or circumstances

3. Shifts of secondary cultural values through time—swings from "core" values over time that impact marketing efforts

4. Summary

Lecture 1— Demographic Data Analysis

This lecture is intended for use with Chapter 6, "Scanning the Marketing Environment." It focuses on the development of marketing environment information for marketing management.

The discussion begins by considering examples of particular approaches in developing demographic-based market research. This leads into a discussion of the implications for the introduction of other research opportunities to the firm and the industry.

Teaching Objectives

- To highlight the role of demographic analysis in marketing decision making

- To stimulate students to think about the critical issues in utilizing demographic analysis

- To offer points to consider in proceeding with a demographic analysis

Discussion

Introduction

For virtually every product or service, demographic data is an important element in the marketing equation. Demographics can help the marketer learn more about the current and potential customers, where they live, and how many are likely to buy the product or service based on prior consumption of various products and services. Demographic analysis also helps marketers serve their customers better by enabling them to adjust to their changing needs.

There are four primary steps in the demographic analysis process:

1. Identify the population or household characteristics that most accurately differentiate potential customers from those not likely to buy

2. Find the geographic areas with the highest concentrations of potential customers

3. Analyze the purchase behavior of the potential customers to establish some understanding of the cause and effect behind their purchasing patterns

4. Determine media preferences in order to find the most efficient way to reach the potential market with an advertising message

From Mass to Target and Niche

Note: Depending on your areas of interest, there are several areas of connection between this material and one or more of the applications computer exercises.

In a mass marketing approach there is one message communicated via the media: newspapers, radio, and broadcast television. The assumption is that the message presumably will reach everyone. No special effort is made to ensure that the message will appeal to or reach the most likely customers.

The result of mass marketing efforts is that substantial resources are expended on marketing products and services to groups in the population that did not want or need them. For example, a motorcycle company expending advertising budget on prime-time television also would reach the housebound elderly as well as the young adult target market. Likewise, a swimsuit manufacturer placing ads in a national magazine would reach potential consumers in Alaska as well as Florida.

The obvious point is that a "shotgun" approach is not the most efficient use of marketing resources.

Target marketing clearly has replaced mass marketing. The guiding principle is "know thy customers." It is essential to obtain answers to a number of important questions about your target market: How old are they? Where do they live? What are their interests, concerns, and aspirations? The answers to these questions provide the basis to determine the specific advertising media or marketing approaches most likely to appeal to those customers and whether you are targeting the right customers. It is also possible that the firm will have more than one group of target markets. Research shows, for example, that young women purchase low-fat frozen dinners for obvious diet purposes, but retired people also purchase the product because they want only a light meal.

The principle also applies in the situation where a firm knows that its customers are predominantly college graduates, and it knows their zip codes. This information could be utilized as follows:

1. First, obtain a tabulation of the number of college graduates by zip code, available through various research organizations and information providers such as the American Demographics Directory of Marketing Information or the U.S. Census Bureau.

2. Second, for any metropolitan area, establish the percentage of all college graduates in the metropolitan area who reside in each zip code. The process is:

    a. Calculate the percentage of existing customers who reside in each zip code.

    b. Divide the percent of college graduates in each zip code by the percentage of customers in the zip code (and multiply by 100). This provides an index of penetration for each zip code. (See application exercises for more explanation.)

    c. If the index of penetration is 100 or above, the market likely is adequately served. If it is below 100, there is more potential that can be developed through direct mail to the specific zip codes.

This analysis is conducted using any group of geographic areas that sum to a total market area, such as counties within a state or metropolitan areas within a region. The object is to compare the percent of customers developed from each submarket area against the percent actually there. The resulting indexes essentially measure marketing performance and potential by specific area.

Demographic information is now readily available for various personal computer systems and formats. Demographic statistics are obtained on CD-ROM or via the Internet, complete with software for accessing the data. The software for highly sophisticated analysis of the data is also readily available.

Although it is possible to analyze the data to provide customized market analysis, such as how many pairs of shoes people own and how often they shop for new ones, there are limits to what the basic census data can provide the marketer. Census demographics can provide basic information to help determine the market, the size of the market, and where potential customers live, but it cannot tell you how many times a week people use diet sodas, dishwashing liquid, or pizza.

Customized Marketing Forecasting, Based on Demographic and Lifestyle Data

With the proper analysis techniques and capabilities, it is possible to merge primary census data with more detailed customer data to form a clearer picture of the market and its potential. This could involve the following:

- A detailed lifestyle analysis as well as demographic data

- A determination of whether the product or service will be sold to an individual or a household.

Refrigerators, for example, are household products, and most households have only one or two refrigerators. On the other hand, everyone within the household has his/her own toothbrush and dozens of other personal-care products. To demonstrate the complexity of this question:

- There are more than 280 million individuals in the United States and more than 100 million households.

- Those classified as "family households" include married couples with children (26 percent), married couples without children (29 percent), single parents living with their children (9 percent), and brothers and sisters or other related family members who live together (7 percent). "Nonfamily households" include people who live alone (24 percent) and cohabiting couples and other unrelated roommates (5 percent).

- Different types of households are more prevalent among certain age groups. For instance, the majority of women who live alone are older than age 65, while the majority of men who live alone are younger than age 45.

- Household types differ between generations as well. Younger people today are much more likely to live in the "other" type of nonfamily household because they may move out of their parents' homes before marriage and live with friends or lovers.

Everyone in the United States (except for the homeless) lives in either a household or group quarters. Many businesses ignore group-quarter populations, reasoning that nursing-home patients and prison inmates probably do not engage in much shopping. However, if the market is computers, beer, pizza, or any number of products that appeal to young adults or military personnel, marketers cannot afford to overlook these populations. This is especially important when marketing a product in an area where a college or military base is present. People who live in these situations may have different wants and needs than those who live in households. In addition, the area may have a much higher rate of population turnover than other locations.

Once the firm determines whether it wishes to market to households or individuals, the next step is to determine which household segment or market segment would be most likely need the product or service. Demographic analysis enables the firm to refine the market definition, the potential market, and how it likely will change over time.

In general, forecasting the U.S. market or that of a specific state is easier to estimate accurately than populations for small areas, such as neighborhoods, which often experience greater population fluctuations. In addition, with shorter time periods, projections tend to be more accurate because there is less time for dramatic changes to take place. We cannot make assumptions for what a market will look like in 15 years because it is not possible to recognize all the possible changes in the marketplace.

However, the firm can have some confidence in educated guesses about the future if researchers in the firm understand past and present population trends, especially with major trends such as the baby boom and baby bust cycle. Accordingly, it is important to understand the differences between a generation and a cohort. The events for which generations are named occur when their members are too young to remember much about them (i.e., the Depression generation includes people born during the 1930s). Cohort groups provide classifications that are more useful for marketers because they provide an insight into events that occurred during the entire lifetimes of the people in question.

Baby Boomers in 2000

To illustrate, consider baby boomers born between 1946 and 1965. In their youth they experienced a growing economy, but they also dealt with competition and crowding in schools and jobs due to the sheer numbers in the cohort. Their lives were shaped by events such as the civil rights movement, the Vietnam conflict, the Women's movement, and Watergate. Baby boomers witnessed increasing diversity and technology and are living longer, healthier lives than prior cohorts. However, they also have not witnessed the level of U.S. and global adversity and conflict of prior cohorts, deeply affecting their view of the world and the challenge of survival in a world changing dramatically in the twenty-first century.

All these factors combine to make baby boomers a very different cohort than the 32 to 51-year-olds of 20 years ago. Traditional ideas concerning the preferences of those aged 50 versus 30 no longer are accurate. Beliefs concerning certain consumption patterns, such as "coffee consumption increases with age" and "younger people drink cola," no longer are as valid as they once were because people who grew up on cola often continue to drink it. The same is true for ethnic foods and a host of other products.

The received wisdom will have to change constantly to reflect new sets of preferences and life experiences. For example, baby boomers remember when the idea of careers for women was considered radical. Not so for Generation X women; most of them work as a matter of course, just like their own mothers. As a result, ideas about marriage, family, and jobs are changing and will continue to change.

If the firm is marketing a product to a certain age range, it should be aware that the people who will be in that age range in five or ten years will not be the same as the ones who are there now. A strategy that has worked for years should be rethought as one cohort leaves an age range and another takes its place.

Therein lies the challenge in contemporary marketing: it is no longer advisable to treat a market as an undifferentiated mass of people with similar fixed tastes, interests, and needs. In the age of target marketing, it is imperative to know who the customers are and how to reach them. When the customer's needs change, it is essential to know that the firm must adjust its marketing efforts accordingly. In sum, a working knowledge of demographics and analytical tools for demographics is important for a firm if it wishes to remain a contender in the market of the next cohort and the next generation.

Lecture 2—The Marketing Environment Takes a Turn, an Older Turn

This lecture is intended for use with Chapter 6, "Scanning the Marketing Environment." It focuses on changing societal and business patterns. Here you should consider using very current examples of developments that augment the material in the suggested lecture. This will enable the students to identify the changes occurring in society as related to their growing knowledge of various marketing management techniques and issues.

Teaching Objectives

- Introduce students to some of the more important issues in the contemporary marketing environment

- Consider the role of marketing and marketers in the societal change and development process

- Discuss specific marketing environment issues

Discussion

Introduction

During the 1990s, U.S. household spending patterns changed dramatically. There were some very different demographics facing businesses during those years, and some of the same variables continue to influence the marketplace into 2002 and beyond.

The U.S. economy grew through the 1990s at a rate not seen since the 1960s, unemployment and inflation were the lowest in decades, and the stock market set records with regularity. Some economists explained the situation by claiming that a new economy was at work, one driven by deficit reduction, low interest rates, and technological advances. Others pointed to the Asian economic bust, the dot-com stock market collapse in 2000, and began to consider the inevitable limits to the economic and marketing environment. Some analysts felt that many firms would not be able to maintain the pace of the new market environment, and they were correct, as the dot-com bust and the market decline demonstrated.

Even with the 2000–2001 market jitters and the Federal Reserve interest rate responses, many felt that the economy was more stable and long-term than we gave credit because consumer spending, which accounted for two-thirds of the nation's economic output, continued to roll along at a steady pace. However, the inevitable slowdown in the economy and consumer spending had already begun, and the attacks on the United States in September, 2001, and the Enron/Anderson corruption scandals at the end of 2001 set the groundwork for not just a rethinking of America's security and growth but also some rethinking about the way we would do business in the future. With this re-evaluation of many issues in the economic, social and political environments, we find the basis of a new economy and a new marketing environment.

New Life-Cycle Pattern

One of the more important predictors of the future direction for the new economy is life-cycle stage. Typically, households headed by twenty-somethings spend less than average on most products and services because their households are small and their incomes are low. Spending reaches the maximum in middle age, as family size increases and incomes peak, then falls again in older age as household size and income decline.

These stages, combined with the baby booms and busts of past decades, have made evaluating and forecasting the marketing environment a complex endeavor. Add in a fundamental change that has been taking place in the life-cycle pattern of spending, and marketers are discovering that doing business today is a lot like building a house in an earthquake zone.

Two big quakes in spending patterns have reshaped consumer markets in recent years. One is the dramatic decline in spending by householders aged 35 to 44. This downturn is of significance to business because the 35–44 age group accounts for the largest share of American households, over 23 percent, and consequently the largest share of most consumer markets. Ten years ago, this group spent 29 percent more than the average household on goods and services. Today, it spends only 16 percent above the average. Between 1987 and 2001, householders aged 35 to 44 cut their spending 9 percent, after adjusting for inflation.

Their spending once matched that of those in the age group (cohort) aged 45 to 54, but the recessions of 1991 and 2001 changed that, and the impact on retailers and manufacturers has been significant. While the number of households headed by 35- to 44-year-olds increased 31 percent from 1987 to 2000, their aggregate spending rose only 19 percent. By contrast, during the same period, the number of households headed by 45- to 54-year-olds rose 44 percent, and their aggregate spending rose an even faster 46 percent. The shift has spelled trouble for toy companies, turmoil among fast-food retailers, and closings and consolidations in the shopping center industry. Even though some of these changes have been beneficial, getting rid of some of the weaker players in these industries, there are some fundamental long-term issues emerging. Depending on your perspective, this can be both good and bad.

What accounted for the younger groups spending decline? The answer is economic insecurity. In this life-cycle stage, people tend to have growing families and huge debts. The two recessions forced 35- to 44-year-old householders to cut their discretionary spending in order to make ends meet. This is the bad side, from the perspective of some analysts, but others argue that given the huge amount of debt and lack of a savings habit with this younger group, the trend could be good for the future. The "big spender" title has moved on to another age group.

Older Americans account for the second quake in life-cycle spending patterns. Between 1987 and 2001, spending by the 65-plus set rose faster than in any other age group, fueled by a more educated and affluent generation entering senior citizen status. Thus, older Americans' spending is rising to approach the average, and the trend will only intensify as the hyper-educated boomers hit their sixties in 2006.

Many businesses still haven't noticed the aging consumer markets. Some are ignoring it entirely. Clearly older consumers are spending money, but they're spending it on the industries that have been courting them. Here's a look at some of the winners and losers as the new consumer paradigm takes hold.

The Casual Consequence

Between 1987 and 1997, the average American household cut its spending on apparel 15 percent, after adjusting for inflation. Spending on women's clothes fell even more, down 20 percent. Householders aged 35 to 54 made the biggest cut. The average household in this age group spent one-third less on women's clothes in 1997 than it did in 1987.

No wonder so many clothing retailers are wondering where their customers went. The growing popularity of khakis and polo shirts, less expensive than business suits, explains part of the decline. "There are a lot more wearing occasions for casual apparel due to a lot of companies going casual in the workplace," explains a Levi Strauss & Co. spokesperson. A 1997 survey commissioned by Levi Strauss found that 53 percent of U.S. workers now dress casually every day of the week, not just on Fridays.

However, more important is the clothing industry's failure to create products that appeal to middle-aged women. The biggest spenders on women's clothes are householders aged 45 to 54, followed by those aged 55 to 64. Yet, most clothing is designed and marketed to teens and young adults. With so little to choose from, women aged 35 and older are spending their money elsewhere.

One forward-thinking company that has captured the attention of older women is DM Management in Hingham, Massachusetts, a catalog retailer that targets a neglected category: affluent women over 35 (see "New Look, Better Numbers," October 1998). Sales through its J. Jill and Nicole Summers catalogs have grown rapidly, up more than 61 percent in 1998–99. Why? Maybe it is because the biggest spenders have nowhere else to shop.

We Just Want to Have Fun

The entertainment industry is booming, and no wonder. Each year since 1987, Americans have devoted more of their budget to entertainment. In 2000, the average household spent over $1,900 entirely discretionary dollars on good times, up from $1,686 in 1987, after adjusting for inflation—an 8 percent jump. Behind this boom is an increasingly affluent population and the growing enthusiasm of older Americans for having fun.

As in almost every other category, the pattern of entertainment spending has shifted markedly. Whereas householders aged 35 to 44 once were the biggest spenders on entertainment, that role has been overtaken, again, by householders aged 45 to 54. Between 1987 and 1997, the average household headed by a 35- to 44-year-old cut its entertainment spending 10 percent. Meanwhile, spending by householders aged 45 to 54 surged 16 percent. By 2000 the 45–54 group spent 33 percent more on entertainment than the average, pushing 35- to 44-year-olds into second place. Rising to third place were householders aged 55 to 64, displacing the 25 to 34 age group.

Nevertheless, the senior citizens have become America's true party animals. The average household headed by a 65- to 74-year-old spends more on entertainment than does the average household headed by someone under age 25. Even the very oldest householders are in on this revolution: Those aged 75-plus spent 98 percent more on entertainment in 2000 than in 1990, the biggest increase of any age group.

The bottom line is that Americans aged 55 and older account for a larger share of spending on entertainment than those under age 35. Despite this fact, the entertainment industry has done little to serve fun-loving older Americans, with some exceptions. Elderhostel is booming, precisely because it targets older consumers. However, many other businesses have risked bankruptcy rather than change their mind-set. The shopping center industry is a prime example, obsessively pursuing teens and young adults when they could reinvent themselves as entertainment venues for older consumers. Mall visits fell from 2.62 to 1.97 per person per month between 1994 and 1997, according to Maritz Marketing Research polls. "What could possibly lure someone who is 49 or 59 years old?" asks a retail consultant. "If anything, they are repelled by congested aisles and merchandise that is not appropriate."

The Stomach Wars

Americans are spending less on food than they once did, and that is a problem for the restaurant industry. Between 1987 and 2000, spending by the average household on food at home fell 3 percent, adjusting for inflation. Spending on food away from home fell a much larger 13 percent. When Americans cut their discretionary spending in the early 1990s, restaurants were hit hard, as people turned to less-expensive take-out food. "Consumers opt for a take-out dinner at home a whopping 61 percent more often than they did 10 years ago, whereas they choose to eat dinner in a restaurant 4 percent less often," reports Restaurants USA, the trade magazine of the National Restaurant Association.

Younger householders have cut their food spending the most. In 1987, the best customers in the food-away-from-home category were householders aged 35 to 44, but the recession took away their appetites. From '87 to '00, they cut their restaurant outlays by an enormous 23 percent, ranking them second to 45- to 54-year-olds in restaurant spending. Not only that, the average household headed by a 55- to 64-year-old now spends more on food away from home than those headed by 25- to 34-year-olds, despite the fact that older households are smaller. Adding insult to injury, householders aged 65 to 74 spent considerably more on food away from home in 1997 than householders under age 25. Good-bye Planet Hollywood, hello early-bird special.

Restaurants will have a difficult time recapturing those lost customers. "The low end of the industry is in for big trouble," says the editor and publisher of a weekly newsletter for food marketers. "It's falling behind because so many supermarket chains have made an effort to supplement their sales with home meal replacements."

Whether they are ready-to-eat or ready-to-heat, home meal replacements are changing the way supermarkets do business. Chefs and nutritionists now create signature menu items that shoppers can buy on the fly—everything from ethnic dishes to all-American comfort foods—and separate checkout counters speed customers on their way. In the battle for share-of-stomach, "supermarkets are winning," In the future, an analyst predicts, restaurant dining "will be more of an occasion."

Note: You or some students may take issue with this view, so it might be interesting to check on the local or regional trends to compare with this perspective.

Upward Spiral: Health Care Costs

No one escaped the rising costs of medical care in the past decade: the average household spent over $2,000 out-of-pocket on health care costs in 2000, a 16 percent increase since 1987, adjusting for inflation. Nearly half that amount was for insurance. But since spending on insurance by the average household grew more than 40 percent across all age groups, the spending pattern did not change significantly. Householders 65 and older spent the most out-of-pocket, 52 percent to 58 percent more than the average. The youngest householders spent the least.

Not surprisingly, health care consumes a sizable share of older householders' budgets. People aged 65 to 74 devote 10 percent of their annual spending to out-of-pocket health care costs. Those aged 75 or older shell out even more—14 percent of spending overall, or $2,930 in 2000. Despite Medicare coverage, 53 percent of seniors' health care dollars go to insurance bills. Out-of-pocket Medicare costs, plus the supplemental insurance purchased by many, boosts their spending on health insurance far above that of any other age group.

These facts are of utmost importance to today's middle-aged adults. Proposals to raise the age of Medicare eligibility could mean boomers would have to devote an even larger share of their retirement income to medical costs. Few boomers are aware of the enormous burden health care costs place on older householders. Their awareness—and their political involvement—is likely to grow as they approach retirement age.

Furniture versus Computers

Perhaps nothing exemplifies the battle for discretionary dollars better than the war between the furniture and computer industries. As spending on computers has surged, spending on furniture has fallen.

By all accounts, these should be golden years for the furniture industry. The economy is up, relatively, homeownership is at a record high, and the baby boomers are in their peak furniture-buying years. However, the average household spent 13 percent less on furniture in 2000 than in 1987. In addition, householders aged 35 to 44, traditionally the biggest hearth-and-home spenders, cut their furniture budgets by a substantial 34 percent. By 1999, householders aged 45 to 54 were the biggest furniture buyers, despite the fact that they, too, were spending 8 percent less than a decade ago.

Forget the new sofa— householders want a computer and Web access. In 2000, the average household spent $260 on computer hardware, software, and online services for nonbusiness use. While that may not sound like much, it is an average and includes those who spent something and those who spent nothing. More impressive: if you rank all the products and services people buy for their homes, computers are in fourth place. The only items that account for a greater share of the household operations budget are telephone equipment and services (average, $909); furniture ($387); and day care ($232). The average household spends more on computer technology than on major appliances, lawn and gardening, or house wares.

The biggest computer spenders are aged 45 to 54, and they spent 61 percent more than the average household in 2000. Second are aged 35 to 44. Seniors aged 55 to 64 are third, spending more on computers than householders aged 25 to 34.

With computer spending surging, other discretionary categories have suffered, and a reversal is unlikely, despite the dot-com bust, as the Internet's popularity grows.

The New Adventurers

Americans spend substantially on travel. In 2000, the average household spent $1,259 on travel-related transportation, food and alcohol, lodging, and entertainment.

The travel market has long been dominated by older Americans, and for good reason: it's one of the few industries that has courted them. "They saw the opportunity. They looked at who had discretionary income and time. The industry has boomed ever since."

In 2000, the biggest travelers were householders aged 45 to 54, 55 to 64, and 65 to 74—in that order. All other age groups spend less than average on travel. Householders aged 55 to 64 devote the largest share of their spending money to travel, nearly 5 percent. In fact, this age group spends more on travel (over $1,900 in 2000, on average) than it does on clothes ($1,753), and almost as much as it spends on furniture, appliances, floor coverings, bed sheets, and bathroom linens combined ($1,755).

Thanks to the aging boomers, the travel industry is likely to experience years of surging growth. When today's workers, regardless of age, are asked what activity they most look forward to when they retire, travel is mentioned by the largest share, 32 percent, according to a Gallup survey. When asked whether there is something workers are waiting to do until they retire, once again travel is the hands-down winner—cited by 45 percent of respondents. Despite, some fall-off in the early months after the 9/11/01 attacks, travel has again begun to increase toward prior levels.

The news could not be better for the travel industry, and it could not be worse for other industries that will lose out to this travel bug. Before the losses mount, businesses should follow the money, targeting the growing numbers of affluent, sophisticated, older consumers.

Travel and retail consultants are optimistic. As boomers inflate the ranks of older consumers, businesses may finally begin to get it. "Boomers are actually going to convince us that youth is something to be endured while you wait for your forties, fifties, and sixties."

Marketing and Advertising

1. Coppertone is always alert to demographic changes that can affect the marketing of its sunscreen products. As this Italian ad demonstrates, the company offers products for both adults and children. In planning the marketing approach for these products, Coppertone managers had to examine Italy's population growth, age mix, and household patterns.

    a. What sources of information can you identify for data about the demographic environment in Italy?

    b. Assume that the birth rate has been dropping, reducing the average household size in Italy. What are the implications for Coppertone's marketing efforts?

    c. What other environmental factors should Coppertone pay particular attention to when planning its advertising for sunscreen products in Italy?

Answer

    a.   One online source is the Instituto Nazionale di Statistica, at http://demo.istat.it/e/. This site provides updated demographics and projections for changes in the future. Another online source (available in printed form, as well) is the CIA's World Fact Book coverage of Italy, at http://www.cia.gov/cia/publications/factbook/geos/it.html. Students will identify other sources in printed and online form, as well.

    b.   If the birth rate is dropping, Italy will have fewer children, which will mean a smaller market for children's sunscreen. However, fewer children also means that parents may be more able to afford to buy higher-quality products, such as a better sunscreen to protect children from the dangers of sunburn. Thus, Coppertone will need to conduct research to learn whether parents in Italy perceive their children as more precious because they have smaller families.

    c.   Other environmental factors that Coppertone should examine when planning sunscreen advertising for the Italian market include: the economic environment (including income levels and forecasts); the natural environment (including governmental restrictions on ingredients or packaging that may adversely affect the environment); the technological environment (including advances in sunscreen formulas and packaging); and the political-legal environment (including rules that govern advertising).

2.   Nearly every state in the United States conducts ongoing marketing campaigns to bring businesses to the area. This ad, which appeared in *Inc.* magazine, seeks to attract businesses to Colorado. Most of the copy focuses on the state's natural environment, although it also mentions the labor force and an existing cluster of high-tech companies.

    a.   Why would a business consider the natural environment of a state when making a decision about relocation or expansion? How does Colorado's ad address these considerations?

    b.   What view of nature does this ad imply through its use of graphics and copy? Relate this view to the company's relocation/expansion decision discussed in (a).

    c.   What other environmental elements are mentioned in the ad that would be meaningful to a business making a relocation decision? Can you suggest additional environmental elements that Colorado marketers should incorporate into this type of campaign?

Answer

    a.   Businesses that tend to attract employees who are particularly interested in outdoor activities will want to learn more about a state's natural environment before making relocation or expansion decisions. The ad addresses this by talking about how the "legendary quality of life" helps companies attract and retain good employees. It also mentions Colorado's "well-educated labor force," indicating that companies can expect to select candidates from among a good labor pool.

    b.   This ad implies a view of nature in which people seek out the harmony of nature, rather than feeling subjugated by it or wanting to master it. As a result, Colorado is appealing to companies whose top managers and work force enjoy nature and participate in outdoor activities made possible by the state's climate and natural resources.

    c.   The ad also mentions "a critical mass of existing high-tech activity," which suggests that businesses can tap into ideas and advances resulting from high-tech suppliers and researchers in the area. In addition, it says that "housing is diverse and plentiful," reassuring employers that their workers will be able to find appropriate housing at a reasonable price. Other environmental elements that marketers might incorporate into such a relocation campaign are the general economic climate, the political-legal climate, and more about the demographic climate.

3. **BONUS AD--See Companion Web site!** Although the technological environment has brought many advances, it has not supplanted some basic, long-standing products such as salt, the subject of this ad from Morton International. Instead of trumpeting salt's vital role in cooking, the ad discusses traditional medicinal uses for salt, such as relieving sore throat pain. At the same time, the ad makes no particular claims for Morton-branded salt.

    a. How does this ad stimulate consumers to think about the technological environment? From Morton's perspective, what is the goal of this approach?

    b. What does Morton stand to gain by promoting salt as a product category? Why would the company choose to promote noncooking uses of salt?

    c. Which environmental forces are likely to have the strongest influence on the marketing of Morton salt? Why?

Answer

    a. This ad puts the technological environment in the context of more traditional, time-tested medical developments based on use of everyday products such as salt. The goal is to encourage consumers who are worried about the long-term safety and efficacy of very recent medical developments to return to salt as a traditional remedy for various ailments.

    b. Because Morton is by far the most prominent brand in the salt category, it stands to gain if consumers buy more salt as a result of a campaign that increases primary demand. Promoting noncooking uses of salt helps Morton grow the market through a market-development strategy that emphasizes new uses of a current product.

    c. One environmental force that could strongly influence the marketing of Morton salt is the natural environment. If naturally-occurring sources of salt become scarce or restricted due to climactic or other changes, Morton might be unable to meet demand. A second environmental force is the emergence of another strong brand to challenge Morton. This would force Morton to use its marketing to increase selective demand for its brand of salt. Students may offer other suggestions, as well.

4. **BONUS AD--See Companion Web site!** Ad number four: This ad discusses how Shell worked closely with a number of stakeholders, including conservation groups and local fishermen, to design a suitable plan for wind-powered energy generation in the United Kingdom. The ad touches on several key factors in Shell's marketing environment.

    a. What concerns related to the natural environment are addressed in this ad—and why are they particularly important for Shell?

b. The ad invites examination of a company report titled "People, Planet and Profits," posted on www.shell.com. Which stakeholder groups would be most interested in such a report?

c. How do ads like this help Shell build relations with consumers who buy gasoline? With its gasoline dealers?

Answer

a. Concerns about the natural environment addressed by this ad are development of nonpolluting energy sources and potential disruption of the natural environment, such as birds or crabs and lobsters that provide the livelihood for local fishermen. These concerns are important for Shell because petroleum companies have previously caused pollution through spills and other problems. Shell wants to maintain a good relationship with all its stakeholders, including local fishermen and conservation special interest groups.

b. Conservation groups and other special interest groups concerned with preserving the natural environment would be particularly interested in Shell's report. In addition, shareholders, gasoline buyers, and government regulators might want to know more about what Shell is doing to protect the environment.

c. Such ads help position Shell as being actively interested in environmental protection and sensitive to the concerns of local fishermen as well as conservation groups. Consumers who go out of their way to do business with socially-responsible companies would be more inclined to buy gasoline from Shell because it is sensitive to environmental concerns, rather than buying than from companies that lack a socially-responsible image. Consumers would also see Shell as sharing their views about the value of preserving nature. Similarly, dealers would rather be associated with an energy firm that is actively protecting the environment, as opposed to associating with an energy firm that is making headlines for oil spills or other environmental mishaps.

Online Marketing Today

Peapod, one of the pioneers of online grocery retailing, has learned to use changes in the marketing environment to its advantage. Increased diversity is opening new opportunities to offer online shopping and home delivery of groceries to Americans with disabilities. In addition, the company closely follows the economic environment, which influences its customers as well as its competitors. Peapod entered the metropolitan Washington, D.C. market by buying the distribution center of failed competitor Streamline.com, which ran out of money during the start of an economic downturn. When venture capital funding ran out for Homeruns.com, a second competitor, Peapod quickly expanded to cover customers in areas that Homeruns.com once served. Peapod is itself influenced by the economic environment, as well: In search of higher profits, the company has stopped offering free delivery in most markets.

Peapod's home page (www.peapod.com), examine the listing of markets served, and read about the benefits for customers. Then follow the "About Peapod" link to learn more about the company's history, goals, and links with employees and affiliates. How has the demographic environment influenced Peapod's choice of markets? How has the economic environment influenced its choice? How do the benefits cited on the home page relate to current trends in the marketing environment?

Answer

The demographic environment has influenced Peapod's choice of markets in terms of the density of population (Peapod chooses highly-populated urban areas and their surrounding suburbs). The economic environment is another important influence because Peapod has chosen markets in which the population has a high income level. The benefits cited on the home page relate to current trends in several ways. First, the increased participation of women in the U.S. workforce means that many households are composed of two working people—who are both pressed for time and therefore would welcome the convenience of having Peapod select, pack, and deliver groceries. Second, more U.S. consumers have access to computers and the Internet, so they are able to quickly and easily order from Peapod's Web site. Third, more consumers want to customize products, and Peapod allows people to order exactly what they want and have it delivered when they want it. Students may identify other trend-related benefits, as well.

You're the Marketer—Sonic PDA Marketing Plan

Every company has to examine its macroenvironment to understand the key developments that shape market opportunities and pose threats to marketing effectiveness. This environmental scanning uncovers emerging trends and changes that can potentially affect the needs and responses of customers, the competition, and the firm's markets.

Jane Melody asks you to scan Sonic's external environment for signs of change that indicate opportunities and threats for the company's PDA product. Review Sonic's current situation and then, using library or Internet resources (or both), locate information to answer the following questions about Sonic's macroenvironment:

- What demographic changes are likely to affect Sonic's two target markets, middle- to upper-income professionals and mid- to large-sized corporations? One source for this kind of data is the government's annual *Statistical Abstract of the United States* publication (www.census.gov/prod/www/statistical-abstract-us.html).

- What economic trends might influence the future of the PDA market? Check the Commerce Department's Stat-USA site (www.stat-usa.gov), especially key topics within the General Economic Indicators section under the "State of the Nation" heading, looking for statistics about changes and trends in consumer buying power and related economic topics.

- What technological changes can potentially affect PDA development, buyer acceptance of PDAs, and the development of substitute products? One online source to search is TechNews World (www.technewsworld.com), which reviews national and international technology developments.

- What current or emerging political-legal issues are likely to affect PDAs? Growing concerns over exposure to cell-phone radiation may lead to new legislation for Web-enabled cell phones that compete with Sonic's PDA. CNET's wireless information site (www.wireless.cnet.com) is only one of many sites to check for updates on this situation.

Once you have completed your environmental scan, analyze the results and their implications for Sonic's marketing efforts. Summarize your findings and conclusions in a written marketing plan or enter them into the Macroenvironment, Market Analysis, and SWOT Analysis sections of a plan prepared with *Marketing Plan Pro* software.

Answer

Students' answers will vary, depending on the latest information available about the macroenvironment, including demographic changes, technological changes, economic trends, and political-legal changes. For example, students will be able to track consumer demographic and economic changes on the U.S. Census Web site or in the *Statistical Abstract* to find out about trends in the size and composition of the professional segment of the consumer market. They will also be able to use U.S. business census data to find out about the size and composition of the business market. These sources will help Sonic's marketers decide whether to focus on specific segments defined by narrow age bands or particular income levels.

Technological changes can quickly affect Sonic's competitive advantage, so students should scan for information about new voice-recognition software and other advances that may surpass the features built into Sonic's PDA. Then Sonic's marketers can determine whether the company has the right mix of products or needs to begin developing new models with new technology. Finally, Sonic must look out for political-changes that could (1) affect its ability to market the PDA in the United States and other countries and (2) enhance or disrupt its ability to import parts from overseas suppliers.

Marketing Spotlight—Mattel

Mattel was founded in 1945 by two Californian dollhouse furniture makers, Harold Matson and Elliot Handler. The decision to sponsor Walt Disney's "Mickey Mouse Club" television show in 1955, the first sponsorship by a toy manufacturer, proved very helpful in attracting young consumers. Mattel can trace its success to the introduction in 1959 of the now legendary Barbie doll. Named after Handler's daughter, Barbie was an instant hit in the doll market despite her dramatic figure and slender proportions, which were not typical of American dolls at the time. Within ten years, over $500 million Barbie dolls had been sold. Barbie became the most successful branded toy in history, and Mattel became a toy and entertainment powerhouse.

Mattel's genius is in keeping its Barbie doll both timeless and trendy. Since Barbie's creation, the doll has filled a fundamental need that all girls share: to play a grown-up. Yet Barbie has changed as girls' dreams have changed. Her themes have evolved from jobs like "stewardess," "fashion model," and "nurse," to "astronaut," "rock singer," and "presidential candidate." Barbie also reflects America's diverse population. Mattel has produced African American Barbie dolls since 1968—the time of the civil rights movement— and has introduced Hispanic and Asian dolls as well. After sales flattened in the mid-1980s, Mattel rejuvenated the famed doll with introductions such as Crystal Barbie (a gorgeous glamour doll), Puerto Rican Barbie (part of its "dolls of the world" collection), Great Shape Barbie (to tap into the fitness craze), Flight Time Barbie (a pilot), and Troll and Baywatch Barbie (to tie in with kids' fads and popular TV shows). Industry analysts estimate that two Barbie dolls are sold every second and that the average American girl owns eight versions of Barbie. Every year since 1993, sales of the plastic doll have exceeded $1 billion.

Much of the renewed success of the classic doll was credited to Jill Barad, who had worked as a marketing director for Barbie before being named president and chief operating officer then gaining the title of CEO in 1997. One of her first moves with Barbie was to make the doll's image more consistent with the empowered woman of the 1980s with a campaign titled "We Girls Can Do Anything." It was a stunning success, and boosted Barbie's sales by more than $100 million within a year. Before Barad came to the company, Mattel had always followed a restrained segmentation strategy, with at most three new doll introductions annually. Barad quickly ramped up these introductions, and before long Mattel was introducing dozens of new Barbie dolls every year in order to keep up with the latest definitions of achievement, glamour, romance, adventure, and nurturing. Her aggressive reinvention of Barbie took the doll from $320 million in domestic sales to nearly $2 billion in global revenues by 1997.

After this peak in 1997, Barbie endured a two-year decline. Contributing to the drop in sales was the "age-compression" trend, marked by children exiting the toy market at increasingly earlier ages. As a result of age compression, one executive noted, Mattel found itself having "to reinvent 80 percent of [its] base volume on an annual basis."(David Finnigan, "A Knock-down, Drag Out Fight," *Brandweek*, Feb. 12, 2001). To keep kids interested in the brand for additional years, Mattel expanded into interactive games and software with a $3.5 billion acquisition in 1998 of educational software firm The Learning Company (makers of popular games "Carmen Sandiego" and "Myst"). The move proved disastrous. A shrinking market for CD-ROM games and software caused The Learning Company to suffer unexpected losses, which in turn cost Mattel $300 million in 1999 and depressed the toy company's stock price by more than 60 percent. Barad was forced to leave the company in February 2000. Kraft Foods veteran Bob Eckert was named as her replacement. After finding a buyer for The Learning Company, he developed plans to revitalize the company by concentrating on its core strengths.

Since Mattel relies on Barbie for roughly 40 percent of its profits, the doll figured heavily in Eckert's comeback strategy. First, Barbie was redesigned and given a slightly wider face that made her look less "waifish." Second, Mattel stepped up its merchandising efforts in stores, adding, for example, 200 Barbie boutiques in Toys 'R' Us stores across the United States. Third, the company segmented its markets further by marketing different styles of Barbie to different age groups.

Outside the Barbie franchise, Eckert pursued conservative growth opportunities that carried minimal risk. For example, rather than design software and games itself, Mattel contracted with experienced software providers to develop electronic entertainment for the company. The company also reduced its licensing commitments, renegotiating with Walt Disney Co. in 2000 to retain the rights to classic characters like Mickey Mouse while forgoing rights to characters from upcoming Disney films, which typically come at great cost and are no longer guaranteed hits. By focusing on the company's core divisions, "Eckert is transforming Mattel from a volatile, hit-driven toy company to a slower-growing but more stable consumer-products company," says one industry analyst. In 2000, sales bounced back, with total worldwide revenue up two percent to $4.67 billion worldwide. Eckert seemed to have Mattel back on track, no small thanks to Barbie, whose sales grew 10 percent domestically and 5 percent worldwide in 2000. After more than four decades on the shelves, Barbie remained the company's blockbuster brand.

Questions

1. How would you compare the marketing success of Mattel and Barbie in the years before and after Jill Barad? Was Barad's approach to marketing Barbie effective or not? Why?

2. What factors contributed to the success or failure of products such as Barbie? Can the success factors provide indicators for other products?

Suggested Responses

1. Barad provided an approach that was indicative of the times, with a contemporary attitude of relatively extreme fashion change to capitalize on the changing attitudes of the baby boomers who frequently had fewer children but did more for those children. There was also a refection of the changing demographics related to marriage and households. With more divorces and alternative lifestyles, both parents often spent much more on their children than other generations, essentially "purchasing" the affections of their children.

It would be difficult to say that Barad did not respond to a need for growth and change that was needed, but on the other hand she effectively changed the culture of the firm in a way that some analysts might consider was too trendy or fashion-oriented. She clearly got caught in the middle of a demographic issue (age compression). However, she also taught the firm some lessons about how far it could extend a brand franchise, primarily for short-term internal performance reasons.

2. Barbie was successful for many reasons, not the least of which was the fact that she generally responded to the look that girls aspired to and matched the image that fit with the times. When Barbie hit the market originally, there was little need to change the look; however, as the product life cycle for many products shortened during the 1980s and 1990s, the marketing environment for toys also changed, encouraging change. Whether this theme can be applied indefinitely is another issue. We have already begun to notice that fashions and attitudes are beginning to shift back to some more moderate views of what is right and wrong, good style and bad style.

Chapter 7—Analyzing Consumer Markets and Buyer Behavior

Overview

In addition to a company's marketing mix and factors present in the external environment, a buyer is also influenced by personal characteristics and the process by which he or she makes decisions. A buyer's cultural characteristics, including values, perceptions, preferences, and behavior learned through family or other key institutions, is the most fundamental determinant of a person's wants and behavior. Consumer markets and consumer buying behavior have to be understood before sound marketing plans can be developed.

The consumer market buys goods and services for personal consumption. It is the ultimate market in the organization of economic activities. In analyzing a consumer market, one needs to know the occupants, the objects, and the buyers' objectives, organization, operations, occasions, and outlets.

The buyer's behavior is influenced by four major factors: cultural (culture, subculture, and social class), social (reference groups, family, and roles and statuses), personal (age and life-cycle state, occupation, economic circumstances, lifestyle, and personality and self-concept), and psychological (motivation, perception, learning, and beliefs and attitudes). All of these provide clues as to how to reach and serve buyers more effectively.

Before planning its marketing, a company needs to identify its target consumers and their decision processes. Although many buying decisions involve only one decision-maker, some decisions may involve several participants who play such roles as initiator, influencer, decider, buyer, and user. The marketer's job is to identify the other buying participants, their buying criteria, and their influence on the buyer. The marketing program should be designed to appeal to and reach the other key participants as well as the buyer.

The amount of buying deliberateness and the number of buying participants increase with the complexity of the buying situation. Marketers must plan differently for four types of consumer buying behavior: complex buying behavior, dissonance-reducing buying behavior, habitual buying behavior, and variety-seeking buying behavior. These four types are based on whether the consumer has high or low involvement in the purchase and whether there are many or few significant differences among the brands.

In complex buying behavior, the buyer goes through a decision process consisting of need recognition, information search, evaluation of alternatives, purchase decision, and postpurchase behavior. The marketer's job is to understand the buyer's behavior at each state and what influences are operating. This understanding allows the marketer to develop an effective and efficient program for the target market.

Learning Objectives

After reading this chapter students should:

- Understand the major factors influencing consumer behavior

- Know and recognize the types of buying decision behavior

- Understand the stages in the buying decision process

Chapter Outline

I.   Influencing buyer behavior

    A.   Cultural factors

        1.   Culture—values, perceptions, and preferences that are the most fundamental determinant of a person's wants and behavior

        2.   Subcultures—nationalities, religions, racial groups, geographical regions

        3.   Social class—hierarchically ordered divisions in a society; members share similar values, interests and behavior (see Table 6-1)

    B.   Social factors

        1.   Reference groups—all groups that have an influence on attitudes or behavior

        2.   Family—the most influential primary reference group

        3.   Roles and statuses—activities a person is expected to perform and the status associated with each

    C.   Personal factors

        1.   Age and life-cycle stage—people buy different goods over their lifetime

        2.   Occupation and economic circumstances

            a)   Blue collar versus white collar

            b)   Spending income, savings and assets, debts, borrowing power, and attitude toward spending versus saving—all impact product choice

        3.   Lifestyle—pattern of living as expressed by activities, interests, opinions

        4.   Psychographics—the science of using psychology demographics to better understand consumers (VALS)

        5.   Personality and self-concept—personality characteristics that influence buying behavior (self-confidence, sociability, etc., and ties to brand personality

        6.   Psychological factors

            a)   Motivation—correlated to the strength of a need (Freud, Maslow, Herzberg)

            b)   Perception—selective attention, selective distortion, selective retention

            c)   Learning—changes in behavior arising from experience

            d)   Beliefs and attitudes—a belief is a descriptive thought a person holds about something; an attitude is a person's enduring favorable or unfavorable evaluations, emotional feelings, and action tendencies toward some object or idea

II.   Buying decision process

    A.   Buying roles—five different roles: initiator, influencer, decider, buyer and user

B. Buying behavior

    1. Complex buying behavior—high involvement, significant difference among brands

    2. Dissonance-reducing buying behavior—high involvement, little or no perceived difference among brands. Purchase is fairly quick

    3. Habitual buying behavior—low involvement, little or no brand difference

    4. Variety-seeking buying behavior—low involvement but perceived significant brand differences. May occur to relieve boredom

C. Stages in the buying decision process

    1. Problem recognition—difference between actual state and desired state

    2. Information search—both internal and external sources

    3. Evaluation of alternatives—different process for every consumer, involves weighing product attributes and their ability to deliver benefits

    4. Purchase decision—form a preference and intention to buy. Actual purchase can be influenced further by attitudes of others and unanticipated situational factors

    5. Post purchase behavior

        a) Post purchase satisfaction—understanding the differences between buyer expectation and the product's perceived performance. Minimizing the gap and achieving truthful representation

        b) Post purchase actions—satisfaction or dissatisfaction will lead to subsequent behavior that can have both positive and negative effects

        c) Post purchase use and disposal—learning more about use and disposal aids follow-on marketing and to enhance ecological awareness

    6. Other models of the buying decision process

        a) Health model—moving people to adopt healthful behaviors (smoking, diet, exercise)

        b) Customer activity cycle model—mapping the *pre, during,* and *post* phases of behavior toward a specific task

III. Summary

Lecture—Consumer Concerns

This lecture is intended for use with Chapter 7, "Analyzing Consumer Markets and Buying Behavior." It focuses on several major new issues in studies and strategies related to consumer marketing. The discussion begins by considering the privacy issue related to the consumer's right to privacy. This leads into a discussion of some of the different types of consumers we find in the U.S. today and the implications for marketers in the future.

Teaching Objectives

- To stimulate students to think about the privacy issue, pro and con, for a firm when it attempts to achieve a better understanding of its customers.

- To communicate the role of various types of information that help the firm achieve a clearer understanding of its customers and the consumer behavior environment of the present and future.

Discussion

Introduction

Americans today feel more protective of their privacy than they did during most of the 1990s. That is the fundamental conclusion of two surveys on privacy issues. Polls by Yankelovich and Louis Harris & Associates indicate continued high levels of concern over the way business obtains, uses, and disperses consumer information.

The more alarming figures arise from the Yankelovich survey, in which nine out of ten respondents favored legislation to regulate business uses of consumer information. Forty-five percent of those polled strongly feel the need for privacy legislation, up from 23 percent in 1990. According to a Yankelovich partner: "Very seldom do we get 90 percent agreement on anything. That really attests to the fact that this is an enormously important issue to people."

The Harris study is more reassuring, providing a less negative message. Although 82 percent of the respondents say they are "somewhat" or "very concerned" about threats to their personal privacy, their uneasiness is more focused on the government than business. The majority of respondents (57 percent) think businesses that handle personal information "are paying more attention to privacy issues these days." An interesting aspect of this poll is, however, that 72 percent of the respondents agreed that "if companies and industry associations adopt good voluntary privacy policies, that would be better than enacting government regulations."

There are some very consistent messages that have gotten clearer in recent years. They are:

- People regard their transaction information as something they feel they have lost control over, and that concerns them.

- People are different. Some don't want any direct marketing, some want everything you can give them, and in between there are people who want some say in what gets to them and what doesn't.

People in the last group (those who want a say in what comes to them) comprise the largest segment of the total (55 percent). This group recognizes the benefits of using personal information for business uses. However, they have to be convinced that the data being sought are relevant and subject to fair information practices. For these people, notice and the ability to opt out are very important. This group "favors voluntary standards, but they will back legislation when they think not enough is being done by voluntary means. As it is, over half the respondents (54 percent) do not believe current laws or business practices adequately protect their privacy.

At the same time, the Direct Marketing Association (DMA) reports that consumers purchased over $700 billion through direct marketing channels in 1998. This is not the contradiction it might seem. A 1994 survey regarding interactive services revealed that the respondents who were most interested in subscribing were also the most likely to have made purchases through direct marketing. They were also the most concerned about privacy, and their willingness to release personal information for interactive marketing purposes was contingent on the presence of policies that protected their privacy.

According to various surveys, the best customers for direct marketing are many of the same people who are looking for proper safeguards in the relationship between the marketer, the service provider, and the consumer. The apparent message here is that it would be a mistake for direct marketers to assume that their customers are not interested in privacy. Clearly, they are the people concerned about privacy.

Respondents to one of the surveys actually expressed a desire for better relationships with marketers. The survey indicated the people are tired of having to be vigilant about everything they do, and they would like to be able to trust a little bit again, but still they are looking for protection. The theme seems to be that it will take more than individual effort. A company could be doing everything right, but ten other companies are doing everything wrong, so in the consumer's mind all marketers stink. The point is that businesses have to make much more of a concerted effort to show that they really do respect privacy.

From the surveys there are some important conclusions. First, companies cannot brandish the survey data and say they can prove that the industry is rock-solid and forthcoming. Secondly, if one considers the process from a broader point of view, it is clear that the public wants industry to be more forthcoming, and they will listen if the industry responds. If the industry does not respond, there could be potential for more regulation. The number of bills to regulate direct marketing passed and pending in various state legislatures is clear evidence of this point. Legislators are showing that this is an issue that people care about.

Behavioral Analysis

There is a substantial question about how well the American consumer is faring in this era of low inflation, downsizing, and global competition. It can be argued that maybe some of this fits VALS 2, but it is likely that one thing is for sure: just when we believe that we have a good understanding of the consumer, some movement or person comes along and upsets our theory. We can learn about the consumer by looking at recent surveys. In general, the surveys tell us the consumer is possessive but despite the events of the latter months of 2001 still somewhat passive.

To support this perspective Langer Associates, Inc., conducts an annual survey of American consumers. Langer specializes in qualitative studies of consumer marketing issues. The firm conducted focus groups with thousands of people across the U.S. and discovered that the following attributes and concerns are widely shared:

- *Self-Security.* As corporate downsizing continues to make headlines, self-employment is increasingly viewed as the safer option. Educational courses and media focused on starting and running a small business still have widespread appeal, as do ads featuring business owners.

- *The "Mine" Generation.* Sensing that resources are becoming sparse and stretched, the "Me" Generation is putting more emphasis on preserving what they do have: jobs, family, community, possessions—a change reflected in economics and politics.

- *Localization.* A new protectiveness following September 11, 2001, has translated into increased interest in issues like school budgets and neighborhood crime. Advertisers can tap into this by localizing their message as well as running national campaigns.

- *More Together.* Coffee bars and the Internet are becoming increasingly popular in part because they satisfy two conflicting desires:

- Connection with others

- Avoiding intrusive interaction

  - The message is that stores, restaurants, and clubs similarly can satisfy both needs by building zones of "alone-togetherness" into their layout.

- *Topsy-Turvy Retail.* Focus group members often give higher marks for customer service to some discounters and off-price stores than the more upscale establishments. Clearly, the higher-price outlets need to work on this, and lower-price stores could promote service along with lower prices.

- *Battle of the Superstores.* Consumers like the more personal atmosphere of small, independent stores, and tend to sympathize more with the owners, but still they spend more at the mega-marts. Although there are signs that the public is beginning to tire of superstores, business remains brisk. Smaller stores will have to maintain excellent personal service, find niches to fill, and do more direct marketing to stay afloat.

- *"Woo-Me" Marketing.* Customers today will not seek out products or services; they assume that offers will come to them. Therefore, businesses need to be more proactive, approaching consumers with free trials and special offers.

- *Yuppies, GenX Style.* Twenty and thirty something's who are settling into careers are spending more, especially the singles. However, they differ from yuppies of the 1980s in that they do not expect to make big money and are less interested in designer labels. Ads that stress value and de-emphasize status as a reason for buying (even if it is the reason) are likely to appeal to this crowd.

- *Clothing Cutbacks.* Until a new style of dressing renders their current wardrobes obsolete, most consumers feel they already have all the clothing they need. The trend toward more casual dress for work and socializing has added to their resistance, even though there are signs that more formality in clothing and other social matters may be on a comeback. The money that would have gone into the closet is being spent instead on homes, travel, and investments despite national and global economic and political issues.

- *High-Tech Polarization.* Attitudes toward technology are polarized, with many people still concerned about the impact of computers on employment, the depersonalization of business and personal relationships, and other issues. Possible remedies: Find ways to offer reassurance, and to maintain the "human touch."

- *Data Glut.* Complaints about being overwhelmed by information are up sharply, indicating a potential market for those who can help simplify it and screen out extraneous communications.

- *Changed Office Structures.* Downsizing means more executives doing clerical work themselves, creating a market for foolproof photocopying and computer products. Other growth areas: outsourcing and products that aid in telecommuting from the home or the road.

- *Solitude Time.* On-the-job stress is creating the need for quiet time. Products that can be positioned as aids to relaxation include aromas, yoga, and reading materials.

- *Working at Relaxing.* Nothing is easy; professional/managerial types put a lot of effort into their down time, scheduling massages, gardening, and redecorating their city apartments. Ads can talk about people deserving to relax, and depict the humor inherent in striving for serenity.

These survey results are all very interesting, but the real question here is: What is the meaning of this for the business thinking of changing products or adding to its current offerings? This is an appropriate question to ask the class to stimulate discussion.

Marketing and Advertising

1.   This ad for Quaker Toasted Oatmeal Squares appeals to personal factors that influence consumer buying behavior, including lifestyle and self-concept. It also provides information so that the targeted segment will recognize and understand the bundle of attributes that this cereal product offers to solve the problem of how to eat a "nice, healthy breakfast."

     a.   Who is the target audience for this ad, and how does Quaker use the concept of consumer lifestyle to effectively communicate with the target?

     b.   Does this ad appeal to the consumer's actual self-concept, ideal self-concept, or others-self-concept? Which is the most appropriate for this product? Explain.

     c.   What bundle of attributes does this ad present for the consumer's consideration? What are the benefits associated with each attribute?

Answer

     a.   The target audience consists of consumers who work ("your briefcase") and are busy ("dashing out the door") but want a "nice, healthy breakfast." The concept of a busy, professional lifestyle is indicated by a graphic of someone running, with a briefcase in one hand and a canister of Quaker in the other, plus the copy. This ad catches the attention of people who identify with the time-starved work world and who often rush to work without being able to have the kind of healthy breakfast they would like.

     b.   This ad appeals to the consumer's ideal self-concept, in that it suggests that people not only want but can have a "nice, healthy breakfast" by eating Quaker products. For consumers who already eat in a healthy manner but are looking for a new breakfast product, it may represent the actual self-concept.

     c.   The main bundle of attributes presented by this ad include: portability (benefit: being able to eat while on the run), packaging (benefit: taking only one serving on the go), nutrition (benefit: a healthy breakfast). Students may identify other attributes and benefits, as well.

2.   Businesspeople also have specific needs and buying behavior when they act as consumers. The BlackBerry ad in Figure 2 targets businesspeople who want to avoid losing touch—even momentarily—with colleagues, clients, and other important contacts. Understanding the nuances of this consumer market's buying behavior, BlackBerry presents its wireless device as a convenient solution to the problem of staying connected at all times.

     a.   What personal and psychological factors in the buying process have been incorporated into this ad?

     b.   What role or roles are being addressed by this ad?

     c.   Which stage of the consumer buying decision process is this ad most likely geared toward? Why?

Answer

    a.   Personal factors incorporated into this ad include: occupation (the ad appeals to busy workers and managers whose work requires them to stay in touch while on the road); lifestyle (people who are very busy and need constant calendar updates as well as communication links with colleagues); and self-concept (people who see themselves as efficient and professional and who want to "always be in the know"). Psychological factors include motivation (staying in touch at any place and time is a satisfier factor, perception (this ad is a stimulus that encourages selective attention because it relates to a current need to stay in touch while on the go), and learning (the ad minimizes any fear of obstacles to learning by pointing out that the product works with existing e-mail addresses).

    b.   The main role is a work one in which someone must coordinate or be aware of the work of others on the team. Secondarily, a BlackBerry can serve as a status symbol.

    a.   This ad seems geared to the problem recognition part of the decision process, because it is calling attention to a common problem ("Berry Busy?" is the headline) and then offering the BlackBerry as a solution.

Online Marketing Today

Who would buy pet health insurance—let alone buy it online? Tom Kurtz founded Premier Pet Insurance a few years ago, after his cat needed $2,000 worth of veterinary treatment. Although pet health insurance has long been accepted in Europe, the U.S. market for pet health insurance remains largely untapped. Fewer than 2 percent of all American cat and dog pets have health insurance, compared with up to 50 percent in Great Britain and Sweden. Now rising costs for sophisticated life-saving procedures such as chemotherapy and kidney transplants are causing more U.S. consumers to consider this type of insurance for their pets. As with other insurance products, many consumers like to shop around and compare policies and rates before making a purchase. That is why Premier maintains an informative, easy-to-navigate Web site.

Visit the Premier Pet Insurance site (www.ppins.com), review the home page, then follow the links to find out more about the various insurance plans, how much buyers can save, FAQs (frequently asked questions), and online quotes and ordering. How does the company address the social and personal factors most likely to affect the purchase of this product? What attitudes and beliefs about this purchase does Premier directly address on its Web site? What type of buying behavior would you expect consumers to follow when buying pet health insurance—and how does the company's online marketing reflect a good understanding of this buying behavior?

Answer

Premier addresses several social and personal factors. First, it implies membership in the aspirational group of people who take good care of their pets. Second, it evokes the "priceless" nature of a pet's "love and companionship," seeming to see pets as part of the family for which a consumer cares deeply. Among personal factors, the site suggests that pet insurance is affordable, alluding to economic circumstances. It also touches on lifestyle with graphics and copy about people who enjoy and value their pets. Finally, it involves self-concept, specifically the ideal self-concept of consumers who want to be the kind of people who get the very best care for their pets.

One belief addressed by the site is that pet health insurance is unlikely to be affordable. The site includes a section titled "How much will you save?" to refute this belief. A second attitude is the value of pets. The copy implies that pets are at least as valuable as homes, cars, and the consumer's health—all of which are insurable. Students may suggest other beliefs and attitudes addressed by Premier's Web site. Finally, consumers probably use complex buying behavior when shopping for pet health insurance, because this is a product about which consumers typically know little and because the price tag is relatively high. The company reflects a good understanding of this buying behavior by offering considerable details of its features, benefits, and costs; offering three levels of insurance at corresponding prices; and providing FAQs and a cost-justification section to allow buyers to become informed and trust Premier as a valuable source of information and a good supplier from which to purchase this insurance.

You're the Marketer—Sonic PDA Marketing Plan

Every company has to study consumer markets and behavior before developing a marketing plan for its products. This enables marketers to understand who constitutes the market, what and why the market buys, who participates in and influences the buying process, and how, when, and where consumers buy.

You are responsible for researching and analyzing the consumer market for Sonic's forthcoming PDA. Look again at the data you have already entered about the company's current situation and macroenvironment, especially the market being targeted. Now answer these questions about the market and buyer behavior:

- What cultural, social, personal, and psychological factors have the most influence on consumers buying PDAs? What research tools would help you better understand the effect on buyer attitudes and behavior?
- Which specific factors should Sonic's marketing plan emphasize—and why?
- What consumer buying roles and buying behaviors are particularly relevant for PDA products?
- What kind of marketing activities should Sonic plan to coincide with each stage of the consumer buying process?

After you have analyzed your markets and consumer behavior, consider the implications for Sonic's marketing efforts supporting the launch of its PDA. Finally, document your findings and conclusions in a written marketing plan or type them into the Market Analysis, Situation Analysis, Target Markets, and Market Summary sections of the *Marketing Plan Pro* software.

Answer

Students will offer a variety of responses to these questions, depending on the rest of their marketing plan ideas developed in earlier chapters. As a sample, students may say that the target market's values of practicality and material comfort are part of the shared culture of the United States. They may also indicate that the roles and statuses play a part by influencing who buys a Sonic PDA as a status symbol. Personal factors influencing this purchase include occupation and economic circumstances and lifestyle. Psychological factors influencing this purchase include perception and beliefs and attitudes. Students may suggest conducting primary research to better understand buyer attitudes and behavior and to determine whether a PDA is considered a high- or low-involvement product; they may also suggest examining secondary research about current PDA owners.

Numerous factors can be emphasized in Sonic's marketing plan. Two sample responses: (1) the plan should stress informative marketing communications targeting consumers who will use PDAs, similar to the way BlackBerry targets users of its wireless e-mail device, to build the brand image and provoke problem recognition to set complex buying behavior in motion; and (2) the plan should stress PDA use among aspirational groups such as top executives or professionals, to bring in social factors that affect consumer buying behavior.

Students may also suggest emphasizing occupation, motivation, perception, learning, beliefs and attitudes, and dissonance-reducing buying behavior. Users are among the most important buying roles for PDA products, although deciders and buyers are also relevant. Complex buying behavior is the most important buying behavior for Sonic to understand, followed by dissonance-reducing behavior in the case of consumers who perceive little difference between Sonic and its competitors.

Finally, Sonic should plan activities for every stage of the consumer buying process. In the first stage, its goal is to help consumers recognize a need for a PDA, using advertising and other activities (students will mention many suggestions). In the second stage, Sonic needs to ensure that it provides a considerable amount of in-depth information, not just from commercial sources but from public and experiential sources, as well. Personal sources will be to Sonic's advantage if friends, colleagues, and others are satisfied with Sonic's PDAs. In the third state, Sonic must use its brand-building activities to create a positive image and contribute to the consumer's evaluation of the product as having the best bundle of attributes and benefits for their needs. In the fourth stage, Sonic should use marketing activities to create a positive buying situation and to lower perceived risk. In the fifth and final stage, Sonic should reassure consumers that they have made the right decision and continue to satisfy customers who need service or have other contacts with the company.

Marketing Spotlight—Nike

The Nike story begins with its founder, running enthusiast Phil Knight. In 1962, Knight started Blue Ribbon Sports, the precursor to Nike. At the time, the athletic shoe industry was dominated by two German companies, Adidas and Puma. Knight recognized a neglected segment of serious athletes who had specialized needs that were not being addressed. The concept was simple: Provide high-quality running shoes designed especially for athletes by athletes. Knight believed that "high-tech" shoes for runners could be manufactured at competitive prices if imported from abroad. Without much cash to do any advertising for his products, Knight crafted his "grass roots" philosophy of selling athletic shoes: Speaking to athletes in their language and on their level; sharing their true passion for running; and listening to their feedback about his products and the sport. Each weekend Knight would travel from track meet to track meet—both high school and collegiate competitions—talking with athletes and selling Tiger shoes from the trunk of his green Plymouth Valiant.

The company's commitment to designing innovative footwear for serious athletes helped it build a cult following that rapidly reached the American consumer. By 1980, after just under two decades in the business, Nike had become the number one athletic shoe company in the United States. Unfortunately for the company, this wave of success was soon to crest as rival companies positioned themselves to take advantage of the aerobics craze, which Nike largely ignored. Companies like Reebok and L.A. Gear developed fashionable and comfortable products aimed at women fitness enthusiasts that sold remarkably well.

Nike refused to join a market it saw as low in quality and heavy on cosmetic properties and continued making durable, performance-oriented products. The company lost millions in sales and allowed Reebok to gain basically uncontested market share points. By 1987, Reebok had nearly doubled Nike's market share, with 30 percentage points compared to Nike's 18. Fortunately for Nike, the company chose to fight back with product innovations and persuasive marketing. The company's "Air" technology revitalized the company with the additional aid of successful advertising campaigns such as the 1987 "Revolution in Motion" spot for the new Air

Max shoes and the "Air Jordan" commercials. When Nike unveiled its now-famous "Just Do It" campaign in 1988, just as Reebok developed the "Reeboks Let U.B.U" slogan, the company was on its way to a full recovery. By 1989, Nike had regained the market leader position in America as market share rose three points above Reebok to 25 percent that year.

In the 1990s, Nike continued its consumer focus. Nike kept its "finger on the pulse" of the shoe-buying public in part through the use of "EKINs" (Nike spelled backwards) – sports-loving employees whose job was to hit the streets to disseminate information about Nike and find out what was on the minds of retailers and consumers. Nike's "Brand Strength Monitor" formally tracked consumer perceptions three times a year to identify marketplace trends. In areas where it felt less knowledgeable, e.g., outside of track and basketball, Nike was more likely to commission customized research studies. Nike's inventory control system, called "Futures," also helped it better gauge consumer response and plan production accordingly.

Innovative product development had always been a cornerstone of the company. By 1998, Nike was unveiling a new shoe style, on average, every day. In 1999, the company put the power to design shoes in the hands of its customers with the NIKEiD project. NIKEiD enabled customers to personalize a pair of selected shoe models using online customization software. The software led consumers through a step-by-step process: customers could choose the size and width of the shoes, pick the color scheme, and affix their own 8-character personal ID to the product. Early reviews of the NIKEiD project were full of criticism of the limited selection and availability, so less than a year after its debut, Nike added additional shoe models and more customization options while increasing site capacity.

Though the company had become a household name throughout the world and, more important, achieved the position of global sportswear leader, Nike was still $3 billion shy of reaching the goal of $12 billion that Phil Knight initially intended the company to reach by 2000. In a letter in Nike's 2000 annual report, Knight addressed the issue of how to jumpstart his company's slowed growth and offered the following formula: "We need to expand our connection to new categories and toward new consumers." This quotation is indicative of Nike's relentless drive to build its brand with a strong consumer focus.

Questions

1. While Nike made significant changes to maintain its global leadership position, there appear to be some problems in maintaining and growing that position. Is Knight correct in his formula for jumpstarting Nike's growth (last paragraph), or is the matter more complicated?

2. Develop and evaluate the types of pro and con marketing environmental changes that you see for Nike. Given the options and challenges that Nike faces, how would you proceed with a strategic marketing plan for the firm?

Suggested Responses

1. Maintaining growth in their business sector requires more than just focus on customers and positive attitudes toward sports and athletes. It also requires a marketing awareness of where the economy and sports are changing and where the future is going, as dictated by the attitudes and actions of the next/younger generation of "players." It would appear that Nike allowed the general market to move away from their products, so if they are going to remain in the game they are going to have to target the heavy-hitters in the sports of today and the future. They cannot sell an unlimited number of shoes to serious athletes, so unless they are willing to also sell some other items (equipment), on a global basis, they will find that what made them great (high tech athletic shoes, etc.) has become a commodity, and they likely will not have a sustainable competitive advantage for the future.

1.   It appears that there is only so much you can do with shoes in a highly competitive environment. Nike is involved in certain high-profile sports (basketball, running, and baseball in particular), but along with the growing diversity of the country (and the world for that matter), there are other sports (and consumers) worth looking at for the future. Knight could be arguing in the last paragraph that they not only need to be more involved in other sports such as hockey, soccer, and even skiing, but they also need to spread the Nike franchise into other equipment for the various sports. Also, they need to move into the sports where there are new consumer and new expenditure opportunities. This could imply golf, hockey, and soccer, and others where there is a significant future. Finally, if a main issue is distribution and the channels, then Nike has to have products that will appeal to new channels and provide new sales profits for those channels that they have not yet fully developed.

Chapter 8—Analyzing Business Markets and Business Buying Behavior

Overview

Business markets consist of individuals and organizations that buy goods for purposes of further production, resale, or redistribution. Businesses (including government and nonprofit organizations) are a market for raw and manufactured materials and parts, installations, accessory equipment, and supplies and services. The variables impacting the business buyer are similar to those of the consumer buyer in some ways but very different in others. In general, the business buyer generally is much more technical, price-oriented, educated for the job, and risk-averse than the consumer buyer. In addition, with the business-buying environment, there is more concern for the status and power of potential vendors, and persuasiveness and empathy play relatively lower roles.

The industrial market buys goods and services for the purpose of increasing sales, cutting costs, or meeting social and legal requirements. Compared with the consumer market, the industrial market consists of: fewer buyers, larger buyers, close supplier/customer relationships, geographically concentrated buyers, derived demand that is relatively inelastic and fluctuating; and professional purchasing with several more buying influences involved, direct purchasing, reciprocity, and leasing. Industrial buyers make decisions that vary with the buying situation or buyclass. Buyclasses comprise three types: straight rebuys, modified rebuys, and new tasks. The decision-making unit of a buying organization, the buying center, consists of persons who play any of seven roles: initiators, users, influencers, deciders, approvers, buyers, and gatekeepers.

The industrial marketer needs to know: Who are the major participants? In what decisions do they exercise influence? What is their relative degree of influence? In addition, what evaluation criteria does each decision participant use? The industrial marketer also needs to understand the major environmental, organizational, interpersonal, and individual influences operating in the buying process. The buying process itself consists of eight stages called buyphases: problem recognition, general need description, product specification, supplier search, proposal solicitation, supplier selection, order-routine specification, and performance review. As industrial buyers become more sophisticated, industrial marketers must upgrade their marketing capabilities.

The institutional and government market share many practices with the business market and has some additional characteristics. Institutional buyers are less concerned with profit than with other considerations when they define the products and services to buy for the people under their care. Government buyers tend to require many forms and favor open bidding and their own nationals when they choose their suppliers. Suppliers must be prepared to adapt their offers to the special needs and procedures found in institutional and government markets.

Learning Objectives

After reading this chapter students should:

- Know the who, what, and how of the business market
- Know the who, what, and how of the institutional and government markets

Chapter Outline

I.   What is organizational buying?

A. The business market versus the consumer market. characterized by:
1. Fewer buyers, larger buyers, close supplier-customer relationships, geographically concentrated buyers, derived demand and inelastic demand
2. In addition: fluctuating demand, professional purchasing, multiple buying influences, direct purchasing, reciprocity, and leasing
B. Buying situations
1. Straight rebuy (reorder on a routine basis)
2. Modified rebuy (product specs, prices, delivery requirements, or other terms may be modified)
3. New task (a purchaser buys a product or service for the first time with major sub decisions involved in the buying decision)
C. Systems buying and selling—purchasers that buy a total solution to their problem from one supplier
D. Participants in the business buying process
1. Initiators, users, influencers, deciders
2. Approvers, buyers, gatekeepers
E. Major influences on buying decisions
1. Environmental factors—level of demand, economic outlook, interest rate
2. Organizational factors—objectives, policies, procedures, structures, and systems. In addition, business marketers should be aware of organizational trends that influence business buying
   a) Purchasing-department upgrading—larger and more important role
   b) Cross-functional roles—purchasing involved product design and development
   c) Centralized purchasing
   d) Decentralized purchasing of small-ticket items
   e) Internet purchasing (and e-procurement)—changing the shape and role of purchasing for the future (B2B)
   f) Other organizational factors—long-term contracts (vendor-managed inventory, etc.), purchasing-performance evaluation and buyers' professional development, improved supply chain management, lean production (JIT)
3. Interpersonal and individual factors—individuals in buying centers have differing interests, authority, status, empathy, and persuasiveness
4. Interpersonal and Individual factors—every business buyer is an individual
F. The purchasing/procurement process
1. Types of purchasing processes (routine, leverage, strategic, and bottleneck products)
2. Stages in the buying process
   a) Problem recognition
   b) General need description and product specification—product value analysis—search for ways to lower costs

3. Supplier search—seeking the most appropriate suppliers—vertical hubs, functional hubs, e-procurement

4. Proposal solicitation—request for proposal (RFP)

5. Supplier selection—each bidder rated on specified criteria; companies increasingly reducing the number of suppliers to insure quality, service and price

6. Order routine specification—final negotiations (blanket contract, stockless purchase plans)

7. Performance review—through both internal and external methods (buyflow map)

II. Institutional and government markets

    A. Institutions tend to have low budgets and captive clienteles

    B. Government a major buyer of goods and services

       1. Decision to purchase is usually based on cost

       2. Paperwork considerable

III. Summary

Lecture—Business Marketing in a Changing Global Environment

This lecture is intended for use with Chapter 8, "Analyzing Business Markets and Business Buying Behavior." It focuses on some of the day-to day considerations the business marketer faces in organizing and operating in the increasingly complex business-to-business marketing setting. Students may have difficulty identifying with the business marketing process because few have had any direct connection with the process. For this reason, the discussion focuses more on some of the rules or guidelines and allows the instructor an opportunity to add various current examples.

The discussion begins with an overview of the changes in the business marketing environment and then moves through some of the most important rules for the business marketer. It concludes with a discussion of the implications of some of these concepts in industry.

Teaching Objectives

- To stimulate students to think about the critical issues in business marketing

- To consider how to proceed with the considerations and strategies related to business marketing

- To discuss some specific approaches to help the marketer more effectively meet his/her business-to-business marketing objectives

Discussion

Introduction

In this era of fast-paced marketing change, mistakes can be and frequently are fatal for the unwary or lackadaisical. This is especially true in the business marketing arena. In fact, some of the "Must" items can turn into "Never!" depending on the industry, product, service, offer, and positioning in the marketplace.

There are as many or more variables in business marketing than in consumer marketing. Everything depends on the way the product or service is distributed and sold, the seasonality of demand for the product, the length of time that it takes to sell the product, whether the product is sold directly through the mail or leads are created for the sales force, the details of the offer, credit availability, size of the order, and much more.

Rules of Business-to-Business Marketing

The first rule is that the business marketer has to invest considerable time and effort to prepare to deal with customers in the business-to-business marketplace. Within the "B to B" arena, it is essential to know what is going on with all the significant players in the industry. It is a well-known rule that professionals ask around in the industry. They take advantage of various business-to-business direct-marketing programs by examining every piece of direct mail received.

Another rule is that if you are likely to be the other firm's customer, they could be your customer as well. Professional buyers check into all the likely, and unlikely, industry periodicals they can think of. One often finds a competitor has just begun, or just been eliminated, and there is some new sales program worth checking. We can learn from the successes and mistakes.

A good and efficient rule is to check out public information about parallel businesses that have the same or similar customer base but are not competitors. For example, both bath soap and corn flakes are sold to supermarkets across the country, but they are not competitors for the same dollar. What do they have in common? Which bath soap ideas can be used to sell more corn flakes? It is likely that there will be selling parallels that can be carried from industry to industry.

An old adage in business marketing holds that typically about 40 percent of business-to-business direct marketing results will come from the firm's choice of database or list. Sadly, it is often the case that the amount of time, thought, and energy put into the selection of the list for a direct-marketing effort is far less than 40 percent, and the campaign suffers for it.

Other Considerations

The next 40 percent of the results will be determined by the offer. Business marketers must consider what they are trading with the audience in exchange for their time, commitment, money, or attention. There are many variables such as credit, delivery, bulk pricing, and other similar arrangements. Overall, the primary variable is the degree to which the potential supplier firm is able to differentiate itself and make dealing with the potential customer firm special and better than dealing with any other option.

The remaining 20 percent of the results are determined by the "creative" copy, art direction, headlines, and the overall appearance of the marketing/advertising effort to create a positive attitude with the client/customer about the supplier's products. However, this is not the only variable, because the best creative in the world is useless if it is not seen by the right people or does not include an offer that provides visible value for the customer.

As in the consumer market, if the business marketer is not really tuned into the business customer, there will be problems. Unless the supplier firm's products or services are perceived as completely new, the supplier's sales and marketing staff will have some historical perspective on who buys those products. It is not enough to know that "50 percent of the sales come from SIC (Standard Industrial Classification) code 12345, 30 percent from SIC 98765, and the last 20 percent from a mix of automotive mechanics and university professors." Rather, it is better to look at the people in the industry as individuals, understand their past buying patterns, their requirements, etc.

The business purchasing process usually has more players involved than the typical consumer purchase effort. The user very often only recommends but does not specify; the user's supervisor also can recommend and sometimes can specify. Above these strata is the level that specifies; these are the people who control the budget and make approvals. Finally, there is the purchasing agent. Every one of these people has a name, a title, a role, a turf to protect, employees to serve, bosses to manage, quotas to meet, budgets to beat, and a thousand other headaches as well.

It is now widely recognized that the best place to invest marketing and sales efforts is in the current customer base, recalling that it is much harder to gain a new customer than to make an existing customer more satisfied. One way to wed customers to a company and its products or services is to show them that they are so important that the supplier firm takes the trouble to learn as much as possible about the customer firm. Every business marketer should start by knowing names, companies, and products, as well as critical buying concerns.

It is useful to keep in mind that the more the business marketer knows about his or her customers at this moment, the better he or she can decide which lists and databases to use when prospecting for new clients. Unless the marketer and company change the product and service mix considerably, future customers are likely to be like the current customers.

A response file is a database of individuals in companies who have responded to a business-to-business direct-marketing message. A list of people in the commercial refrigeration business who accepted an offer for a free book on "Developments in Commercial Refrigeration" would be an example of a response file.

The alternative is a "compiled" file: a database that has been constructed from researched information. For example, a list of purchasing agents, vice presidents of purchasing, and purchasing executives in the umbrella industry compiled from membership rosters in various umbrella and purchasing industry organizations would be a compiled file. There may be a tremendous amount of overlap between a response file and a compiled file.

Why is one type of "file" preferable to the other? The answer is that there is one thing we know for sure about the people in the response file: they have shown that they respond to direct marketing. Individuals on a compiled database may or may not be responder material. Using a response list helps the business marketer to stack the deck in her or his favor.

Other ways of stacking the deck include testing for affiliations and other objective correlatives that mean they are the kind of people you want to hear your business-to-business message. Look for people who attended industry conventions, who read industry publications. Among buying professionals these are key contact points.

Another less-used area for the business marketer is to use SIC codes to advantage. If the product is used to move liquids from one place to another on dairy farms, then the SIC code is 0241. Anther possible SIC is 2033, Canned Fruits and Vegetables Manufacturing, or SIC 2061, Cane Syrup, Made from Sugar Cane; or even SIC 2013, Canned Meats. All of these options could provide additional business that might use the equipment. Then the marketer could seek out lists of other food or cosmetics producers to see if there is a reasonable fit with the product.

Business marketers also improve marketing operations and success by approaching others in the potential customer company. They talk to sales people, staff engineers, etc., to identify the sales process at the customer firm: who to talk to, titles, how long it takes to get an appointment, how many visits over how many months it takes to make a sale; who the players are in a company, by title, and by function.

Another approach is to ask company sales people for the names, titles, and addresses of 50 individuals they want to sell to but who are buying from the competition; then market to their hit list.

It also pays to identify the "worst" customers, too. The comparison can be useful in designing a program to migrate the "worst" customers into a better category.

Achieving and measuring results is very important in business marketing. An ad for a retail store in the local newspaper can be measured by the number of cars in the parking lot and the amount of cash in the cash register the following morning. It can take a lot longer to fine-tune business-to-business marketing activities into a moneymaking machine.

Marketing and Advertising

1. As the ad in Figure 1 shows, Ford Credit provides commercial lending services for businesses buying Ford vehicles. The Ford logo is prominently featured in this ad, which invites businesspeople to call toll-free or visit the Web site (www.commtruck.ford.com) for more information about financing Ford truck and car purchases.

    a. Would an established business with an existing truck fleet be making a straight rebuy, a modified rebuy, or a new task purchase when it orders a new Ford truck? How might Ford Credit use this information to create a suitable advertising campaign to encourage usage of its commercial lending services?

    b. Which members of a business's buying center are most likely to be involved in decisions about choosing and using a commercial lending service to finance a vehicle purchase? What are the implications for Ford Credit's marketing planning?

    c. People who participate in business buying decisions also make consumer buying decisions in private life. Which stages of the business buying process are likely to be most influenced by a business buyer's personal perceptions of and experience with Ford consumer vehicles and financing? What should Ford do to leverage positive impressions (or counter negative impressions) among consumers who participate in business buying decisions?

    Answer

    a. An established business with an existing truck fleet would most likely be making a modified rebuy when ordering a new Ford truck. This is because the company would already be familiar with such a purchase but would need to modify the specifications, prices, or other terms based on current needs and current model availability. Ford Credit could use this information in an advertising campaign by stressing that it understands the needs and process of businesses that buy vehicles from time to time. Ideally, the company would show how its approval and disbursement methods streamline rebuys to save companies time and money.

    b. Several members of a business buying center are likely to be involved in decisions about choosing and using a commercial lending service such as Ford Credit. First, influencers such as financial management would have a say in the decision to pay cash or finance the purchase, although approvers such as top management would authorize the final decision based on financial guidelines or other policies. These people may prefer that Ford Credit present more detailed financial information in its communications. Second, users—those who actually

146

drive or supervise the driving of company vehicles—might suggest Ford Credit to pave the way for requests for new vehicles. An ad such as the illustration is general enough to appeal to this group. Students may be able to identify the role of other buying center participants and suggest how Ford Credit should allow for these participants when planning its marketing strategy.

c. The stages of the business buying most affected by a buyer's personal perceptions of and experiences with Ford as a consumer include supplier search, proposal solicitation, and supplier selection. Consumers who have good experiences or positive perceptions of Ford vehicles and financing will be more likely to include Ford in its supplier search, proposal solicitation and—ultimately—as the supplier selected. On the other hand, consumers who have poor experiences or perceptions of Ford will be less willing to include Ford in these stages. Ford is already leveraging its "Ford tough" consumer slogan by adding it to the illustrated ad for the business market. Students may suggest various ways in which Ford can leverage its positive image or counter negative impressions among consumers involved in business buying decisions. For instance, Ford Credit might advertise a very high consumer satisfaction rating (backed up by research), as proof that consumers are happy with its products, implying that businesses will be happy, as well.

2. The Cessna ad combines a dramatic photograph with descriptive copy focusing on attributes and benefits that are important to buyers of corporate aircraft. It also makes a head-to-head comparison with a competitive product to establish its superiority with specific evidence that is meaningful to the target market.

a. Which environmental and interpersonal factors are likely to have the strongest influence on a company's purchase of a new aircraft? How can Cessna incorporate the influence of these factors in its marketing planning?

b. Which stage of the business buying decision process is this ad most likely geared toward? Why would Cessna want to emphasize that stage in its advertising efforts? In what other stages might advertising be a particularly important part of Cessna's marketing efforts?

c. What attributes might be most critical for a company that is assessing aircraft suppliers prior to a purchase? Explain.

Answer

a. Environmental factors that may strongly influence the purchase of a new aircraft are: level of demand for the purchaser's product coupled with economic outlook, which contribute to the future performance of the buying company and its willingness to buy a new private plane; rate of technological change, which would help the company decide whether to buy a Cessna or wait for a more advanced model (from Cessna or a competing manufacturer). Interpersonal factors that can play a major role include: authority (Cessna should target managers with the authority to make such a major purchase) and status (Cessna can use its marketing to emphasize the high status of executives who travel on corporate planes).

b. This ad seems to be geared toward problem recognition, because it hints at retiring an existing turboprop plane and lists the benefits of buying a new Cessna Citation (faster travel time and lower operating costs). This stage is important because owners of corporate planes may not be aware of speedier and less expensive alternatives, or they may not even be thinking of replacing the current plane. This ad secondarily contributes to the general need description stage of the buying process, during which businesses work out the attributes they seek in a corporate aircraft. The ad refers to speed (472 mph), noise (quiet cabin), cabin size (expanded center-club cabin), performance ("outruns, outclimbs, and outcarries"), and costs (to own and operate). Cessna's aim is to not only provoke problem recognition but ensure that buyers frame the general and product characteristics in terms that fit the Cessna Citation, encourage buyers to include Cessna in their supplier search and proposal solicitation, and ultimately choose Cessna.

c. As Cessna's advertising implies, companies that are assessing aircraft suppliers prior to a purchase will be looking at speed, comfort, performance, and costs. They will also be examining safety, terms of purchase (including financing and warranty period), and repair and maintenance costs and issues.

Online Marketing Today—Bayer

German-based Bayer, which markets chemicals, polymers, and health care products around the world, has created a series of Web sites to connect with its business customers. The strategy is to combine "our traditional strengths—a comprehensive product portfolio, R&D expertise, and customer contact—with the new opportunities offered by the Internet," says Werner Spinner, a member of Bayer's management board. BayerOne, the company's main portal for chemical and polymer products, is available to business customers in North America and Europe, complete with multilingual options. Customers can place orders, track shipments, and examine as many as 50 account reports generated on the site or delivered by e-mail. The specialized Web sites, such as BayerRubberOne, offer more detailed information about products, applications, and industry news.

Visit BayerOne (www.bayerone.com) and review the look and contents of the welcome screen. Then go to the BayerRubberOne site (www.bayerrubberone.com). Examine the home page and follow the links to see the product information, applications, news, and services areas. Which members of the buying center would probably be most interested in each site? Would these sites be most useful for straight rebuy, modified rebuy, or new task purchasing situations? How does BayerRubberOne address some of the organizational, interpersonal, and individual factors that influence business buying behavior?

Answer

Students' answers will vary depending on the current material posted on BayerOne and BayerRubberOne. BayerOne is geared toward buyers who make the actual product decisions as well as deciders and users. BayerRubberOne targets these members of the buying center as well as initiators, influencers, and approvers (as indicated by the more general nature of the industry and product information available at this site). BayerOne seems better suited to straight rebuy situations, while the other site seems better suited to modified rebuy and new task purchasing.

BayerRubberOne addresses other major influences on business buying in several ways. First, it provides industry-related news to enhance an individual's knowledge ("The World of Rubber," for example) and influence risk attitudes concerning Bayer as a supplier and its products. Second, it has information suited to various interpersonal interests, authority levels, and status levels. Third, it offers details needed by buying-center members concerned about different organizational factors such as long-term contracts, Internet purchasing, and centralized purchasing. Students may offer other ideas, as well.

You're the Marketer—Sonic PDA Marketing Plan

Like their counterparts on the consumer side, business-to-business marketers have to understand their markets and the behavior of members of the buying center in order to develop appropriate marketing plans.

At Sonic, you are learning more about the business market for the company's PDA products. Jane Melody has defined this market as mid- to large-sized corporations that need to help their workforce stay in touch and input or access important data from any location. Given Sonic's current situation and your knowledge of business marketing, answer the following questions about this business market:

- What specific types of businesses appear to fit Melody's market definition? How can you research the number of employees and find other data about these types of businesses? Check the U.S. Census Bureau online listing of NAICS business classifications (www.census.gov/epcd/www/naics.html) as part of your research.
- What s
- pecific needs could Sonic's PDA product address for these businesses?
- What type of purchase would a Sonic system represent for these businesses? Who would participate in and influence this type of purchase?
- Which environmental, interpersonal, and individual influences are likely to be most important to business buyers of PDA products—and why?

Think about the opportunities, threats, and issues represented by the business markets you have researched. Also consider how this information could affect Sonic's marketing efforts in targeting prospective customers in each stage of the business buying process. Now report your findings and conclusions in a written marketing plan or type them into the Market Analysis, Situation Analysis, Target Markets, and Market Summary sections of the *Marketing Plan Pro* software.

Answer

The information that students gather about business-to-business prospects and influences will affect what they include in their written marketing plans. They may suggest targeting specific NAICS sectors, such as information (code 51), finance and insurance (code 52), and professional, scientific, and technical services (code 54). Following links on the U.S. Census Bureau site, students can find out exactly how many companies are in each industry grouping, determine how many are in specific geographic markets, and identify the number of employees. Many state sites also offer state-specific data. Business data for Connecticut can be found at www.state.ct.us/ecd, for example.

Students should try to match closely particular needs to the industry or business sectors they have identified. For instance, businesses such in the professional, scientific, and technical services sector (code 54) may share certain common needs, such as wanting employees to be able to send messages to or receive messages from headquarters or branch offices when they are on the road. Finance and insurance services businesses (code 52) may have additional needs, such as providing data updates to satisfy time-sensitive customer requirements during real estate deals and other transactions.

For business customers that have no PDAs, a Sonic PDA would represent a new-task buy. Any and all of the buying-center members may be involved in a new-task buy. A gatekeeper, for example, may allow Sonic's marketing communications to reach buyers but prevent Handspring's communications from getting through. For those seeking to replace older PDAs, a Sonic PDA would represent a modified rebuy, because the buyer is taking a new look at changing product specs, prices, delivery requirements, and other aspects of the purchase. Although any buying-center participant may be involved, those most directly involved in formulating new specifications and evaluating suppliers are likely to be influencers (especially internal information technology experts), deciders, approvers, and buyers.

Various environmental, interpersonal, and individual factors influence business buyers of PDA products. Important environmental factors include: economic outlook, which offers hints as to the likely strength of the company's own performance and profitability; rate of technological change, which would influence the timing of a PDA purchase (buyers expecting a major breakthrough might postpone their purchase in favor of better technology or negotiate for a better deal to buy PDAs that are soon to be outdate); and competitive developments in the PDA industry (to learn whether other products will be soon be released or if Sonic could be under such severe competitive pressure that it goes bankrupt in the near future).

Important interpersonal factors include: company objectives, which influence the use of PDAs as tools for improving productivity and performance; and organizational structures, especially decentralization that results in the need for devices to improve communication and coordination between units and employees. Important individual influences include: age (younger professionals are often more eager to embrace new technology such as Sonic's voice recognition PDA); education (more educated individuals may be better able to operate the technology; and job position (most critical: companies will issue PDAs only to individuals whose positions require such products). Students may be able to make a convincing case for additional factors that influence business buying behavior.

Marketing Spotlight—Branding Energy

Deregulation of the energy industry in some states during the mid-1990s enabled energy companies to compete for retail customers. The competition led many companies to step up their marketing programs in efforts to reach consumers recently empowered with the right to choose their energy provider. Spending on advertising in the energy industry rose from $80 million in 1996 to $180 million in 1997. Several companies also changed their names to make them more consumer-friendly, as when Panhandle Eastern became PanEnergy and Natural Gas Clearinghouse changed its name to NGC and later became Dynegy (for "Dynamic Energy"). Some power companies began offering loyalty programs while others appealed to consumers with cross-promotions with other utilities such as telephone and plumbing.

One of the first companies to make a significant investment in raising its public profile was Cinergy Corporation. In 1995, the company signed a $6 million, five-year deal to rename Cincinnati's Riverfront Stadium as Cinergy Field. Right before the deal was made, name recognition of the company stood at 50 percent in the greater Cincinnati area. Nine months after the renaming, name recognition in Cincinnati rose to 94 percent. Because of national television coverage for football and baseball, the Cinergy name became known all over the nation. Another energy company, Edison International, signed a $30 million, 20-year deal with the Walt Disney to rename the Anaheim Angels "Big A" stadium Edison International Field.

Energy companies also used traditional advertising methods to build brand awareness. Following its 1998 name change, Dynegy was still relatively unknown amongst financial analysts and wholesale energy buyers according to a 2000 brand awareness study conducted by the company. The company suffered from a low-profile image despite the fact that it was one of the top three transporters in each interstate gas pipeline in North America and had annual revenues of $29.4 billion in 2000. To raise awareness, Dynegy debuted its first national television advertising campaign in 2001, comprised of several 30-second spots that used humor to illustrate the company's services. In one ad, an actress playing a Dynegy employee arranges food on the dinner table so it resembles a power grid. Subsequent surveys revealed that recognition of the Dynegy brand increased significantly.

150

Power company's emphasis on marketing did not necessarily lead to a change in consumer behavior. In the two largest deregulated states, California and New York, only two percent of consumers switched utility companies. Allan Adamson, the managing director of brand expert Landor Associates, said of the energy industry, "This is a very difficult category to brand. Coming up with anything that's differentiating to customers beyond consistent power delivery is hard." This may help explain why spending on advertising in the category peaked at $180 million in 1997. In 2000, only three power companies (Enron, Southern, Pacific Gas & Electric) had ad budgets that exceeded $10 million.

Further troubles for the energy industry occurred when energy giant Enron, the leading energy marketer in the world and the seventh largest company in the United States, declared bankruptcy in December 2001. Enron had been a major advertiser, boasting the largest ad budget of all the national utility companies at $18 million in 2000. Enron also sponsored a stadium called Enron Field in Houston, where baseball's Astros play. After investors and analysts raised questions about Enron's business model, however, it was revealed that Enron had employed unorthodox accounting principles to misstate earnings. The company could not recover when credit rating companies downgraded Enron's debt to junk status in November 2001.

Enron's woes caused concern for the fate of the energy trading industry. Dynegy's stock fell 37 percent in the three weeks after it abandoned a rescue acquisition of Enron. Share prices for energy firms slumped in the wake of Enron's collapse. One energy consultant asserted, "Without a doubt, Enron's collapse has given the energy trading industry a black eye." Other energy companies tried to shake the stigma. Dynegy CEO Chuck Watson predicted that the intense focus on the energy industry would help the major players by forcing weaker competitors to exit the business, and insisted that the "Enron failure [wasn't] the failure of the energy merchant business." Other energy trading companies lined up to assure consumers that Enron's troubles were not indicative of an industry-wide problem. A spokesperson for California-based Calpine said, "Calpine is not another Enron."

Sources: Neil Weinberg and Daniel Fisher. "Power Player." *Forbes*, December 24, 2001, p. 53–58; Bethany McLean. "Why Enron Went Bust." *Fortune*, December 24, 2001, p. 58–72; Charlene Oldham. "Energy Traders Tidy Up." *Dallas Morning News*, December 18, 2001, p. 1D; Todd Wasserman. J. Dee Hill. "Feller Creates Dynegy's Premiere TV Campaign." *Adweek*, September 24, 2001, p. 4; Greg Hassell. "'Screaming People' Create Awareness." *Houston Chronicle*, September 19, 2001, p. 1; "Where's the Power Surge?" *Brandweek*, August 13, 2001, p. 31; Leonard S. Greenburger. "The Name in the Game." *Electric Perspectives*, July 1, 1999, p. 52; Peter Fritsch and Lisa Brownlee. "Energy Firms Try To Create Image for the Invisible." *Wall Street Journal*, August 28, 1996, p. B6.

Questions

1. Can branding overcome the consumer tendency not to identify with innocuous or nondifferentiated products/services? Using Enron as an example, what evidence is there of long-term value in the branding process, especially for commodity-type products?

2. Evaluate the positive side of energy branding and the inherent advantages? Do likewise with the disadvantages. Can branding recognition create negative as well as positive images? Discuss.

3. For Dynegy, Calpine, and others in the energy marketing business, what marketing strategies or tactics would you suggest that they do to reacquire the confidence that might have been lost in the Enron matter?

Suggested Responses

1. There is considerable research that indicates that for products/services that are less "visible" to the average consumer, the less likely it is that a firm or organization in that product/service category will be able to achieve a lasting brand recall impact. In the case of energy products and services the general rule should apply. However, there is some contradiction of the point with the major oil retail firms (Exxon, Shell, etc.), but because these firms have many retail locations that are often closely involved with the community, and have been there for decades, the recall can be high. It is likely that Enron attempted to achieve a similar position in the marketplace.

    However, Enron's primary target market in their branding effort was not the general public. Enron's emphasis was on creation of a positive image with key organizations and decision-makers, including:

*   Potential investors who could add to Enron's equity capital base

    *   Major wholesale distribution firms that use Enron's energy trading services

    *   Banks and investment banking houses that would provide ongoing loan facilities

    *   Various officials in government who would provide input to achieve favorable legislation

    As a number of analysts and articles have noted, Enron wanted these key individuals and organizations to know that they were dealing with a major player in the energy and energy trading business. Enron management intended, in turn, to provide the company and its officers with a basis for political and economic influence on a rather broad scale. Retail energy consumers and the general public were secondary recipients of the branding effort and heard about Enron only through various contributions, sponsorships, and secondary reminder efforts such as the former Enron Stadium (home of the Astros) in Houston.

3. For the firms engaged in energy branding, the primary value occurs in two basic areas. It can positively position the firm against others in the industry and potentially it can provide the firm with more market leverage related to pricing and negotiations. In this manner, the firm can influence markets and people in a manner that it could not do otherwise. As with vegetable and fruit branding, energy branding provides recognition for the product to move it beyond consideration as a mere commodity. This occurred to some degree in the Enron situation. The company obtained world recognition for their products, activities, and services and effectively purchased a perceived position as the leading company on their playing field.

4. As to the disadvantages, the Enron case demonstrates that the branding and other public relations image-creation activities, in retrospect, created an unhealthy attitude and feeling of superiority and power for their corporate officers. As a result, they developed a view that with their enhanced image investors and others would continue to believe that the firm would go up in market value, indefinitely. Company management also continued to believe that their position and image allowed them to buy or bully their way into positions of unfair influence with legislators and regulators. This, in turn encouraged them, and their auditors, to believe that they could conduct their business beyond the law without fear of retribution due of their perceived importance to the nation's economy. Certainly, this was not the initial purpose of the branding effort, but the Enron case demonstrates that the downside can have even more cumulative impact than the upside, leading to greater public awareness of the negative versus the positive aspects.

5. The Dynegy and Calpine comments (last paragraph) show the cumulative downside of a failed branding and image creation effort. The Enron situation created unfavorable consumer awareness for other firms attempting to carry on normal energy branding activities. Dnyegy, Calpine, and others that had nothing to do with the way Enron did business, clearly received negative responses that forced them to respond from a defensive position. Eventually, with careful control over their operations, their stakeholders and the public should recognize that they did not operate like Enron. Only then will those firms be able to go back to business as usual. To demonstrate this point, within six months of the Enron debacle, Dnyegy regained their lost stock market value.

Chapter 9—Dealing with the Competition

Overview

In the marketplace, many companies develop effective products, channels, pricing and advertising. However, many of these companies lose in the marketplace. There may be many reasons, but a critical variable may be an inability to understand the competitive environment and to gather and utilize data on that environment.

To prepare an effective marketing strategy, a company must consider its competitors as well as its actual and potential customers. This is especially necessary in slow growth markets because firms generally gain sales by winning them away from competitors.

A company's closest competitors seek to satisfy the same customers and needs and make similar product and service offers. A company should also pay attention to its latent competitors that may offer new or different ways to satisfy the same needs. The company should identify its competitors by using both an industry and market-based analysis.

A company should gather information on competitor strategies, objectives, strengths, weaknesses, and reaction patterns. The company should study and understand competitor strategies in order to identify its closest competitors and take appropriate action. The company should know the competitor's objectives in order to anticipate further moves and reactions. Knowledge of the competitor's strengths and weaknesses permits the company to refine its own strategy to take advantage of competitor weaknesses while avoiding engagements where the competitor is strong. Understanding typical competitor reaction patterns helps the company choose and time its moves.

The firm should collect, interpret and disseminate competitive intelligence continuously. Company marketing executives should be able to obtain full and reliable information about any competitor that could have bearing on a decision. As important as a competitive orientation is in today's markets, companies should not overdo their focus on competitors. Changing consumer needs and latent competitors are more likely to hurt a firm than the existing competitors. Companies that maintain a good balance of consumer and competitor considerations are practicing effective market orientation.

Teaching Objectives

After reading this chapter students should:

- Know the difference between the industry and market concepts of competition

- Understand how to identify competitor strategies

- Understand how to determine competitor objectives

- Understand how to estimate competitor reaction patterns

- Know how to design competitive intelligence systems

- Know how to select competitors to attack or avoid

- Understand what it means to balance a customer and competitor orientation

Chapter Outline

I. Introduction

II. Porter's five forces

    A. Three (first three) Porter forces focus on competitors

    B. Internet is rapidly altering many of the existing patterns of competition, especially for the existing middleman and distribution channels

III. Identifying competitors—four levels: brand, industry, form, and generic

    A. Industry concept of competition

        1. Number of sellers and degree of differentiation (monopoly, oligopoly, monopolistic competition and pure competition)

        2. Entry and mobility barriers—ease of entry into market and various segments

        3. Exit and shrinkage barriers—ease of exit and reduction in size

        4. Cost structure

        5. Degree of vertical integration

        6. Degree of globalization

    B. Market concept of competition—in addition to companies making the same product, look at companies that satisfy the same customer need

IV. Analyzing competitors

    A. Identifying competitor strategies

    B. Determining competitor objectives

    C. Assessing competitor strengths and weaknesses

        1. Share of market

        2. Share of mind

        3. Share of heart

    D. Rule for evaluating companies

        1. Those that make steady gains in mind share and heart share

        2. Inevitably, they make gains in market share and profitability

    E. Estimating competitor reaction patterns

        1. Laid-back (does not react)

        2. Selective (reacts only to certain types of attacks)

        3. Tiger (reacts to any assault)

        4. Stochastic (no predictable reaction)

V. Designing the competitive intelligence system (focus today on Internet and competitor Web sites)

    A. Four main steps

        1. Setting up the system

        2. Collecting the data

        3. Evaluating and analyzing the data

        4. Disseminating information and responding

    B. Selecting competitors to attack and void—major steps in customer value analysis are:

1.   Evaluating major attributes that customers value

    a)   Assess quantitative importance of the different attributes

    b)   Assess company and competitor performance on the different customer values against their rated importance

    c)   Examine how customers in a specific segment rate the company's performance against a specific major competitor on an attribute-by-attribute basis

    d)   Monitor customer values over time

2.   Classes of competitors—following customer value analysis:

    a)   Strong versus weak

    b)   Close versus distant

    c)   Good versus bad

3.   Customer value analysis helps a marketer perceive company/product value to a customer relative to competitor product value(s)

VI.   Designing competitive strategies

    A.   Market-leader strategies

        1.   Expanding the total market, with new users, new uses and more usage

        2.   Defending market share, with position, flank, preemptive, counteroffensive, mobile, and contraction defensive strategies

        3.   Expanding market share (note Procter & Gamble and Caterpillar case studies)—line-extension, brand-extension, multibrand, etc., strategies

    B.   Market-challenger strategies

        1.   Defining the strategic objective and the opponents

        2.   Choosing a general attack strategy

        3.   Choosing a specific attack strategy

    C.   Market-follower strategies

    D.   Market-nicher strategies

VII.   Balancing customer and competitor orientations—marketers should not become so competitor-centered that they focus on customers already lost

VIII.   Summary

Lecture 1—Competitive Intelligence

This lecture is intended for use with Chapter 9, "Dealing with the Competition." It focuses on the uses of various sources of information for marketing. It is useful to update the examples so that students will be able to identify readily with this concept based on their general knowledge of the techniques, companies and products involved in the lecture/discussion.

The discussion begins by considering examples of particular approaches in developing competitor research. This leads into a discussion of the implications for all marketers.

Teaching Objectives

- To stimulate students to think about the need for and value of competitive analysis

- To present points to consider in proceeding with development of a competitive analysis program

- Recognize some of the better sources of information for various marketing questions

Discussion

Introduction

In the marketplace, many companies do a first class job of developing a great product, great channels, great pricing and great advertising. You might say—wow! That is great. However, many of these companies not only lose in the marketplace, but they lose big. The reasons may be management, financial, etc., but when we get right down to it the answer may be much more interesting. The critical variable may be the competitive intelligence that the firm failed to get at the right time, with the right detail. In this discussion, we will look at some of the issues and questions behind choosing the right sources as well as approaches that might be useful in preparing the competitive intelligence program that will do the job.

First, the Kotler text gives some excellent examples of how to scan the competitive environment. As part of this framework, it also is useful to determine where to get the information, that the analyst is able to determine where and how to use the questions asked, and that the data developed is based on the marketing and strategic plans, not just collected in a random manner. This requires knowledge of a number of variables and then bringing it all together to be utilized in the firm's marketing positioning effort. Remember, to achieve an effective competitive analysis it is essential to place the process in perspective.

Competitive Analysis

The logical starting point for the strategy analysis is to understand effectively the competitive structure and attractiveness of the industry. It is important to recognize that some industries are and will be more profitable than others. It is important also to know the real strengths of the industry, and the firms within the industry, not only in overall terms but also in specific detail. Many times appearances can be deceiving. Consider, for example, companies that project a great public relations image but in reality are quite the opposite. (Enron could serve well as an example.)

A logical overview of this process comes from Porter's five basic forces of competition:

- Threat of new entrants

- Rivalry among existing competitors

- Bargaining power of suppliers

- Bargaining power of buyer—price sensitive

- Threat of substitutes

What determines the strength of each of these five forces in the industry? The process is shaped by a number of underlying structural determinants. It is important to remember that any of the forces that undermine the structure of an industry likely will cause profitability to decline. A good example is the dot-coms that raced to steal markets from the existing well-organized physical retailers but had little to offer except investor hype. Their inability to show quality and superior results immediately led to investor disenchantment and the loss of confidence that they could produce a profit against the existing competition. This, in turn, led to massive dot-com failures, consolidation in the industry, and finally the successful entrance of many major retailers with name, cash and ability to stay the course.

To begin this process, the firm should develop a complete evaluation of the competitive framework and the specific competition. This would include a detailed compilation of the competitors, both real and potential, along with their products, marketing capability, service, production strength, financial strength and management. Next, you must detail where each firm, including your own, fits into the industry in terms of products, marketing capability, service, production strength, financial strength and management. At this point, you should be able to develop a thorough analysis of the following, for the past, present and future:

- Degree of industry concentration
- Changes in type and mix of products
- Market "segments" in the firm and industry (and changes)
- Companies that have left or entered the industry (and why)
- Industry market share changes (and why—technology, substitution, etc.)
- Company market shares and share changes
- New technology substitution
- Each firm's vulnerability to new technology

In addition to these specific competitive characteristics, the firm should focus on the various financial, economic, technological, and socio-political factors in the industry environment. This information is available through a variety of sources, including:

1. Company Web sites and literature

2. Industry trade show observation and contacts

3. On-line databases including Lexis-Nexis, EBSCO, First Source, PROMPT, Trade & Industry and Investext, along with various other on-line sources such as the TV networks, Hoover, investment houses (Schwab, Merrill Lynch, etc.), The Wall Street Journal (WSJ), Business Week (BW), and so forth

It is important to understand each firm's position within the industry. Companies in large or small industries have varying levels of profitability, and it is important to understand what it takes to be a superior performer in industry. Information that may assist in this process might include some or all of the following:

- How the industry might change, in the short to long term

- How the competing firms within an industry differ in the way in which the competitive forces influence each of the competitors

- Identify the companies that have the power to shape the industry. These companies could either make the industry or cause the demise

- New product development potential within the industry and which firms have the ability to make it happen

This analysis should first provide a detailed and technical description of the products and services offered, including product mix, depth and breadth of product line. This should lead to a clear understanding and listing of market position, by product, citing product strengths and weaknesses, individually and in the overall product line. Among the sources for this information are company Web sites, company product literature, WSJ, BW, and on-line databases including DIALOG, Lexis-Nexis and Hoover.

Another important area is R&D expenditures (industry and by company), analysis of each company's research and development expenditures and capabilities, along with a run down on technical personnel and expertise. Sources for this information include EBSCO, Lexis-Nexis, DIALOG, Hoover, PROMPT, Trade & Industry, and Investext.

Next, it is important to understand clearly who holds which patents (current and pending), the product standards and specifications, including a quality and technical analysis. Some of the better sources for this could include: Claims, World Patent Index, Derwent, IFI/Plenum Claims. Company Web sites and trade show industry contacts also can provide valuable clues in this part of the effort.

The last piece of information needed in this section of the competitive intelligence analysis includes a new product introductions analysis (past, present and expected). Some good sources for this information include press releases (company/industry Web sites), Predicast New Product Announcements and sales force contacts. In addition, EBSCO, Lexis-Nexis, DIALOG and various investor sources can provide valuable insight.

Markets

Often, firms have a good overall understanding of the markets they are in or wish to compete in, but they tend to operate with the same attitude and perspectives that have existed in the company and industry for many years. To truly understand the market, the potential new competitor should have a solid grasp of the factors that make and drive the market for the product or service. For example, the firm should have a detailed compendium of the following, by firm within the industry:

- Market segmentation

- Customer base (markets targeted, regional sales analysis, penetration, importance to each firm)

- Profiles of markets and customers (including product mix and sales data by product line)

- Market growth and potential for future growth

- Market share by product line

- Market and geographic areas targeted for expansion

- Marketing tactics and strategies (4 Ps, especially price and promotion)

- Distribution network/channels of distribution

- Advertising/marketing/sales efforts including budgets and advertising/marketing firms used

Among the sources that could be used on this activity are: PTS MARS, magazine ads, PROMPT, Investext, Trade & Industry, SEC reports, Newspapers, Newswires, BW, Fortune, WSJ, company Web sites, and so on.

International/Global

Depending on the expected competition and market activity, it is essential that the competitive intelligence effort include a foreign trade analysis. Without access to some expensive databases that provide specific product sales and market share information, it would be best to look at and evaluate recent order information, government contracts and individual sales forces overseas (performance, experience, compensation, etc.). For U.S. firms, StatUSA provides an excellent data source, along with PIERS Exports & Imports, Commerce Business Daily, Newspapers (especially WSJ, NYT, BW), Lexis-Nexi,s and DIALOG.

Strategy/Decision Making

Identification of marketing and corporate strategies probably is one of the more important requirements of any competitive analysis. For this, most firms need experienced professional input, along with extensive use of the Internet, DIALOG and other similar tools noted above. Below, we have established for each firm in the industry several important the intelligence needs, followed by selected sourcing:

1. Apparent strategic (long-range) plans, including details of acquisition and divestiture strategy, etc. (SEC filings)

2. New products on the horizon—with indications of a new direction for the company (PROMPT, press releases, newspapers)

3. Apparent strategic objectives: corporate/divisional/subsidiary company priorities; business unit/segment goals; basic business philosophy/targets (suppliers, employees, wholesalers)

4. Analysis of company's decision-making process. Overall company image and reputation. Company's ability to change. How will the company look/perform in the future? Anti-takeover measures instituted; the firm's key success factors? The key objective: Why has the firm been successful, overall? (shareholder lawsuits pending, Lexis-Nexis)

5. Corporate attitudes toward risk (legal databases, employees, suppliers)

6. Statements of plans to enter new markets, improve market position and/or increase market share (trade journals, top executive speeches, PROMPT, marketing analysts)

Following this exercise, the analysis should provide a clear understanding of the operation of the industry, and the competing firm should be able to utilize this information to provide an overall planning framework, strategy plan and marketing plan to take advantage of current and future market opportunities.

Lecture 2—Does Preemptive Marketing Work?

This lecture is intended for use with Chapter 9, "Dealing with the Competition." It focuses on Porter's framework for preemptive strategy in a marketing setting, and the role and value of this concept in the overall marketing process and strategy for the company. Many students will be able to identify readily with this concept based on their general knowledge of the companies and products involved in the lecture/discussion.

The discussion begins by considering why a leader firm would consider preemptive strategy as a means of maintaining or increasing the firm's market position. This leads into a discussion of the implications for the introduction of a preemptive strategy for other firms in the industry in the medium and long-term.

Teaching Objectives

•   Stimulate students to think about the critical issues, pro and con, for a firm when it moves toward adoption of a preemptive strategy approach

•   To consider how to proceed with a preemptive strategy

•   To discuss the role of preemptive strategies in helping the firm achieve a position in the industry

Discussion

Introduction

Preemptive marketing involves many different possibilities for the leader to assume a defensive or offensive position in the market and with competitors. The primary elements for a firm to consider in a preemptive action are that delay and/or position are critical and that nothing is forever. The firm must recognize that eventually it will be essential to conduct some type of preemptive action if it is to maintain control or partial control of the niche or share position.

There are many reasons for a leader to adopt a preemptive strategy approach, but often it is a consequence of product maturity. The leader firm recognizes that another firm(s) has developed a superior capability in product or service. While it is possible for a challenger or other strategic planning firm to develop a preemptive position, the reasons tend to be more to disrupt the course of the industry in order to gain advantage against an entrenched leader.

While this can be a very beneficial move, it has a tendency to convey a message to other firms in the industry that the firm could be posing a serious threat to all others in the industry. Firms that have done this, such as People Express, often find they are able to ride the crest of the wave of success only so far and so long, unable to sustain against the retaliatory moves of the industry in general. The primary preemptive objective of the leader or challenger is to maintain or occupy more of the critical or prime positions in the industry. This could include positioning their company or product in the mind of the consumers or distributors, preemptive control of the physical locations for retail facilities, preemptive control of critical raw materials and/or preemptive control of other resources critical to success in the industry.

Identifying Preemptive Opportunities

There are many ways to succeed to achieve a preemptive advantage, but identification of a weak link in the commitment from one or more firms in the industry is a good starting point. Among the various positions that Porter demonstrates is the attempt to secure access to raw materials or components. This ploy has worked primarily in those industries where raw or primary industries are critical to operations or success.

In a like manner, programs to preempt production equipment have worked effectively. This situation works best where the production equipment involves proprietary processes or patents. Efforts to dominate supply logistics, such as brokers, transportation or similar settings, have made an impact. *Note: There are many current examples of these and other preemptive approaches. Current examples, or examples the students may know, will enhance the discussion.*

Moving to the various functional area activities, in products and/or services, a number of other preemptive methods are utilized. For example, introducing new product lines and expanding production aggressively, such as IBM and many other firms have done, a competitor attempting to follow the lead of the leader can find it a very expensive and likely a losing proposition.

In the area of production systems, there have been in recent years some very good examples of firms able to develop proprietary production methods, expand capacity aggressively and secure scarce and critical production skills. In addition, in the production systems area, firms that achieve some level of vertical integration with key suppliers can create a considerable barrier for competitors without the same economies of scale.

In the 1980s, IBM, among others, applied the principle that if a firm provides the dominant product design in the industry it will be able constantly to keep the competitors as followers. Constantly expanding the scope of the product is another variation on this theme. A classic example of this approach is Merrill Lynch with the Cash Management Account of the late 1970s, and many others more recently.

"Positioning" the product more effectively also can be an effective preemptive strategy. This can be an effective and relatively inexpensive strategy, given that there are many different types of positioning in the marketplace, including positioning in the mind of the consumer, distributors, suppliers and others. *Note: There are and will be many current examples where firms have successfully achieved both challenger and leader positions with various positioning and re-positioning efforts.*

Other examples of preemption relate to situations where a firm is able to secure accelerated government agency approval because of strong technical capabilities and/or market recognition. This situation obviously occurs most often in medical and pharmaceutical products or other related areas where there are health and safety concerns.

Keeping the competitors off balance by constantly adding to the market segments in the marketplace is another useful preemptive action. Coke achieved this effectively with New Coke. Even though the company had to return to the earlier formula and publicly back down from the decision, they were able to further fragment the market and take more share from the smaller competitors with fewer resources.

Lastly, it is useful to consider the role of the preemptive in working with distributors. It is appropriate for the leader firm engaging in preemptive marketing to capture key accounts, occupy prime locations, develop preferential access/key distributors, control supply systems and distribution logistics, and insure access to superior service systems. In addition, one of the most important areas for great potential is to engage in educational and promotional activities that are designed to develop the skills of the distributors. This could include a number of activities designed to enhance the capabilities for the distributors to better serve their customers.

Note: In all of these examples there are many firms both winning and losing with this strategy. Clearly among the best examples are firms winning, but there are many situations where those losing provide an interesting story.

Marketing and Advertising

1.   Ad number one: Few product categories have as many competing products and brands as the detergent category, each vying for share of market, mind, and heart. The ad in Figure 1 shows how Surf is responding to competitive pressure from other brands—by suggesting that customers try one of the other Surf products.

      a.   What kind of competitive strategy does this ad represent? Explain.

      b.   What are the arguments for and against Surf using a price-discount strategy instead?

      c.   Does Surf appear to have a customer or a competitor orientation?

Answer

      a.   This ad represents a market-challenger strategy, with Surf attacking the market-leader in detergents. This particular attack is a flanking attack, targeting the segmental dimension of consumers who choose detergents based on fragrance. Surf launched a product proliferation attack by adding product variety based on different fragrances.

b.   If Surf used a price-discount strategy, it would lower its profit margins, which could threaten its overall profit performance if the company did not cut costs to compensate. On the other hand, price discounting could help Surf gain market share at the expense of the market leader. Students may provide additional explanations.

a.   This is a good opportunity to compare and contrast competitor-centered and customer-centered companies. Surf seems to be balancing competitor concerns with customer concerns. It is obviously keeping a close watch on competitive moves yet its ads incorporate consumers' need for variety in fragrances. Some students may argue that Surf is being reactive in advertising the product feature of new fragrances in response to competitive pressure rather than being proactive in directly addressing the underlying consumer needs. Other students may say that product proliferation is a good way to take shelf space away from competitors and, through advertising, build consumer demand that will take market share away from competitors.

2.   Ad number two: This ad for Listerine Essential Care Toothpaste is promoting a mouth-care product closely related to Listerine's well-known mouthwash products. The highlighted feature (germ-killing ability) is the same as the main feature of Listerine mouthwash. In this case, however, the highlighted benefit is preventing (or reversing) gingivitis.

a.   Does Listerine appear to be a market leader, market challenger, market follower, or market nicher in the toothpaste category?

b.   How does this ad incorporate competitive strengths and weaknesses?

c.   Colgate is one of the leading toothpaste brands. From its perspective, how can Listerine be classified as a competitor?

Answer

a.   Listerine appears to be a market nicher because it is targeting the narrower sub segment of consumers who are most interested in gum care. Cavity-fighting capabilities are assumed of all toothpaste products, so brands are seeking specific segments to target with particular features and benefits. Listerine's reputation as a germ-killer may be transferred to the gum-care niche, which also depends on germ-fighting capabilities.

b.   This ad leverages Listerine's favorable brand image and strong market share among mouthwashes as a carryover to a different product category. Listerine may be counting on high brand recognition and positive associations to induce consumers to try its toothpaste and continue using it. However, Listerine lacks market share and brand image in the toothpaste category, which may prove to be a significant weakness if Colgate and other major rivals decide to counterattack.

c.   From Colgate's perspective, Listerine is a relatively distant competitor but a potentially strong one. Over time, Colgate will be able to monitor Listerine's continued marketing activities in the toothpaste category to determine whether it is actually strong or weak, which will affect Colgate's competitive response. Listerine does not appear to be a "bad" competitor, because it is targeting a specific niche and differentiating its product based on valuable features and benefits. This is a good opportunity to discuss classes of competitors in more detail and have students justify their responses.

Online Marketing Today—NetFlix

NetFlix is a fast-growing DVD rental site that has carved out a popular niche between retail giants like Blockbuster and online retailers like Amazon.com. The company invites movie fans to pay $19.95 per month for all the DVD movies they can see in a month. Although customers can only rent three movies at one time, they can rent up to three more as soon as they return the first three. DVDs arrive in the mail and include a postage-paid envelope for customers to use in returning their rentals. NetFlix doesn't levy late fees or set deadlines for returning DVDs, so customers can watch at their leisure without incurring penalties. This combination of convenience and value propelled NetFlix into the top five e-commerce sites and helped it attract more than 300,000 regular monthly customers in less than two years of operation.

Go to the NetFlix site (www.netflix.com) and read about what the company offers. Next, move to the Customer Service page and browse the top customer questions. As a nicher, which of the specialist roles does NetFlix appear to be adopting? What are the risks of this niche competitive strategy? What entry, mobility, and exit barriers can you identify for the industry where NetFlix is currently operating?

Answer

NetFlix appears to have adopted the product specialist role, because it offers only one product: DVDs. Some students may say that NetFlix is a channel specialist, because it uses only direct channels (the Internet supplemented by telephone access) as its distribution channel. One risk is that another company may adopt the same specialist role with a competitive advantage such as a larger product selection or lower prices based on lower costs. Another risk is that DVDs may become less popular if video-on-demand services gain significant penetration. Students may identify additional risks, as well. A major entry barrier is the need for significant capital to buy DVD stock and set up an ordering and fulfillment system. A major mobility barrier to entering the mainstream retail rental market is the entrenched leadership of Blockbuster, which is working on an Internet rental system and testing flat monthly fees for rentals. A major exit fee is the low salvage value of used DVDs and the possibility that the DVD format may become obsolete in a relatively short period. Students may also suggest additional barriers.

Marketing Spotlight—Microsoft

Microsoft was founded in 1975, when Bill Gates left Harvard at age 19 to work with high school friend Paul Allen on a version of the BASIC programming language. After moving the company from Albuquerque, New Mexico, to Seattle in 1979, Gates and Allen began writing operating system software. What happened to the company since it's founding is a well-known and oft-told story. Here we highlight a few of the key strategies that enabled Microsoft to achieve such remarkable growth in the competition-laden computer industry:

Product innovation: Microsoft achieved early success because of a single product innovation. In 1980, IBM contracted Microsoft to write the operating systems for its new PCs, which led to the creation of Microsoft Disk Operating System (MS-DOS). Since other PC manufacturers desired compatibility with IBM machines, Microsoft was soon adopted as the standard PC operating system. Another, even bigger innovation followed. In 1983, the company introduced the now-ubiquitous Windows, based on a graphical interface common to Apple's Macintosh system. Since it was the first "windowing" software to work on PCs from any brand, Windows—like DOS before it—became the standard for personal computers.

While Windows enabled the company to vault to unforeseen heights, it continued to develop innovative software and other products. Microsoft's current big project is a next-generation operating system called Microsoft .Net (pronounced "dot-net"), designed to merge Windows with the Internet directly. Microsoft .Net will allow multiple devices—PCs, wireless phones, pagers, digital cameras, PDAs, and other "smart devices"—to work together over Web connections with unprecedented ease.

Brand-extension strategy: Microsoft uses its strong brand name to launch new software products. Some examples include Microsoft Word, Microsoft Office, and Microsoft Internet Explorer. In 1989, Microsoft passed Lotus to become the world's largest seller of software worldwide. At that time, the company boasted the broadest array of software products and applications as well as the highest profit margin in the industry, at close to 25 percent.

Launching a new product under a strong existing brand name gives the new brand instant recognition and credibility with much less advertising outlay.

Heavy advertising: In the early years, Microsoft used advertising sparingly. In the mid-1990s, however, it began to advertise aggressively. In 1994, the company made two major moves: it hired the head of marketing and advertising from Procter & Gamble and developed its first global advertising campaign. The campaign doubled the company's ad budget to $100 million, and the following year that figure ballooned to $200 million for the Windows 95 launch. Today, it is common for the company to spend $50 million marketing a single product. Its global marketing budget for 2001 exceeded $500 million.

Competitive toughness: Microsoft's aggressive competitive practices enabled the company to establish a leadership role in many product categories, but also led to legal battles. In one of the most publicized antitrust suits ever, the U.S. Justice Department filed antitrust charges against Microsoft, claiming that it had limited consumer choice and stifled competition in part by bundling software, such as Internet Explorer, with its operating system. The presiding judge ruled to split Microsoft into two separate companies—an operating system company and an applications company, but the company continues to operate as a whole while its appeal is pending.

Product expansion: Microsoft was quick to expand its business beyond operating systems into software applications for home and business PC users, educational software, and computer games. The company also expanded its operating system business. In 1993, the company introduced its Windows NT operating system, which was designed to compete with UNIX as the operating system of choice for large networks. After overcoming initial reluctance to embrace the Internet, Microsoft developed the Internet Explorer Web browser as an answer to Netscape, and developed the Web portal Microsoft Network (MSN) to compete with the likes of Yahoo! and AOL. MSN was not successful and endured major alterations before being reborn as MSN.com. The company also expanded into media development in the 1990s. It formed a joint venture with NBC to create the cable station MSNBC, which featured news, financial, and talk show programming. The company added another television venture in 1997 when it bought the set-top box system WebTV (later to become UltimateTV). The company rolled out a video game console called Xbox intended to compete with advanced game systems from Sony and Nintendo.

(Sources: Rebecca Buckman, "About Advertising: Microsoft Ad Campaign Touts Its Software for Big Business." Wall Street Journal Europe, January 23, 2001; "Windows of Opportunity." Marketing Week, December 9, 1994; "Microsoft Hires P&G Marketer." Marketing Week, November 18, 1994; www.microsoft.com;)

Questions

1. Could Microsoft be considered one of the best and worst examples of marketing success in America during the 1980s and 1990s? Discuss.

2.   The Marketing Spotlight notes some of the effective competitive marketing strategies that Microsoft has exhibited in a short but very successful history. Could a similar firm entering the market today operate in the same manner?

3.   Do any of the Microsoft strategies belie future issues that Microsoft and other technology-oriented firms should prepare to deal with in coming years?

Suggested Responses

1.   Microsoft clearly has applied successfully most of the critical marketing strategy concepts related to the 4 Ps. They successfully exploited virtually every window of opportunity and applied product development, consumer behavior and competitive analysis, etc., concepts that have created the basis for many new concepts in consumer and B-to-B marketing.

However, despite the fact that they were great innovators, they were not always the inventors. Instead, they did a superb job of scanning the environment and determining what they could get away with in certain situations and products rather than merely survive. Clearly, they learned effectively from their mistakes and those of others.

2.   Probably not. Microsoft basically was allowed to do what it wanted in the beginning, and the market was highly appreciative of their efforts. Further, Microsoft had almost no competition and set the pace for the future, pushing their marketing strategies to the limit in order to achieve a preemptive and sustaining competitive advantage. It was able to make huge strides, in terms of marketing and technology, in a rather short timeframe. In a world hungry for technology, early Microsoft technology and marketing approaches brought success after success. Today, however, that marketplace has been replaced with one that is much more knowledgeable and skeptical about everything and assumes much more with regard to technology and actions toward competitors. Many of Microsoft's competitive actions and strategies today are considered more preemptive than innovative and receive a much different public response than in the past.

3.   Technology firms typically do not follow consumer wants and needs but create them because there is no conceptual understanding in the marketplace when they develop and introduce new products. In addition to some very clever and hard-nosed approaches to marketing, Microsoft also utilized some forward and very unusual thought processes to arrive at new approaches that often effectively changed many traditions and expectations. Students could argue that Microsoft has been successful because it remained focused on what would be best for themselves and the consumer rather than merely responding. Gates and Microsoft took some existing concepts and looked way out on the horizon to identify some possibilities that were literally beyond the horizon. However, in the future, given the public knowledge of their actions, and constant media scrutiny, Microsoft and other similar technology-based firms are unlikely to achieve as many competitive marketing advantages as in the past.

Analytical Tools for Marketing Management—Specialized Buying Power Indexes

Students may question whether it is possible to add numbers representing households, dollars, and various other elements to create an index. We often do it when we want to obtain the effect of important variables that interact in the market place. The technique is called an "Arbitrary Factors Index." It is assumed that anyone using this technique can justify each factor that is chosen.

Problems

See Student Guide for question details. The task is to evaluate four top metro areas in Connecticut, and allocate a $750,000 annual promotional budget to them. To do this the analyst will have to construct index numbers for each market based on the following criteria:

1. Consumers are adults, aged 18–34, living in metro areas surrounding a large city. For example, Hartford also includes the communities of New Britain and Bristol.

    a. Consumers are in the $10,000 to $24,999 income class.

    b. The product category is Health & Beauty Aids sold in drug stores.

2. If you were selling air conditioners, which factors would you use to create a custom-made Buying Power Index? Explain.

Answers

2. Data should come from an analysis of four Connecticut markets as follows:

    a. Bridgeport, Stamford, Norwalk and Danbury

    b. Hartford, New Britain, Bristol

    c. New Haven, West Haven, Waterbury, Meriden

    d. New London, Norwich

    e. For the sake of simplicity, identify each market by the first name in the market group.

    Here are preliminary data for population of 18–24, 25–34, and income classes $10,000 to $14,999 and $15,000 to $24,999:

Metropolitan area covered	% 18-24	% 25-34	Total*	$10K-14.9K	$15K-24.9K	Total**
Bridgeport	10.7	15.2	25.9	6.5	17.9	24.4
Hartford	12.9	16.8	29.7	8.4	24.4	32.8
New Haven	12.5	16.7	29.2	10.0	27.1	37.1
New London	14.7	17.2	31.9	9.8	28.1	37.9

* Each percentage is multiplied by the population in each area. (See tables in S&MM data.)

**Each percentage is multiplied by the number of households in the area. (See S&MM.)

- Now the following table can be prepared from the data above:

Specially Created Buying Power Index					
1	2	3	4	5	6
Pop. Aged 18–34	No. Households with incomes $10K–14,900	Retail sales, health / beauty aids	Sum of factors	Index	Allocation of budget
Bridgeport 209,505	$69,955	$18,968	298,428	24.47%	$183,525
Hartford 312,296	124,870	29,573	466,739	38.27%	$287,032
New Haven 222,679	103,286	16,501	342,466	28.08%	$210,607
New London 75,714	31,836	4,384	111,934	9.18%	$68,836
TOTALS 820,194	329,947	69,426	1,219,567	100.00%	$750,000

Notes/Procedure

- Data from columns 1, 2 and 3 added across and the sum placed in Column 4

- Column 4 figures added down to obtain total

- To obtain an index, each figure in column 4 divided by the total (1,219,567)

- Total allocated budget ($750,000) multiplied by each index to obtain allocation for each metro area

2.   If you were selling air conditioners you might want to assemble data on:

   a.   Number of dwelling units in each area

   b.   Number of households in the area

   c.   Income above a certain level, such as above $20,000 a year. This would depend on how expensive (price, relatively, the air conditioning unit you are selling)

   d.   Mean yearly temperature in the area

   e.   Mean yearly humidity in the area

   f.   Number of yearly days over 95 degrees

There could be other factors depending on the planning needs.

Chapter 10—Identifying Market Segments and Selecting Target Markets

Overview

Sellers can take three approaches to a market. Mass marketing is the decision to mass-produce and mass distribute one product and attempt to attract all kinds of buyers. Product-variety marketing attempts to offer a variety of products to broaden the customer base. Target marketing is the decision to distinguish the different groups that make up a market a to develop corresponding products and marketing mixes for each target market. Sellers today moving away from mass marketing and product differentiation toward target marketing because the latter is more helpful in spotting market opportunities and developing winning products marketing mixes.

The key steps in target marketing are market segmentation, market targeting, and product positioning. Market segmentation is the act of dividing a market into distinct groups of buyers with different needs or responses. The marketer tries different variables to see which reveal the best segmentation opportunities. For each segment, a customer segment profile is developed. Segmentation effectiveness depends upon arriving at segments that are measurable, substantial, accessible and actionable.

Next, the seller has to target the best market segment(s). The seller must evaluate the potential of each segment, which is a function of segment size and growth, segment attractiveness, and company objectives and resources. Then the seller must decide how segments to serve the seller can ignore segment differences (undifferentiated marketing), develop different market offers for several segments (differentiated marketing), or go after one or a more market segments (concentrated marketing). In choosing target segments, marketers need to consider the ethical choice of market targets, segment interrelationships and super segments, and potential segment invasion plans.

Learning Objectives

After reading this chapter students should:

- Understand what it means to "segment" a market

- Know the basic steps in segmenting a market

- Understand the bases used to segment consumer and business markets

- Know how to evaluate and select segments for targeting of marketing programs

Chapter Outline

I.   Introduction—Target marketing requires the following: identify and profile distinct groups of buyers with distinct needs/preferences, select one or more market segments, establish and communicate distinctive benefits of the market offering to each target segment.

II.   Levels and patterns of market segmentation—buyers differ in many ways

    A.   Levels and patterns of market segmentation

        1.   Levels of market segmentation

            a)   Mass—one product/marketing mix available for all buyers

            b)   Micro marketing—the response to the decline in favor for mass marketing

2. Segment marketing—a large identifiable group within a market.Midpoint between mass and individual marketing

3. Niche Marketing—a narrowly defined smaller group whose needs not currently met effectively

4. Local Marketing—programs targeted to the needs and wants of local customer groups

5. Individual Customer Marketing—"one to one" marketing

   a) Mass-customization and choiceboard.

   b) Customerization—empowering customers with the means to design their own products.

6. Self—a form of individual marketing in which the consumer takes more responsibility for determining which brands and products to buy. (i.e., shopping over the Internet)

B. Patterns of market segmentation—homogenous, diffused, clustered preferences

C. Market segmentation procedure—survey, analysis, profile

   1. Focus on needs-based market segmentation and market portioning

D. Effective segmentation—segments must be: measurable, substantial, accessible, differentiable, actionable

III. Segmenting consumer and business markets

A. Bases for segmenting consumer markets

   1. Geographic—nations, states, regions, counties, cities, neighborhoods

   2. Demographic—age and life cycle, gender, income, generation, social class

   3. Psychographic—lifestyle, personality, values

   4. Behavioral—based on purchase occasions, benefits, user status, usage rate, loyalty status, buyer-readiness stage, and attitude

B. Multi-attribute segmentation (geoclustering): assumes people who live near each other and exhibit similar traits from all of the above segmentation bases

   1. Geoclustering via PRIZM clusters (American dreams, rural industria, gray power, country squires)—focus on increasing diversity.

   2. Targeting multiple segments—because consumers no longer can be neatly pigeonholed into one segment.

C. Bases for segmenting business markets

   1. Based on their stage in the purchase decision process, channel preferences

   2. Types of buyers: programmed, relationship, transaction, bargain hunters.

   3. Customer groups: price-oriented (transactional selling), solution oriented (consultative selling), strategic value (enterprise selling)

IV. Market targeting

A. Evaluating and selecting the market Segments (factors: Segment size and growth, segment structural attractiveness, company objectives and resources)

   1. Single-segment concentration—firm concentrates on one market only for its one product

170

2. Selective specialization—firm selects a number of attractive and appropriate segments and develops products that appeal to each segment

3. Product specialization—firm focus is on a product it can sell to several segments

4. Market specialization—firm satisfies multi-faceted needs of one particular group

5. Full market coverage—firm serves all customer groups with products they might need

a) Undifferentiated marketing—entire market receives the same program

b) Differentiated marketing—different programs for different segments

B. Additional considerations

1. Ethical choice of market targets—targeting sometimes generates controversy

2. Segment-by-segment invasion plans—enter one at a time to avoid revealing total expansion plans

3. Intersegment cooperation—all segment managers work together to improve overall company performance

V. Summary

Lecture—Understanding Market Segments

This lecture is intended for use with Chapter 10, "Identifying Market Segments and Selecting Target Markets." Students should now begin to understand that marketing and marketers cannot be all things to all people, and there is a need for increasing focus and segmentation.

Teaching Objectives

- To appreciate the value of segmenting and targeting markets
- To comprehend the process through which marketers engage in segmentation
- To learn about companies/industries making use of segmentation

Discussion

Instructor note: consider one or more of the computer applications exercises as a basis for some of the discussion related to this subject

Introduction—Understanding the Issue

Market segmentation is a process based on factual information rather than marketer intuition. The value of market segmentation is obvious. Customers are different and are likely to be attracted to different products throughout various stages in their lifetimes. For an illustration of this concept, consider the automobile industry.

Note: To develop this issue, ask students to offer the names of various brands and models (placed on the board). Then, ask them to identify which brands and models are likely to appeal to specific characteristics—age, income, gender, etc. From this illustration, it will become obvious that not all products appeal to everyone on a mass level.

The segmentation process involves dividing a market into distinct groups of buyers who might require separate products or marketing mixes, recognizing that all buyers have unique needs and wants. Still, it is usually possible in consumer markets to identify relatively homogeneous portions or segments of the total market according to shared preferences, attitudes, or behaviors that distinguish them from the rest of the market. These segments may require different products and/or separate mixes, and in the contemporary one-to-one marketing approach segmentation is a critical step.

Targeting and Positioning

Market targeting is the follow-up to the segmentation process and is the process of evaluating each market segment's attractiveness and selecting one or more segments to enter. Given effective market segmentation, the firm must choose which markets to serve and how to serve them. In targeting markets to serve, the firm must consider its resources and objectives in setting strategy.

Market positioning is the process of formulating competitive positioning for a product and a detailed marketing mix. The firm must have a plan for how to present the product to the consumer, and the product's position is defined by how consumers view it on important attributes. The Text discusses this concept in detail.

The consumer market is often segmented according to variables such as: demographics, psychographics, geographic location, behavior, etc. Major segmentation variables for business markets obviously vary from the consumer market. The important variables here are as follows:

Demographics: Industry segmentation focuses on which industries buy the product. Company size can be used. Geographic location may be used to group businesses by proximity.

Operating Variables: Business markets can be segmented by technology (what customer technologies should we focus on?), user/nonuser status (heavy, medium, light), or customer capabilities (those needing many or few services).

Purchasing Approaches: Five approaches are possible.

1. Segment. "Segmentation" can be by purchasing function organization (centralized or decentralized)

2. Power structure (selecting companies controlled by a functional specialty)

3. The nature of existing relationships (current desirable customers or new desirable customers)

4. General purchase policies (focus on companies that prefer some arrangements over others such as leasing, related support service contracts, sealed bids)

5. Purchasing criteria (focus on noncompensatory criteria such as price, service, or quality).

    In addition, there can be situational factors that influence the business market segmentation effort. Situational segmentation may be based upon urgency (such as quick delivery needs), specific application (specific uses for the product) or size of order (few large or many small accounts)

Personal Characteristics: Personal comparisons can lead to segmentation by buyer-seller similarity (companies with similar personnel and values), attitudes toward risk (focus on risk-taking or risk-avoiding companies), or loyalty (focus on companies that show high loyalty to their suppliers.

There are several steps in the segmentation and target marketing process, but first it is necessary to establish that the market can be segmented. As mentioned in the text, some of the questions a company should answer with regard to determining candidates for segmentation are:

- Can the market(s) be identified and measured?

- Is the segment large enough to be profitable? Related issue: Is the segment stable and long-term?

- Is the segment reachable?

- Is the segment responsive?

- Is the segment expected not to change quickly?

- Can the segment be protected (protectability)? In other words, can competitors choose to target this segment easily and with a high level of success

- Interaction with other segments? Meaning: will the different messages received cause confusion about the product among different segments?

- What is the risk with this segment or segmentation action?

Examples of this process in action follow:

Finding "Healthy" Customers in the Medical Industry

As members of its industry begin to understand the mass-market approach is no longer viable, health care providers are moving from a product orientation to a marketing orientation. Market segmentation has become a tool that is widely used by a financially squeezed health care industry. Aiming their marketing efforts at those segments of the market that are likely to prove most profitable helps to conserve their limited resources. Some of the characteristics health care providers use to choose the proper target markets include: underlying needs, demographics, and patterns of behavior.

Because hospitals maintain detailed information on patients, the information necessary to determine the "typical" patient is available. Through medical and business records, health care marketers have access to usage rates for a predetermined number of years, services received, payment (or nonpayment) history and, at the simplest level, name and address information. The search for data also can extend to external sources, such as state agencies, trade associations, and syndicated sources. Once the marketer has gathered this data, he / she can begin the process of analyzing it to determine market share for the various lines of health care services.

Overlaying demographic with psychographic information allows hospitals to learn about the people who compose the market. By combining this information with its own product line mix, and disease incidence rates, segmentation opportunities become readily apparent. For example, one hospital recently recognized the potential for outpatient substance-abuse counseling services among upscale members of the business community. Although a competitor currently offered an in-patient program, the target group most likely to utilize the service found the in-patient option unappealing for many reasons, one of which was that many potential patients lived in close proximity to the hospital.

Based on an understanding of its target market, the marketing-oriented hospital developed an outpatient program and spoke directly to the target audience via promotional efforts in publications and television. A direct mail effort also targeted the businesses where those upscale patients were likely to be found. As a result, the hospital gained significant market share and won the favor of the community. This was no small feat in today's competitive health care marketplace.

Senior Citizens Enjoy Surfing . . . the Internet

Many members of the older generation are out to dispel beliefs that they are resistant to new technology. Internet clubs, consisting of members who are in their later years, have been formed all over the United States. The seniors use the Internet to obtain many types of new information, order products, and meet and / or "chat" with other seniors throughout the country. A number of marriages have evolved out of these connections.

Smart marketers realize that this segment of the market represents a substantial audience for products advertised via the Internet. Why? One reason is the information explosion. Consider the amount of information that is available on the Internet. In today's society, few of us in the work force have the leisure time available to spend learning about the power of the Internet. We tend to bookmark the information we need on a regular basis but rarely venture out on extensive "surfing" expeditions. Retired persons do have this kind of time, so when they log on to the Internet, they are likely to stay a while. In addition, many of the people in their golden years have physical limitations that may restrict their mobility. The Internet is an ideal way to stay connected to the outside world and beat the loneliness that may ensue from an inability to venture beyond their home.

Note: It is important to note here that when a marketer considers the needs of one segment over all other segments, controversy is likely to ensue. A good way to begin a discussion in this topic area is to ask students for some of the dangers and/or disadvantages that may result from segmenting and targeting markets.

Source: Adapted from a report presented on *Good Morning America*.

Marketing and Advertising

1. With the headline "Adult Entertainment," the ad in Figure 1 beckons to a particular segment of the consumer market. Bahlsen knows that consumers of all ages generally like cookies, yet the company is signaling its segmentation strategy through the headline, body copy, and illustration.

   a. Which variables is Bahlsen using to segment the overall consumer market?

   b. Based on these variables, how would you describe the targeted segment?

   c. Why would segmentation be effective for identifying market segments in this situation?

Answer

   a. Bahlsen appears to be using the demographic variables of age (signaled by the word "adult" in the headline and copy) and family life cycle ("the kids are finally tucked away" and "the kids are going to grow..."). It is also using the behavioral variables of occasions (implied usage during the evening, after the kids have been taken care of) and benefits ("adult entertainment" and "indulge yourself" phrases signal the benefit of enjoyment. Students may also mention the behavioral benefit of cost-savings (because of the in-ad coupon), among other variables.

   b. One way to describe the segment is: parents who want to enjoy themselves during child-free evenings and who want to save money on such indulgences.

c.   Segmentation is effective in this situation because Bahlsen knows that an adult's taste in cookies is often different from a child's taste in cookies, so adults can be singled out as a substantial, differentiable, and measurable segment. In addition, Bahlsen believes that adults would react differently to marketing programs targeting them as a segment, compared with programs targeting children as a segment. Finally, Bahlsen can measure the size, purchasing power, and characteristics of the adult segment it is targeting. Students may offer other appropriate explanations, as well.

2.   Hertz is a well-known brand among consumers and business travelers who need to rent a car. As shown in Figure 2, the company targets specific segments within business markets.

a.   Which of the major segmentation variables does Hertz appear to be using on its business markets?

b.   Which of the three business buyer groups identified by Rackham and Vincentis might Hertz be stressing in this ad?

c.   What personal characteristics might be particularly important in this segment of Hertz's business markets?

Answer

a.   Hertz is using company size ("small business"), situational factors (use of rental cars), and purchasing approaches ("tight budgets" indicates cost-saving purchasing criteria) to segment the business market. Students may suggest additional factors, as well, such as geography and age (in tiny type, the ad specifies that customers must be 25 years old and U.S. or Canadian residents).

b.   Hertz seems to be addressing price-oriented business customers in this ad, because of the emphasis on special low rates and Club Express membership at "no extra cost." Some students may argue that Hertz is stressing solution-oriented business customers, because the ad discusses how customers can "save time with Hertz #1 Club Express," a value-added feature that provides the benefit of helping small business owners expedite the rental process.

c.   Loyalty may plan an important role in the segment of the business market that Hertz is targeting. By encouraging customers to enroll in and use Club Express membership, Hertz can deliver faster and more convenient service; coupled with special low small-business rates, this combination may lead business customers to become loyal users of Hertz services. Students may also may a good case for attitudes toward risk, because renting from a well-known agency can reduce the risk that business customers might perceive in the process.

Online Marketing Today

For Levi Strauss, the key to successful mass customization is to make clothing that meets customers' expectations for fit as well as style. Customers can customize an existing Levi's style (such as the 502 button-fly model) or start from scratch to create a one-of-a-kind pair of jeans, khaki pants, and shorts by mixing and matching color, length, and other style choices. Still, the company recognizes that there is no substitute for accurate body measurements. As a result, its Original Spin site allows online visitors to learn about the process, review their options, and even fill out an order form. To complete the transaction and place an order, however, customers must go to a local store to be measured.

Visit the Original Spin site (www.originalspin.com) and follow the links to learn how the process works. Also, follow the links to find the nearest Original Spin retail site and to examine the order form. Which of the four types of segmentation variables is Levi Strauss applying in its mass customization strategy? How does the Web site support or reinforce the segmentation strategy? Why would Levi Strauss insist that reorders be funneled through the stores rather than submitted online? What improvements can you suggest to make the Original Spin site more effective in attracting or serving customers?

Answer

Levi Strauss appears to be applying all four major types of segmentation variables. First, it has designated certain stores as Original Spin stores, which is a geographic variable that effectively segments the market by proximity to these stores. Second, it uses the demographic variable of gender to segment the market by offering different styles for men and women. Third, it uses the psychographic variables of lifestyle and personality by inviting consumers to customize pants for work (khakis) and play (jeans and shorts) and allowing them to express their personalities through the design of this clothing. Finally, it applies behavioral variables such as benefits (because customers seek both good fit and unique styling) to segment the consumer market.

The Original Spin site supports the segmentation strategy in several ways. For example, the featured models are both male and female, sending a signal that both genders can enjoy the benefits of Original Spin. In addition, the site offers a store locator so customers can find out where to get measured and submit orders. Because Levi Strauss has an extensive store network, it can offer customers more personalized attention and check incoming orders for errors or omissions by having reorders funneled through the stores rather than submitted online. Students may offer a variety of innovative improvements to make the Original Spin site more effective in attracting or serving customers. As just one example, they may suggest that Levi Strauss offer live text chat with customer service representatives who can view options with customers and offer advice.

You're the Marketer—Sonic PDA Marketing Plan

Defining a target marketing strategy through market segmentation is a critical aspect of any marketing plan. The purpose is to identify and describe distinct market segments, target specific segments, and then pinpoint the differentiating benefits to be stressed.

In your role as Jane Melody's assistant, you are responsible for market segmentation and targeting for Sonic's new PDA product. Look back at the SWOT analysis, market needs information, and competitive data you previously documented in the marketing planning process. Then answer the following questions about Sonic's market segments and target markets:

- Which variables should Sonic use to segment its consumer markets? For example, in addition to income and geography, does Sonic want to focus on consumers who have specific lifestyles, needs, or attitudes?

- Which variables should Sonic use to segment its business markets?

- How can Sonic evaluate the attractiveness of each identified segment? Should Sonic market to one consumer segment and one business segment or target more than one in each market? Why?

- Should Sonic pursue full market coverage, market specialization, product specialization, selective specialization, or single-segment concentration? Why?

Next, consider how your decisions about segmentation and targeting will affect Sonic's marketing efforts. Depending on your instructor's directions, summarize your conclusions in a written marketing plan or enter them in the Market Analysis and Target Markets sections of the *Marketing Plan Pro* software. Also, note any additional research you may need in the Marketing Research section of the software.

Answer

The answers to these questions depend, in part, on the data students have gathered for earlier marketing-plan exercises and the decisions they made for those exercises. In general, Sonic would benefit by targeting specific consumer segments based on their busy work and home lifestyles; their needs for a product that delivers the benefit of helping organize their lives and stay in touch while away from home and office; and positive attitudes toward PDA (personal digital assistant) technology, including wireless Web and e-mail access. Students may suggest additional variables for Sonic to use, as well.

For business markets, Sonic can use demographics (such as industry and company size) and situational factors (need for specific applications such as on-the-go access to e-mail or ability to input data in the field). Again, students may offer other ideas for suitable variables to segment the business market.

Sonic can evaluate the attractiveness of each identified segment by determining whether it is measurable, substantial, accessible, differentiable, and actionable. The company will probably need to conduct research to support this evaluation. The decision to market to one or more segments in each market depends on how well each segment fits with Sonic's goals and objectives and its resources, such as the marketing budget.

Students can make a compelling case for Sonic pursuing either product or selective specialization. With product specialization, the company will sell its PDA products to both consumer and business segments that need the primary communication and information exchange benefits. With selective specialization, the company will identify specific segments that would respond to the PDA offer, thereby diversifying the risk. However, Sonic should not pursue full market coverage at this time, in part because different segments may have different needs and in part because the cost is too much for a start-up. In addition, single-segment concentration may prove too narrow to be profitable for Sonic.

Marketing Spotlight—Marriott International

Marriott International grew to an international hospitality giant from humble roots as a single root beer stand started by John and Alice Marriott in Washington, D.C. during the 1920s. The Marriotts added hot food to their root beer stand, renamed their business the Hot Shoppe, which they incorporated in 1929. They began building a regional chain of restaurants. As the number of Hot Shoppes in the Southeast grew, Marriott expanded into in-flight catering by serving food on Eastern, American, and Capital Airlines beginning in 1937. In 1939, Hot Shoppes began its food service management business when it opened a cafeteria in the U.S. Treasury building. The company expanded into another hospitality sector in 1957, when Hot Shoppes opened its first hotel in Arlington, Virginia. Hot Shoppes, which was renamed Marriott Corporation in 1967, grew nationally and internationally by way of strategic acquisitions and entering new service categories, and by 1977 sales topped $1 billion.

In the pursuit of continued growth, Marriott continued to diversify its business. The 1982 acquisition of Host International made it America's top operator of airport food and beverage facilities. Over the course of the following three years, Marriott added 1,000 food service accounts by purchasing three food service companies, Gladieux, Service Systems, and Saga Corp.

Determining that its high penetration in the traditional hotel market did not offer many opportunities for growth, the company initiated a segmented marketing strategy by introducing the moderately priced Courtyard by Marriott hotels in 1983. Moderately priced hotels comprised the largest segment of the U.S. lodging industry, a segment filled with established competitors such as Holiday Inn, Ramada, and Quality Inn. Research conducted by Marriott registered the greatest consumer dissatisfaction in the moderately priced hotels, and Courtyard hotels were designed to offer travelers greater convenience and amenities, such as balconies and patios, large desks and sofas, and pools and spas.

Early success with Courtyard prompted Marriott to expand further. In 1994, Marriott entered the vacation timesharing business by acquiring American Resorts Group. The following year, the company purchased Howard Johnson Company, selling the hotels and retaining the restaurants and rest stops. In 1987, Marriott added three new market segments: Marriott Suites, full service suite accommodations; Residence Inn, extended-stay rooms for business travelers; and Fairfield Inn, an economy hotel brand. A company spokesman explained this rapid expansion: "There is a lot of segmentation that's going on in the hotel business. Travelers are sophisticated and have many wants and needs. In addition to that, we saw there would be a finite . . . ability to grow the traditional business."

Marriott Corp. split into two in 1993, forming Host Marriott to own the hotel properties and Marriott International primarily to engage in the more lucrative practice of governing them. In 1995, Marriott International bought a minority stake in the Ritz-Carlton luxury hotel group (Marriott purchased the remaining share in 1998). In 1996, the company acquired the Forum Group, an assisted living and health care services franchise, and merged it with Marriott Senior Living services. Marriott added a new hotel brand in 1998 with the introduction of SpringHill Suites, which provide moderate priced suites that are 25 percent larger than standard hotel rooms. The following year, the company acquired corporate housing specialist ExecuStay Corp. and formed ExecuStay by Marriott. To capitalize on the online travel and accommodations boom, the company developed Marriott.com, which offers customized content to registered visitors such as a vacation planner, golf course information, express reservations, and business content. In 2000, the company announced plans to join with rival Hyatt Corporation to launch a joint B2B e-commerce venture that will provide procurement services for the hospitality industry.

The last Hot Shoppe restaurant, located in a shopping mall in Washington D.C., closed on December 2, 1999. This closing was fitting, since the tiny restaurant in no way resembled the multinational hospitality leader it spawned. Today, Marriott International is the largest hotel and resort company in America and one of the leading hospitality companies in the world, maintaining more than 2,200 operating units in 59 countries that brought $20 billion in global revenues in 2000.

Questions

1.   What target marketing and marketing segmentation concepts discussed in the text did Marriott apply to get to where it is today?

2.   Has it picked its market segments and target markets effectively? Discuss the bases of Marriott's segment interrelationships.

3.   Does the evolution of Marriott's "businesses" indicate that the firm is well positioned for the coming decades of the twenty-first century? What opportunities and problems will

[1] Henderson, Nell. "Marriott Bares Courtyard Plans." *Washington Post*, June 12, 1984.
[2] Tucker, Elizabeth. "Marriott's Recipe for Corporate Growth; Plan to Buy Denny's Reflects Aggressive Strategy." *Washington Post*, June 1, 1987.

Marriott encounter as it pursues their marketing strategy in planning toward the year 2010?

Suggested Responses

1. Marriott appears to be successful in developing a clear understanding of where and how it can create business value and opportunity, with a profit, based on existing corporate capabilities. As a leader in the hospitality business, the firm has made a conscious and consistent effort to avoid mass marketing, attempting to serve only distinct groups of customers with different needs. In addition, Marriott has conducted effective marketing research over the years to determine which segments are measurable, substantial, accessible and actionable. It has gradually widened the list of target markets, constantly evaluating the ongoing potential of each target in terms of attractiveness and fit with the company objectives and resources. Lastly, it has developed different market offers for each segment, capitalizing on segment interrelationships that could lead in the future toward possible super segments.

2. Marriott attempted to ensure that the market segments were measurable, substantial, accessible, and actionable. Further, they defined target markets that would contribute to customer relationships and lead to enhancement of their name franchise position in their other lines of interrelated business activity. Finally, Marriott appeared to recognize that they should be able to obtain future new target opportunities as they evolved from the overlaps that existed within their current activities.

3. The interrelationships between the institutional catering (universities, hospitals, and businesses), combined with the in-flight catering and hotel businesses, led naturally to overlapping name recognition in the resort and senior living facilities, businesses, and possibly other areas. Of course, because there were also operational overlaps in these businesses, the company not only gained purchasing and management synergies but opportunities for future profitable business development and expansion (e-commerce and so on).

4. Although it appears that Marriott is well-positioned for the future, there are two critical variables that could provide constraints for the future:

a. Any service-oriented business faces the critical fact that operational success relies largely on the capabilities of its employees. Because the majority of Marriott's operations are in the United States, it will require access to continuing sources of high quality, low-cost labor. This could be a problem in the future.

    b. Since Marriott operates in business sectors that depend largely on a traveling public and substantial public sector input (universities, senior care facilities, etc.), major changes in travel patterns or decreases in public spending could impact the firm negatively.

Part III—DEVELOPING MARKET STRATEGIES

Chapter 11—Positioning and Differentiating the Market Offering Through the Product Life Cycle

Overview

Positioning is the act of designing the company's offer and image so that the target understands and appreciates what the company stands for in relation to its competition. The company's positioning must be rooted in an understanding of how the target defines value and makes choices among vendors. The positioning tasks consist of three steps. First, the company has to identify possible product, services, personnel, and image differences that need to be established in relation to competition. Second, the company has to apply criteria to select the most important differences. Third, the company has to effectively signal to the target market how it differs from its competition. The company's product-positioning strategy will then enable it to take the next step, namely, to plan its competitive marketing strategies.

Products and markets have life cycles that call for changing marketing strategies over time. Every new need follows a demand life cycle that passes through the states of emergence, accelerating growth, decelerating growth, maturity, and decline. Each new technology that emerges to satisfy that need exhibits a demand-technology life cycle. Particular product forms of a given technology also show a life cycle, as do brands within that product form.

The sales history of many products follow an S-shaped curve made up of four stages. The introduction stage is marked by slow growth and minimal profits as the product is pushed into distribution. The company has to decide during this stage among the four strategies of rapid skimming, slow skimming, rapid penetration, or slow penetration. If successful, the product enters a growth stage marked by rapid sales growth and increasing profits. During this stage, the company attempts to improve the product, enter new market segments and distribution channels, and reduce its prices slightly. There follows a maturity stage in which sales growth slows down and profits stabilize. The company seeks innovative strategies to renew sales growth, including market, product, and marketing-mix modification. Finally, the product enters a decline stage in which little can be done to halt the deterioration of sales and profits. The company's task during this period is to identify the truly weak products; develop for each one a strategy of continuation, focusing, or niching; and finally phase out weak products in a way that minimizes the hardship to company profits, employees, and customers.

Not all products pass through an S-shaped PLC. Some products show a growth-slump-maturity pattern, others a cycle-recycle shape, and still others a scalloped shape. Some investigators have discovered more than a dozen PLC shapes, including those describing styles, fashions, and fads. Because of the globalization of the marketplace, an international PLC shape has also emerged. PLC theory has been criticized because companies cannot predict the shapes in advance, nor can they know what stage they are in within a given shape or predict the duration of the stages. In addition, PLCs are the result of chosen marketing strategies rather than independent of the chosen marketing strategies.

Product life-cycle theory must be broadened by a theory of market evolution. The theory of market evolution holds that new markets emerge when a product is created to satisfy an unmet need. The innovator usually develops a product for the mass market. Competitors enter the market with similar products leading to market growth. Later growth slows down and the market enters maturity. The market undergoes increasing fragmentation until some firm introduces a powerful new attribute that consolidates that market into fewer and larger segments. This stage does not last, because competitors copy the new attributes. There is a cycling back and forth between market consolidation based on innovation and fragmentation based on competition. The market for the present technology will ultimately decline upon the discovery of superior technologies.

Companies must try to anticipate new attributes that the market wants. Profits go to those who introduce new and valued benefits early. The search for new attributes can be based on customer survey work, intuition, dialectical reasoning, or needs-hierarchy reasoning. Successful marketing comes through creatively visualizing the market's evolutionary potential.

Learning Objectives

After reading this chapter students should:

- Understand the concepts of positioning
- Be able to identify competitive advantages of specific attributes in the marketplace
- Be able to discern differentiation attributes
- Be able to review how different firms are trying to communicate their positioning strategy to the market
- Know how firms can choose an effective position in the market
- Know the concept of the product life cycle
- Know the stages of the product life cycle
- Understand the possible strategies to be used during each stage of the PLC
- Understand the concept and stages of market evolution
- Relate marketing strategy to market evolution

Chapter Outline

I.   Introduction

II.   Competitive differentiation tools for:

     A.   Volume industry

     B.   Stalemated industry

     C.   Fragmented industry

     D.   Specialized industry

III.   Product differentiation

     A.   Features—characteristics that supplement the product's basic function

     B.   Performance quality—the level at which the product's primary characteristics operate

     C.   Conformance quality—the degree to which all the produced units are identical and meet the promised target specifications

     D.   Durability—measure of the product's expected operating life under natural or stressful conditions

     E.   Reliability—a measure of the probability that a product will not malfunction or fail within a specified period

F.   Repairability—a measure of the ease of fixing a product that malfunctions or fails

G.   Style—the product's looks and feel to the buyer

H.   Design: the integrating force—the totality of features that affect how a product looks and functions in terms of customer requirements

IV.   Services differentiation

A.   Ordering ease

B.   Delivery—speed, accuracy, and care

C.   Installation—making a product operational

D.   Customer training—instruction on proper and efficient use

E.   Customer consulting—data, information systems, and advising services

F.   Maintenance and repair—keeping products in good working order

G.   Miscellaneous services—finding other ways to add value

V.   Personnel differentiation

A.   Competence

B.   Courtesy

C.   Credibility

D.   Reliability

E.   Responsiveness

F.   Communication

VI.   Channel differentiation

VII.   Image differentiation

A.   Identity versus image—company intentions versus consumer perceptions

B.   Symbols—logos, objects, people, colors

C.   Written and audiovisual media—to convey company or brand personality

D.   Atmosphere—physical space in which the organization produces or delivers its products

E.   Events—sponsorships

VIII.   Developing and communicating a positioning strategy

A.   Criteria for differentiation—price/quality, service, attributes, benefits, against competition, application, users, against product category

B.   How many differences to promote—single versus double or triple benefit positioning

C.   Which differences to promote—with many ways to go, a firm still must choose

D.   Communicating the company's position—to all publics, both internal and external. Other marketing mix elements should help support the position, not detract from it

IX.   Product life-cycle marketing strategies

A.   Concept of the product life cycle

1.   Demand/technology life cycle—to describe changing need levels as well as the level of technology available to satisfy these changing needs

2.   Stages in the product life cycle—introduction, growth, maturity, decline

3.   Product-category, product-form, and brand life cycle—the PLC concept can be applied to any of these cycles

4.   Other shapes of the product life cycle—from six to seventeen different patterns

      a)   Style, fashion, and fad life cycles

5.   International product life cycle—United States manufacturers export product, foreign production starts, then foreign production becomes competitive in export markets and import competition begins.

B.   Marketing strategies: introduction stage

1.   Marketing strategies in the introduction stage—rapid-skimming, slow-skimming, rapid-penetration, slow-penetration

2.   Market pioneers—research shows those first in the market gain the greatest advantages, both consumer- and producer-oriented

3.   Competitive cycle—sole supplier, competitive penetration, share stability, commodity competition, withdrawal

C.   Marketing strategies: growth stage

1.   Marketing strategies in the growth stage—a wide variety available

D.   Marketing strategies: maturity stage

1.   Marketing strategies in the maturity stage—market modification, product modification, marketing mix modification

E.   Marketing strategies: decline stage

1.   Marketing strategies during the decline stage—identifying the weak products, determining decline marketing strategies (increasing investment, maintaining investment, decreasing investment, harvesting, divesting), the "drop" decision

F.   Product life-cycle concept: critique

X.   Market evolution

A.   Stages in market evolution

1.   Emergence stage—latent market that consists of people who share a similar need or want for something that does not yet exist. One company enters to satisfy that need or want

2.   Growth stage—new firms enter into what is now considered an attractive market

3.   Maturity stage—heavy competition causes market fragmentation and, with the emergence of new attributes, market consolidation

4.   Decline stage—either society's total need level declines or a new technology begins to replace the old

B.   Dynamics of attribute competition—firms can discover new attributes through customer-survey, intuitive, dialectical, and needs-hierarchy processes

XI.   Summary

Lecture—Product Positioning in the New Economy

This lecture is intended for use with Chapter 11, "Positioning the Market Offering Through the Product Life Cycle." It focuses on development of data required to achieve a global marketing strategy. The format utilized here will enable students to utilize the concepts in a broader domestic, as well as international, setting.

Teaching Objectives

- To stimulate students to recognize and evaluate the critical issues in positioning a product, along with the research and analysis that goes with it

- Points to consider in proceeding with a positioning strategy—what to stress and not stress

- Awareness of the need for a positioning policy and strategy

Discussion

Introduction—Creating Continuity

In the text and several of the applications exercises, it is clear that segmentation is an important element in managing a new or existing market. Image, perceived rank, customer perception, product features, and competitive advantages are the primary tools for positioning a product in the marketplace. A firm may position its product in numerous ways, by attributes, price, quality, use/application, and type of end user, all with respect to a competitor(s). To turn this into a positioning strategy, it is essential to identify the competitors, assess the customer's perception of the competitors, identify competitive positions, research and understand the customers, choose the positioning strategy, and monitor the effectiveness of the positioning choice.

There are many examples of positioning strategies that have either succeeded or failed (see Kotler text). The business literature is replete with winners and losers, but the process by which the positioning strategy has been implemented proves by far to be the most critical variable for determining success.

The Positioning Concept

Positioning as a strategy started with positioning the product itself. Positioning refers to efforts to position the product in the mind of the consumer. As Reis and Trout pointed out in the 1960s and 1970s, the United States is very overadvertised, and any firm or product that seeks a more effective market position will have to achieve mental positioning before undertaking further marketing activity. If the position achieved is too general, the resulting image will be of no value to the customer who will not be able to differentiate clearly between the product choices. For example, a shampoo cannot maintain a strong position by claiming as its primary benefit its ability to get the consumer's hair clean.

Many companies have repositioned, or are attempting to reposition, their products in recent years. A growing number of firms have repositioned based on one or more service variables. This may appear on the surface as incongruous, but when one recognizes the level of competition in the United States and the world today, it makes sense. Declining profit margins and the need to differentiate many products that have become virtual commodities make it is easy to see the value of repositioning so that the consumer sees the entire product and service package in the broadest sense. Because a lawyer or hospital, for example, generally is distinguishable on any basis other than service, many providers in these areas today are focusing on a specialty or specific service in their marketing as the means to get the customer mentally repositioned on who and what they are compared to their competitors.

To conclude, the primary means for promoting differences include focusing on those differences that are important, distinctive, superior, communicable, preemptive, affordable, and profitable.

Teaching Suggestion

Break the class into several groups and ask each group to discuss and identify several (four to six) brands and products/services within one or more chosen goods or service industries. The students should then evaluate the positioning activities or advertising used to differentiate, position, and reposition these goods and services. What they may find is that virtually everyone will agree on the ways in which the chosen products are positioned, but the larger challenge has to do with how to position or reposition in the future. For example, few would argue that Trix is positioned as a kid cereal or that Colgate fights cavities. Nevertheless, there likely will be disagreement about what Colgate (P&G) is going to do now that it is losing market share, and fighting cavities is a less important position than whiter teeth and other positioning variables used by the competition. This presents an applied example of positioning in action. Some industries to consider are: beverages, toothpaste, retailers, snack chips, entertainers, hospitals, lawyers, and ice cream.

Marketing and Advertising

1. When T-Fal sells its pans around the world, it takes into account each market's unique characteristics. The headline of the ad in Figure 1 reads "Pan for the Index Finger," showing how Japanese customers can use one finger to detach the handle so the pan can be used in different ways and stored in tight spaces.

    a. What unique selling proposition is this ad promoting?

    b. Which of the nine product differentiation variables is being communicated in this ad? Why is this variable important to the target market?

    c. State the value proposition suggested by this T-Fal ad.

Answer

    a. The unique selling proposition is that consumers can quickly remove the pan's handle for easy usage or storage.

    b. Features are the main product differentiation variable being communicated in this ad. The features variable is important because the target market has a wide choice of cooking pans but also must deal with the constraint of limited storage and the desire for multiple usage.

    c. One sample value proposition this ad suggests is: "T-Fal pans are the most convenient and easiest to use and store." Students may offer variations on this statement.

2. The ad in Figure 2, placed by the U.S. Postal Service for its NetPost Mailing Online service, targets businesses that use direct mail to reach their customers.

    a. Is this ad illustrating attribute, benefit, use, user, competitor, product category, or quality/price positioning?

    b. Which of the main service differentiators is being communicated by this ad? Why would customers value this difference?

    c. The market for postal services is in the maturity stage. Does U.S.P.S. appear to be using market modification, product modification, or marketing-mix modification to stimulate sales?

Answer

    a. The ad is illustrating benefit positioning, by emphasizing the convenience of

185

sending information to the U.S.P.S. Web site for 24-hour production and mailing. Students may also suggest that the ad is illustrating use positioning (for businesses that need to have a direct mail piece printed and mailed).

b. Ordering ease is one service differentiator being communicated by this ad. Students may also suggest that speedy/easy delivery (as in having information printed and mailed) is another key service differentiator being communicated by this ad.

c. The U.S.P.S. seems to be using product modification, by offering additional features beyond the basic mail delivery service it has traditionally provided for consumer and business markets.

3. **BONUS AD--See Companion Web site!** As this ad explains, Snyder's of Hanover offers "more flavor intensity" and "more flavor varieties" than all other flavored pretzels. In all, four flavors are pictured and two more are mentioned in the ad.

a. How is Snyder's differentiating its pretzel products in this ad? Why is this difference worth establishing?

b. Where do pretzels seem to be in the product life cycle? What are the implications for the way Snyder's markets its pretzel products, as seen in this ad?

c. How does the ad develop a distinctive image for the Snyder's brand?

Answer

a. Snyder's is using product differentiation to set its pretzel products apart. Specifically, the company is using flavor (a feature) as a point of differentiation—an appropriate difference because new and unusual flavors help Snyder's stand out from more traditional pretzel products. In addition, snack lovers are presumably interested in taste, so flavor intensity and variety should be important considerations when these buyers choose between competing products.

b. Pretzels are in the mature stage of the product life cycle, because after being on the market for many years, overall sales growth is either small or stagnant. As a result, Snyder's is looking for ways to modify the market (by converting nonusers who like nontraditional flavors such as honey mustard and onion), modify the product (by improving the taste through more varieties), and modifying the marketing mix (by advertising the new flavors).

c. This ad helps Snyder's establish an image as the pretzel brand with more flavors and more flavor intensity. That image sets Snyder's apart from brands that emphasize more traditional pretzel flavors. The headline, copy, photo of a chef and baker's paddle, and prominence of featured flavors all support this image.

4. **BONUS AD--See Companion Web site!** This ad uses play on words to create an emotional appeal for using Hefty OneZip storage bags, which incorporate their product differentiation into the brand name.

a. What product variable(s) are being used to differentiate Hefty OneZip bags from competing storage bags?

b. Describe the target customers, benefits, and value proposition for Hefty OneZip bags.

c. Which of the product life cycle patterns are likely to apply to this product? Why?

Answer

186

a. Hefty OneZip bags are being differentiated based on features (zip-closing slider), performance quality (slider stays closed), conformance quality (all OneZip bags stay closed as expected), and reliability (food will be protected as expected). Students may identify other points of differentiation, as well.

b. Target customers are consumers who need to store, freeze, and protect all kinds of foods. Benefits: bags are easy to close, stay closed, protect foods. Value proposition: an easy-closing freezer bag that stays closed to protect food while frozen. Students may offer variations on these descriptions.

c. Hefty OneZip bags are likely to follow the traditional bell-shaped product life cycle pattern unless new technology produces storage containers that make this product obsolete or offer significant improvement over this product's features and benefits. Thus, this product can be expected to have a lengthy maturity stage during which it will have to battle many competitors and use promotion to defend market share and sales.

Online Marketing Today

Although pioneering a market can be expensive and difficult, companies that do it effectively will reap first-mover advantages. The online auction site eBay is a good case in point. When the Internet was in its infancy, eBay invented the online auction concept and revolutionized the way consumers buy and sell products among themselves. Now 30 million consumers are registered as eBay buyers or sellers, and 2 million more register every month. In recent years, companies have begun using eBay's auction facilities to sell a range of new products. J.C. Penney, for example, has auctioned clothing on eBay, while Mitsubishi Electric has auctioned factory automation equipment.

Visit the eBay site (www.ebay.com) and see how the company orients new users to its services. Also look at the goods and services featured on the home page; follow the link to eBay Motors or another of the specialty sites; and follow the link to read "About eBay." Based on your observations of eBay's online marketing efforts, does this market appear to be in the emergence, growth, maturity, or decline stage? How are eBay's marketing efforts intended to affect the market? How is eBay using its site to create an effective image?

Answer

The market appears to be in the growth stage, because eBay has a number of competitors and it has been adding new features and improvements; it is also entering new market segments such as autos. Marketing efforts used by eBay are intended to retain current users through new features and improvements; attract new customers from new segments, such as auto and art buyers; and develop brand preference for eBay. Students may be able to discuss how specific aspects of the eBay site relate to these marketing efforts. Students may say that eBay is using its site to create an effective image through its use of colorful text and graphics, which convey the idea that online auctions are fun and entertaining; by prominently featuring interesting products being auctioned; by providing links to charity and other specialized auctions. They may cite additional ways, as well.

You're the Marketer—Sonic PDA Marketing Plan

In the course of developing a marketing strategy, marketers must select and communicate an effective positioning to differentiate their offerings. They also have to plan appropriate marketing strategies for each stage of the product life cycle and the market's evolution.

As before, you are working with Jane Melody on Sonic's marketing plan for launching a new PDA. Review your work on previous sections of the marketing plan. Then answer these questions about positioning and life cycle strategies for Sonic:

- Which of the differentiation variables related to product, services, personnel, channels, and image are best suited to Sonic's situation, strategy, and goals? Include the rationale for your selection.

- In developing your positioning, identify the benefits most valued by your target customers. Will you stress one or more than one benefit in your positioning? In a sentence, what is the value proposition for Sonic's PDA?

- Knowing the stage of Sonic's PDA in the product life cycle, what are the implications for the marketing mix, product management strategy, service strategy, and R&D strategy?

- In which stage of its evolution does the PDA market appear to be? What does this mean for Sonic's marketing plans?

Once you have answered these questions and considered the effects on Sonic's marketing, either summarize your ideas in a written marketing plan or type them in the Positioning sections of the *Marketing Plan Pro* software. Also, note any additional research you may need in the Marketing Research section of the software.

Answer

Students' answers may vary, depending on their answers and decisions related to marketing plan exercises in earlier chapters. In general, some of the key differentiation variables they may suggest for Sonic are: features (especially the voice recognition system, for product differentiation); maintenance and repair (through the warranty, for services differentiation); competence (of customer service representatives, for personnel differentiation); and image (based on the marketing mix that Sonic uses to create a quality, value-added image).

Among the benefits most valued by Sonic's target customers are ease of communication (delivered by Sonic's voice recognition system) and portability (for information access and communication anytime, anywhere). Sonic should probably stress these two benefits in its positioning and its marketing programs, because both are important to the target market and help differentiate Sonic's product from competing models. The value proposition for Sonic's PDA might be summarized as: "the most versatile, convenient way to communicate and exchange information on the go." Students may suggest other appropriate value propositions.

Marketing Spotlight—Monsanto Company

In the 1980s, St. Louis–based Monsanto Company repositioned itself as a cutting-edge biotech firm with a concentration on food and nutrition. During the next two decades, the company dedicated millions of dollars to scientific research in biology and life sciences for the purpose of developing genetically modified (GM) agricultural and food products. In 1996, then-CEO Robert Shapiro spun off Monsanto's $3 billion chemicals business, the old core of the company. Three divisions remained: a pharmaceuticals division, a food ingredients division, and an agricultural products division that produced GM foods. Such foods included a potato designed to fight potato beetles without pesticides and corn that is resistant to herbicides.

The new Monsanto, bearing little resemblance to the small pharmaceuticals company founded in 1901, became a leader in the biotech revolution. The company felt that biotechnology would be the key to feeding the world's rising population—currently growing at a rate of 800 million per decade—and improving global nutrition standards. Monsanto claimed that genetically superior crops of corn, wheat, tomatoes, and soybeans will yield larger harvests, while biotech improvements in the food supply will help prevent illness and boost human productivity. In the company's view, the next two decades would bring a biotechnology revolution that would blend the pharmaceutical, agricultural, and food and nutrition businesses into a single "life science" industry. To improve the company's reach in this industry, Monsanto spent millions amassing biotech patents by acquiring smaller companies and making deals with agribusiness firms. Such moves included the 1995 acquisition of Merck's specialty chemicals unit and the purchase of Unilever's wheat-breeding business in 1998.

Monsanto's aggressive move into the biotech industry met with approval on Wall Street. In 1997, Monsanto stock sold for close to 23 times earnings, compared with pure chemical company Dow's stock, which sold for 10.5 times earnings. In addition to being a favorite of investors, however, Monsanto became a target for environmentalists and consumers opposed to GM products. Backlash was particularly harsh in Europe, where the mad-cow scare made food products an especially sensitive consumer issue. British newspapers repeatedly referred to the company as a "Frankenstein food giant" and "biotech bully boy," while Prince Charles vowed never to eat food containing Monsanto products. Monsanto's attempt to win over U.K. citizens with an expensive public relations campaign failed: following the campaign, 51 percent of British consumers expressed negative feelings about GM foods, compared with only 44 percent beforehand. This sentiment was shared throughout much of Europe. In 1998, the European Union declared a moratorium on the approval of new GM seeds for planting. Several European countries, such as Austria and Luxembourg, banned GM foods altogether. Other hotspots for public criticism of the company included Japan, Australia, and India.

Monsanto's financial fortunes turned as hostile public receptions throughout the world left it unable to either sell expected volumes existing products or introduce new products. Following a merger with drug company Pharmacia & Upjohn, the pharmaceuticals division of Monsanto became part of the new Pharmacia Corporation in 2000. The remainder of the Monsanto Company is now a subsidiary of Pharmacia and strictly a biotechnology corporation. Pharmacia spun off part of Monsanto into a public company while retaining majority ownership. In 2000, Monsanto issued a statement apologizing for its insensitivity and arrogance and formally pledged to be "honorable, ethical, and open" in all its future actions. New CEO Hendrik Verfaille admitted that the company "missed the fact that this technology raises major issues for people of ethics, of choice, of trust, even of democracy and globalization. When we tried to explain the benefits, the science and the safety, we did not understand that our tone, our very approach, was arrogant."

Amid mounting consumer concerns about GM crops, in November 2000 Monsanto adopted a restricted planting schedule for a GM corn product and delayed introduction of another variety until 2002. The growth potential for the company is huge: Monsanto estimates that more than 70 percent of the world's insect- and herbicide-resistant crops come from the company. Anywhere public contempt for GM products lessens, Monsanto's opportunities improve dramatically. The company has undertaken various advertising, public relations, and education campaigns to improve public perception of its products. The prevailing attitude at the company is now much humbler than it was during the mid-1990s, when then CEO Robert Shapiro declared that "worrying about starving future generations won't feed them. Biotechnology will."

Sources: Amy Barrett, "Rocky Ground for Monsanto?" Business Week, June 12, 2000; Scott Kilman and Helene Cooper, "Crop Blight: Monsanto Falls Flat Trying to Sell Europe on Bioengineered Food." Wall Street Journal, May 11, 1999; "Pledge to Turn Over a New Leaf." The Guardian, December 14, 2000.

Questions

1. What marketing mistakes did Monsanto make to cause the firm to receive such bad press in Europe and elsewhere?

2.	What lessons about public relations marketing do the Monsanto spotlight case indicate? Are there additional issues that Monsanto should consider for the future?

Suggested Responses

1.	On the surface, it appeared that Monsanto did nothing wrong. They realized that the commodity chemical business was going nowhere, and they saw a future in the GM and related products. However, beneath the surface, it appears that Monsanto, apparently a very product-oriented company, did little or nothing to understand the complicated nontechnical issues involved with GM products before they moved aggressively forward. There is no mention of any consumer marketing attitude research regarding GM products inside or outside the United States.

2.	It is common knowledge that in Europe and many other regions of the world there are deep and strongly-held public expectations of socially, environmentally and ecologically responsible corporate actions, especially related to medical and health-related products. Because Monsanto adopted in its public relations efforts a defensive and typically American attitude that implied what is good from an American perspective is good for everyone, everywhere, they came across as highly arrogant. Attempting to sway public opinion on this deep-seated ethical and social issue only made matters worse.

3.	Monsanto's eventual recognition of the cause of the problem indicates that they may have learned a lesson. But in retrospective it would not have occurred if Monsanto had been more market- and marketing-oriented and paid closer attention to the variables required to reposition the products that caused the public concern. They forgot a key lesson in repositioning strategy: never try to reposition when the facts do not justify the reposition.

4.	Even the articles utilized for the Spotlight discussion tend to indicate that because Monsanto has agreed to be more "honorable, ethical and open" they should be able to reposition the products with time and national acceptance. However, students might argue that it is unwise for the company literally to wait out the opposition to GM products. Presumably, Monsanto is working closely with various grass-roots political, environmental and related groups in Europe and elsewhere to make available all sides of the research that enable the countries and people themselves to determine whether or not GM products are the best for the long-term future of their nations.

Analytical Tools for Marketing Management—Market Segmentation

Problems—Using the Student Guide and the Interactive Spreadsheet

1.	Calculate the index number for the users in the 25–34 age group, from the following data:

Total homemakers, all ages	74,975
Total users, all ages	25,202
Total homemakers, age 25–34.	17,130
Users, age 25–34	6,028

2.	SMRB data for Automatic Dishwashing Detergent Usage. Using only the "All User" column, select two personal and two geographic segments that best represent the target market for this product category:

3.	Primary personal demographic _____

4. Secondary personal demographic _____

5. Primary geographic demographic _____

6. Secondary geographic demographic _____

7. Prepare a rationale (based on the data) to prove that the choices you made above are the best of all alternatives.

8. If you had to select any one of the six alternatives (such as heavy, medium, light users, etc.), which would you select for special promotional efforts? Explain why.

This applications activity continues and adds depth to the discussion of index numbers. The numbers in this exercise are derived from Simmons Research Bureau (SMRB) data for segmentation and targeting. The exercise may be used either as a take home problem or as an exercise to be discussed and completed in class.

Listed below are some considerations in using SMRB index numbers for making segmentation analyses:

1. These numbers look authentic. There are so many numbers on any one Simmons' page, and there are so many pages, that most students begin to perceive the data to be very accurate. However, the data is compiled from a questionnaire that is exceedingly long. Some marketers complain that respondents who fill out these questionnaires reach a point of diminishing returns in filling them out. As a result, they tend to tire and do not answer the product usage and/or demographic questions accurately. This in turn makes the raw data and index numbers somewhat suspect.

2. Small demographic segments should not to be selected. When marketers face the problem of communicating with very small segments, they may not be able to find media vehicles that can reach those segments without buying a great deal of audience waste (nonprospects). Further, unless the firm is a small niche player in the industry, it is not worth the money or effort to attempt to sell to most small markets. Therefore, larger segments are usually preferred to very narrow, small segments.

3. Demographic segments are often misleading. For example, if index numbers should lead one to select a demographic segment composed of college graduates, the results could be misleading. College graduates will come from different social classes and may live radically different lives, and therefore they may have different purchasing patterns.The marketer, however, cannot glean that information by looking at the index number. Alternatively, two persons may be in the same income category, but they also may live different lives and therefore buy different kinds of products. For that reason, lifestyle segmentation, either as a replacement for demographics or in addition to demographics, may be necessary to achieve the best segmentation.

Answers to Questions

1. Index number for the users in the 25–34 age group:

Index for 25–34 age users		%	Index
Total homemakers, all ages	74,975		
Total homemakers, age 25 -34	17,130	0.228	
Total users, all ages	25,202		
Users, age 25–34	6,028	0.239	105

191

Rationale: Age group as a percent of the total, and age group users as a percent of total users

2.   The largest personal demographic segments for automatic dishwasher detergent are:

INCOME $35,000+	199	1	5,493*
Income $25,000+	178	2	11,902
Home value $40,000+	163	3	15,526
Graduated college	152	4	4,660*
Professional/manager	149	5	4,668*
Ages 45–54	138	9	5,107*
Other (Latino, etc.)	136	6	1,346*
Ages 35–49	134	7	8,266
Children 12–17	133	8	7,127
Ages 55–64	128	10	3,534*
Attended college	125	11	4,855*
Employed part time	125	12	3,380*
Married	122	13	20,257
Families with 5+ people	122	14	4,568*'
Ages 25–54	121	15	16,937
Families with 3–4 people	121	16	10,965
Incomes $20,000 to $24,999	126	10	3.958*

The best choices are the segments with the largest index numbers. However, an examination of the "users" column, suggests that some of these segments are too small. Those marked with an asterisk are much too small (arbitrarily decided, but based on an examination of the entire range of segment sizes).

The next step should be to see if some of these segments could be combined.

Here are some likely combinations:

Segments	Combined User Segments
Ages: 25–54 and 55–64 (16,937 + 3,434)	20,471
Incomes: $25,000+ and $20,000–$24,999 (11,902 + 3,958)	15, 860
Families with 3–4 and 5+ people (10,965 + 4,668)	15, 633
Attended and Graduated college (4,855 + 4,660)	9,515

The following would not make good choices for the reasons given:

a. Homes valued $40,000+—no media to reach these people and there is too much variation in lifestyles of those who own such homes.

b. Married—no media to reach these people, and there is too much variation in lifestyles of married people.

	Index	Rank	Users
Marketing: Pacific	119	1	4,981
Census West	117	2	6,130
Metro suburban	115	3	12,116
County size A	109	4	10,243
Marketing: Northeast	104	5	6,148
Marketing: West Central	104	6	4,515
County size B	99	7	7,250
Census: Northeast	99	8	5,456
County size C	98	9	4,290

Decision

- For the <u>personal demographic segments</u>, the following were chosen, tentatively:

    - Choose age combination group: 25–54 and 55–64 for the <u>primary personal demographics</u>

    - Choose combined income grouping of $25,000+ and $20,000 to $24,999 for <u>secondary personal demographics</u>

    Note: The main reason each was chosen was their large user bases. They provide the largest overall segment.

1. For the <u>geographic segments</u>, the following were chosen, tentatively:

    a. The first choice for <u>primary geographic segments</u> would be a combination of markets in County sizes A, B and C with 21,783,000 users in them.

    b. The likely best choice for <u>secondary geographic segments</u> is Metro suburban, alone, because the segment is so large: 12,116,000 users.

    c. The only other choices would be a combination of various geographic regions such as Pacific Northeast, and West Central.

    d. Such choices are not as good as the first choice (A, B and C markets) because these regions are too broad.

Therefore, the "best" answers are:

1. Primary personal demographic: Ages: 25 to 64

2. Secondary personal demographic $20,000+ income

3. Primary geographic segment: County sizes A, B, and C

4. Secondary geographic segment: Metro suburban

2. Prepare a rationale (based on the data) to prove that the choices you made above are the best of all alternatives.

Rationale for Decisions

1. Tentative choices are made based on index numbers. It is also important, however, to select segments with correspondingly high numbers of users. Thus, the second criterion can modify the first and lead to a final decision.

2. *The primary personal segment* is: *ages 25–64* because this segment has the largest number of users: 20,471,000

   a. The *secondary personal segment* chosen is a *combination of two income segments of $20,000+ equaling 15,860,000 users, second largest.* This provides a sharp delineation to the age segment selected as the primary group.

   > *Note: Some students may argue that a demographic segment with a higher index number ought to be preferable to the 121 index of the 25–54 age segment. But the reason that 121 segment is chosen is that when combined with the adjacent segment with the second highest index number, incomes over $25,000, we have the largest overall segment.*
   >
   > *Second, this segment, combined, provides the second highest index number, 121.*
   >
   > *Third, this segment is relatively easy to reach with mass media. Fourth, this segment brings in some users who are not in the primary group.*

   b. The *primary geographic segment* chosen is *A, B, and C county markets.* This selection made it easy to choose individual markets in which to sell and advertise. There are more than 200 markets within these A, B, and C groups distributed in every state of the country. This segment also had the largest number of users in it: 21,783,000.

   c. The *secondary geographic segment* chosen, East and West central, contains the largest single index number (122), and it also has the second largest number of users: 16,710,000. Although there is some overlap between the primary and secondary targets, presumably the secondary targets will be used for adding extra advertising weight in a marketing campaign.

3. If you had to select any one of the six alternatives (such as heavy, medium, light users, etc.), which would you select for special promotional efforts? Explain why.

   a. The answer to this question comes from common sense and some experience in marketing. It would not be wise to use the heavy user segment alone because it has only 14.9 of all homemakers in it, 7,684,000 users. Perhaps it could be added to one of the other segments.

   b. Medium users represent a large category (11 of all homemakers and a total of 13,487,000 users). It may be a good target for promotion, especially when combined with heavy users.

   c. The light user segment is the largest of the three, with 23.2 of all homemakers and 16,621,000 users. However, there is a question concerning whether it is possible to convince light users to become medium or heavy user (to convince these people to buy more detergents), especially if they do not own a dishwasher. In other words, it is difficult to expand the detergent market because, generally, light users are very fickle, and promotion is usually not strong enough to change people's minds.

- Thus, the best answer is to combine heavy and medium user segments. Clearly, it will be easier to sell detergents to people who already buy dishwasher detergents of some kind.

    a.   17,130 / 74,975 = .228

    b.   12681/ 54321=. 233

    c.   .223/. 228 x 100 = 102

4.   Additional SMRB Database

As an adjunct or addition to the Simmons materials above, we have included in the Analytical/Computer student materials an interactive spreadsheet of data from SMRB (Diet or Sugar Free Carbonated Cola Drinks). This data includes the following:

- Raw consumer questionnaire results

- User consumption data, based on demographic data similar to that found in the dishwasher example

- In addition, the user data includes readership and viewer information. This data provides an additional exercise/analysis source

Note: For a problem or research set you could provide the students with various forms of altered data or other requirements and request various analyses. Because the spreadsheet is "live," students can proceed and focus on the analysis without the need to construct a spreadsheet from scratch.

Chapter 12—Developing New Market Offerings

Overview

Most firms recognize the necessity for and advantages of regularly developing new products and services. Mature and declining products eventually must be replaced with newer products. New product development strategy thus is one of the most important activities for any firm in the contemporary marketplace. If the firm does not obsolete its own products, eventually someone else will, and all firms should remember that a good idea might not be a good investment.

New products can fail, and the risks of innovation are as great as the rewards. The key to successful innovation lies in developing better organizational arrangements for handling new product ideas and developing sound research and decision procedures at each stage of the new-product development process.

The new-product development process consists of eight stages: idea generation, idea screening, concept development and testing, marketing strategy development, business analysis, product development, market testing, and commercialization. The purpose of each stage is to decide whether the idea should be further developed or dropped. The company should minimize the chances that poor ideas will move forward and good ideas will be rejected.

With regard to the adoption of new products, consumers and/or organizations respond at different rates, depending on their characteristics and the product's characteristics. Manufacturers try to bring their new products to the attention of potential early adopters, particularly those with opinion leader characteristics.

Learning Objectives

After reading the chapter the student should understand:

- The main risks in developing new products

- The organizational structures used in managing new-product development

- The new-product-development process

- The consumer-adoption process

Chapter Outline

I. Introduction—categories of new products:new to the world products, new product lines, additions to existing product lines, improvements and revisions of existing products, repositionings, cost reductions

II. Challenges in new-product development

    A. Companies that fail to develop new products put themselves at risk; at the same time new product development is risky

    B. Factors that hinder new-product development:

        1. Shortage of important ideas in certain areas
        2. Fragmented markets
        3. Social and governmental constraints
        4. Cost of development
        5. Capital shortages

6. Faster required development time

7. Short product life cycles

III. Organizational arrangements—successful new-product development requires top management commitment and planning

A. Budgeting for new-product development

B. Organizing new-product development: new-product managers, venture teams, "skunkworks," stage-gate system for innovation

C. Managing the new-product development process: ideas come from a variety of sources

1. Idea generation—ideas—idea generating techniques

a) Interacting with others (attribute listing, forced relationships, morphological analysis, reverse assumption analysis, new contexts, mind-mapping

b) Idea screening—not all ideas can be pursued, but must be sent to a committee where they are considered either: promising, marginal, or a reject

(1) Themes: idea manager, idea committee, drop-error, go error

(2) Risks of either accepting a bad idea or rejecting a good one

IV. Managing the development process: concept to strategy

A. Concept development

1. Attractive ideas must be refined into testable product concepts

2. A product concept is an elaborate version of the idea expressed in meaningful consumer terms

B. Concept testing

1. Product concepts should be presented to an appropriate group of target consumers to gauge their reactions

2. Customer-driven engineering is an engineering effort that attaches high importance to incorporating customer preferences in the final design. Consumer preferences can be measured through conjoint analysis

C. Conjoint analysis—deriving the utility values that consumers attach to varying levels of a product's attributes (See Applications exercises)

D. Marketing-strategy—development of preliminary marketing strategy plan:

1. Target size, structure and behavior, positioning, sales, share, profits

2. Planned price, distribution strategy, marketing budget

3. Long run sales, profit goals and mix strategy

E. Business analysis—performing sales, cost and profit projections on the proposed product to determine satisfaction of company objectives

1. Estimating total sales—sum of three different types of sales (first-time, replacement, repeat) must yield a satisfactory profit

2. Estimating costs and profits—illustrated in the text

V. Managing the development process: development to commercialization

A. Product development

1. Represents a substantial jump in investment. Product continues to move through functional and consumer tests

2. Techniques for measuring consumer preferences—simple rank-order method, paired comparison, and monadic-rating

B. Market testing

 1. Consumer-goods market testing—least costly to most costly

  a) Sales-wave research—consumers who initially try the product at no cost are re-offered the product, or a competitor's product, at slightly reduced prices

  b) Simulated store technique—consumers are questioned about brand familiarity and preferences, shown advertisements, given a small amount of money and sent to a mock store where there purchases are recorded and analyzed

  c) Controlled test marketing—organizations work with a panel of stores willing to test market a product for a fee

  d) Test markets—organizations choose entire market areas in which to introduce their products

C. Business-goods market testing—testing also offers benefits. Examples of testing are alpha, beta and trade show

 1. Commercialization—contract to manufacture, marketing (sequenced mix of marketing tools)

 2. When (timing)—first entry, late entry, parallel entry

 3. Where (geographical strategy), single market, many markets, national

 4. To whom (target-market prospects)—identifying prime prospects

 5. How (introductory market strategy)—involves many activities

VI. The consumer-adoption process—how do potential customers learn about new products, try them, and adopt or reject them? Followed by a consumer-loyalty process

A. Stages in the adoption process (awareness, interest, evaluation, trial, adoption)

 1. Factors influencing the adoption process—people differ markedly in their readiness to try new products

  a) Readiness to try new products (Rogers adopter groups: innovators, early adopters, opinion leaders, early majority, late majority, laggards)

  b) Personal influence—varies but more impact on late adopters products

  c) Characteristics of the innovation

   (1) Relative advantage, comparability, complexity, divisibility, communicability

   (2) Also risk and uncertainty, scientific credibility, social approval

  d) Organizations' readiness to adopt innovations—various based on variables in the organization's environment (community organization itself, public opinion)

VII. Summary

Lecture—Developing New Products: When and How?

This lecture is intended for use with Chapter 12, "Developing New Market Offerings." The discussion focuses on new product development strategy in a marketing setting.

Teaching Objectives

- To stimulate students to think about the critical issues, pro and con, for a firm when it considers new product development strategy

- Points to consider in evaluating new products

- Role of new product development strategies and policies in helping the firm achieve a balanced position in utilizing effectively what is there and what should be on the horizon for the future

Discussion

Introduction—Whether or Not to Develop a New Product

A strategy for new product development is one of the most important activities for any firm in the contemporary marketplace. Reasons for this include the fact that if the firm does not obsolete its own products, a competitor will obsolete them. In creating a new product approach and strategy, there are some very important questions to consider in the process. Throughout the effort, it is useful to remember that a good idea may not be a good investment.

For example, one of the most important but overlooked questions is: Is there a current need for the product? This question may appear obvious, because the text has focused heavily on developing a clear understanding of the need for a customer-oriented and integrated marketing concept and orientation. However, for firms in the middle of many daily problems and crises, it is sometimes difficult to get beyond the challenge of staying alive in business by concentrating on currently available products.

Another important question relates to the size of the market. Is it big enough for the company and its current or future competitors to operate in and make a profit? This appears to be an easy question to deal with, especially with all of the research available on the Internet and many other readily available resources. However, here again we find that most firms take a local and narrow product specific perspective without thinking where the future might lead, and the competition that can come from within, or even outside, the product category.

Other questions include the number and types of customers that the firm plans to target, as well as the attitudes of the potential customers toward the product category. Each of these activities requires looking beyond the obvious and general descriptions of people and numbers, and toward sources such as Markets and Audits, Predicasts, Simmons and A.C. Nielsen, and many regional research firms. (See Analytical Exercises)

Not only is the size of the market a major issue, but the firm should consider how much of the market it can capture (%), whether the volume is attractive and whether the firm can be the best in the market or likely will be a quality or value follower. These are important issues that if ignored could lead to numerous problems down the road. Likewise, it is important to note whether the market for the product category is growing or declining. This can be a critical indicator because it indicates the amount and type of inertia the firm will have to deal with in the marketplace.

Deciding How to Develop New Products

The strongest possible one-to-one marketing role for a firm is to constantly tailor new products to the tastes and needs of individual consumers. The routine, cost-efficient customization of products, referred to as "mass customization," is an increasingly efficient manufacturing activity, made possible by the same information processing advances that make tracking individual customer relationships possible.

Mass customizers use computer-controlled production processes to manufacture individually customized products, combining any of a wide array of production capabilities. However, to be successful, they must also put in place an efficient mechanism for learning an individual customer's product specifications before manufacturing a product for that customer. As a result, there is an intrinsic link between mass customization and interactive, one-to-one marketing.

The population of successful mass customizers is growing rapidly and will continue to grow. There are companies that mass customize bicycles, automobiles, windows, bathing suits, and greeting cards. Motorola mass customizes pagers. Custom Clothing Technology Corporation has a system for mass customizing blue jeans for Levi Strauss. So why not soup, or paper towels, or dry cereal? If you want raisins and nuts in your Cheerios today, you have to mix them in yourself. General Mills cannot accommodate you, for a number of very good reasons:

- First, they have not yet incorporated mass-customization technology into their dry-cereal production process.

- Second, even if they were to do so, they have no efficient way to distribute a mass-customized cereal to individual consumers through supermarkets, and if they were to distribute directly, it might poison their relations with their current distribution network.

- Third, they have no mechanism at present to gather preferences and specifications from individual consumers. Why should they? They cannot use the feedback anyway. Feedback from an individual is not useful if you cannot act on it. In the interactive, one-to-one future the only way to be successful as a packaged-goods manufacturer will be to mass customize.

Mass customization provides a platform for sustaining a direct relationship with the consumer. The alternatives may increase as brands are reduced in importance, and more traditional packaged-goods companies will have to shift to commodity manufacturing. Today these firms are bidding against each other to be the lowest-cost supplier to the retailers as well as other relationship gatekeepers that are closest to the consumer and, in many ways, are key to consumer demand.

The Basis of Future New Product Planning and Development

Clearly, the strength of any marketer in the one-to-one future will be measured not by brand equity alone, but by customer equity. We can quibble over the question of who should or will succeed in owning this interactive consumer, whether it is a delivery service, the store, or the mass customizer, but one thing should be very clear: one-size-fits-all advertising and mass marketed new products will be reduced to relatively meaningless roles.

Some truly mass products or services like McDonald's, or Madonna CDs, or Diet Pepsi is promoted to everyone the same way because part of their attraction is that they are predictably the same. Among other benefits, they help consumers fit in. People are social animals, and some products are socially unifying experiences. The Super Bowl, the Academy Awards, and the last episode of *Friends* or *Seinfeld* are popular partly because they represent shared experiences. The same is true for a wide variety of products and services, from blue jeans to bikes.

For expensive, high-involvement products, "one-to-one marketing" refers to deliberate alliances between marketers and their customers, designed to invite the customer into deeper and ever more collaborative relationships. Such relationships will reward customers with tailored products, customized services, and personalized communications. However, for routine, low-involvement products, especially those bought with a regular frequency, such as packaged goods, "one-to-one marketing" will provide the customer with convenience-automating, and even anticipating a customer's everyday needs.

In the next generation, it is likely that many of today's great packaged-goods brand names simply will not be around. The mass marketing of packaged goods will be nearly supplanted by one-to-one marketing (on-line and otherwise), with totally new services acting as "stores without storefronts" for the benefit of individual consumers, and totally new manufacturing companies mass customizing their products, again for the benefit of individual consumers. To conclude: as marketers give consumers more, they will demand more. That is the way it is and will continue to be well into the twenty-first century.

Marketing and Advertising

1.   The ad in Figure 1 introduces a new blend of seasonings from Mrs. Dash, along with a recipe in which it can be used. The inset showing ripe tomatoes, fresh basil leaves, and garlic cloves highlights the flavors featured in the new product, one in a line of other seasoning blends.

    a.   How could this idea have been described as a product concept during the product-development process? Suggest an appropriate concept statement.

    b.   What forms of consumer testing would be appropriate for this seasoning product? Why?

    c.   Which of the four consumer-goods market-testing methods do you think Mrs. Dash should have used to gauge consumer reaction prior to launching this product? Explain your answer.

Answer

    a.   Students may suggest differing product concepts based on the ad's description of this seasoning blend and on the product label, which includes the key phrase "salt free." One sample concept statement would be: A tasty blend of seasonings for adults who want to minimize salt intake.

    b.   Mrs. Dash's marketers could test this product concept by allowing consumers to read the concept statement, examine a prototype jar, and even taste the product in a recipe during focus groups or other concept-testing research. In this way, marketers could determine consumer reaction to the concept and specific aspects of the offer (including the packaging and labeling). They can also determine whether consumers understand that the product is designed to offer a tasty seasoning alternative to salt.

    c.   Later in the product development process, the company may want to use simulating test marketing, controlled test marketing, or a full market test to gauge consumer reaction and make any needed adjustments before introducing this product.

2. Office furniture manufacturer Steelcase recently introduced the new product shown in Figure 2, an interactive sign system for managing meeting rooms.

    a. Into which of the six categories of new products does this sign system fit? Explain.

    b. In estimating total sales for the RoomWizard sign system, would Steelcase consider this a one-time purchase, an infrequently purchased product, or a frequently purchased product? What are the implications for the product life-cycle sales curve?

    c. Would Steelcase have benefited from alpha testing of this new product? What other market testing methods would you recommend for this product—and why?

Answer

    a. According to the ad, this is "the first Web-based system of interactive signs for managing meeting rooms." Therefore, it is a new-to-the-world product, creating an entirely new market.

    b. Steelcase should consider this a one-time purchase, because once a company has installed this sign system, it would not need to buy a similar product (although it might upgrade to a more sophisticated system in the future). Thus, the company cannot count on repeat purchases to drive the product life-cycle sales curve. Instead, it must base its estimates on first-time sales.

    c. Yes, Steelcase would have benefited from alpha testing its new product to identify both strengths and weaknesses and obtain internal feedback to improve the product before its introduction. Students may also suggest beta testing, among other testing methods, to gain experience in installing and training companies in the use of this kind of Web-based product, which depends on proper system connections.

3. **BONUS AD--See Companion Web site!** As this British ad shows, Ariel and Hoover have joined forces to advertise two new products, a washing machine with larger load capacity and a pouch of liquid laundry detergent.

    a. If you were creating a product-positioning map for Ariel Liqui-Tabs, what two dimensions would you include? Why are these dimensions important to consumers?

    b. What consumer needs are addressed by the new Hoover washing machine? What customer segment should Hoover be targeting for this new product?

    c. What are the advantages and disadvantages of Hoover and Ariel using joint advertising to introduce their new products?

Answer

    a. Students may suggest various dimensions for a product-positioning map for Ariel Liqui-Tabs, including: convenience, cost, ease of use, and cleaning effectiveness. Each of these dimensions is important to consumers evaluating detergents for home use.

    b. One need is to wash more effectively a larger load of laundry. Another is the need to more easily use the machine and plan laundry chores by watching the electronic display as a load progresses through the wash cycle. Students may cite other needs, as well. Hoover should probably target consumers with large families for this model.

   c.   Students may suggest various pros and cons. Some of the advantages of jointly advertising the washing machine and laundry detergent: (1) share the cost of reaching the same target market; (2) use the power of two well-known brands to introduce two new products. Some of the disadvantages: (1) risk that a poor consumer experience with one brand will cause a negative reaction to the other; (2) risk that consumers will be confused or tune the ad because there are too many brands and benefit points on which to focus.

Online Marketing Today

Intuit, which makes Quicken, QuickBooks, and other financial management software packages, is well known for applying customer-driven engineering in its new product development process. Many months before a new program is scheduled for release, the company invites individuals and business users to become beta testers of a "prerelease" version. Then Intuit's marketers and technical specialists ask beta testers to comment on all aspects of the software, including the ease of use and the value of the features.

Visit Intuit's Web site (www.intuit.com) and browse the home page. Follow any visible links to the beta testing page (located at http://beta.intuit.com/public/default.cfm) or use the search function to find the location if this page is not available through a direct link. Why would consumers and business customers want to participate in the beta testing of an Intuit software package? Why does Intuit impose restrictions on prospective beta testers? What does Intuit stand to gain from testers' feedback? How early in the development process do you think Intuit should start beta testing?

Answer

Consumers and business customers often want to be the first to try new products, because they enjoy the challenge of learning and they feel it gives them status. Many are so interested in improving products that they are willing to be testers and report on their observations and recommendations. Intuit imposes restrictions because it does not want competitors to learn about new features until a product is officially released. As a result, it screens prospective testers to be sure that they are not connected with any competing products.

Intuit stands to gain from testers' feedback in several ways: it will learn which features are valued, whether product operation is easy and intuitive, what additional features testers would like to see in future products, and what parts of the program testers don't like or can't easily use. Intuit cannot start beta testing until it has developed a working model of the product. However, it should probably invite beta testing as early as possible in the development process, so it has time to analyze feedback and refine features and operation.

You're the Marketer—Sonic PDA Marketing Plan

Product strategy is based on the choices companies make as they segment their markets, research and target customer groups and create an appropriate market positioning. With this foundation, marketers are ready to plan for new-product development and management.

You are considering Sonic's new product development options for its line of personal digital assistants (PDAs). In light of what you know about the company and the recommendations you have made so far in the marketing planning process, answer these questions to continue with the Sonic marketing plan:

What specific needs of the targeted customer segments should Sonic seek to profitably satisfy with a second PDA product?

Working alone or with other students, generate at least four ideas for new PDA products, and indicate the criteria Sonic should use to screen these ideas.

Develop the most promising idea into a product concept and explain how Sonic can test this concept. What particular dimensions must be tested?

Assuming that this idea has tested well, develop a marketing strategy for the introduction of the new product. Include a description of the target market; the product positioning; the estimated sales, profit, and market-share goals for the first year; your channel strategy; and the marketing budget you will recommend for this new product introduction. If possible, estimate Sonic's costs and conduct a break-even analysis.

Into which of the six categories of new products identified by Booz, Allen & Hamilton does Sonic's first PDA product fit? Into which of these categories does your suggested new product fit? What are the implications for Sonic's marketing plan?

As your instructor directs, summarize your ideas in a written marketing plan or enter them in the Marketing Mix, Marketing Research, Break-Even, Sales Forecast, Budgets Analysis, and Milestone sections of the *Marketing Plan Pro* software. Be sure to include your estimates of sales, profits, and budget requirements for the new product, along with a schedule for its introduction.

Answer

Sonic's weaknesses include a slightly heavier product and a monochrome screen. Its second product should therefore try to satisfy customer needs in a way that will address these two weaknesses. For example, customers need an easily portable device for communication and information exchange on the go. Making the second product a bit lighter would underscore Sonic's portability; offering a color screen would allow Sonic to better satisfy the Web-browsing needs of users. Students may suggest other needs to be satisfied, as well.

This is an excellent opportunity for students to be creative in thinking up new product ideas that will help Sonic meet its goals and objectives and compete more effectively. For example, one product might allow users to record memos of up to 30 seconds long. New product ideas can be screened through an idea committee and by rating against preset criteria. In addition, they may be tested by asking members of the targeted segments to consider the concept or handle a prototype, among other testing methods. Testing will help Sonic determine the portability and usability of a possible new product and examine reaction to specific features described in the concept, such as visibility of a color screen or quality of the recorded memos. The marketing strategy suggested by students should fit with the overall goals and ideas proposed in their marketing plans, including an examination of the costs and an appropriate break-even point.

The first Sonic PDA is a new product line for the company, because it entering an established market for the first time. The second Sonic PDA is an addition to an existing product line. Thus, Sonic must consider how the second product may cannibalize sales of the first product. It also must be sure that the second product is sufficiently differentiated from the first. Students may suggest additional issues for Sonic to consider.

Marketing Spotlight—3M

Minnesota Mining and Manufacturing (3M) fosters a culture of innovation and improvisation evident in its very beginnings. In 1904, the company's directors were faced with a failed mining operation, but they turned the leftover grit and wastage into a revolutionary new product: sandpaper. Today 3M makes more than 60,000 products, including sandpaper, as well as adhesives, computer disks, contact lenses, and optical films. Each year 3M launches scores of new products, and the company earns about 35 percent of revenues from products introduced within the past five years. The company regularly ranks among the top 10 U.S. companies each year in patents received. 3M has an annual R&D budget of $1 billion, which is a healthy portion of its annual $16.7 billion in sales.

3M has a long history of innovation. In addition to inventing sandpaper, the company has developed numerous product innovations in its 99-year history that were the first of their kind. Here is a brief timeline:

    1925—Scotch™ masking tape
    1930—Scotch™ transparent tape
    1939—First reflective traffic sign
    1956—Scotchgard™ fabric protector
    1962—Tartan Track™, first synthetic running track
    1979—Thinsulate™ thermal insulation
    1980—Post-it™ Notes
    1985—First re-fastening diaper tape
    1995—First nonchlorofluorocarbon aerosol inhaler
    2000—First laminating products that do not require heat

3M is able to consistently produce innovations in part because the company promotes a corporate environment that facilitates new discoveries. The following are some tactics 3M uses to ensure its culture remains focused on innovation:

3M encourages everyone, not just engineers, to become "product champions." The company's "15 percent rule" allows all employees to spend up to 15 percent of their time working on projects of personal interest. Products such as Post-it Notes, masking tape, and the company's microreplication technology developed because of 15 percent rule activities.

Each promising new idea is assigned to a multidisciplinary venture team headed by an "executive champion."

3M expects some failures and uses failed products as opportunities to learn how to make products that work. Its slogan is "You have to kiss a lot of frogs to find a prince."

3M hands out its Golden Step awards each year to the venture teams whose new products earned more than $2 million in U.S. sales or $4 million in worldwide sales within three years of commercial introduction.

In the late 1990s, 3M struggled as sales stalled and profits fell. The company restructured, shed several proprietary noncore businesses, and cut its work force. Because of these moves, 3M had record sales and income in 2000. When 3M named GE executive James McNerney its new chairman and CEO that year, he vowed he would continue to improve the company's bottom line while keeping its culture of innovation intact.

Sources: www.3m.com; 3M 2000 Annual Report.

Questions

1. How can 3M hold on to the notion of accepting failures to achieve the winners during recessionary times and shorter product life cycles (PLC)?

2. What changes would you make in the 3M marketing strategy if it became apparent that generic competitors were consistently able to copy the innovative 3M products?

3. How well has 3M applied the marketing concepts discussed in the text chapter?

Suggested Responses

1. With its vaunted positive attitude toward accepting failure on the way to successful new products, it appears that 3M will be able to continue the remarkable stream of new product developments. Firms such as 3M operate above the day-to-day recession and shorter PLC issues, focused more on achieving product innovations and improvements than responding to economic conditions.

2. Possibly to look more toward marketing organizational and supportive improvements, along with ways to get closer to consumers and their needs. Because 3M constantly works to innovate out of and beyond its existing products (35 percent of their profits come from products introduced in the prior five years), copycats and generic competitors are assumed and of no particular consequence in the larger 3M product development picture.

3. It appears that 3M could be one of the prime examples for many of the concepts discussed in the text. They have the organizational culture, attitude of questioning and innovation, and the willingness to take risks that belie an organization that could and should succeed when others go astray while trying to take shortcuts to innovation. 3M's culture is so deep and positive that the company likely is happy to see competitors attempt to use keep up with 3M because it spurs 3M researchers and scientists on to find even more effective products. In addition, because 3M also owns many brand names, trademarks and patents, competitors will have to engage in costly efforts to work around the 3M legal protection.

Analytical Tools for Marketing Management—New Product Planning

Problems

Create a three-year payout plan based on the following information:

- The year one estimate for the number of cases sold is 8,000,000. Estimates indicate that the market will grow at a rate of 10 percent per year

- The average share estimated for year one is 10 percent; for year two it is estimated at 12 percent, and for year three, 20 percent.

- The distribution pipeline will purchase: .4 MM, .2 MM, and .1 MM for each of the three years. (MM = million)

- Factory income is $10 a case, and factory cost is $5 a case.

- At least 50percent of a three-year budget should be spent in year one. Year two should be 30 percent

- Advertising should receive 80percent, and sales promotion should receive 20percent of the budget in each of the three years.

Answer (See Student Materials and Interactive Spreadsheet for Details)

Three year payout plan:	1	2	3	Totals
1. Size of total market (in cases)	8,000,000	8,800,000	8,880,000	

	10%	12%	20%	
2. Average market share for new brand	10%	12%	20%	
3. Cases bought by pipeline	400,000	200,000	100,000	
4. Cases bought at consumer level	1,200,000	1,300,000	1,900,000	
5. Total shipments from factory	1,600,000	1,500,000	2,000,000	
6. Factory sales (based on input price)	$12,000,000	$13,000,000	$19,000,000	
7. Less cost per case (input)	$6,000,000	$6,500,000	$9,500,000	
8. Dollars available for promotion and advertising	$6,000,000	$6,500,000	$9,500,000	$22,000,000
9. Reallocation of dollars	11,000,000	6,600,000	4,400,000	$22,000,000
10. Percent of total dollar	50.0%	30.0%	20.0%	100.0%
11. Allocation of dollars: To advertising (80%)	$8,800,000	$5,300,000	$3,500,000	$17,600,000
To sales promotion (15%)	$2,200,000	$1,300,000	$900,000	$4,400,000
12. Profit (or Loss)	($5,000,000)	($100,000)	$5,100,000	
13. Cumulative investment	($5,000,000)	($5,100,000)	$0	

The creator of this plan estimated that the investment could be paid back in three years. Other plans for other products may indicate payback sooner or later. Everything depends on the market dynamics and the resulting sales estimates.

Explanation of Payout Plan (line by line):

Size of the market: Market sizes can be described in people, dollars, ounces, pounds, or cases. Cases used here.

Average share estimates: An important line because if estimates are too high, and market share does not develop, then the plan may have to be changed quickly and realistically.

Year-end market share: Also an important estimate, but it is not used in the calculations.

Pipeline (or channel) sales are the first factory sales. Represents sales to distributors, wholesalers, and retailers.

Cases sold at the consumer level calculated by multiplying the average share by total market size.

Total factory sales: The sum of pipeline plus consumer sales .

Factory sales price: 12 per case times the total factory sales (units).

The cost per case ($7) is multiplied by the number of cases sold to indicate profit. This amount subtracted from factory sales. The result is the dollar amount available for advertising and sales promotion.

Dollars available for advertising and promotion: Note that the increasing availability runs counter to the need to have more funds available in the first year to create brand recognition and market positioning.

The *reallocation of dollars* available is redistributed in a more logical (market-directed) manner. The advertising/promotion budget set higher and smaller amounts in the next two years. This allows the brand to receive more emphasis in the first year.

Percent of total dollar sales: Reflects the reallocation percentages. The brand will not make enough money the first year to earn the budgeted allocation. As a result, the company must make an investment in the brand during year one. The year two investment shows up as a loss in line 13. In year two the company must invest an additional $700,000 in the brand.

Allocation to Advertising: Budget for year one is 43 percent of the three-year total, and years 2 and 3 allocated accordingly. The allocation to sales promotion (separated from advertising) also increased according to the marketing needs of the brand.

Profit/loss: Although the brand has a loss in the first year, in year two the loss is considerably less than year one, and the brand owes the total payout (payback) for year three.

Cumulative Investment: By year three the brand's sales are sufficient to pay back the cumulative investment. In year four, the brand should make a profit.

Chapter 13—Designing Global Market Offerings

Overview

Companies can no longer focus only on their domestic market, no matter how large the market. Many industries are global industries, and their leading firms achieve lower costs and higher brand awareness. Protectionist measures can only slow down the invasion of superior goods; the best company defense is a sound global offense. At the same time, global marketing is risky due to shifting borders, unstable governments, foreign exchange problems, technological pirating, high product- and communication-adaptation costs, and other factors. The steps in going international include:

1. Understand the international marketing environment, particularly the international trade system. In considering a particular foreign market, the firm must assess the economic, political, legal, and cultural characteristics.

2. Consider what proportion of foreign to total sales to seek, whether to do business in a few or many countries, and what types of countries to enter.

3. Decide which particular markets to enter, and this calls for evaluating the probable rate of return on investment against the level of risk.

4. Decide how to enter each attractive market. Many companies start as indirect or direct exporters and then move to licensing, joint ventures, and finally direct investment; this company evolution has been called the internationalization process.

5. Decide on the extent to which the product, promotion, price, and distribution should be adapted to individual foreign markets.

6. Develop an effective organization for pursuing international marketing. Most firms start with an export department and graduate to an international division. A few become global companies, which means that top management plans and organizes on a global basis.

Learning Objectives

After reading the chapter the student should understand:

*   The importance of international markets
*   The riskiness of international markets
*   How to make international marketing decisions
*   Differing entry strategies
*   Differing marketing organizations

Chapter Outline

I.   Introduction: competing on a global basis

II.   Deciding whether to go abroad—consider factors that might draw a company into the international arena

      A.   Pro—global exposure, counterattack to home attacks, higher profits/margins for international, reduce dependence, international servicing domestic customers

B.   Con—understand overseas preferences, foreign business culture, underestimate foreign regulations and costs, lack managers with international experience, commercial laws/currency/political/expropriation problems

III.   Deciding which markets to enter—firm should define its international objectives and policies

    A.   How many markets to enter

    B.   Regional free trade zones

        1.   the European union

        2.   NAFTA

        3.   Mercosul

    C.   Evaluating potential markets

        1.   Where to start—psychic proximity

        2.   Risk variables—high rank on market attractiveness, low in market risk, competitive advantage

IV.   Deciding how to enter the market

    A.   Indirect and direct export

        1.   Indirect—work through independent intermediaries to export products

        2.   Direct—company handles its own exports, through a domestic department, overseas sales branch, traveling reps, or foreign-based distributors/agents

    B.   Licensing—sell a foreign company the rights to your manufacturing process, trademark, patent, trade secret, etc., for a fee

    C.   Joint ventures—join with local investors to share ownership and control

    D.   Direct investment—direct ownership of foreign-based operations

    E.   Internationalization process:

        1.   No regular export activities

        2.   Export via independent reps

        3.   Establishment of one or more sales subsidiaries

        4.   Establishment of production facilities abroad

V.   Deciding on the Marketing Program

    A.   Product—straight extension, product adaptation, product invention

    B.   Promotion—communication (promotion) adaptation, dual (product and promotion) adaptation

    C.   Price—uniform price, market-based price, cost-based price

    D.   Place (distribution channels)—links include seller's international marketing headquarters, channels between nations, and channels within nations

VI.   Deciding on the marketing organization

    A.   Export department—firm ships goods to other countries.

    B.   International division—firm becomes involved in several international markets and ventures

    C.   Global organization—firm no longer thinks of itself as a national marketer, all management and staff are involved in worldwide pursuits

VII.   Summary

Lecture 1—Winning in the Global Consumer Marketplace

This lecture and discussion focuses on product development strategy in a global marketing setting.

Teaching Objectives

- To stimulate students to think about the critical issues, pro and con, for a firm when it considers international or global market development
- Points to consider in evaluating global markets
- The role of global marketing strategies and policies in helping the firm achieve a balanced international corporate and brand strategy and to plan possible actions for the future

Discussion

Introduction and Background—the Global Shaving Legacy

Gillette, the $10 billion Boston-based consumer products giant, has for more than 100 years built a corporate culture around finding better ways to remove unwanted hair from human beings. In addition, Gillette is as much a part of the American lifestyle as Campbell Soup and Coca-Cola.

Gillette also sells Duracell batteries, Braun appliances and Parker pens around the world. Still, blades and razors are the bedrock of Gillette's global branding effort. Like other great marketers, Gillette simply knows its customers better than its competitors. It tests, measures and rates products and preferences ceaselessly around the world.

The company has parlayed its focus on its marketplace, and its unmatched ability to forecast what men and women will buy, into a 72 percent market share in both the United States and Europe. This dominance is born from a relentless pursuit of better shaving technologies, a willingness to invest whatever is required to manufacture its products effectively, with an integrated marketing strategy that works everywhere.

BLADE HISTORY

- In 1971, Gillette dramatically changed the shaving marketplace when it introduced TracII, the first twin-blade razor with two parallel blade edges housed in a single cartridge.

- With Atra in 1977, Gillette increased performance and pressed its "comfort and closeness" marketing line with an innovative pivoting head. During the same time period, Gillette fought with Bic, the French company that developed Good News, the first twin-bladed disposable.

- By the mid-1980s, with disposable razors taking up a whopping 50 percent of the market, Gillette executives decided to break out of what they saw as a dead-end strategy. With disposables, the razor had become a commodity, and the buying decision was based solely on price and convenience. For a company like Gillette, this was a debilitating situation.

- Gillette needed a differentiator, a product upon which the brand could be elevated and market share substantially increased. Rather than compete on the existing playing field, Gillette simply created a new category, the shaving system, and took control of it while at the same time eroding the market share of the disposables category.

- In 1990, after 10 years of research and development, Gillette introduced the Sensor twin-blade shaving system. As with TracII and Atra, the blade cartridges were disposable. But there was more. With blades mounted on springs that allowed the razor to adjust to a man's face as he shaved, Sensor raised the shaving bar to new heights. The shave really was better—significantly better. The design not only produced markedly closer shaves but also brought Gillette out of the disposables morass and back into an indisputable leadership position.

Gillette, never a firm to rest on its laurels, decided that if two blades could produce a close shave, three blades could do even better. In order to insure that consumers would not simply scoff at three blades as a marketing gimmick, the shave had to be demonstrably better. The goal: "The closest shave ever in fewer strokes—with less irritation."

Like other great marketing companies, Gillette acknowledges that product quality is the core value proposition around which everything else swirls. "If you have a significantly and demonstrably superior product or service, it really is quite meaningful."

"Procter & Gamble has traded on the same concept. When they introduce a new and improved product, it really is new and improved. It really solves a personal problem. What Gillette has done is develop a new technology that worked. The tougher task is getting people to try it."

Many superior technologies have slipped away, unnoticed and unrewarded, in the history of consumer products. At Gillette, gaining consumers' confidence is an art form. Getting them to try a new product and offering a "reason to believe" has never been better orchestrated than with Mach 3. The first and most important step is creating a clear value proposition for the consumer.

New Product Goals

For a new product that a firm wishes to take global, the value proposition has to be compelling, succinct and easily understood by a vast consumer base around the world. The value has to be there for a wide cross section of shavers, from the serious system user to the disposables user. It has to work for the blue-collar worker in Des Moines as well as the executive in Milan.

Not surprisingly, men around the world crave the same thing: a close, clean, comfortable shave without nicks and cuts. Most men take between 100 and 500 strokes when they shave, often going over the same area again and again. So a bridge was needed to get from the idea of a close shave to a less irritating shave. Add to that mix the disposables user, who values the quickness of a shave

Accordingly, the Gillette value proposition, a proposition that sounded so simple and obvious, was in fact a "Eureka" revelation inside Gillette. With this statement, all marketing efforts would have a common foundation upon which to build. Gillette could not only woo its own Sensor Excel customers to move up, but it could also grab market share among disposables users.

"If you don't put it into language that gives a promise of something better, people won't try it," says a Gillette manager. "But if you can create an appeal that gets them to try the product, the product will sell itself."

- Enter the Mach 3—before the Sensor

In May1994, several months before Gillette shipped the highly successful Sensor Excel razor in the United States, marketing plans were already under way for the product that would succeed the Sensor Excel. That month, four Gillette marketing executives met with B.B.D.O., the firm's advertising agency, to set the marketing agenda for a new razor that would render Sensor Excel all but obsolete. That new razor, which would later be named Mach 3, was introduced with the attendant fanfare in the summer of 1998.

- Marketing Lessons from the Razor Business

At Gillette, there is no such concept as getting ahead of yourself. New products go on the drawing board as much as a decade before they are introduced. When it comes to blades and razors,

Gillette is not content with merely having an innovative product. The company has also turned marketing into a quantitative science, pouring time and resources into marketing plans that are almost military in their precision and implementation.

- Mach 3 and the Global Market

The Mach 3 shaving system is a blend of leading-edge technology and constant consumer testing; it took seven years and $750 million to develop. The first industrial design of the sleek new razor existed in 1993.

The product was named two full years before it was first shipped. The efforts were so secretive that the directors, including billionaire and major shareholder Warren E. Buffett, were not allowed to see the product until nine months before its launch.

Gillette has poured another $300 million into marketing the new product, making Mach 3 the world's only billion-dollar razor, but the results soon were off the chart. Sales of the Mach 3 far surpassed Sensor and Sensor Excel, and both of those razors dominated the market in their day, and exceeded even Gillette's lofty expectations. Despite the skepticism of some in the financial press, who felt the new razor was gimmicky and too expensive, in just six months Mach 3 became the top-selling razor and blade in North America and Europe. If success can be choreographed, Gillette has done it.

Going Global

Gillette's vaunted marketing machine is actually the sum of many parts, all tied inextricably together by time-honored traditions within the company. The goal of the Horizon Committee, for example, is capture the future, looking five to 20 years ahead for what the hair removal experience is likely to be. Even today, Gillette is looking beyond wet shaving to lasers and other forms of technology for potential products.

To Gillette's chief executive, the company looks at the world "as one nation," and global product positioning is expected and required. The Mach 3 gave Gillette a distinct advantage; the company had essentially been there before. The company's experience with both the Sensor and the Sensor Excel created a template for the manufacturing and global market and promotion of a shaving system. Sensor was so successful that had turned the company's earnings around and set off a string of straight profitable quarters at Gillette. The lessons were clear:

Because the product would probably take off immediately, manufacturing had to insure that it had enough capacity to avoid shortages at the outset.

To facilitate a smooth global introduction of all packaging, point of sale and other promotional and support material had to be the same, simply translated into 30 languages for other geographies.

In the same vein, all marketing and advertising was based on a single campaign released in every market, with only minor local adjustments and translations.

Pricing needed a built-in elasticity, but by carefully testing the concept with consumers, Gillette fixed a profitable price point based on the expected number of blades per user per year.

Planning the 4 Ps

The plans were thorough, coordinated and highly secretive. Like a military strike, a global introduction had to be carefully planned and orchestrated to be successful. Gillette had introduced Sensor in all of its markets in just 18 months. But Mach 3 would be completely introduced around the globe in less than one year.

For Gillette, the faster the product is in the market globally, the faster existing Gillette customers will trade up to the new product and the faster new users will be drawn from competitors. Such quick-strike thinking not only leads to better financial results, but prevents competitors from thwarting Gillette's efforts in remote markets before the product is shipped.

They had many name options, such as Vector, Synchro and Triad. But the eventual name had to work as well in Germany and Latin America as it did in North America. Thousands of one-on-one interviews around the world with consumers confirmed that the name Mach 3 would fly. Keeping it a secret became a CIA–like operation, with all executives required to sign confidentiality agreements—telling spouses was strictly verboten—and no one was exempt.

By 1996, specific plans started to come together. The task force drew up advertising budgets, capital costs, sampling costs and formulas for achieving more profit per user per year. In this manner, Gillette developed the strategic business plans for 1997 and eventually 1998.

Gillette has always carefully tracked blade usage. With the Atra razor, men used an average of 30 to 32 blades a year. The number dropped to the high 20's with Sensor, and, because of its superior performance, the number was expected to drop even more for Mach 3. Based on these estimates, the company set out pricing strategies.

Based on the success of Sensor, priced at a 25 percent premium over the previous offering, Gillette was extremely aggressive in its pricing for Mach 3. Mach 3 was priced 35 percent higher than Sensor Excel—at $6.49 to $6.99 for the razor and a similar increase for blades, but consumers did not blink. In their consumer-use test study, they asked questions about what consumers would be willing to pay. As they increased the price, the preference actually improved. That was a first.

Global Marketing—Advertising/Packaging/Promotion

To orchestrate the product unveiling successfully, Gillette followed strict guidelines about all advertising, marketing and promotion. Everything from packaging to point-of-sale displays to retail sales guidelines was created with a single audience in mind rather than individual geographies.

All packaging, point-of-sale displays and support materials were the same around the world. The color scheme, an aqua green, and all typefaces and design elements are also the same. Mach 3 packages from Spain, Germany, Britain and Italy were identical except for the language on the package. The company purposely keeps the number of words on the front of the package to a minimum to avoid the need for design alterations to the packaging.

Gillette knows its markets intimately. For countries like Italy and Spain, where many stores are small, Gillette created a special display for the Mach 3. More than 100,000 of these displays were sold in the first six months after the premiere.

Even the television and radio advertising is the same. A single Mach-3 television commercial used in all countries. Though some local production had to be done in certain markets, the commercial is essentially the same everywhere—male models have to have faces that are "acceptable" in all regions.

By creating a single look and feel to the entire global campaign, the Mach 3 achieved a branded look almost instantaneously. A believer in big-budget advertising, Gillette seeks to surround the consumer with its message, embracing every medium, from television to billboards to the Internet. It stepped up its public relations efforts for Mach 3 and received 10 times as many mentions in the media, called share of voice, for the product rollout as it had for Sensor.

To obtain share of voice in certain key markets they know they have to do things different. For example, they spent more in Italy than Germany. The Italian market is much more devoted to disposable razors, so they concentrated more media in Italy. With Sensor, Gillette used basically a television plan, with heavy television advertising. With Mach 3, they used more print, outdoor, radio and the Internet. It was more of a multifaceted media effort.

As a result, the Mach 3 will be "advertising driven" for its first two years and then, as the product becomes entrenched in the marketplace, advertising efforts will slow while a sampling campaign commences. Research shows that 75 percent of Mach 3 sales go to Sensor Excel users who are moving up to the new product.

To win over disposable users, sampling is crucial. From their focus groups they learned that many customers are dedicated disposable users until they receive a Sensor in the mail.

What Is Next—Another Winner?

By early 1999, Mach 3 blew away the skeptics and became the type of whirlwind success that product developers and marketers dream about. The Mach 3 easily supplanted the Sensor Excel as the No.1 brand on the market. In fact, it took Sensor two years to reach the sales level that Mach 3 achieved in six months.

Mach 3 razors already have a 15 percent market share in the United States and as much as 17 percent in Italy. It took Sensor two full years to reach that market share.

Gillette expected a 20 percent to 30 percent market share for Mach 3 razors and blades over the next two years, and it now sells more than a billion blades annually around the world. For a follow-up, Gillette recognized an opportunity to move Mach 3 into the women's market, much as it did with Sensor.

In a competitive global economy, Gillette understands that every consumer it can get to try a new product sooner is one less customer who is likely to get away.

Possible Discussion Questions

- What makes Gillette so good? Innovation or execution?

- Does Gillette follow or create markets?

- What are the primary marketing tools behind Gillette's success?

Lecture 2—Making Decisions in a Complicated International Marketplace

This lecture focuses on development data required for making decisions needed to achieve various international marketing strategy goals and objectives. The format utilized here will assist student learning in the domestic as well as international marketing environment.

It is critically important today to prepare thoroughly before attempting to tackle the global marketplace. There are many difficulties in finding useful data for making international marketing decisions. The prospects, however, for the medium- and long-term global marketing environment make it almost impossible for a firm that is serious about the future to ignore the international market.

Teaching Objectives

- To stimulate students to think about the critical issues in international marketing analysis and research

- Points to consider and steps to take in proceeding with a global marketing data acquisition program

- Become more aware of specific marketing policy and strategy planning needs in the international marketplace

Discussion

Introduction

During the 1950s and 1960s, market research became increasingly important in the U.S. marketplace. Businesses started to rely heavily on market research to make decisions about asset allocation. Businesses today are at that same point in the international market. Many firms, however, remain hesitant and uncertain about how to define and enter the international market. This is where international marketing research enters the process. The bottom line for any business is resource allocation. Knowledge about where potential market growth exists, and understanding the consumers in those markets, is the foundation for making solid decisions about international market resource allocation.

Most companies realize that going global is more important than ever before and that they can no longer avoid it. In order to be successful in the global marketplace, firms need a global strategy. That strategy must enable them to assess global opportunities, carry out distribution and advertising, and maintain a tracking system to evaluate their efforts. International market research is the key to the development of global strategies.

International Research for Developing Global Marketing Strategy

For the firm that has a research department that is knowledgeable about international research and large enough to do the necessary coordination among countries, evaluating a new international marketing opportunity is not a big deal.If the firm does not, however, have this capability, it must either turn to a marketing research firm with familiarity and experience in the global market, or it has to develop the capability in-house. Because international research is expensive and because of the cost of making a mistake can be even more expensive, this is an important decision.

There are more differences than similarities between international and domestic market research, so it is appropriate to consider the differences first. Most of the differences occur in the up-front stages of the research process rather than in the execution. Obtaining consensus within the firm on several key questions is the first step. These questions include: What is the problem? How should the problem be approached? What kind of research should be used? What is the research design and how do we utilize the research? Who pays for the research within the company?

These are just a few of the critical issues that must be addressed before taking on a major international research effort.

The Design Stage and Data Development

The design stage is first substantive step. Here the sponsor company can think "domestically" because just as when the firm is conducting research in the United States, the focus should be on what it wants to accomplish, overall, in the program. Clearly, these design decisions are critical to achieve the project goals. There is no easy answer here, and each project will vary considerably.

In order for it to be comparable, international research must be standardized in terms of concepts and issues. This can be accomplished by having one central coordinator design and analyze the data across countries. Another way to keep data and analysis consistent across countries is to have a "traveling" focus group leader, one person who leads the focus groups in all of the study countries. Another option is to have one person who is involved in all the group interviews. Either of these options can be expensive and difficult to implement, but they are worthwhile in the long run.

Of course, the fewer the number of countries involved in the research design, the more focused the results. The firms, however, must go where the problem exists. If the goal is to know more about consumers in Japan, then the research must be done in Japan.

Conducting Research Across Boundaries

There are considerable differences between international qualitative and quantitative research. When doing qualitative research internationally, it is important to be very careful about the composition of focus groups. In most countries outside the United States, there are clear distinctions and rules of behavior between income levels, age groups, and even gender. Accordingly, in a mixed group, younger people are likely to defer to older people, and women are likely to defer to men. Developing a mixed focus group is something that firms generally do not have to worry about in the United States, but in international research the best results occur only if participants are of similar demographic backgrounds.

There are other cultural differences that complicate qualitative research. For example, the interviewer must always be alert to "yea saying." In many cultures, it is considered discourteous to disagree or to speak openly. As a result, respondents will try to figure out what they think the interviewer or the sponsor company wants to hear, and give that as their response. On the other hand, in some countries such as Norway, you will always get a response. Culturally, there is no such thing as "no answer," and that response will always be honest, no matter what.

Quantitative research also can become complicated in the international marketing environment. Questions about brand preference, or how much and how often a consumer buys a certain product, just do not apply in the former Eastern Bloc countries. Those countries are still struggling with shortages of goods, so people will buy what they can, when they can.

International Marketing Research as a Career Field

It is a specialized field now and will remain so for quite some time because of the number of new developing countries. In these emerging economies, good research will be a nightmare, and expensive. The challenges in international research are enormous and complex, but if the firm is aware of them, knows about them in advance, builds them into the corporate planning and coordination effort, keeps an open mind, and listens to the locals. At this point, the problems can be addressed and execution carried off effectively.

International Data Sources in the Twenty-first Century

Deciding which markets to enter abroad requires much information and a willingness to accept risk. To reduce the risk, it is appropriate to develop a number of international data sources. There are several proprietary (and expensive) international databases, but the National Trade Data Bank (U.S. Dept. of Commerce), the United Nations and the Organization of Exporting Developed Countries (OEDC) are among the better, and more reasonably priced, sources.

Use of the Internet and other on-line or CD ROM capabilities makes the search much easier than before. International marketing research, however, generally cannot be done entirely on the Internet and requires intensive analysis of many different information sources and formats, on-line and in print. In addition, there are diverse locations for various information sources. This is especially true with the development of marketing decision support systems. The objective of such systems is to collect, interpret, and present data for international marketing research, and the results are far superior to what they were even a few years ago.

An international decision support system operates on the basis that firms need a decision-making tool to work from the information collected inside and outside the firm as to the market and the competitive environment. Various universities and research organizations have international marketing decision support systems and expert systems to help the prospective exporter and international marketer research the global marketplace. Schools such as Michigan State, Indiana University and the University of Texas have developed these or similar programs.

There are four major steps in the international marketing decision support system research process:

- Determine basic data about the company and its product(s)

- Use import statistics to determine one or more countries with potential markets

- Analyze each of these countries in detail

- Evaluate each country and compare the results with other potential global markets

Expert systems provide an additional level of capability in international marketing research, enabling the researcher to minimize research time, provide access to a wide variety of information sources and apply expert knowledge to the data. Expert systems include literally hundreds or thousands of questions, but typically they address the following areas:

- Does the region, industry and/or firm have the ability to develop a "global" mentality or attitude?

- Does the product fit an identifiable international niche or market opportunity?

- Is the prospective or current firm willing to spend considerable time and effort to assess, test and cultivate the new international markets?

- Is the firm fully aware of its strengths and weaknesses compared to the competition it will find beyond the home environment?

Research Levels for Expert Systems

To implement this structure into an expert system, a fairly high level of detail will have to be specified. Each step focuses on a certain issue relevant for a country evaluation. The order is determined by interviewing several marketing experts. Every step should be interpreted as a research effort dealing with a unique issue. The steps should be structured from broad to more detailed research issues and to identify the different steps as "research levels". These issues or levels may include the following:

1.   General product assessment

2.   Specific product assessment

3.   Economic environment

4.   Socio/cultural environment

5.   Political and legal environment

6.   Geographic environment

7.   Export/import data and analysis

8.   Product marketability

9.   Trade shows opportunities

Research levels one and two are applied to screen different countries and regions to determine potential international markets. Levels three to six analyze specific issues regarding the foreign market. Levels seven and eight provide the researcher with detailed information about the foreign market, and level nine would include dates and addresses for trade shows and distributors.

Research Level Structure

Through the use of the different research and search levels, a general pattern of potential actions can be specified in order to ensure a successful end result. For each research level there are certain questions relating to the company and the product that will provide specific needed information. Before conducting country or regional research, information regarding the company and its products must be developed to ascertain the general situation in the foreign market. For example, product category and related information will enable the researcher to evaluate the tariff and legal considerations for the product in the target market.

After clarifying information needs, data can be retrieved based on the research level. Even if the task is clearly formulated, this step in the marketing research effort normally creates problems. The general question that has to be answered can be formulated to determine the location of information. The company internal database usually can to guide the user to the most valuable information sources. The different interfaces of the system can be used to access information directly through Internet, CD-ROM, fax, or on-line database services.

The next step includes the evaluation of the data to rank the countries on a scale from very export favorable to export unfavorable. After retrieving the appropriate detailed information to make a final evaluation.

The researcher can evaluate different topics during the search and calculate an overall ranking score for each country. By summarizing the information about a target market into a single number, different countries can be compared easily. Weighting the various factors compensates differences in location or history. All entered and retrieved data is stored in a format that allows the user to stop and start the research as many times as necessary. The system also provides the functionality to create a final report.

The planning approach and supporting database works on the premise that effective data collection and analysis will enable firms to assess international trade potential by first applying an importance weight and a ranking to each of the internal and external business considerations related to the region. Following this step the researcher could sum the scores before working with the company to make a decision on where to place its global marketing priorities.

Marketing and Advertising

1. Kellogg's ready-to-eat breakfast cereals are sold in many countries, including Germany, as the ad in Figure 1 shows. This ad highlights an in-package prize promotion rather than the taste or nutrition of the featured cereals. Kellogg's Frosties and Kellogg's Pops bear a strong resemblance to the U.S. products Kellogg's Frosted Flakes and Kellogg's Corn Pops.

    a. Neither Kellogg's Frosties Spice nor the cell-phone logos featured in this ad are available in the United States. Therefore, which of the five international product and promotion strategies does Kellogg's appear to be using?

    b. Which of the ten commandments of global branding are being applied in this ad? Why are these appropriate for Kellogg's international strategy?

c.   Can Kellogg be considered a global firm? Can ready-to-eat breakfast cereals be considered a global industry? Explain.

Answer

a.   Kellogg's is using dual adaptation, adapting both the product and the promotion to the German market. Frosties Spice is a variation of Frosted Flakes, and offering cell-phone logos in the package is a variation of other in-package prizes that Kellogg's has offered in the United States and other countries.

b.   Kellogg's understands the similarities in consumer behavior, because cereal eaters in many countries like to look for in-package prizes. It also is balancing standardization and customization by using the basic cereal adapted to local tastes and the basic packaging adapted to the local language and including local promotional copy and graphics. Finally, it is leveraging its valuable brand elements, including the look and color of the Kellogg's logo and trademarked cereal names, plus well-known brand mascots and identifiable graphics.

c.   Yes, Kellogg's can be considered a global firm, because it operates in numerous countries and creates production, marketing, R&D, reputation, and other advantages not available to single-country competitors. Ready-to-eat breakfast cereals can definitely be considered a global industry, because the relative positions of General Mills, Kellogg's, and other giant competitors are affected by their overall international operations and advantages.

2.   The ad in Figure 2 announces that HSBC, which is based in London, provides financial services (such as corporate banking, commercial lending, and personal banking) through 6,500 branches serving 29 million customers in 79 nations.

a.   Which distribution channels does HSBC have to use to make its financial services available to customers around the world?

b.   Do you think HSBC's financial services would tend to be more standardized or would they tend to require considerable adaptation for each country? Why?

c.   Does HSBC's global branch system represent a market entry strategy of licensing, joint venture, direct investment, or direct exporting?

Answer

a.   HSBC goes beyond its international headquarters in London to use its local branches as channels within foreign nations to reach financial services customers. This allows local customers to make deposits and withdrawals and use many other services that can only be provided in-person. Because of HSBC's international presence, however, the bank can also offer financial services for consumers and businesses that need to cross national borders, such as foreign exchange.

b.   HSBC's basic banking services would probably tend to be standardized, because checking accounts do not need to differ from country to country. Yet banking laws and regulations often vary from country to country, so HSBC would have to adapt its products and operations as necessary to meet local requirements.

c.   HSBC's branch system represents direct investment, because the bank itself owns either the lease or the building in which each branch operates. This also helps HSBC build its reputation as a good corporate citizen in each locality, because the bank is supporting the local economy and participating in the community more fully than if it was not using direct investment.

Online Marketing Today

Marketers participating in global e-commerce need to speak the languages and understand the customs and interests of their target customers. For example, the main Reebok.com Web site has links to country-specific sites for the United Kingdom and France. The Reebok brand name is prominently displayed on all three sites, but the specific products and promotions being highlighted differ from country to country.

Point your Web browser to the Reebok site (www.reebok.com), examine the U.S. site, then visit the U.K. and French sites. Bearing in mind the ten commandments of global branding, what differences and similarities do you notice when browsing these three Reebok sites? How does Reebok leverage key brand elements on-line? Which of the sites (if any) allow on-line purchases? What conclusions can you draw about Reebok's on-line balance of standardization and customization and its balance of global and local control?

Answer

Although all three sites will change from time to time, students should notice that the Reebok brand and logo appears on all three. The sites do not all have exactly the same look, and they generally feature different products and promotions. However, when Reebok has a particularly hot new product, it may feature that product on more than one of these sites. The distinctive letters of the Reebok brand and the exciting sports-related graphics are common brand elements that the company uses in print and on-line marketing. When this book went to print, the U.S. site was referring buyers to other retailers' sites; the French site had a retail store locator; and the U.K. site had a link to a Reebok on-line store. Apparently, Reebok is using standardization for brand elements and some products and promotions but customizing its on-line marketing to local tastes, distribution arrangements, and government regulations. The differences among the three sites also suggest that Reebok allows some local control of on-line content, although the branding and products appear to be globally available and therefore under headquarters control.

You're the Marketer: Sonic PDA Marketing Plan

Global marketing offers a way for companies of all sizes to grow by expanding their customer base beyond the domestic market. The complexities of global marketing, however, demand careful planning and proper implementation.

As Jane Melody's assistant, you are researching non-U.S. markets for Sonic's first personal digital assistant product. Review the data you previously collected and your other recommendations for Sonic's marketing plan. Then answer these questions about how Sonic can approach global marketing:

- Should Sonic use exporting, licensing, joint ventures, or direct investment to enter the Canadian market? To enter other markets?
- If Sonic wants to start marketing a PDA in other countries, which of the international product strategies is most appropriate? Why?
- What international markets seem most promising for Sonic? Using online or print sources (such as the Global Edge Web site at http://globaledge.msu.edu/ibrd/ibrd.asp or the U.S. Business Advisor at http://www.business.gov), identify at least one foreign market that Sonic could consider entering.

- Is global standardization or adaptation most appropriate for Sonic's entry into the market(s) identified above? To answer, you will have to research electronics standards in the chosen market(s) as well as consumer behavior and competitive products. How can you collect such data?
- What brand partnerships might be of most value to Sonic in entering one or more global markets? Why?
-

When you have examined potential global markets and strategies, summarize your ideas and additional research needs in a written marketing plan or enter them into the Markets, SWOT and Issue Analysis, Marketing Strategy, and Marketing Research sections of the *Marketing Plan Pro* software.

Answer

Sonic should begin by exporting its products to other countries, minimizing the risk, investment and commitment. This also allows the company to evaluate response and, if warranted, stop selling in one or more countries. Sonic must consider some adaptation, because of variations in electrical standards around the world. Also, consumers in other countries may have different needs and preferences, and the competition in PDAs is likely to vary in each market, which will affect Sonic's marketing efforts. Collecting this data may require contacting numerous sources, such as major distributors, import-export specialists, and U.S. trade agencies.

Because of proximity, Sonic should consider exporting to large North American markets such as Canada and Mexico, depending on the state of each country's economy and the local distribution and competitive situation. Shipping PDAs to these markets is less expensive than shipping to overseas markets. Also, Canada and Mexico are major U.S. trading partners and therefore Sonic can get considerable assistance from U.S. government sources. Through research, students may be able to identify other promising markets. Remind students to review Sonic's mission, objectives and goals, and other strategy elements to be sure that global expansion fits with its direction and resources.

Sonic may be able to work with well-known software and hardware companies when entering foreign markets. If these companies make products for the Sonic PDA, such as a phone adapter or financial software, Sonic could mount a joint promotion to leverage the power of both brands. Another option is to work with a local cell phone service provider to jointly promote the wireless communication features of Sonic PDAs. Students may offer other creative ideas, as well.

Marketing Spotlight: Coca-Cola

The most recognized brand name in the world got its start in an Atlanta pharmacy, where it sold for five cents a glass. The name Coca-Cola, registered as a trademark on January 31, 1893, was based on two of the drink's ingredients: extracts from coca leaves and the cola nut. In its early days, when the drink contained a form of cocaine, a drug made from coca leave extracts, the Coca-Cola was marketed as an "Esteemed Brain Tonic and Intellectual Beverage." The company's first president, Asa Candler, was a savvy businessman who implemented numerous marketing strategies to increase consumption. At Candler's behest, the company printed coupons offering complimentary first tastes of Coca-Cola, and outfitted distributing pharmacists with clocks, calendars, and scales bearing the Coca-Cola brand. The drink soon became a national phenomenon; by 1895, the company had established syrup plants in Chicago, Dallas, and Los Angeles.

Coca-Cola expanded beyond the American borders in the early 1900s into numerous countries including Cuba, Puerto Rico, and France. In the 1920s, Coca-Cola pursued aggressive global branding, finding creative placements for its logo such as on dogsleds in Canada and on the walls of bullfighting arenas in Spain.

During World War II, the U.S. Army shipped bottles of the beverage abroad to supply American soldiers in Europe and Asia. Its popularity throughout the world was fueled by colorful and persuasive advertising that cemented its image as the "All-American" beverage. When the Vietnam War tarnished the American image, Coke developed more globally aware advertising. In 1971, the company ran its legendary "I'd like to buy the world a Coke" television spot, in which a crowd of children sang the song from atop a hill in Italy. Coke's moves into formerly restricted markets, such as China in 1978 and the Soviet Union in 1979, bolstered its image as a global company. By 1988, Coca-Cola was voted the best known and most admired brand in the world.

One ad agency executive said, "There are about two products that lend themselves to global marketing—and one of them is Coca-Cola."

Still, Coca-Cola did not institute a uniform marketing program in each of its global markets. Rather, the company often tailored the flavor, packaging, price, and advertising to match the tastes in specific markets. For example, Coke's famous "Mean Joe" Green TV ad from the United States—in which the tired, weary football star reluctantly accepts a Coke from an admiring young fan and then unexpectedly tosses the kid his jersey in appreciation—was replicated in a number of different regions using the same format but substituting famous athletes from those regions (e.g., ads in South America used the Argentine soccer star, Maradona, while those in Asia used the Thai soccer star, Niat). Additionally, local managers were assigned responsibility for sales and distribution programs of Coke products to reflect the marked differences in consumer behavior across countries. In Spain, Coke has been used as a mixer with wine; in Italy, Coke is served with meals in place of wine or cappuccino; in China, the beverage is served at special government occasions. The company used the phrase "think global, act local" to describe its marketing strategy during the 1990s.

Today, Coca-Cola conducts business with more than 230 brands in 200 countries. More than two-thirds of Coca-Cola's revenues come from outside the United States, a fact which makes the company vulnerable to downturns in international economies, as evidenced by shallow earnings during the global economic upheaval in the late 1990s. In response to the depressed sales brought by international recessions, the company pursued a restructuring plan that would recast the beverage giant as "a collection of smaller, locally run businesses." When Douglas Daft took over as chairman and CEO in 2000, he expressed his desire for Coca-Cola managers to adopt a new mantra: "think locally and act locally."

Sources: "The Story of Coca-Cola," www.coca-cola.com; Betsy McKay, "Coca-Cola Restructuring Effort Has Yet to Prove Effective." Asian *Wall Street Journal,* March 2, 2001; Andrew Marshall, "Focus: Can They Still Sell the World A Coke?" *The Independent,* June 20, 1999.

Questions

1. What is the primary basis for Coke's past international marketing success? Is it only advertising?

2. Given the growing political and economic uncertainty, what changes can Coke make to it's global marketing strategy?

3. What is the real meaning of "think locally and act locally"? Can and should this marketing philosophy always work? Why?

Suggested Responses

1. Many will say that it is the level of advertising, but the better answer may be the consistent and effective, locally oriented global marketing, aimed carefully at targeted

markets around the globe. Coke and other brands have become leaders in their product categories by understanding consumer motivations and desires and by creating relevant and favorable image associations. There is nothing fly-by-night in such activities.

2.   Coca Cola has struggled since the late 1990s to find new direction(s) against the rise of new global competition, nationalism and various internal management philosophies arguing for new and different marketing directions and/or activities. Accordingly, some analysts have argued it may be time for Coke to look for new direction(s), especially in marketing and advertising because it appeared that during the past few years Pepsi consistently introduced more innovative and creative marketing campaigns.

It may be useful to note to the class that Interbrand's annual list of the 100 most valuable global brands shows that 62 of them are U.S. based. American companies account for nine of the 10 most powerful brands in the world (Coca-Cola, Microsoft, IBM, General Electric, Intel, Disney, Ford, McDonald's and AT&T). The irony is that in most areas where there have been some of the more strident anti-American attacks, especially in Muslim regions, those attacks are against locally-owned companies. Many of the restaurant chains, such as KFC and McDonalds, for example, operate on a franchise basis. Thus, while the brand may be global, the business itself is locally owned.

3.   The phrase ("think globally, act locally"), in the original Coke setting, was designed to achieve effective planning and strategy at the global level, with tactics and application at the local level. The new concept (think and act locally) argues for a much more decentralized decision-making and application process. The "pro" to this is that it places more responsibility and control at the local level, but the "con" is that it also enables much more diverse and often divisive attitudes and actions that may in the end actually detract from the ultimate corporate goal.

It is easy to argue that in this day of increasingly nationalistic orientation, that if local franchises of multinational firms like Coke are owned and operated at the local level there will be much more support and less likelihood of local political and social interference. If, however, operational control is largely separated from the more centralized corporate management, the end result can be very different, and possibly negative.

Part IV—SHAPING THE MARKET OFFERING

CHAPTER 14—Setting the Product and Branding Strategy

Overview

Product is the first and most important element of the marketing mix. A product is anything that can be offered to a market for attention, acquisition, use, or consumption and that might satisfy a want or need. Products can be physical objects, services, people, places, organizations, and ideas. Product strategy calls or making coordinated decisions on product mixes, product lines, brands, packaging, and labeling.

A product can be considered on five levels. The core benefit is the essential use-benefit, problem-solving service that the buyer primarily buys when purchasing a product. The generic product is the basic version of the product. The expected product is the set of attributes and conditions that the buyer normally expects in buying the product. The augmented product is additional services and benefits that the seller adds to distinguish the offer from competitors. The potential product is the set of possible new features and services that might eventually be added to the offer.

All products can be classified according to their durability (nondurable goods, durable goods, and services). Consumer goods are usually classified according to consumer shopping habits (convenience, shopping, specialty, and unsought goods). Industrial goods are classified according to how they enter the production process (materials and parts, capital items, and supplies and services).

Most companies handle more than one product, and accordingly product mix can be described as possessing a certain width, length, depth, and consistency. These four dimensions are the tools for developing the company's product strategy. The various lines making up the product mix have to be periodically evaluated for profitability and growth potential. The company's better lines should receive disproportionate support; weaker lines should be phased down or out; and new lines should be added to fill the profit gap.

Each product line consists of product items. The product-line manager should study the sales and profit contributions of each item in the product line as well as how the items are positioned against competitors' items. This provides information for making several product-line decisions. Line stretching involves the question of whether a particular line should be extended downward, upward, or both ways; line filling, whether additional items should be added within the present range of the line; line modernization raises the question of whether the line needs a new look and whether the new look should be installed piecemeal or all at once; line featuring, which items to feature in promoting the line; and line pruning, how to detect and remove weaker product items from the line.

Companies should develop brand policies for the individual product items in their lines. They must decide on product attributes (quality, features, design), whether to brand at all, whether to do producer or distributor branding, whether to use family brand names or individual brand names, whether to extend the brand name to new products, whether to create multiple brands, and whether to reposition any of them.

Physical products require packaging decisions to create such benefits as protection, economy, convenience, and promotion. Marketers have to develop a packaging concept and test it functionally and psychologically to make sure it achieves the desired objectives and is compatible with public policy. Physical products also require labeling for identification and possible grading, description, and promotion of the product. Sellers may be required by law to present certain minimum information on the label to inform and protect consumers.

Learning Objectives

After reading the chapter the student should understand:

- The levels of the product
- How a company can build and manage its product mix and product lines
- How a company can make better brand decisions
- How packaging and labeling can be used as a marketing tool

Chapter Outline

I. Product and the product mix
- A. Product levels (five)—core benefit, basic product, expected product, augmented product (beyond expectations, where most competition takes place), and potential product (future augmentation possibilities)
- B. Product hierarchy—seven levels of product hierarchy: need family, product family, product class, product line, product type, brand, and item
- C. Product classifications
  1. Durability and tangibility—nondurable goods, durable goods, services
  2. Consumer-goods classification—convenience, specialty, shopping, unsought
  3. Industrial-goods classification—materials and parts, capital items, supplies and business services
- D. Product mix—a product mix (product assortment) is the set of all products and items that a particular seller offers for sale to buyers. The marketer must consider width, length, depth, and consistency

II. Product-line decisions—a product line is a group of products that are closely related because they perform a similar function, are sold to the same customer groups, are marketed through the same channels, or fall within given price ranges
- A. Product-line analysis—sales and profits of each item
  1. Sales and profits—margin differences related to core product, staples and convenience items
  2. Market profile—positioning against competitors
- B. Product-line length—a line is too short if the manager can increase profits by adding items; the line is too long if the manager can increase profits by dropping items
  1. Line-stretching
     a. Downmarket stretch—enter on the low end
     b. Upmarket stretch—enter on the high end
     c. Two-way stretch—both directions

        d.   Line-filling—adding more items (live filling and just-noticeable difference)

C.   Line modernization, featuring, and pruning

    1.   Updating product line to reflect current trends and themes

    2.   Line-featuring—select one or a few items in the line to feature

    3.   Line-pruning—when a product is depressing profits, or a company is short of production capacity

III.   Brand decisions—traditionally, market power has rested with brand-name companies.

A.   What is a brand?

    1.   A name, term, sign, symbol, or design, or a combination of them, intended to identify the goods or services of one seller or group of sellers and to differentiate them from those of the competition

    2.   A brand has six levels of meaning (attributes, benefits, values, culture, personality, and user)

    3.   Researching the position the brand occupies in the consumer mind (key concepts include word associations, personifying the brand, and brand essence

B.   Building brand identity (issues related to brand name, logo, colors tagline, and symbol)

C.   Building brands in the new economy

    1.   Clarify the corporation's basic values and build corporate brand

    2.   Use brand managers to carry out the tactical work (with top management involvement)

    3.   More comprehensive plans about total positive customer experiences

    4.   Define the brand's essence everywhere

    5.   Use brand value as key to company strategy

    6.   Measure brand-building by customer-perceived value, satisfaction, share of wallet, retention, and advocacy

D.   Brand equity—brand awareness, brand acceptability, brand preference, brand loyalty. High brand equity provides a number of competitive advantages

    1.   Value of brand equity (positive differential effect of brand on the customer)

    2.   Brand valuation (total financial value of the brand)

    3.   Competitive advantages for high brand equity:

        a.   Trade leverage in channel bargaining

        b.   Higher price

        c.   Line extensions easier

        d.   Defense against price competition.

    4.   Managing brand equity (mismanagement is a problem today in the quest for ever-increasing profits—brand loses focus)

E.   Branding challenges

    1.   Branding decision: to brand or not to brand?

    2.   Brand-sponsor decision

        a.   Manufacturer brand, distributor brand, licensed brand name

      b.   Brand ladder (customer ranking of brands)

      c.   Growing power of retailer brands (price orientation)

      d.   Blurring of brand identity

      e.   Internet considerations

F.   Brand name decision

     1.   Strategies

         a.   Individual names (General Mills Bisquick)

         b.   Blanket family names (Heinz and GE)

         c.   Separate family names for all products (Sears Kenmore and Craftsman)

         d.   Corporate name combined with individual product names (Kellogg Rice Krispies)

     2.   Brand name qualities

         a.   Suggest product's benefits, product, or service category

         b.   Concrete "high imagery" qualities

         c.   Easy to spell, pronounce, and remember

         d.   Distinctive

         e.   No negative international carryover meanings

G.   Brand building tools

     1.   Public relations and press releases

     2.   Sponsorships

     3.   Clubs and consumer communities

     4.   Factory visits

     5.   Trade shows

     6.   Event marketing

     7.   Public facilities

     8.   Social cause marketing

H.   Brand strategy decision—varies based on whether: functional brand (satisfy functional need); image brand (difficult to differentiate between brands); experiential brand (consumer involvement)

     1.   Line extensions—additional items in the same product category

     2.   Brand extensions—existing brand name in a new product category

     3.   Multibrands, new brands, and co-brands

         a.   Multibrands—additional brand names in the same product category

         b.   New brands—new brand names in a new product category

         c.   Co-brands—two well-known brand names combine in one product offering

I.   Brand asset management (many areas beyond advertising and public relations)

J.   Brand auditing and repositioning

     1.   Note brand report card

     2.   Brand repositioning (changing customer preferences, competition)

IV.   Packaging and labeling
    A.   Packaging (all the activities of designing and producing the container for the product)
    B.   Levels of material (primary, secondary, shipping package)
    C.   Promotional value
        1.   Self-service
        2.   Consumer affluence
        3.   Company and brand image
        4.   Innovation opportunity
    D.   Labeling
        1.   Identify, grade, describe or promote the product
        2.   Legal concerns for labels and packaging
V.   Summary

Lecture 1—Reinventing Products and Companies

The general purpose of this lecture and discussion is to tie together the product and branding aspects of the course and bring in the strategy and planning elements as well. The lecture focuses on achieving implementation in the overall marketing strategy process. Students should be able to identify readily with this concept because it brings together concepts they have studied and draws on their general knowledge of companies and products discussed to date.

Teaching Objectives

- To comprehend the major elements of the product planning and control effort

- To understand how and where the product control effort serves as a linchpin for much of the rest of the marketing strategy effort

- To appreciate the distinction between defining the product plan and actually committing to carrying out the program

- To define a structure, with examples, for improving skills in composing and submitting a marketing plan

Discussion

Introduction—What the Best Companies Do to Reinvent Themselves, Again and Again

It is often said that the best companies can time and time again pull out of mistakes with their strong cultures and will to succeed. This may be true, but more importantly their success or failures rest on how well they conduct and control the product strategy that often drives the rest of the marketing strategy process. There are many examples in the marketplace of the winners and losers, but clearly one of the top winners has to be Gillette (previous lecture). The company operates in just about the most mundane of product categories, but due to their product and strategic planning excellence they have become one of the most successful and resilient companies in the world. Their success is no accident.

To begin with, consider some of the things that Intel, Microsoft, General Motors, IBM and other major firms have done right and wrong at various times in their product and branding strategy, and then compare that to what Gillette learned and did, often just before the brink of disaster. With this discussion you can begin to see the real meaning of product and branding strategic planning excellence. The message is that regardless of size or category dominance, if firms do not reinvent their corporate charter and product franchise, someone else will. The meaning here: Nothing is forever or sacrosanct in the world of global product marketing, and the only thing that we know for certain is that if a firm sits on its laurels for very long they will be undercut or flanked, sooner or later.

The Requirements for Reinventing Products—and Companies

Reinventing a company's product and brand franchise requires foresight. It also requires the courage to challenge conventional wisdom. It requires the confidence to think outside the comfort zone. This activity taps all of the company's resources to leverage its assets and skills. It has the power to increase sales and profits, or if performed badly it can cost the firm everything it has worked to gain.

Focusing more specifically on Gillette, razors and blades account for a third of Gillette's sales and two-thirds of its operating income. But we should remember that there was a period when the advantages of this lucrative business were almost lost. After dominating the category for years, Gillette found itself fending off corporate raiders because it lost sight of what drives the business engine. Gillette fortunately woke up soon enough and turned its fortunes around to again become a world-class leader. It is, in a phrase, the story of a successful reinvention.

In the mid-1970s, BIC introduced the disposable razor in Europe. Gillette management was wary about moving into disposables, fearing the product would cannibalize sales of its far more lucrative shaving systems. Nonetheless, Gillette introduced Good News as the first disposable razor in the United States.

Gillette continued to develop superior shaving systems, improving upon the twin-bladed Trac II with the pivot-headed and Atra in 1977. Unfortunately, following on the Trac II and Atra system successes, the company quickly incorporated improvements into the disposable models. Competitors followed, and consumers saw little reason to pay a 40–50 percent premium for system razors. The result was that they flocked to disposables. Gillette's share of 70 percent of the wet-shave market declined to under 60 percent, and this was only the beginning.

Disposables grew by 17 percent a year, while system sales were declining by 1 percent. By 1985, Gillette put more than 60 percent of its consumer ad spending behind disposables. As a result, disposables captured 60 percent of category units and 53 percent of dollars at drastically lower price points and profit margins. In 1987, Gillette spent only one-fourth of the $61 million it spent in 1975 on media advertising.

Coincidentally, at the same time this was happening, the company was already in the throes of responding to another challenge that was to lead Gillette toward a reinvention of itself with a response that saved the company from some of its own mistakes.

Note: There are many contemporary examples of the same type of mistake; this could include IBM, Oracle, and others discussed in the text.

In 1986, the chairman of Gillette, in the heat of a proxy battle, promised stockholders that Gillette management would increase their value more than the raiders. Accordingly, the company had to take a chance, a very big chance.

For years, design engineers had tinkered with a system that set thin blades on springs so the razor followed the contours of the face. Eventually this system would be called the Sensor. Development costs exceeded $200 million before the first unit was sold at retail. The simultaneous launch of Sensor in the United States and Europe in 1990, supported by a $100 million marketing budget, was hugely successful. By 1992, sales of Sensor and Lady Sensor exceeded $500 million. Gillette successfully reinvented its franchise by doing what it did best, better. Sensor returned Gillette to providing the consumer with a superior shave, and away from competing on price.

Reinvention of existing products or services is much more likely to succeed than new product development, new business development or acquisition for two major reasons:

- The costs and risks of reinventing the franchise are substantially lower because the tools, systems, talents and skills are already in place

- The rewards can be considerably higher, because a company is starting with what it knows and the learning curve is flatter

Microsoft, Intel, Ford, GM and others also have learned how to play this game. To generate real growth, even managers of successful brands cannot just respond to change. They must anticipate change. They must be a catalyst for change. They must continually reinvent their franchise.

Lecture 2—Brands, Are They Dead? And a New Look at Packaging

This lecture and discussion focuses on strategy in a marketing setting, and the challenges and opportunities related to branding in the overall marketing process and strategy for the company.

The lecture considers a topic of considerable importance in today's marketplace: the "death" of brands. Ask your students what they find important in making purchase decisions. Is brand name as important as it used to be? The discussion continues by providing examples of several brands and their strategies for "staying alive." This leads into a discussion of the implications for the introduction of various branding strategies into the firm and the industry.

Teaching Objectives

- To stimulate students to think about the important issues in branding and packaging strategy

- To present points to consider in proceeding with a specific branding/packaging strategy

- To emphasize the role of branding/packaging strategies and policies in the overall marketing strategy

Discussion

Introduction—Brand Equity: Dead or Alive?

One aspect of branding that has required a shift in focus has been the declining power of brand equity. The invention of the checkout scanner, which allows a company to see sales data instantaneously, has fueled price wars in the packaged goods arenas. With increasing promotional activity in the marketplace, consumers have become more value-driven in their purchases, and retailers have responded with the introduction of private label goods (goods sold under the retailer's name) in many packaged goods categories. Frequently, the perceived difference in quality between manufacturers' and private label goods is minimal, spurring the growth of the private labels. Brands thus have also been a party to their own decline. With a long period of prosperity, primarily based on the consumers' one-time obsession with brands, the brands became complacent in efforts to differentiate themselves and justify their premium prices.

Responding with the Fighting Brand

The result is that a number of variables have put the brand names on notice, but today the brand-holders have been fighting back with so-called "fighting brands." This approach is not new, with brand marketers using such a ploy as a temporary measure to hold customers during recessions. Today, however, many marketers see the wave of fighting brands as more than a temporary phenomenon.

The fighting brand has been seen as a response to the fragmentation of the mass marketplace, based on taste and economic insecurity. Many consumers have become switchers, trading back and forth between branded products and store brands. The trend has spurred the growth of private-label products, which have risen from approximately 18 percent of supermarket unit sales in 1990 to around 22 percent last year.

Despite the problems that micro beers, import beers, discount beers, etc., have brought to the brewers, there has been some positive development for at least one of the big U.S. brewers. Miller Brewing Co. has found there's still some sparkle in the brand, but not as a premium-priced brew. Miller is one of a small number of U.S. brand marketers trying to breathe new life into their old brands. They're slashing the prices of some well-known products and repositioning them as higher-grade alternatives to the store brands and other low-priced fare that appeal to budget-minded shoppers.

Miller dropped prices on Miller High Life and revived the old "Miller Time" ads to go after store and discount brands. Over the last few years Procter & Gamble also has dropped prices on some products to put pressure on store brands and rivals while protecting its higher-priced brands. Cereal makers, including Kellogg, General Foods, General Mills and Quaker, all have responded in a similar manner. Kodak, another example, launched Funtime, a new low-price film aimed at store brands. It will be offered only in the spring and fall.

For manufacturers, the mid-tier brands offer several benefits. They can help to control the switchers in the marketplace without setting off price wars on premium brands. The mid-tier brands keep them producing branded product while they save the old brands from dying. This allows them to continue to profit from the efforts of years of advertising.

Now, fighting brands are being used with success on a wider scale. A number of brand-holders have used price-tiering before, on a limited basis. P&G has utilized this approach with shampoos in the United States, with diapers in Venezuela and Germany, and with laundry detergents in the developing world. The market share for Luvs' (also P&G) disposable diapers in unit volume is up from 11percent to 14percent since its price was cut by 16percent, arresting a severe slide. Even so, it appears that Luvs initially cannibalized some of Pampers' sales; Pampers recovered when it introduced a new, thinner diaper. P&G's total unit share rose shortly after and has maintained the pace since then.

In beer, using another example, despite a flat beer market, High Life's sales jumped 9 percent, to 5 million barrels after Miller cut its price 20 percent or more in most markets. A 12-pack of High Life that cost $6.99 two years ago in Ohio can now be had for $4.99. 'The impact was fairly immediate," says the director of pricing for the Philip Morris Companies unit. The challenge is to calibrate a fighting brand to make it good enough to draw consumers from low-priced rivals but not so good that it will clobber the company's top brands or its profit margins. To offset the lower margins on its Funtime film, for example, Kodak is also launching a high-end film for special occasions, Kodak Royal Gold. For Luvs diapers P&G eliminated jumbo packages, streamlined package design, simplified printing on the diapers, and trimmed down promotions.

Other brand marketers figure that if they cannot beat store brands, they might as well make them. That's what RJR Nabisco began doing recently. It test-marketed private label cookies and snackers in some stores. This underscores, again, the power of retailers who love the fat margins on store brands. Research has shown that retailers, for example, make 8 percent to 12 percent on store-brand diapers. As part of the Luvs repositioning, P&G said it has increased the retail margins to over 8 percent from just over 3 percent. As a result, while it may pull back some retailers, others will not respond. For example, most divisions of Safeway Inc., no longer stock Luvs.

Conclusion—Fighting Brands

Clearly the fighting brands won't effect any change in the process if the retailers don't give them a chance. This has led a number of brand manufacturers to make presentations to retailers regarding the strength of brand names in attracting the most profitable shoppers. This category of shopper on average purchases more during a typical visit. In addition, the brands have altered their promotional strategies to create a new image for the brands and rebuild consumer loyalty. These efforts, to some degree, are working; and some consumers have begun to trust again because the companies are making brands worth trusting. Private label brand sales have plateaued recently, and there has been less emphasis on promotional price incentives overall.

Thus, the idea of branding is far from passé. When a brand is managed properly it can and will provide credibility and attract attention in the marketplace.

A New Look at Packaging—Packaging: the Five Second Commercial

A point increasingly driven home to marketers of food, health and beauty product lines and over-the-counter drugs is that the package is the brand. Once the brand has done everything possible to make the product taste good, work effectively, or cost less, it is still possible to distinguish it with a package that no competitors can copy.

As products and media channels proliferate, prospective customers split into increasingly more difficult-to-reach audience, market and readership segments. Without an impressive return on investment from mass media advertising, the role of packaging as a key influencer on the customer, especially during the moments before and during purchase, has expanded dramatically.

Many marketers are paying more attention to package design because the products increasingly are more alike in the marketplace. This is the argument of some marketing professionals who point out that when differentiation through taste, color and other product elements has reached parity, packaging makes the critical difference.

An example of this is found in the Pepsi-Cola Co. reaction to Coca Cola's plasticization of its hallowed curved bottle. Pepsi found that it could not follow suit, but they responded in a manner designed again to level the playing field. Pepsi set out to do a new package, as they do every few years. As a Pepsi executive has noted, operationally it is very complicated to make a major shift like this, but clearly in this type of the product category this is necessary occasionally. Pepsi and other similar companies can build business on distribution and price, but packaging is a way for them to build excitement without changing the formula or adding products that will cannibalize the rest of their product line. That is the challenge.

The result is that Pepsi is building a whole new round of designs based on themes such as: Fast Break, a 20-oz. resealable, curved bottle; "Big Slam," a one-liter bottle geared to convenience stores. "Pepsi Junior is a resealable 12-oz. plastic "can"; and "Block Party, " is a 30-can version of "The Cube." Pepsi's has turned the 24-can multipack into a promotional tool, carrying coupons from Breyer's (a Nabisco label), Thermos and Spalding.

Other examples include:

- Perrier—The firm made its distinctive package the centerpiece of promotion, shrink-wrapping original artwork on to bottles sold through restaurants

- McDonald's—Licensees are cashing in on the recognizability of McDonald's packages by selling neckties in mock fry and burger boxes in department stores

Beyond good looks, the best designs extend the brand and its image by adding some intrinsic value to the product itself. As many marketers look at it, it is a constant dance to balance identity and utility; brands want to be different and to offer benefit to the consumer,"

Packaged goods marketers are paying special attention these days to delivery systems. That is prompted in part by the success of club stores (Sam's Club, B.J. Wholesale Club, etc.) whose giant packs sell better when they are resealable. A unique delivery system, like Mentadent toothpaste's double pump, can cement a brand's image. And designs that take into account how consumers use the product and the package, make consumers feel like the manufacturer cares about them.

Other companies also have capitalized on this as they fight off private labels.

- Procter & Gamble has an easy-to-open yet childproof cap on its Aleve analgesic.

- Tylenol touts its Fast Cap, designed for older adults. This is a convenience move that adds value. If a competitor can copy it, it's more of a tactical move than a strategic brand-protection, It ends up being a bonus for container makers, though, giving them a ready market for innovative packages that may have required expensive retooling to produce.

Proprietary packaging, especially patented designs, prevents knockoffs. As a result, it has become common practice for marketers to patent a specific design and then build a moat around that design by copyrighting several similar designs.

Consumer concerns for the environment now pressures marketers to avoid wasteful packaging. Although these moves cut down the surface area for graphics, it is better for marketers in the long run. Greater ecological pressure may even reawaken interest in proprietary shapes. The most likely candidates are jarred and bottled items like condiments; glass is easy to shape, and a distinctive jar means an added value to consumers. Cartons, on the other hand, are more expensive to shape and more difficult to protect from infringement.

Ecological advances, however, come at a cost. When Hanes dropped the plastic egg for L'eggs hosiery in 1991 and moved to a gabled box, there was no question they lost something. The egg structure had been tied to a function; without the function, it is not clear whether the shape was relevant to the future equity of the brand. And the question is, how do you capture the shape graphically?

Companies tend to adjust the graphics more often than product structure because it is a cheaper and faster way to update a brand. Category leaders often use well-recognized graphics to extend their clout into new categories. For example, Sun Diamond Growers of California developed new packaging for Sun-Maid dried fruits that uses the Sun Maid woman and bright red used by the No. 1 raisin brand. Frito-Lay (Pepsi Co.) took the same approach by using the Taco Bell name and graphics with its supermarket line of Taco Bell–branded food.

In sum, package design has to be very carefully integrated with product, distribution and service design. Brand name companies cannot just slightly modify the package to fend off private label marketing. There has to be a more systematic design change that adds some intrinsic value. Without this, the brand will end up competing in some very small consumer niches, creating interest with either very rich or very naive consumers.

Marketing and Advertising

1.   Ad number one: Pepperidge Farm cookies are positioned as premium cookies. This magazine ad features a larger-than-life Milano cookie, plus a simple headline, logo, and the tagline "Never have an ordinary day."

      a.   Identify the basic, expected, and augmented products that Pepperidge Farm is offering.

      b.   How would you classify this consumer product?

      c.   How do the elements of this ad help convey the brand's attributes and benefits?

Answer

      a.   The basic product is a sweet snack finger food, delivering the core benefit of a treat or reward. The expected product is a sugary baked good that can be eaten in one or two bites. The augmented product is a high-quality, sophisticated cookie with special ingredients and chocolate, protected from breakage by careful packaging.

      b.   This consumer product can be classified as a convenience good, purchased frequently and immediately with little effort. Students may further classify cookies as impulse goods, although Pepperidge Farm clearly wants customers to seek out its particular brand of cookies.

      c.   The enlarged cookie shows off the crispy cookie and chocolate filling, two attributes that would be valued by cookie lovers and the help deliver the benefit of a rewarding treat. Other pictured cookies look tasty and inviting. The headline suggests that Pepperidge Farm cookies are real treats, and the tagline "Never have an ordinary day" reinforces that these cookies make a day feel special. The cookie name adds to the feeling of sophistication, elevating the product from the everyday and conveying a European feeling. The Pepperidge Farm brand and farm graphic suggests freshness. Students may offer other ideas, as well.

2.   Ad number two: Binney & Smith is well known for marketing Crayola crayons in a wide variety of colors, including jack-o-lantern orange, as shown in this seasonal ad.

      a.   Can the Crayon Treat Pack be considered a line or brand extension? Why would Binney & Smith choose this strategy?

      b.   Discuss Binney & Smith's packaging strategy for the Crayon Treat Pack. How does this strategy reinforce the company's company and brand image?

      c.   Are Crayola crayons convenience goods, goods, specialty, or unsought goods? How does this classification affect Binney & Smith's marketing of its Crayon Treat Pack?

Answer

      a.   The Crayon Treat Pack is a line extension, because it involves existing products (crayons) being packaged in a new way (three-packs). Binney & Smith might choose this strategy to increase sales seasonally and reinforce the Crayola brand without the higher risks of launching brand-new products. This strategy also helps Binney & Smith combat competition by encouraging purchasing and consumption in a nontraditional yet highly acceptable way. Students may have other ideas, as well.

b.   Although Binney & Smith crayons are usually offered in larger packages, this holiday three-pack is an innovation that offers parents a desirable alternative to traditional candy giveaways for Halloween. The brand is prominently displayed on the treat pack bag and on individual three-packs, reinforcing the Crayola brand and enhancing its image as a brand appropriate for every occasion.

c.   Crayons are typically convenience goods, purchased with minimal effort and often on impulse. Binney & Smith's marketing of its Crayon Treat Pack is designed to encourage more impulse purchasing of this product as a replacement for Halloween candies. Students may also make a case for crayons as shopping goods, because consumers seek out Crayola-branded products in particular.

Online Marketing Today—Virgin

As noted earlier, Richard Branson is aggressively building his Virgin brand on and off the Internet. Virgin.com has evolved into a major U.K. portal with links to every Virgin company Web site and offers of goods and services in numerous product categories, from travel and transport to house and home and business and finance. This site also serves as a central recruitment point for Virgin companies with job openings.

Visit the Virgin site (www.virgin.com), review the offers on the home page, and follow several links to featured offers and companies. Return to the home page and click to read about at least one "travel and transport" offer and one "house and home" offer. Which brand-name strategy is Virgin using? Why is this strategy appropriate for Virgin? Select two offers and determine whether they can be characterized as convenience goods, shopping goods, specialty goods, or unsought goods. Why would Virgin choose to highlight these type of products?

Answer

Virgin is combining its company trade name with individual product names. In many cases, the product names incorporate the name of the basic product (Virgin Cola), directly communicating what customers can expect from that product. This strategy helps Virgin widen recognition and awareness of its company trade name while using the brand's existing strength to expand into other product categories. Students may choose any of the Virgin products, which range from wedding services to rail services and banking services. Wedding services, for example, are specialty goods; buyers make a special purchasing effort when considering this type of service. Ask students to explain their reasoning for classifying the chosen products as they do. Virgin appears interested in offering goods and services where branding can make the difference in the customer's purchasing decision. Thus, visitors to the Virgin site are already predisposed to the company's branded products and more likely to seriously consider—and buy—products featured on its site.

You're the Marketer—Sonic PDA Marketing Plan

Decisions about products and branding are critical elements of any marketing plan. During the planning process, marketers must consider a variety of issues related to product mix, product lines, brand equity, and brand strategies.

You are helping Sonic manage its soon-to-be-expanded line of personal digital assistant products, as well as branding for this line. After reviewing the company's current situation, target market, positioning, and other issues previously addressed in your marketing plan, consider the following questions:

1.   What is the core benefit of the first PDA product Sonic will soon introduce?

2. What elements of the potential product should Sonic consider incorporating into the higher-end second product to be developed next year?

3. What are the attributes and benefits suggested by the Sonic brand?

4. How can Sonic use packaging and labeling to support its brand image and help its channel partners sell the PDA product more effectively?

Think about how your answers to these questions will influence Sonic's marketing activities. Now, as your instructor directs, summarize your ideas in a written marketing plan or type them into the Marketing Mix and Marketing Strategy sections of the *Marketing Plan Pro* software. Also indicate (in the Marketing Research section) any additional studies you will need to support decisions about managing the product line and brand.

Answer

The core benefit of Sonic's first PDA is to enable users to communicate and exchange information on the go. As they identify elements of the potential product to be incorporated into Sonic's second PDA product, students may be creative in suggesting features that extend the versatility of the product for consumers and business customers, such as GPS mapping capabilities (benefit: help business travelers find their destinations), stereo speakers (benefit: allow consumers to play downloaded MP3 music), and fax transmission capabilities (benefit: allow businesspeople to send faxes to people who do not have PDAs or e-mail access).

The Sonic brand name clearly suggests sophisticated electronics technology, a desirable attribute for a brand that wants to deliver the benefit of allowing users to easily and conveniently communicate and exchange information while on the road. Students may suggest other associations, as well. Sonic can reinforce these associations on the packaging by prominently displaying its brand and create an accompanying logo (such as a "thunderbolt" graphic or some other appropriate graphic). Other ways to use the packaging to reinforce the brand image include: listing important product specifications to show how the PDA's advanced technology delivers on the brand promise (this also helps retail salespeople compare the product to competing models); and including an enlarged photo or illustration of the PDA highlighting key competitively-superior features and the benefits they deliver (again, this helps retail salespeople discuss the product's competitive strengths). Encourage students to think creatively about packaging and labeling as part of the marketing package that will help the product's introduction.

Marketing Spotlight—Anheuser-Busch

Budweiser Lager was first brewed in 1876 by E. Anheuser & Co., St. Louis. Today, Anheuser-Busch is the largest brewer in the world in terms of volume and competes across a diverse range of markets. The company oversees more than 30 different beer brands, including the domestic market leader Budweiser, a number of other beverages, a group of theme parks, and a real estate enterprise. A broad brand portfolio has been a boon to Anheuser-Busch in the past. During the Prohibition era (1920–1933), the company kept revenues pouring in by selling products as diverse as yeast, refrigeration units, truck bodies, soft drinks, and chocolate syrup. After Prohibition, Anheuser-Busch continued to grow with its core malt beverages. In 1957, Budweiser surpassed Schlitz to become the leading beer in the United States In 1980, the company had a 28 percent share of the domestic beer market, a figure that would rise steadily over the next two decades to 47 percent in 1995. Anheuser's market share climbed to 50 percent by 2000, leaving competitors Coors and Miller far behind with 21 percent and 12 percent, respectively.

The table displays Anheuser-Busch's brand portfolio:

Marketing the Flagship Beer

Anheuser-Busch has earned a reputation as an expert marketer, due in large part to its success with the flagship Budweiser brand. Budweiser receives much of the marketing support and attention of the company. Of the $396 million Anheuser-Busch spent on measured media in 2000, $146 million was spent on Budweiser, compared with $107 million for Bud Light. Advertising for Budweiser takes a three-pronged approach: ads emphasizing product quality, ads focusing on values and social responsibility, and ads with contemporary appeal designed to humor and entertain the audience. With this multi-pronged approach, Budweiser is able to create a rich brand image that resonates with a broad audience base. One marketing analyst recently proclaimed that "Budweiser, originally the beer of choice for blue-collar workers, is now beer for all demographics."

Anheuser-Busch conducts extensive and sophisticated market research in order to develop engaging ad campaigns. It is no surprise, then, that advertising for Budweiser routinely garners both critical and audience acclaim, and is credited for much of the brand's success. One of Budweiser's most popular campaigns in recent years—the "Whassup?!" series—earned the company top honors during the Super Bowl ad frenzy, and spawned a host of Internet parodies and television spoofs.

Anheuser-Busch moved to the Internet and launched Budweiser.com in 1996. The site offers information about the brand, company history, information about sporting events sponsored by Budweiser, downloads such as screensavers and television ads, and free e-mail addresses ending in Budweiser.com. During the first two months of 2001, Budweiser.com received almost 2 million more average monthly page visits than similar sites from Miller, Heineken, and Coors. In addition to these effective pull strategies, Anheuser-Busch uses various push strategies in retail outlets to help sell beer, from price cuts to instant-win packaging to in-store promotions. Because summer is the peak season for Budweiser, Anheuser Busch steps up its in store push strategies with its annual Bud Summer promotions.

Anheuser-Busch Looks Ahead

As Anheuser-Busch continues to expand, it will need new products to attract new drinkers. The company is planning on introducing a new super-premium beer using its flagship Budweiser brand as a launch pad. The company will test the new product, called Budweiser Red Label, in certain markets before launching it nationally. The company hopes the extension will attract import drinkers without alienating Budweiser purists. Other recent new products, including 180 energy drink and Tequiza beer, have not been successful. Still, Anheuser-Busch continued to set earnings records in fiscal 2001, and the strength of its brand portfolio continued to prove itself as the company gained market share at the expense of its competitors.

(Sources: Al Stamborski. "A-B Looks to Expand Its Horizons." St. Louis Post-Dispatch, February 19, 2001; David A. Aaker. Managing Brand Equity. The Free Press. New York: 1991, pp. 78–84; Hillary Chura. "Bud Set to Test Upscale Brew." Advertising Age, May 7, 2001; www.budweiser.com; Gerry Khermouch and Theresa Howard. "Core Brands Receive Primary Marketing Focus." Brandweek, June 21, 1999; Thomas Lee. "A-B Tries New Ad Approach on Internet." St. Louis Post-Dispatch, March 20, 2001; David Armstrong. "E-Commerce (A Special Report): Here's to the Net." Wall Street Journal, April 23, 2001.

Questions

1. Provide a concise analysis of the basis for the Anheuser-Busch marketing strategy that has worked so well for so long.

2. If we can assume that great brand and product management is one of Anheuser-Busch's primary strengths, what are some of the contributing factors in that process, and who is affected, primarily?

Suggested Responses

1. Anheuser-Busch has become a master at the game of balancing channel and corporate interests to achieve market share. In addition, they have maintained control of the fine art and science of developing effective and winning product quality and managing life cycle and product positioning strategies so that the long-term corporate needs are met. They constantly balance the types and placements of their various offerings, recognizing that the consumer mind (and that of distributors) has become increasingly fickle. Anheuser-Busch constantly must find different uses for and with the same product base and extend their brand franchise carefully so as not to over-extend in any particular area. This, combined with their attitude of social responsibility and legendary humor and contemporary appeal in their advertising make for a winning combination.

2. The purpose of the question is to point out that A-B is highly successful at the marketing game, but that there is much more to the process than merely good advertising. They have done well to continually differentiate themselves from other products and competitors, in products and in the marketing behind those products, and they have striven to operate at the highest standards in product, advertising and social responsibility. In addition, they are well diversified into complementary, but very focused, areas directly related to the products that put them ahead of the rest. This, of course, helps them to continue the brand recognition that has made them so successful in the past and also as one of the premier performers in the capital markets. With widespread support for their actions, they have no problem maintaining their position in the mind of the consuming public.

With regard to the other variables, the Anheuser-Busch control over their channels of distribution and keen sense of the market, largely due to a first-class market research capability, puts them in a strong position with both their channels and the competition. They are able to see trends well ahead of others, adjusting advertising and product only enough to keep them differentiated. As part of this, they also have managed to constantly widen their demographic base of consumer appeal. As a result, the only real losers in the process are the smaller and less well-heeled competitors that cannot act quickly and effectively to respond to the A-B juggernaut.

Problem

Assume that you are the brand manager for the VW Jetta. You would like to know how to position your car in national advertisements. You start by measuring perceptions of your car versus the top three competitors. The data is shown below:

Table 1 represents data from research conducted to determine the attributes that consumers consider important in the purchase of an automobile. The survey research was performed with 100 subjects.

Table 1	Rating						
Benefits	1	2	3	4	5	6	7
Fuel efficiency					25	35	40
Styling & design		15	15	10	35	15	10
Low maintenance		5	15	15	20	20	25
Low cost of parts	10	10	15	15	15	20	15
Good reputation	10	15	15	10	15	20	15

Table 2—When asked to rate each car on each benefit, on a scale of 1 to 7, where 7 is the highest rating, the subjects provided the following:

TABLE 2	Average Ratings for Each Brand on Each Benefit				
	Toyota	VW	Chevy	BMW	Infiniti
Benefits	Tercel	Jetta	Camaro	525	Q45
Fuel efficiency	7	4	4	3	5
Styling & design	4	1	1	5	7
Low maintenance	7	1	3	6.7	5
Low cost of parts	7	1	4	2	3
Good reputation	5	2	1	6.5	7

Questions

1.   Calculate the means and share of perceptions for the brands.

2.   Develop a semantic differential for each vehicle.

3. Create a 2-dimensional map and position the vehicles in this 2-dimensional space.

4. Which positions should you take to advertise your brand in the marketplace? Explain.

5. In terms of advertising strategy, should you attack competitors through comparative advertising? Explain.

Answers

1. Calculate the means and share of perceptions for the brands.

Consumers were asked to rank the importance of each benefit when making a decision to purchase a car. Having rated each benefit's importance on a scale of 1 to 7 (7 is the most important). Calculate the results as follows: multiply each benefit rating times the number of responses for that rating.

Table 1

Benefits	Rating (Calculated)							
	1	2	3	4	5	6	7	Total
Fuel efficiency					25	35	40	615
Styling & design		15	15	10	35	15	10	450
Low maintenance		5	15	15	20	20	25	510
Low cost of parts	10	10	15	15	15	20	15	435
Good reputation	10	15	15	10	15	20	15	425
								2435

When asked to rate each car on each benefit, on a scale of 1 to 7 where 7 is the highest rating subjects gave the following as shown in Table 2.

Table 2

Benefits	Average Ratings for Each Brand on Each Benefit				
	Toyota	VW	Chevy	BMW	Infiniti
	Tercel	Jetta	Camaro	525	Q45
Fuel efficiency	7	4	4	3	5
Styling & design	4	1	1	5	7
Low maintenance	7	1	3	6.7	5
Low cost of parts	7	1	4	2	3
Good reputation	5	2	1	6.5	7

Multiply the importance rating by the average rating for each car to obtain the relative perceptions for each car, as shown in Table 3.

Table 3

	(all Calculated)				
	Toyota	VW	Chevy	BMW	Infiniti
Benefits	Tercel	Jetta	Camaro	525	Q45
Fuel efficiency	1.77	1.01	1.01	0.76	1.26
Styling & design	0.74	0.18	0.18	0.92	1.29
Low maintenance	1.47	0.21	0.63	1.40	1.05
Low cost of parts	1.25	0.18	0.71	0.36	0.54
Good reputation	0.87	0.35	0.17	1.13	1.22

2.   Develop a semantic differential for each vehicle:

a.   Dimension 1

Fuel efficiency	
Low maintenance	From the one dimension called Economy
Low cost of parts	

b.   Dimension 2

Styling and design	From the dimension called Image
Good reputation	

Dimension 1—Economy (calculated)

Benefits	Toyota Tercel	VW Jetta	Chevy Camaro	BMW 525	Infiniti Q30
Fuel efficiency	1.77	1.01	1.01	0.76	1.26
Low maintenance	1.47	0.21	0.63	1.40	1.05
Low cost of parts	1.25	0.18	0.71	0.36	0.54
Total	4.48	1.40	2.35	2.52	2.85
*(Total / 3)	1.49	0.47	0.78	0.84	0.95

Dimension 2—Image (calculated)

Benefits	Toyota Tercel	VW Jetta	Chevy Camaro	BMW 525	Infiniti Q30
Styling & design	0.74	0.18	0.18	0.92	1.29
Good reputation	0.87	0.35	0.17	1.13	1.22
Total	1.61	0.53	0.35	2.05	2.51
*(Total / 2)	0.805	.265	.175	1.025	1.255

3.   Create a 2-dimensional map and position the vehicles.

Image Map (Product Positioning)

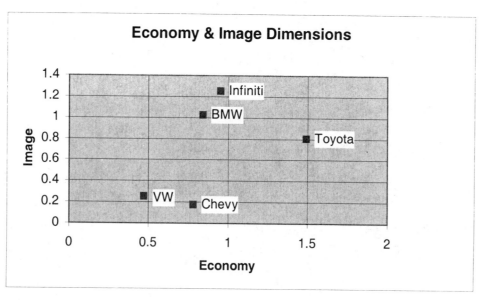

Questions (continued)

4.   Which positions should you take to advertise your brand in the marketplace? Explain.

Answer

The highest perceptions are price and styling. Therefore copywriters should feature these two positions, primarily. Although the car's roominess is not much worse than any of the other cars, roominess is relatively unimportant, and advertising alone cannot make it important.

          What should the company ignore or play down?

Answer

Miles per gallon or safety should not be stressed, especially if the issue has received any publicity.

5.   In terms of advertising strategy, should you attack competitors through comparative advertising? Explain.

Answer

Generally, in a highly competitive market, a brand may resort to comparative advertising if perceptions of the brand are obviously favorable to the brand and not to the competitors. If one can assume the data is valid, then such a strategy should be implemented, but the differential must be significant and the message must be bonafide. If, however, the comparisons are of unimportant benefits then they should not be made.

Chapter 15—Designing and Managing Services

Overview

As the United States moves increasingly toward a service economy and beyond, marketers need to know more about marketing service products. Services are activities or benefits that one party can offer to another that are essentially intangible and do not result in ownership of anything tangible. Services are intangible, inseparable, variable, and perishable. Each characteristic poses problems and requires strategies. Marketers have to find ways to make tangible the intangible; to increase the productivity of providers who are inseparable from the product; to standardize quality in the face of variability; and to influence demand movements and supply capacities better in the face of service perishability.

Because services generally are intangible, customers perceive them as a more risky proposition and evaluation more difficult. Accordingly, they tend to rely more on personal references or information sources, reputation (brand name and image), and the price and/or facilities of the service provider as an indication of quality. Among the means by which the service provider can reinforce these elements and overcome the perceptions of risk is to reduce the complexity involved with the service (paperwork and bureaucracy), stress the positive elements of tangibility in the service, make all communications with the customer very clear and unambiguous, and focus constantly on service quality.

Service industries have typically lagged behind manufacturing firms in adopting and using marketing concepts, but this is changing. Services marketing strategy calls not only for external marketing but also for internal marketing to motivate employees, and interactive marketing to create skills in the service providers. Further, in the future customers will use more technical and functional criteria to judge the quality of services.

Even product-based companies must provide and manage a service bundle for their customers; in fact, their services bundle may be more critical than the product in winning customers. The service mix includes presale services such as technical advice and dependable delivery, as well as postsale services including prompt repair and personnel training. The marketer has to decide on the mix, quality, and source of various product support services for customers. Service marketers, to succeed, must create competitive differentiation, offer high service quality, and find ways to increase service productivity without reducing the perceived service level.

Learning Objectives

After reading the chapter the student should understand:

- How services are defined and classified
- The distinctive characteristics of services as opposed to goods
- How service firms can improve their differentiation, quality, and productivity
- How goods-producing companies can improve their customer-support service

Chapter Outline

Introduction

I.   The nature of services

       1.   Definition: any act or performance one party can offer to another that is essentially intangible and does not result in the ownership of anything

       2.   May or may not be tied to a physical product

B.   Categories of service mix

       1.   Pure tangible good

       2.   Tangible good with accompanying services

       3.   Hybrid

       4.   Major service with accompanying minor goods and services

       5.   Pure service (degree of people and equipment based service activity provides an important variable in the goods-to-service mix)

C.   Characteristics of services and the marketing implications

       1.   Intangibility—services cannot be seen, heard, touched, tasted or felt. A critical element here is the signs or evidence of service quality to transform intangible services into meaningful benefits

       2.   Inseparability—services are produced and consumed simultaneously, and the provider-client interaction is an important aspect in the outcome

       3.   Variability—the quality of a service depends on when, where and by whom they are provided, with training a crucial differentiator

       4.   Perishability—services cannot be stored for later use. There are several strategies that can be used for producing a better match between service demand and supply

II.   Marketing strategies for service firms

A.   Three additional "Ps"

       1.   People (should be competent, caring and responsive)

       2.   Physical evidence (development of a look and observable style)

       3.   Processes (how the service is delivered)

           a)   Goal: achieve a high level of interactive marketing between provider and client

B.   Managing differentiation—offering, faster and better delivery, image (perceived by customers, and to develop a differentiated offer, delivery or image as the alternative to price competition)

C.   Managing service quality—one way to differentiate is through consistently higher quality service that meets or exceeds customer expectations (perceived versus expected service)

       1.   Gaps that cause unsuccessful service delivery

           a)   Consumer expectation and management perception

           b)   Management perception and service-quality specification

           c)   Service-quality specifications and service delivery

           d)   Service delivery and external communications

           e)   Perceived service and expected service.

       2.   Determinants of service quality

           a)   Reliability

           b)   Responsiveness

           c)   Assurance

           d)   Empathy

           e)   Tangibles

    3.   Excellently managed service companies—commonalities:

           a)   Strategic concept: "customer obsessed"

           b)   Top-management commitment

           c)   High standards

           d)   Self-service technologies

           e)   Monitoring systems

           f)   Satisfying customer complaints

           g)   Satisfying employees as well as customers

  D.   Managing productivity (approaches to improve service productivity and to reduce costs)

    1.   Goal is to avoid pushing productivity too hard

    2.   Enhance perceived quality ("high-tech" versus "high-touch")

III.   Managing product support services

    1.   Product-based industries must provide a service bundle to customers and respond to specific customer worries related to

           a)   Reliability

           b)   Service

           c)   Dependability

           d)   Maintenance.

  B.   Postsale service strategy

  C.   Major trends in product support service (building in more reliability, service unbundling, third party service organizations, service contracts, rising customer service choices, rising quality of company call centers and CSRs)

IV.   Summary

Lecture—Services Marketing in the Twenty-first Century

This lecture focuses on the changing role of strategy in an important services marketing setting and the broader value of effective services marketing.

Teaching Objectives

- Stimulate students to think about the differences between service and product marketing

- Develop an understanding of some of the areas where service marketing has changed and become effectively marketing-oriented

- Role of service strategies and policies in helping the firm achieve a better market position

Discussion

Introduction

There are many areas of service marketing that have long have been recognized and others that are just beginning to emerge more prominently for future attention. The latter includes tourism (excluding airlines, hotels and travel agencies), childcare, and business services. This discussion will consider developments in one or more of these areas.

Tourism Marketing

Tourism and related areas of service marketing in the United States traditionally have operated in a relatively fragmented and disjointed manner. Interestingly, despite the vast amount of attention given to tourism in the United States, there has been very little effort to market it properly. In fact, many of our competitors for the international tourism dollar place far more creativity and raw spending on tourism than the United States. The United States. ranks thirty-third in the world in marketing dollars spent on tourism, coming just after Tunisia.

The main concern of many professionals in the tourism industry is that the industry must focus much more on pleasing customers and keeping them happy and secure. Otherwise, as we saw following September 11, 2001, tourists and other visitors will defect to competitors who provide a better solution for their needs.

Fortunately, there were signs even before September 11, 2001, that the process had begun to change. As the U.S. economy became more mature and service-oriented during the late 1990s, many American cities, states and firms jumped on the tourism bandwagon. They recognized that even though tourism was the second largest industry in the United States, the lack of a unified marketing approach worked against establishing coherent marketing plans and programs.

States and cities traditionally conducted most public sector tourism marketing, and while the federal government did some tourism marketing, the focus on other special interest programs resulted in cuts from the meager sums of the past. The private sector, hotel, motel, chains, etc., have done and continue to do the majority of the tourism marketing in the United States.

Mainstream marketers, who avoided direct involvement in tourism in the past, are beginning to take a position on the matter. Further, the importance of marketing in the process is becoming even more evident in discussions throughout the United States. Concerns are rising as we look at our infrastructure in terms of whether or not it provides a pleasing situation for visitors. Unfortunately, even before the recent security concerns, customs officials and others at airports were chided for slow and sometimes ungracious behavior. This is a prime cause of tourism dissatisfaction. Perceived feelings of danger also often are mentioned as a catalyst for a spoiled trip, and there are efforts in many states and cities to correct the problem and the perception even though the security pressure increased markedly after September 11, 2001. But there are other issues. For example a substantial number of tourists arrive at our borders with no provision available to exchange currency. This would not happen in any other major developed nation.

There is, however, an effort in many areas to spotlight cultural resources that attract tourists. Many top proponents of American culture are developing very marketing-oriented stances, portraying the vital role of America's cultural heritage as a major treasure that deserves to be carefully marketed. Increasingly, there is also an interest in the development of a national strategic marketing analysis.

There is recognition given to well marketed attractions such as the "New Orleans Delta Blues Festival" that are the wave of the future. The view is that it is nice to have excellent transportation and smiling customs officials, but tourists will stay away if there's nothing of interest to experience.

Garrison Keillor, of "Prairie Home Companion" fame, and one of the most important figures in American culture today, points out that while infrastructure, an educated workforce, and superior technology are important to the health of travel and tourism, in the final analysis most people travel to America to experience and celebrate its diverse cultural heritage.

We have to be careful, however, that we do not over-market our culture. Keillor notes that although New Orleans recently built fine hotels and a convention center, the strategic planners seemingly forgot to nurture young jazz players. Thus, the city has extraordinary tourism facilities and a reputation for excellent music, but the best examples of the American jazz culture are found in small, obscure towns, not in New Orleans.

We should recognize the impact of marketing in tourism. Considering the traditional 4 Ps of marketing to be only the tip of the iceberg, we need to take a macro-approach in tourism marketing by planning and developing optimum, long-term marketing strategies for the tourism industry, focusing on the best in our culture rather than some of the less savory sides of American life.

Marketing and Advertising

1.   CIGNA offers a range of financial services for individuals, businesses, and corporate employees. The ad in Figure 1 focuses on the benefits of buying the company's life, accident, and disability insurance.

      a.   Who is the target market for the CIGNA insurance products featured in this ad? What does CIGNA do in this ad to make its services seem more tangible to this market?

      b.   What elements of perishability and variability might CIGNA have to consider when marketing its services?

      c.   What postsale service issues would be particularly vital for CIGNA customers? How can the company address these issues in its postsale service strategy?

Answer

      a.   The target market is businessmen with children, particularly entrepreneurs or small business owners (judging by the copy wording "plans that make sense for your company and for you"). To make insurance seem more tangible, CIGNA mentions some of the costly things that parents often buy for their children, such as braces and college. The ad also shows a father hugging his children, which makes the situation more tangible.

      b.   CIGNA might need to consider perishability in terms of higher demand for its services while its ad campaign runs. During that period, CIGNA would have to be ready to respond to customers as they make inquiries about insurance policies. Also, end-of-year periods tend to be busier for business insurance, so CIGNA must be ready to handle high demand at that time. Regarding variability, CIGNA must ensure the same high quality customer service regardless of the way in which customers contact the company or the location of the service reps. This requires consistent and ongoing training, as well as consistent supervision. Students may offer other ideas about perishability and variability, as well.

      c.   After the sale, CIGNA customers would be likely to contact the company with questions about their coverage, to file claims for payment, and to discuss pricing for renewal or for additional coverage. CIGNA could address these issues through a postsale service strategy focusing on availability of customer service representatives, periodic contacts (by mail, phone, e-mail, etc.) to update customers about the status of their accounts, and through ads and other communications that reassure customers that they have made the right decision by choosing CIGNA. Students may have additional suggestions as well.

2. Ad number two: Concierge.com, the travel planning Web site featured in this ad, provides informational services as "the online home of *Condé Nast Traveler.*"

    a. Can Concierge.com be considered a pure tangible good or a pure service? Does it fall in between the two extremes? What are the implications for its marketing strategy?

    b. Why is inseparability a particularly important issue for online service providers like Concierge.com?

    c. How might Concierge.com use self-service technology to enhance its offering?

Answer

    a. Concierge.com is a major service with accompanying minor goods and services, because it helps customers with travel planning—which entails tangibles such as ticket stubs, airline amenities, and so on. Therefore, Concierge.com must pay close attention to the reliability of its online services as well as the quality of the tangibles that accompany the service.

    b. Customers cannot separate the production and consumption of an online service such as Concierge.com. Therefore, if customers experience difficulties using the service—such as an inability to access some parts of the Web site—they will be dissatisfied because they perceive that the service is not complete or lacks the expected quality.

    c. Students can use their creativity in answering this question. For example, Concierge.com might use self-service technology to provide one-click live text or voice chat with representatives, which would add a human dimension to the offering.

Online Marketing Today

As discussed earlier, Schwab.com combines high-touch and high-tech services to allow its brokerage customers to place trades, research securities, or access account information at any hour. Geoff Penney, chief information officer, says the company's strategy emphasizes "people and technology working together" to deliver service "across all of our customer touch points . . . in our investment centers, on the phone, on the Web site, and with our software products." On the high-tech side, Schwab continually upgrades its technology for different customer segments, including special software for active traders. On the high-touch side, the company focuses on hiring, training, and motivating its skilled work force.

To see Schwab's online approach to service, visit its home page at www.schwab.com. Note the different links for customers and noncustomers. Also look at the array of information available on the home page. How does Schwab make its services seem more tangible on this site? What aspects of the site would be particularly valuable to a very active trader? To a first-time investor? What are the implications for Schwab's service strategy?

Answer

Schwab makes its online services seem more tangible by showing a range of services that customers can use to explore investments and make financial services decisions, such as research, market news, stock quotes, and a free demonstration. A very active trader would particularly appreciate the free real-time quotes, while a new investor would find the "how to" investment information valuable. Schwab must therefore prepare a service strategy that would satisfy the divergent needs of this wide spectrum of investment customers, from novices to experienced traders.

You're the Marketer—Sonic PDA Marketing Plan

All marketers need to develop a service strategy when preparing their marketing plans. If they are marketing an intangible product, they will want to consider how to manage customers' expectations and satisfaction; if they are marketing something tangible, they will want to create suitable support services.

You are planning product support services for Sonic's new personal digital assistant. Start by looking over the information and decisions already documented in your marketing plan. Then respond to the following questions to map your service strategy (indicating, where necessary, any additional data or research you may need):

- What support services do buyers of PDA products want and need? Review what you know about this market and its needs; also think about what Sonic's competitors are offering.

- How can Sonic manage gaps between expected and perceived service to satisfy customers?

- What postsale service arrangements must Sonic make to handle repairs and other issues that arise after the purchase?

- What kinds of guarantees should Sonic offer to be competitive?

- What type of internal marketing does Sonic need to be able to implement its service strategy?

Consider how your service strategy will support Sonic's overall marketing efforts. Summarize your recommendations in a written marketing plan or, if you are using *Marketing Plan Pro* software, enter the information under the Product Offering heading and the Service section under the Marketing Mix heading.

Answer

Sonic may need more research to uncover specifics, but in general, PDA buyers would want convenient access to repair services if needed, as well as a good warranty offer and information about upgrades and updates. Sonic can manage the gaps between expected and perceived service by (1) managing expectations through communications that explain what the company offers so customers do not have expectations that exceed actual service delivery and (2) researching customer satisfaction and perceptions of service to uncover problems that can be addressed. To be competitive, Sonic will have to offer at least the same guarantee as it major rivals Palm and Handspring. If Sonic's products are better quality than those of rivals, it can take a small risk and offer a better guarantee. Sonic's internal marketing must include training of company employees, distributors, and repair or service centers; students may suggest additional internal marketing programs.

Marketing Spotlight—Merrill Lynch

Merrill Lynch was founded when Charles Merrill and Edmund Lynch opened an underwriting firm on Wall Street in 1914. The company built a legacy of personalized service, and became the first major firm to introduce investing to the mass market. Charles Merrill coined the phrase "Bringing Wall Street to Main Street" and is credited with helping to change consumer attitudes about investing. Merrill advocated sound investment strategy and made it accessible to the American public using advertisements with titles like "How to Invest." Merrill Lynch had 400,000 clients by 1956, making it the largest brokerage in the country. In 1971, the company unveiled its now-famous bull icon with an advertising campaign titled "Merrill Lynch Is Bullish On America." In 1977, Merrill Lynch introduced one of its most innovative and successful products, the Cash Management Account, which combined checking, money market, and margin accounts.

A Modern Merrill Lynch

As more Americans turned to investing to protect and build their wealth, Merrill Lynch distinguished itself from other brokerages with the financial security it could provide, the high level of service it offered, the personal contacts it established with its retail offices, and the advanced financial research it performed. As Merrill aggressively expanded into institutional investing and banking in the 1980s, its image as a main street brokerage became somewhat muddled. The company's association with high finance and corporate Wall Street became a negative after recession and scandals shook the economy in the 1980s and early 1990s. So Merrill streamlined its operations and developed advertising campaigns with themes like "A Tradition of Trust" that were intended to inspire confidence in the everyday investor. The company continued to grow its retail brokerage businesses and other financial services during the rest of the decade.

Recently, Merrill Lynch found itself under assault from an unlikely segment: discount brokers. Online trading sites set up by discount brokers like Ameritrade and Charles Schwab attracted waves of new investors as the Internet took hold in the latter half of the 1990s. Merrill was slow to move online, primarily because its brokers were reluctant to see the company give total control of trading to investors via an online portal, and the company was concerned about the effect of a proprietary Internet e-commerce site on its heritage as a full-service, customer-focused broker. At the same time, Merrill Lynch was losing current clients and failing to attract new ones as Internet technology gained popularity among investors. In 1998, Schwab's assets under management grew by 39 percent, while Merrill's grew by only 18 percent. By March of that year, Merrill Lynch executives were exhorting the rest of the company to embrace the Internet. The company's vice-chairman, John L. Steffens, argued that Merrill Lynch "had to offer an online-only account or it would lose too many assets, not to mention the next generation of investors."

Merrill Arrives Online

Merrill Lynch decided that it would provide online trading tools that augmented its traditional off-line services. First, the company opened a bare-bones online site, called Merrill Lynch Online, that enabled high-value customers to access accounts and information using the Internet. In December 1999, the company created Merrill Lynch Direct, a full-service, online-only retail trading site. To provide content and technology, the company invested in or partnered with a number of technology companies, such as IBM, Cisco, Microsoft, Bloomberg, and Real Networks. For $29.95 a trade, Merrill Lynch Direct gave customers broker-less trading, real-time market updates, a spectrum of services from the vaunted off-line side of the business, such as Merrill research, access to Merrill initial public offerings, and portfolio management tools. Many customers continued to work closely with their brokers, whom the company encourages to provide consulting-type service to clients. To better combine its off-line strengths with its emerging on-line capabilities, the Merrill Lynch developed a strategy called "Merrill Anywhere" that links clients to their accounts via the Internet, the telephone, and eventually a host of wireless platforms.

Merrill Lynch Direct was recognized by Financial NetNews as the best in their categories in 2000. The award for the individual investor portal applauded Merrill for "outshin[ing] its counterparts in the full service space" by combining its traditional off-line service with the Internet site. The addition of online trading technology helped Merrill Lynch achieve revenue records in every category and region in 2000. Its institutional clients made a record $1.9 trillion in trades using Merrill's online technology. The company earned $3.8 billion in 2000, a 41 percent increase from record earnings of $2.7 billion in 1999. Merrill Lynch may have been slow to adopt the online trading model, but today the company is combining the Internet with its traditional financial services to yield impressive results.

Sources: Leah Spiro. "Merrill's E-Battle." *Business Week,* November 15, 1999; "A Legacy of Leadership." www.ml.com; "Merrill Lynch Reports Record $1.9 Trillion in E-Commerce Volume in 2000." *Business Wire,* January 15, 2001; Jaqueline Doherty. "Ride 'Em Dave." *Barron's,* November 30, 1998; Stephen Power. "Credit Where Credit Is Due." *Dallas Morning News,* October 9, 1994.

Questions

1. What are the service marketing strategy differences between Merrill Lynch online, Merrill Lynch Direct and Schwab?

2. Given the direction of investment firm marketing, do you believe that the Merrill Lynch marketing service strategy is heading in the right direction? Could the Merrill Lynch marketing strategy backfire? Discuss.

3. How would you compare the service marketing concepts discussed in the text with how Merrill Lynch operates? Why did it take Merrill Lynch so long to get on board with the twenty-first century?

Suggested Responses

1. Merrill Lynch On-line is designed to support or augment the regular full service, broker-based, operations for the "Priority Client" investor demographic that Merrill Lynch seeks to replace the middle-America demographic of the 1950s and 1960s. Merrill Lynch Direct is a discount competitor to Schwab and essentially copies or responds to the Schwab concept. Merrill Lynch Direct, however, is totally separate from the Merrill Lynch Online and corporate operations and effectively is a separate brand and company. This could present some image and branding problems for Merrill Lynch as they work through adjustment to the fact that they have very different demographics to work with in the future.

2. The problem with the Merrill Lynch model is that it really has created some overlapping images for its primary brand (full-service brokerage), with the result that their image is not as clear as in years past. Because they have been one of the most significant brokers in the marketplace, it is easy to understand why they were slow to change and why they were forced to make major adjustments in their operations and culture when they finally decided to respond to the drop in their clientele base. If Merrill Lynch had dealt with these issues earlier, when the handwriting was on the wall in terms of the impact of Schwab and others, the transition might have been less traumatic. Because they did not respond, however, the combination of the earlier investor defections and September 11, 2001, led to much more internal adjustment and management upheaval than expected.

3. Merrill Lynch took so long to get on board because it had to struggle with the brokers to bring in the modern and competitive twenty-first century product. Merrill Lynch had to recognize that computers and the Internet brought the process much closer to the average customer. Many of their customers were no longer were willing to sit back and let someone else handle their affairs. Customers learned from many other cultural and economic changes during the last quarter of the twentieth century that they could do much more to cope with the changing economic, competitive and investment environments. This and the transparency that evolved in pricing and other areas of marketing (discussed in this course) made it likely that there would be substantial change for firms providing brokerage and investment services.

Like Schwab and others saw and responded to the coming changes, Merrill Lynch finally recognized that a more egotistical and self-confident generation of Baby Boomers and Generation Xers wanted more control and wanted it faster. This fit with much of what Kotler talks about as the key response variables for successful marketers. Although there will always be room for Merrill Lynch and other full service brokers, it is also likely that with ups and downs in the market there will always be those who feel they have the ability to do their own investment planning and action and will turn to the competition if they do not get what they want from the dominant firms. There is considerable marketing data that even affluent investors have become more interested in on-line trading as a way to build awareness and maintain control. They are less interested in merely handing over his/her investment funds to someone who may or may not have greater investing insight.

Chapter 16—Developing Price Strategies and Programs

Overview

Price has become one of the more important marketing variables. Despite the increased role of nonprice factors in the modern marketing process, price is a critical marketing element, especially in markets characterized by monopolistic competition or oligopoly. Competition and buyers that are more sophisticated has forced many retailers to lower prices and in turn place pressure on manufacturers. Further, there has been increasing buyer awareness of costs and pricing, and growing competition within the channels, which in turn provides the consumer with even more awareness of the pricing process.

In setting the price of a product, the company should follow a six-step procedure. First, the company carefully establishes its marketing objective(s), such as survival, maximum current profit, maximum current revenue, maximum sales growth, maximum market skimming or product-quality leadership. Second, the company determines the demand schedule, which shows the probable quantity purchased per period at alternative price levels. The more inelastic the demand, the higher the company can set its price. Third, the company estimates how its costs vary at different output levels, production levels, different marketing strategies, differing marketing offers, and target costing based on market research. Fourth, the company examines competitors' prices as a basis for positioning its own price. Fifth, the company selects one of the following pricing methods: markup pricing, target return pricing, perceived-value pricing, value-pricing, going-rate pricing, and sealed-bid pricing. Sixth, the company selects its final price, expressing it in the most effective psychological way, coordinating it with the other marketing mix elements, checking that it conforms to company pricing policies, and making sure it will prevail with distributors and dealers, company sales force, competitors, suppliers, and government.

Companies will adapt the price to varying conditions in the marketplace. Geographical pricing is one marketplace adjustment based on a company decision related to pricing distant customers. Price discounts and allowances are a second area for adjustment where the company establishes cash discounts, quantity discounts, functional discounts, seasonal discounts, and allowances. Promotional pricing provides a third marketplace option, with the company deciding on loss-leader pricing, special-event pricing, cash rebates, low interest financing, longer payment terms, warranties and service contracts and psychological discounting. Discriminatory pricing, the fourth option, enables the company to establish different prices for different customer segments, product forms, brand images, places, and times. Lastly, product-mix pricing, enables the company to determine price zones for several products in a product line, as well as differential pricing for optional features, captive products, byproducts, and product bundles.

When a firm considers initiating a price change, it must carefully consider customer and competitor reactions. Customer reactions are influenced by the meaning customers see in the price change. Competitor reactions flow either from a set reaction policy or from a fresh appraisal of each situation. The firm initiating the price change must also anticipate the probable reactions of suppliers, middlemen, and governments.

The firm encountering a competitor-initiated price change must attempt to understand the competitor's intent and the likely duration of the change. If swiftness of reaction is desirable, the firm should preplan its reactions to different possible competitor price actions.

To summarize, pricing involves the customer demand schedule, the cost function, and competitors' prices. The question is how should a company integrate cost-, demand-, and competition-based pricing considerations? In setting a price the firm, for example Kodak, will have to consider the following cost-, demand-, and competition-based pricing decisions:

Cost-based pricing decisions: Marginal analysis and break-even analysis are the two primary methods in cost-based pricing decisions:

- What is the impact of a 5 percent cost increase in the price of silver on film costs?

- Should Kodak attempt to purchase silver futures to reduce the volatility of silver costs?

- What is the impact on film manufacturing and marketing costs of a 10 percent demand reduction?

Demand-based pricing decisions: Among the variables here are the type of demand for the product (prestige, price-oriented, etc.), changes in buyer attitude toward price with changes in the economic environment (uncontrollable variables), and the elasticity of demand

- What is the elasticity of demand by market segment (amateur photographer, professional photographer, and X-ray market)?

- Are the short- and long-range effects of price increases the same?

- Will consumers switch to slow-speed films that contain less silver?

Competition-based pricing decisions: To set prices effectively, an organization must be aware of the prices charged by competitors.

- Among the major questions here are: Will all competitors raise their prices by the same percentage? Will competitors react to cost increases more slowly to try to increase their market share? Will some competitors try to absorb much of the cost increases to induce brand switching?

Learning Objectives

After reading the chapter the student should understand:
- The six-step procedure in establishing product or service price
- How varying situational considerations influence price
- The factors considered in making a price change

Chapter Outline

I.   Introduction—Developing the point that price and pricing are increasingly important in the marketing mix and process. The issue that it communicates much about the firm's intended value positioning. There are many emerging issues related to price-cutting, channel pricing, international pricing and pricing improved products.

II.   Setting the price

    A.   Step 1: Selecting the pricing objective

        1.   Survival

        2.   Maximum current profits

        3.   Maximum market share (market-penetration pricing)

        4.   Market skimming—appeals to high end market segments

        5.   Product-quality leadership—premium quality connotes premium price

        6.   Other pricing objectives—cost recovery (partial or full), social pricing

B.   Step 2: Determining demand

      1.   Price sensitivity

            a)   Unique-value

            b)   Substitute-awareness

            c)   Difficult-comparison

            d)   Total-expenditure

            e)   End-benefit

            f)   Shared-cost

            g)   Sunk-investment,

            h)   Price-quality

            i)   Inventory effects

      2.   Estimating demand curves

            a)   Statistical analysis

            b)   Price experiments

            c)   Buyer input

      3.   Price elasticity of demand

            a)   Determination of the affect of a change in price on overall demand

            b)   If demand changes considerably with a change in price, it is elastic. If demand does not change significantly or in parallel with the price, it is inelastic

C.   Step 3: Estimating costs

      1.   Types of costs and levels of production (fixed, variable, and total costs)

      2.   Accumulated production (learning curve pricing)

      3.   Differentiated marketing offers

      4.   Target costing—determine price that must be charged according to market research

D.   Step 4: Analyzing competitors' costs, prices, and offers (evaluate from customer perspective, compare, value, and reaction)

E.   Step 5: Selecting a pricing method

      1.   Markup pricing—standard markup, but can vary according to product categories

      2.   Target return pricing—to make a fair return on investment

      3.   Perceived value pricing—based on buyer perceptions

      4.   Value pricing—fairly low price for a high quality offering, everyday low pricing, and so on

      5.   Going rate pricing—base price on that of competitors ("follow the leader")

      6.   Auction-type pricing—ascending, descending, and sealed-bid

      7.   Group pricing (Internet-based methods for group buying, pool pricing)

F.   Step 6: Selecting final price

      1.   Psychological pricing (indicator of quality, reference price, odd pricing)

2.   Gain-and-risk sharing pricing (risk losing customers if cannot deliver full promised value)

3.   The influence of other marketing-mix elements—note relationships between relative price, relative quality, and relative advertising

4.   Company pricing policies—contemplated price must be consistent

5.   Impact of price on other parties—distributors, sales force, competitors, suppliers, government, and so on

III.   Adapting the price

A.   Geographical pricing (cash, countertrade, barter)

B.   Price discounts and allowances

1.   Cash discounts

2.   Quantity discounts

3.   Functional (trade) discounts

4.   Seasonal discounts

5.   Allowances, trade-in or promotional

C.   Promotional pricing

1.   Loss-leader pricing—to stimulate traffic

2.   Special event pricing—to draw customers

3.   Cash rebates—to encourage purchase within a specified time period

4.   Low-interest financing—to facilitate purchase

5.   Longer payment terms—for lower monthly payments

6.   Warranties and service contracts—added value

7.   Psychological discounting—set an artificially high initial price

D.   Discriminatory pricing

1.   Customer-segment pricing—different prices for different groups

2.   Product-form pricing—different versions priced differently

3.   Image pricing—same product at two different levels

4.   Channel pricing (location pricing)—same product priced differently at different locations

5.   Time pricing—same product priced differently at different day, time or season

E.   Product-mix pricing

1.   Product-Line Pricing—price steps

2.   Optional-feature pricing—in addition to main product

3.   Captive-product pricing—main products that require ancillary products

4.   Two-part pricing—fixed fee plus variable fee based on usage

5.   Byproduct pricing—to recoup production costs of main product

6.   Product-bundling pricing—less costly when purchased together

IV.   Initiating and responding to price changes

A.   Initiating price cuts

1.   Excess capacity

2.   Drive to dominate the market. *Note: This strategy has high risks.*

B.   Initiating price increases

    1.   Cost inflation

    2.   Anticipatory pricing

    3.   Overdemand

    4.   Options

        a)   Delayed quotation pricing

        b)   Escalator clauses

        c)   Unbundling

        d)   Reduction of discounts

C.   Reactions to price changes

    1.   Customer reactions

    2.   Competitor reactions

D.   Responding to competitors' price changes

    1.   Maintain price

    2.   Raise perceived quality

    3.   Reduce price

    4.   Increase price and improve quality

    5.   Launch low-price fighter line

V.   Summary

Lecture—Measuring the Impact of Price: How Important Is the Pricing Variable

This lecture deals with pricing strategy in a marketing setting, and the role and value of effective pricing in the overall marketing strategy and implementation effort. The discussion begins with examples of pricing problems and options as a means of maintaining or increasing the firm's market position. This leads into a discussion of the implications for the introduction of various pricing strategies for the firm and an industry.

It is useful to update the examples so that students will be able to identify readily with this concept based on their general knowledge of the companies and products involved in the lecture/discussion.

Teaching Objectives

- To stimulate students to think about the critical issues, pro and con, for a firm when it moves toward adoption of a formal or informal pricing strategy

- Points to consider in proceeding with a specific pricing strategy

- Role of pricing strategies and policies in helping the firm achieve a balanced position *vis á vis* the customer and the competition

Discussion

Introduction

Pricing policies in many companies tend to be based more on intuition and what the market will bear more than scientific or objective criteria. This approach, however, is beginning to change, in line with many other changes taking place in marketing and in the U.S. and global economies. Pricing has become a key issue for both consumer and business marketers, and sadly it is a problem area where few managers are well prepared. Pricing is not part of most university programs, largely because it long has been considered part of the world of economics, "the dismal science."

Marketing professionals have tended to ignore pricing theories and concepts, and in the past they did not even consider it as an equal part of the marketing equation. Accordingly, pricing and the impact of price have been studied very little, but clearly it is and should be one of the more important aspects of the marketing process. To most contemporary marketing professionals, pricing is a final and very important marketing strategy focal point. Without an effective pricing analysis and price decision, the rest of the marketing process is left unfinished.

Role of Pricing

Pricing can and does help a company attain its other marketing objectives. As a result, pricing strategy should be tied closely and carefully to the overall business, competitive and marketing strategy. Further, the pricing program should be supported with a focused plan of implementation. Pricing enables the marketer to segment markets, define products, create customer incentives, and even send signals to competitors.

For example, if the company wants to enter a crowded field, such as the credit card business, it may opt for a penetration strategy. This is what Sears did with the Discover card. The retailer obtained as many customers as possible through a low price (i.e., no membership fee), and established a position in the market. Skimming would be the opposite strategy, pricing a product at a high level to "skim" the innovators. That way, the firm obtains high profits at the beginning of the product life cycle, effectively covering the development costs. After the firm pays for the development costs, it has the option to move the price down to the next level to achieve other marketing objectives. Either strategy can work, but the decision, implementation, and results all depend on the firm's marketing objectives.

Many marketing professionals argue that pricing is a valuable strategic weapon that helps companies enhance and capitalize on competitive vulnerability, and there is no question that pricing decisions have an immediate impact on a company's bottom line. From this perspective, it is easy to argue that to a large degree, pricing decisions can determine whether a product or a company will succeed or fail.

Pricing Limits

One of the first things a pricing strategy process can determine is that there is an upper and lower price boundary, and each has to be considered. The upper boundary, the economic value of the product, is the most an informed consumer is willing to pay for the product. Marketers determine this boundary by comparing the product with a reference product, and asking what attributes the product has that are above, or below, the value of the product offered by the competitors. Clearly, if a product is below the value of the competition, it is almost impossible to set the price higher than the competitive price.

Next, the marketer should identify the best available alternative product for the most important customer market or segment. The marketer could ask: "Other than the obvious benefit, what additional benefits does this product provide?" Many times the benefit is labor savings or additional productivity. Other times there could be emotional benefits, or some other intangible benefit.

Once the list of benefits is completed, it is time to assign a value to each benefit. Some benefits are quantifiable directly, such as labor savings. The analyst can calculate the number of hours saved times the wage rate. If there is another specific benefit, the firm may try to determine the value. For example, the marketer may analyze possible substitute products to determine if there are other benefits that related products might have that eventually prove important in the competitive process. It is appropriate to make an effort to determine the approximate value of each such benefit to determine when prices should be adjusted.

Another technique that can be useful in determining the upper boundary of a particular product's price is a conjoint study, or survey, of various customers. With this approach, prospects are invited to select from a series of pricing options for the product. In the survey, the researcher attempts to determine the value of the product's particular attributes. Once the firm has obtained this data, it has identified the upper boundary of the product's potential price.

It is critical to approach the process from the customer perspective, separating what the company thinks is the economic value and the customer's perceived economic value. Unfortunately, some companies care so much about the product that they consider every benefit at the high end. The result is that the survey research has to determine whether people will believe what the company believes concerning price and value.

The Role of the Customer

There are many examples of the role of the customer in the pricing process, and one of the better examples comes from Datastorm, a software firm that made the Procomm Plus, an early software product that linked computers to networks through a modem. The market for this software was already beginning to grow in 1991, just when ProComm Plus was scheduled for its debut, and competing products were already on the shelves, priced at a premium. Datastorm believed that it could tap pent-up demand for lower-priced communications software in the consumer market, so the strategy was to set the price of the product at $179, dramatically less expensive than the competition. The company maintained that pricing point for four years. Datastorm dominated the field, with an 85 percent market share among IBM computer users, until 1995–96. Many analysts credit the company's pricing strategy as the key to its success.

What the marketing managers at Datastorm did, consciously or unconsciously, was to follow a well-defined market-oriented process to pick new product prices. The focus was on the three Cs: customer, company, and competition. To employ this simple marketing tool, Datastorm managers set the price of a new product based on the customer's perception of a fair price. Of course, the customer's perception of what was a fair price often was based on the competitor's price that typically the consumer perceives as on the high (economic) end of the scale. This approach can be quite useful for those selling into an established market, or even if they are selling into a new market, whether the measurement was performed properly.

Micro-marketing also plays an important part in pricing strategy. Stores, such as the midwestern grocer Dominick's, engaged in micro-marketing by using pricing data obtained from scanners and measured by Information Resources Inc., and A.C. Nielsen. Nielsen's program measured the differences in elasticity between stores and matched prices so that customers who cared more about price got discounts, and customers who cared about other factors could receive those benefits.

To determine low-end pricing for a particular product, it is important to adopt a customer perspective. As noted above, companies often are so aware and care so much about the product that every benefit is considered at the high end in price-value. Of course, the obvious question is whether individual consumers and the marketplace have the same perception of value and price.

The marketer also must examine the variable costs, or incremental costs, that matter to the consumer. A common error is that companies consider variable costs as part of fixed costs. In an airline, if you have a seat, and you consider the average cost of the plane and the crew it might turn out that the average cost per seat was $10. If, however, the plane is sitting on the runway, ready to take off, the variable cost might be as low as $1. At this point, the differences between fixed and variable costs look very different. This is the way it is with highly perishable and time-sensitive goods and/or services. The variable cost tells you what you are gaining for each additional customer. If you raise that price too high, you likely consider additional customers as not as valuable as they truly are in the final analysis (such as when the plane is setting on the runway, ready to take off).

Firms that inflate their variable costs tend not to cut their prices very often. They do not realize the true incremental revenue they can gain from a discount. Experts advise against putting overhead costs into the price of the product because they are fixed, not variable, costs. By folding overhead costs into the equation, the firm may be distorting the pricing decision. The essence of the matter is that empty hotel rooms or plane seats are revenue never to be regained. It is better to have something than nothing. This is an attitude that has gained considerable popularity since September 11, 2001 as the airlines and other industries watched their carefully developed strategies based on their perceptions of value go down the drain.

The relationship between the quality of a product and a particular price is always an issue. Price sensitivity research has provided much information that can help determine the relationship of price to quality. Consumers ask: "Is this better if it is more expensive?" In response, marketers apply the principles of "odd" versus "even" pricing. Research in pricing indicates that something at $9.99 versus $10 is generally associated with Sears, Kmart, and J.C. Penney. It puts the emphasis on the first digit. The implication or perception is that the retailer is trying to save the consumer money. If a retailer sells a Packard-Bell computer for $1,999.95, there is only a five-cent difference between that and $2,000. Many people, however, place emphasis on the first number. On the other side of the scale, Nordstrom and other high-end retailers price in even numbers. This lends an aura of quality to the product. There is also prestige pricing, where you effectively advertise that you have the most expensive perfume in the world. This is strictly a matter of old-fashioned snob appeal, but it works, depending on your market segment.

Art of Naming a Price

After the price limits, high and low, are determined, we enter into what essentially is the "art form" of pricing, often referred to as "the art of pricing." There are particular aspects of pricing that will determine where the firm will price, based on these upper and lower boundaries, without much price sensitivity or elasticity. Here there are issues such as "fairness."

Fairness is gauged by thinking about how a customer feels about the price of a product. Research shows that price increases are perceived as fair if they are based on increased costs, but those based on the characteristics and/or circumstances of the customer are considered unfair. One of the major pricing issues in recent years is that of "everyday low pricing". This is where the retailer charges a constant, lower price at all times, with no temporary price discounts. This approach reduces uncertainty among consumers, and it helps to restore faith in the price of a brand. It also contrasts sharply with the so-called "high-low" strategy of companies that rely on constant price promotions. Discounters such as Wal-Mart led the trend toward "everyday low pricing," but the concept generally remains more popular in the South than in the North.

Whatever pricing tactics the firm chooses, it is important to remember that pricing is essential to strategy and should not be treated as an afterthought. Strategic pricing should be one of a business's most potent competitive weapons, and substantial sales potential may well be lost without an effective planning and control effort in this important area of marketing activity.

Marketing and Advertising

1. Ad number one: In this ad, 1-800-Contacts reaches out to price-sensitive contact-lens users with an offer to "Get the exact same contacts delivered for less than you're paying now."

    a. What specific elements might affect price sensitivity in the consumer market for contact lenses?
    b. What pricing method does 1-800-Contacts appear to be using in this ad?
    c. How might 1-800-Contacts use product-bundling pricing to increase sales to its target market?

Answer

    a. Price sensitivity among consumer contact lens buyers might be affected by: the substitute-awareness effect, because buyers know they can buy glasses or have surgery as substitutes; difficult-comparison effect, because buyers may have difficulty comparing the quality of substitute products; total-expenditure effect, because contact lens purchases are a small part of total consumer income; price-quality effect, because consumers perceive that some branded products are higher quality.
    b. 1-800-Contacts appears to be using market penetration pricing to achieve higher sales volume and higher long-term profit.
    c. 1-800-Contacts could use product-bundling pricing to increase sales to its target market by bundling contact lens cleaning products, lens cases, or other items that consumers typically need when using contact lenses. The company could also bundle services such as optometry exams with local specialists. Students may suggest other ideas, as well.

2. The ad in Figure 2 shows how the online auction site eBay attracts price-sensitive business buyers to auctions for electronic gear such as projectors, monitors, PCs, and television monitors.

    a. Because product prices are never mentioned, what benefits does eBay emphasize to encourage business buyers to visit its Web site?
    b. Is business demand for slide projectors likely to be elastic or inelastic? What are the implications for the auction prices of projectors sold to business customers on eBay's site?
    c. Which of Nagle's nine factors affecting price sensitivity are most applicable to business demand for slide projectors?

Answer

    a. The copy in this ad emphasizes that buyers may find bargains on eBay and stresses that "millions of items" are listed so buyers can find "just about every presentation tool you could want." It also focuses on convenience and timesaving benefits.
    b. Business demand for slide projectors is likely to be elastic. Because this is not an essential item for businesses, buyers are likely to buy more at lower prices.
    c. Of Nagle's nine factors, the following are most applicable to business demand for slide projectors: unique-value effect, because buyers will be less price sensitive to distinctive products; substitute-awareness effect, because buyers will be less price sensitive when they are unaware of substitutes such as electronic presentation technology; total-expenditure effect, because projectors are a

relatively small purchase compared with business revenues; and the sunk-investment effect, because many businesses have existing slide shows to use with projectors.

3. ****BONUS AD--See Companion Web site!** Baymont uses value pricing to attract business travelers as well as vacationers to its 180 inns and suites around the United States, as this ad shows.
    a. According to this ad, what is Baymont doing to adapt its price for lodgings?
    b. Identify some of the fixed and variable costs that Baymont might experience.
    c. How does Baymont communicate quality in this ad to differentiate itself from competing chains?

Answer

a. Baymont is adapting its price using geographical pricing to vary the price of renting a room from location to location. It is also promotional pricing to offer a rewards program that allows frequent customers to enjoy free hotel stays.

b. Students will identify a number of different fixed and variable costs. For instance, real estate taxes and mortgage payments are fixed for each hotel, regardless of volume. Variable costs include laundry costs for used linens and the cost of in-room amenities such as soap and shampoo.

c. Baymont communicates quality to differentiate itself by highlighting the "Best Hotel Value Award" from *Entrepreneur Magazine*. It also mentions the size of the room ("big, comfortable") and the many amenities.

Online Marketing Today—Priceline.com

The online market for travel services will reach $63 billion within a few years, and Priceline.com aims to capture a significant share; already, it is high on the top-ten list of travel Web sites. After a brief period of diversification into name-your-price sales of groceries and gasoline, the company has refocused on its core travel and financial services offerings, including airline tickets, hotel rooms, rental cars, and mortgage loans. The company guarantees that a Priceline.com mortgage is the "lowest-cost loan on the market" and backs this up by paying $300 to any customer who finds a better price.

See how the system works by visiting the Priceline Web site at www.priceline.com. Follow the link marked "How it works" to read about the name-your-price process. Then return to the home page and follow several of the links promoting discounted offerings. What can you say about the price sensitivity of Priceline's customers? What effect would Priceline's prices be likely to have on the reference prices customers bear in mind for travel and mortgage services? How does the company's lowest-cost loan guarantee affect a customer's perception of the product's value?

Answer

Priceline's customers are likely to be very price sensitive, which drives them to set their own (presumably low) prices for travel services. If consumers consistently see low prices for Priceline's travel and mortgage services, they will keep these in mind as they compare prices from other sources. Thus, sources that offer higher-priced travel and mortgage services may be perceived as out of the range these consumers believe is normal and acceptable for those products. The company's lowest-cost loan guarantee will reassure customers and enhance their perceptions that they are getting the best possible value at Priceline.

You're the Marketer—Sonic PDA Marketing Plan

Pricing is a critical element in any company's marketing plan, because it directly affects revenue and profit goals. To effectively design and manage pricing strategies, marketers must consider costs as well as the perceptions of customers and the reactions of competitors—especially in highly competitive markets.

You are in charge of pricing Sonic's first personal digital assistant for its launch early next year. Review your current situation, especially the SWOT analysis you previously prepared and your competitive environment. Also think about the markets you are targeting and the positioning you want to achieve. Now continue working on your marketing plan by responding to the following questions about pricing:

- What should Sonic's primary pricing objective be? Explain your reasoning.
- Are PDA customers likely to be price sensitive? Is demand elastic or inelastic? What are the implications for your pricing decisions?
- How will the introductory product pricing work with the other parts of Sonic's marketing mix?
- What price adaptations (such as discounts, allowances, and promotional pricing) should Sonic include in its marketing plan?

After you have developed your pricing strategies and programs, document your recommendations in a written marketing plan or type them into the Marketing Mix section of the *Marketing Plan Pro* software, depending on your instructor's directions.

Answer

Sonic's primary pricing objective should be market penetration, because they are operating in a difficult and highly competitive market. If they fail to achieve a decent market share, they will not be able to effectively compete and they will not be able to lower unit costs through higher volume. Students may argue that survival is an appropriate pricing objective, but this is probably not the case because Sonic is not yet in trouble. Nor can Sonic set prices to maximize current profits at this time, because it needs to establish its brand.

PDA customers are likely to be fairly price sensitive, because there are many well-known PDAs already on the market (substitute-awareness effect) and because current users of other brands may perceive switching costs (sunk-investment effect). Demand is relatively elastic, with more buyers willing to buy when prices are substantially lower. Thus, Sonic must price at the low end of its acceptable range to implement a market penetration strategy. Sonic's introductory product pricing must be supported by the other parts of the marketing mix. For example, Sonic's advertising might mention the price or tout the value, and its choice of distributors should be consistent with it's pricing. Students may suggest other ideas, as well.

Price adaptations to be included in Sonic's marketing plan include: cash discounts for resellers buying PDAs (because these encourage early or on-time payment of invoices) and promotional allowances for encouraging distributors to stock the new PDAs. Sonic might also use promotional pricing on a limited basis to jump-start consumer purchases of its new PDA. Ask students to consider how other tactics mentioned in the chapter might apply to Sonic's product introduction.

Marketing Spotlight—Louis Vuitton Moet Hennessey (LVMH)

Luxury leather goods maker Louis Vuitton was established in Paris in 1855. For more than a century and a half, the company made quality handcrafted luggage and other leather goods. It remained a small, family-controlled company until the 1970s, when French businessman Henry Racamier married a Vuitton heiress, and rapidly expanded and diversified the business. When Racamier took over in 1977, the company had only two shops in France and had combined sales of less than $50 million. By the mid-1980s, the company had 95 stores across the globe and revenues topping $500 million.

In 1987, the merger of Louis Vuitton with famed French spirits, champagne, and perfume group Moet-Hennessey marked a new era of consolidation in the luxury-goods industry. The newly formed Louis Vuitton Moet Hennessey (LVMH) instantly became the world's largest luxury goods company, raking in $4 billion in revenues in 1991. The company continued to grow in the 1990s by acquiring a number of other luxury-goods companies, including fashion label Christian Lacroix and shoe designer Berluti in 1993, TAG Heuer watchmaker in 1999, and the Donna Karan brand in 2000. Today, LVMH has a portfolio of 50 luxury brands and is the number one worldwide seller of champagne, cognac, fashion and leather goods, and the number three worldwide seller of perfumes and cosmetics. The company's revenues topped $10 billion in 2000.

Here are some of the famous luxury brands LVMH controls:

Champagne, Wine, Cognac, And Brandy	• Moet & Chandon
	• Dom Perignon
	• Hennessey
Fashion	• Berluti
	• Christian Lacroix
	• Givenchy
	• Louis Vuitton
	• Donna Karan
Fragrances	• Christian Dior
	• Givenchy
Cosmetics	• Hard Candy
	• Fresh
	• Urban Decay
Watches	• Ebel
	• Tag Heuer

LVMH also owns several business and financial media publications, including La Tribune newspaper, and two art magazines. The company owns all or part of a number of retail franchises, including the Sephora chain of cosmetic stores, DFS Group duty free shops, Miami Cruiseline Services duty free shops, and French department stores Le Bon Marche. Other businesses the company owns include auction houses Phillips, de Pury & Luxembourg and Etude Tajan, Omas luxury pens, and a development capital business called LV Capital. LVMH maintains an Internet presence (www.lvmh.com), but its Web site is mostly informational. It does, however, feature an e-commerce site called eLuxury, which debuted in June 2000 and in which LVMH is a principal investor. The site strives to maintain an "exclusive" image by prohibiting advertising, providing editorial content on trends, travel, and entertainment, and partnering with more than 60 luxury brands.

Luxury Pricing, LVMH Style

LVMH has consistently pursued a luxury pricing strategy, which means high markups, limited availability, and few if any markdowns. When asked by a reporter whether the Louis Vuitton store in Paris would have a post-Christmas sale, the company's president Yves Carcelle answered "No," saying, "That would devalue the brand." Louis Vuitton sells its products only through a global network of company-owned stores. This keeps margins high and allows the company to maintain control of its products through every step in the channel. Bernard Arnault explained, "If you control your factory, you control your quality; if you control your distribution, you control your image." Today, LVMH maintains a global network of 1,286 stores, a 28 percent increase over 1999. Its 284 Louis Vuitton stores and 461 Sephora locations comprise over half of the stores in this network.

Recently, Louis Vuitton built several flagship concept stores located on high-fashion avenues around the world like Rodeo Drive and Fifth Avenue. These stores sell an estimated average of $1,800 per square foot. Some of the best-selling stores sell as much as $8,000 per square foot. Additionally, since maintaining an upscale image is vital to a luxury brand, LVMH devotes over ten percent of annual sales to promotion and advertising. The company advertises its brands primarily in fashion and lifestyle publications. Some of the leading brands sponsor major international events with luxury cachet, as Louis Vuitton does by sponsoring the America's Cup. Because image is an essential part of marketing luxury goods, LVMH is careful to evaluate every advertising and promotional opportunity for consistency with the image of its brands. As a result, the company manages a portfolio of luxury brands unparalleled in both size and sales.

Sources: William Echikson. "Luxury Steals Back." *Fortune,* January 16, 1995; www.lvmh.com, www.eluxury.com; Thomas Kamm. "Latest Fashion." *Wall Street Journal,* December 28, 1987; Lisa Marsh. "LVMH Thinks of Vuitton Globally, Acts on 5th Ave." *New York Post,* December 5, 2000; Joshua Levine. "Liberté, Fraternité—But to Hell with Égalité!" *Forbes,* June 2, 1997.

Questions

1. What constitutes a luxury good such as those in the LVMH stable of products? What pricing concepts does LVMH apply effectively? Likewise, what actions has LVMH taken that belie a different and less effective approach? How would you characterize the LVMH marketing strategy?

2. Suggest possible changes that LVMH could make to its marketing strategy in the future. Assume that their objective is to develop new market segments for LVMH.

Suggested Responses

1. LVMH has worked hard to secure a prized position, "snob appeal," in the marketplace. Snob appeal, combined with the "luxury good" classification, is as good as it gets for virtually any branded product. Snob appeal implies to the customer that if you (the customer) are concerned about the price you have no business considering purchase. Achieving such an august position is both very difficult and can involve luck as well as marketing skill. LMVH has, until recently, done very well in this arena.

   The other side of the scale, however, is that the buyers of such goods can be very fickle, and the firm must operate very carefully so that it does not lose the prized luxury good position. Any actions that pull luxury goods out of the stratosphere and place them in merely the specialty good category can be very costly to the bottom line. Being the best, knowing it, and pricing accordingly is the goal of every marketing manager, but only a very few firms every reach this point. To contradict this theme, however, and be caught in the hinterland would be tantamount to disaster for LVMH and the fall could be much faster than the rise. Several expansion and brand extension moves LVMH has made in recent years have negatively affected the franchise.

   LMVH moved aggressively into the United States in a losing business (Sephora) and into increasingly more tourism-oriented product categories (via duty free, etc.). This could be a problem because if there are prolonged declines in tourism/travel, they could be impacted negatively. In addition, some of the moves they made into related businesses (auctions) indicate that the name is going too far afield. It may also be that LVMH has moved to a more corporate-oriented strategy; as a result, it could hurt the specific brands associated with the corporate move(s).

2.   One of the primary actions that LMVH has taken is to extend the brand franchise well beyond where they established their position. A related action was to purchase a lower price retailing/merchandising operation (Sephora) that was intended to provide an "approachable" concept for young buyers of cosmetics and start-up brands such as Hard Candy. To LMVH, Sephora was also a way of attacking the U.S. market. Following September 11, 2001, this division, a loser before, became a major loser. This, along with the failure of e-retailing, has impacted image, margins and profits.

By moving into the more popularly priced, self-serve, duty-free and other product categories they have set themselves up for many more problems. It would appear that in the extension effort, they have brought on some issues that could sink the image. To respond to this they must quickly remove themselves from positions and strategies that smack of over-extension and lower quality. As per the concepts discussed in the text chapter, if they are going to engage in brand extension they should do it under other brand and corporate names that are entirely unrelated to the LMVH name so that it does not confuse the consumer image of LVMH as the premier luxury good player.

Analytical Tools for Marketing Management—Using Costs in Setting Prices

When setting prices, marketers usually use some costing method as a base. There are, however, two major costing methods as choices. This application exercise is a brief introduction to the problem of choosing one of these methods.

One of the first steps in setting prices is planning for the recovery of costs. Although costs are not the only element in setting prices, they certainly play a major role. A general approach to price setting is to set it high enough to recover production and selling costs and make a profit. But a problem exists on which major costing method to use: (1) direct costing, also called "variable" costing," or (2) absorption costing, also called "full costing."

The problem hinges around the differences between these two costing systems that are, essentially: Should fixed costs be charged to the product, or handled separately?
A fixed cost (sometimes called an "overhead cost") is one that is not affected by changes in production or sales. A variable cost, on the other hand, is affected by such changes, and rises and falls in a rather precise ratio. Theoretically, the level of fixed costs remains the same from month to month (although some adjustments can be made over time). Examples of fixed costs are heat, rent, light, building depreciation, real estate taxes, supervisory salaries, plant guard salaries, and advertising. Advertising is a fixed cost because the percent level is dependent on a management decision and not on rises or falls in production.

In absorption costing, fixed costs are included in the computation of the product cost and affect gross profit. All costs have been absorbed in the process. Prices, therefore, would be set high enough to cover all costs. On the other hand, product costs in direct costing are found in the contribution margin (also called gross margin). Fixed costs, however, are omitted from the cost of the product. Because gross profit and contribution margin are so different, they usually cannot be compared. Contribution margin has been defined as the profit that a product contributes to the total business operation.

To show how gross profit and contribution margin appear in an income statement, note the following example.*

	Direct costing	Absorption costing
Sales revenue	$770,000	$770,000
Variable manufacturing costs	550,000	550,000
Add: Fixed manufacturing costs	-	100,000
Total costs of goods produced	$550,000	$650,000
Less inventory at year's end:		
Variable cost	- 100,000	-
Fixed and variable cost	-	- 115,000
Cost of goods sold	$450,000	$535,000
CONTRIBUTION MARGIN	$320,000	-
GROSS PROFIT	-	$235,000
Variable selling & Adm. exp.	60,000	60,000
FINAL CONTRIBUTION MARGIN	$260,000	-
Fixed manufacturing costs	$130,000	-
Capacity variance*	-	$ 40,000
Fixed selling & Adm. exp.	$ 60,000	$ 60,000
Total	$190,000	$160,000
Net income before taxes	$ 70,000	$ 75,000

*Capacity variance is a portion of the fixed manufacturing costs that are not allocated to the product because the plant is not operating at full capacity. It would be unfair to charge the product this cost.

The preceding illustration shows that variable and fixed costs are combined in absorption costing, but they are separated in direct costing.

How would these two techniques be used in pricing? Here is an example, with four different prices sampled to see how they fare in terms of either gross profit or contribution margin.

---

[1] Source: Carl L. Moore, <u>Profitable Applications of the Break-Even System</u>, Prentice-Hall, Inc. Englewood Cliffs, NJ, 1971.

	Possible Prices			
	$4.00	**$3.80**	**$3.60**	**$3.40**
ABSORPTION COSTING				
Estimated unit sales	10,000	12,000	16,000	20,000
Estimated dollar sales	$40,000	$45,600	$57,600	$68,000
Mfg. cost @ $3. 40 unit (includes fixed cost)	$34,000	$40,800	$54,000	$68,000
Gross profit in dollars	$ 6,000	$ 4,800	$ 3,200	0
Gross profit %	15.0%	10.6%	5.5%	0
DIRECT COSTING				
Estimated unit sales	10,000	12,000	16,000	20,000
Estimated dollar sales	$40,000	$45,600	$57,600	68,000
Variable costs @ $2.70 a unit (no fixed costs)	$27,000	$32,400	$43,200	54,000
Variable selling cost @2% sales	800	912	1,152	1,360
Total Direct Cost	$27,800	33,312	44,352	55,360
Marginal contribution $	12,200	12,288	13,448	12,640
Marginal contribution %	30.5%	26.9%	23.3%	18.6%

From this table, it is apparent that if the marketer utilizes absorption costing the best cost in both dollars and percentages would be $4.00. In direct costing, however, the best cost would be $3.60. This cost would provide the most benefit to the company (or $13,448 versus $6,000 gross profit with absorption costing).

Which Is Best for Marketing?
Many analysts think that neither of these is better than the other. They both present different values. Nevertheless, there is a strong argument that direct costing is best for market planning. Here are some of the reasons for using direct costing:
1.   It is easier than absorption costing to find the most profitable price, especially when lowering the price will increase sales.
2.   Many times companies sell their products at different prices in different territories. Each territory may have a different contribution margin. The marketer, therefore, can concentrate efforts in more profitable territories and minimize efforts in others.
3.   In absorption costing, the effects on profits of a change in price that cause an increase in volume will be more difficult to calculate. Although the unit manufacturing cost will be reduced, the amount of reduction may have to be calculated department by department because fixed costs are spread that way. Direct costing, however, does not have fixed costs calculated in product costs.

Pricing may be done by adding a markup percentage or an amount to the unit costs to find the price.

Problem

A manufacturing company produced a product costed by the absorption method. The data for the absorption method and the pricing are shown below:

	Absorption Costing
Cost of materials	$ 2,891
Labor costs	1,479
Estimated tool maintenance	430
Total cost	$ 4,800
Plus 10% markup	400
Target selling price	$5,200

Armed with a $5,200 selling price, the salesman for this product went into the marketplace, only to find that there was a great deal of protest about the price. Almost everyone told the salesman that the "going" price for this product on the market was $4,400, and that his product clearly was overpriced.

In response, the marketer recalculated the costs using the direct costing method and arrived at a lower price as shown below.

	Direct Costing
Cost of materials	$ 2,891
Labor costs	725
Estimated tool maintenance	430
Total cost	$ 4,046
Competitive selling price	4,400
Potential contribution	$ 354

The problem is this: What should the salesman do about the situation? Even with direct costing, the company may not break even on the product. Explain which costing method he should use and the rationale for doing so.

The value of this exercise is that it focuses on one of the most important underlying bases for setting prices: although most students understand the importance of product costs, they may not have thought much about the different bases for calculating them. This exercise is only an introductory discussion of the subject. Hopefully, it will lead to a more in-depth study of the value of both absorption and direct costing methods.

Answers

The salesman should accept the order at the competitive selling price of $4,400, if the plant is not operating at full capacity. If the plant is operating at full capacity, then taking the work may result in overtime and other extra costs that could effect a loss for the company.If the plant is not operating at full capacity, however, the sale would contribute something, potentially $354, to the business.

Keeping the price at $5,200 in order to recover all costs probably means that the sale would be lost. After all, customers can buy competing products at lower prices. To lose the sale would mean no profit contribution.

---

[2] Spencer A. Tucker, Business Formulas (Englewood Cliffs, N.J.: Prentice-Hall, 1981), pp. 18-19.

On the other hand, if other work is competing for the use of the same production facilities, then the work with the highest contribution margin should be accepted.

Part V—MANAGING AND DELIVERING MARKETING PROGRAMS

Chapter 17—Designing and Managing Value Networks and Marketing Channels

Overview

Value network and marketing channel decisions are among the most complex and challenging decisions facing the firm. Each channel system creates a different level of sales and costs. Once a particular marketing channel is chosen, the firm usually must adhere to it for a substantial period. The chosen value network or channel will significantly affect and be affected by the other elements in the marketing mix.

Middlemen typically are able to perform channel functions more efficiently than the manufacturers. The most important channel functions and flows are information, promotion, negotiation, ordering, financing, risk taking, physical possession, payment and title. These marketing functions are more basic than the particular retail and wholesale institutions that may exist at any time, and when a channel member no longer provides value-added service it can and often is replaced by another channel member or a new means of distribution.

Manufacturers face many channel alternatives for reaching a market. They can choose selling direct or using one, two, three or more intermediary channel levels. Channel design calls for determining the service outputs (lot size, waiting time, spatial convenience, and product variety), establishing the channel objectives and constraints, identifying the major channel alternatives (types and number of intermediaries, specifically intensive, exclusive, or selective distribution), and the channel terms and responsibilities. Each channel alternative has to be evaluated according to economic, control, and adaptive criteria.

Channel management calls for selecting particular middlemen and motivating them with a cost-effective trade relations mix. The aim is to build a "partnership" feeling and joint distribution programming. Individual channel members must be periodically evaluated against their own past sales and other channel members' sales. Channel modification must be performed periodically because of the continuously changing marketing environment. The company has to evaluate adding or dropping individual middlemen or individual channels and possibly modifying the whole channel system.

Marketing channels are characterized by continuous and sometimes dramatic change, especially with the changes brought by the growth of the Internet as a major marketing tool and channel of distribution. For example, the new competition in retailing no longer involves competition between individual firms but rather between retail systems. Three of the most significant trends are the growth of vertical, horizontal, and multichannel marketing systems. All channel systems have a potential for vertical, horizontal, and multichannel conflict stemming from such sources as goal incompatibility, unclear roles and rights, differences in perception, and high dependence. Managing these conflicts can be sought through superordinate goals, exchange of persons, co-optation, joint membership in trade associations, diplomacy, mediation, and arbitration. Marketers should continue to explore and respond to the legal and moral issues involved in channel development decisions.

273

Learning Objectives

After reading the chapter the student should understand:

- The role and function of intermediaries
- The issue of channel levels
- How service outputs determine channel design
- How to evaluate channel alternatives
- What are the major channel management decisions
- Channel dynamics

Chapter Outline

I.   Introduction—notes the emergence of the value network view of the individual businesses. Deals with all the upstream (suppliers) and downstream (customers) variables

II.   What is a value network and marketing-channel system
    A.   Value network—a system of partnerships and alliances that a firm creates to source, augment and deliver its offerings
        1.   Firm decision regarding emphasis upstream versus downstream
        2.   Makes firm more aware of where problems can occur
        3.   Encourages more online development with business partners
    B.   Marketing channels
        1.   Interdependent organizations
        2.   Making product or service available for use or consumption
        3.   More use today of "hybrid" channels (direct, online, indirect)
        4.   Customers expect more channel integration (buy from any of the hybrid channels and obtain from any of the others)

III.   What work is performed by marketing channels?
        1.   Smooth the flows of goods and services
        2.   Save manufacturer money, time and specialized effort
    B.   Channel functions and flows
        1.   Information
        2.   Promotion
        3.   Negotiation
        4.   Ordering
        5.   Financing
        6.   Risk taking
        7.   Physical possession
        8.   Payment
        9.   Title
    C.   Channel levels—zero to three levels, can be longer
    D.   Service sector channels—focus on location and minimizing levels
    E.   Information highway channels (information industry)
        1.   Expansion of bandwidth, internet, extranets, intranets
        2.   Companies to provide this: content (Disney); consumer devices (Palm, etc.), components (Lucent); conduit (AT&T)

IV.   Channel-design decisions
    A.   Analyze customers' desired service output levels (lot size, waiting time, spatial convenience, product variety, and service backup)
    B.   Establish objectives and constraints—based on:
        1.   Product characteristics
        2.   Strengths and weaknesses of intermediaries
        3.   Competition's channels

4. Environmental changes
C. Identify major channel alternatives
1. Types of intermediaries
2. Number of intermediaries
a) Exclusive distribution—one or a select few
b) Selective distribution—more than a few, less than all
c) Intensive distribution—as many outlets as possible
3. Terms and responsibilities of channel members
D. Evaluate the major alternatives
1. Economic criteria—sales versus costs
2. Control and adaptive criteria—degree of intermediary commitment
V. Channel-management decisions
A. Selecting channel members—evaluate experience, number of lines carried, growth and profit record, solvency, cooperativeness, and reputation
B. Training channel members—prepare the channel member employees to perform more effectively and efficiently
C. Motivating channel members—coercive, reward, legitimate, expert, or referent power
1. More sophisticated companies try to form partnerships
2. Can evolve into long-term distribution programming
D. Evaluating channel members—sales quota attainment, average inventory levels, customer delivery time, treatment of damaged and lost goods, and cooperation in promotional and training programs
E. Modifying channel arrangements—system will require periodic modification to meet new conditions in the marketplace
VI. Channel dynamics
A. Vertical marketing systems
1. Corporate and administered VMS—corporate (under single ownership), administered (one member emerges as dominant in channel)
2. Contractual VMS—program integration
a) Wholesaler-sponsored voluntary chains
b) Retailer cooperatives
c) Franchise organizations
d) Manufacturer-sponsored retailer franchise (Ford dealers) or manufacturer-sponsored wholesaler franchise (Coca Cola bottlers)
3. The new competition in retailing—between systems, not individuals
B. Horizontal marketing systems
1. Two or more unrelated firms put together resources or programs.
2. Each firm lacks the capital, technology, marketing resources or other variables to take on the venture alone
3. Can be permanent or temporary
C. Multichannel marketing systems
1. Multichannel marketing—single firm uses two or more marketing channels to reach one or more customer segments—advantages: increased coverage, lower cost, customized selling
2. Planning channel architecture (companies thinking through their channel architecture—which are efficient and not, and developing new means)
3. Roles of individual firms in a multichannel system: (insiders, strivers, complementers, transients, outside innovators)
D. Conflict, cooperation, and competition

1. Types of conflict and competition
    a) Vertical channel conflict
    b) Horizontal channel conflict
    c) Multichannel conflict
2. Causes of channel conflict
    a) Goal incompatibility
    b) Unclear roles and rights
    c) Differences in perception
    d) "Over" dependence
3. Managing channel conflict (responses)
    a) Adoption of superordinate goals
    b) Exchange of people between channel levels
    c) Co-optation—winning support at different levels
    d) Joint membership in and between trade associations
    e) Diplomacy, mediation, arbitration

E. Legal and ethical issues in channel relations
    1. Exclusive dealing
    2. Exclusive territories
    3. Tying agreements
    4. Dealers' rights

VII. Summary

Lecture—Measuring Channel Performance

This lecture provides a discussion of distribution/channel strategy in the contemporary marketing setting and the role and value of effective channel strategy in the overall marketing process and strategy. It is useful to update the examples utilized so that students will be able to identify readily with this concept, based on their general knowledge of the companies and products involved in the lecture/discussion.

Teaching Objectives

- To stimulate students to think about the critical issues, pro and con, for a firm when it develops or modifies its channel strategy

- Points to consider in proceeding with a modification of the distribution strategy

- Role of various channel and distribution strategies and policies in helping the firm achieve a balanced position *vis á vis* the customer and the competition

Discussion

Background

One of the more important functions in today's complicated marketing environment is how to measure the performance of channel members. Whether the analysis involves an independent or vertical marketing environment, the problem is similar. There are means for following and measuring the results of this activity, and this discussion will focus on one such method.

Before beginning the formal evaluation of the channel, there are several considerations.

- *Degree of manufacturer control over the channel members.* If there is a strong contractual relationship there will be a much greater expectation for information on performance.

- *Importance of channel members.* If the manufacturer uses many intermediaries, the evaluation will be more comprehensive versus those using fewer intermediaries. For example, major appliance dealers receive much more comprehensive analysis from manufacturers largely due to the number and degree of service and support involved, versus a tire dealer. Major tire dealers in the past tended to be company stores, so the companies did less analysis on the independents.

- *Nature of the product.* Obviously, the more complex the product, the more the evaluation. Because complexity can usually mean more after sale services, the criteria tend to be focused more on issues of target market satisfaction.

- *The number of channel members.* Intensive distribution normally involves cursory examination, but for selective distribution the analysis tends to be much more comprehensive.

Performance Evaluation

Performance evaluation clearly will be more comprehensive than day-to-day monitoring efforts. Accordingly, there are typically three levels in developing a performance audit vehicle:

- Develop measurement criteria

- Evaluate channel members against the criteria

- Take corrective actions, as needed

The measurement criteria for the channel member should include the following:

- *Sales performance:* This critical measurement includes both sales to the channel member and member sales to its customers. This may or may not be a reliable measure, depending on the perishability of the product. For example, convenience stores tend to get a great deal of information from its franchisees. The key variables here are current versus historical sales, comparisons to quotas, and cross comparisons to other channel members. The 80/20 rule is important in the last measure.

- *Inventory maintained:* This major indicator provides information on the degree to which the member maintains stock or meets stocking requirements as specified in any agreements between the manufacturer and the channel member. It is important to understand whether this agreement is formal or informal. Also, although this is an area which often is difficult to perform, there are six key questions that can help with the measurement:

  1. Total inventory level

  2. Breakdown by units/types/prices

  3. Comparisons between the member estimates and purchases of related and competitive lines

  4. Condition of the inventory holding facilities

  5. Quality of inventory control and record-keeping

  6. Selling capabilities—it is worthwhile to evaluate the abilities of the channel member by appraising their salespeople. One way to do this is to cross-check this information with other members of the channel. You should check the number of salespeople working with the manufacturer's line, the technical knowledge and

competence of the sales people and the level of interest the salespeople have in the manufacturer's products.

- *Attitudes of the channel member:* Usually this is not done until there is a drop in performance. The best way to handle it is to survey the attitudes through face-to-face contact and also solicit feedback from the member's clients, salespeople, the competition and related sources.

- *Competition faced by the member:* This refers to competition from other intermediaries and from other product lines carried by the manufacturer's direct channel members. The questions might include how does the member do against the competition. Then, the issue is of more support required from the manufacturer. To probe this issue further, it would be appropriate to ask for names of the competitors and how they rank them. This will help you determine the degree to which the member understands the competitive arena.

- *General growth prospects for the channel member:* This measurement provides you with an awareness of how knowledgeable and sophisticated the member is regarding the general and area economies and the potential growth in each of them.

- *Other criteria :* Includes financial status, character, reputation and quality of services.

Applying these performance criteria involves three different approaches:

1. First, there is a separate performance evaluation, utilized primarily when there is intensive distribution and a limited sales, inventory and selling capability. The goal here is easy and fast, but it offers little insight into the operations of the business.

2. Second, the multiple criteria are combined informally. The goal here is to combine the criteria into an overall judgment. There are, however, some pros and cons:

   a. One advantage of this approach is that it is not only still fairly informal but also flexible in use and application

   b. This measure adds in the element of experience, but it can be arbitrary when the member does well in one area but not so well in other areas

   c. In addition, it is tough to use the same comparisons between channel members, and there is no one quantitative index to show overall performance

3. The third measure is the multiple criteria combined informally. The steps here are:

   a. Complete all criteria operational measures

   b. Assign weights in terms of importance

   c. Evaluate on the basis of a scale of 1 to 10

   d. Multiply the score times the weight to achieve a product for each factor

   e. Sum the factors to obtain an overall status

The advantage of the third method is that it provides weights and measures to provide an explicit and overall quantitative index. Although this may be viewed as a bit artificial in some ways, it also is easier to rely on a number to start with and then develop ameliorating qualitative data to make a final conclusion.

Marketing and Advertising

1. Ford has introduced a certification program to identify dealerships that are among the best in customer satisfaction. This ad alerts car and truck buyers to look for the blue thumbprint symbol at their local Ford dealerships.
    a. What type of vertical marketing system does the Blue Oval Certified Ford Dealership program represent?
    b. How might the Blue Oval certification program affect Ford's channel dynamics?
    c. Over time, how might Ford establish and apply criteria to evaluate its channel members?

Answer

    a. The Blue Oval Certified Ford Dealership program is a form of manufacturer-sponsored retailer franchise. Each dealer is independent but must meet Ford's specifications.
    b. This certification program might divide Ford's dealer base into two distinct groups: those with certification and those without. Consumers might then perceive that dealers without the certification are not as good as those with the certification, which could change the sales volume at both dealer groups. Students may offer other reactions, as well.
    c. Ford could develop a certain set of criteria to evaluate channel members according to sales, customer satisfaction levels, cooperation, and so on. Then it would evaluate all dealers at least once per year based on these criteria, communicate the results to the dealers, and plan to either upgrade the activities of low-scoring dealers or drop the low-scorers. Ask students to discuss the implications of warning and dropping dealers.

Online Marketing Today—Peoples Bank

As mentioned earlier, Peoples Bank, based in Connecticut, uses its Web site as a key channel for reaching individuals, business customers, and prospects. Not only can customers e-mail the bank with questions, they can click on a link to have a bank representative call them with further information or choose another link if they want to chat online. In addition, prospects can open new accounts online, print out and fax account applications, and even order printed checks with a few keystrokes. Now the company has expanded its financial services offerings by adding insurance products for consumers and businesses.

Visit the Peoples Web site (www.peoples.com). After looking at the home page, follow the link to read about Online Services and click for a demonstration of People's Online. Next, follow the Insurance link and dig deeper by clicking on Auto, Home, and Other Personal Insurance. What role is Peoples.com playing in the distribution of these insurance products? What is the length of the channel the bank uses to distribute its own checking account products? How would you describe the channel positioning of People's Bank?

Answer

Peoples.com is not the provider of the insurance products featured on its Web site, merely a distributor in the channel. On the other hand, it is the provider of the checking account products it offers directly to consumers and businesses, which means a zero-level channel. The channel positioning of People's Bank can be described using words such as convenient and value-added. Ask students to discuss a possible People's Bank positioning statement based on their perceptions of what the bank is trying to accomplish with its Web site.

You're the Marketer: Sonic PDA Marketing Plan

Manufacturers need to pay close attention to their value networks and marketing channels. By planning the design, management, evaluation, and modification of their marketing channels, manufacturers can ensure that their products are available when and where customers want to buy.

At Sonic, you have been asked to develop a channel strategy for the company's new personal digital assistant (PDA). Based on the information you previously gathered and the decisions you have already made about the target market, the product, and the pricing, answer the following questions about your marketing channels:

- What forward and backward channel flows should Sonic plan for?
- How many levels would be appropriate for the consumer and business markets you are targeting?
- In determining the number of channel members, should you use exclusive, selective, or intensive distribution? Why?
- What levels of service output do Sonic customers desire? How do these levels affect Sonic's channel strategy?
- How should Sonic support its channel members?

After you have answered the questions, document your recommendations about marketing channels and strategy in a written marketing plan. Alternatively, type them into the Marketing Mix and the Channels sections of the *Marketing Plan Pro* software.

Answer

Sonic must plan forward channels to allow consumers and business customers to buy its PDAs from suitable dealers and retailers. It must also plan backward channels to allow for the return flow of defective or broken PDAs and unsold merchandise being returned by dealers. Sonic may have to use two levels (wholesalers and retailers) to reach the consumer and business markets; it may also have to sell directly to business markets that buy in volume, such as large corporations. Sonic should plan for selective distribution, because—as a new company entering an established product category—it may not be able to sign up all the distributors it would like. Also, Sonic will want to use only channel members who are knowledgeable about PDAs, can offer the right levels of service, and who reach the targeted customer segments.

In terms of service output levels, consumers would like to buy in lots of one (or two), although business customers may require larger lot sizes. Customers will generally want to avoid delays in receiving their purchased items, and they will want easily accessible locations for buying the PDA (spatial convenience). Service backup, particularly availability of service and credit, will also be important. These are all considerations that Sonic must bear in mind when selecting and evaluating channel members. Finally, students will have various suggestions for ways that Sonic can support its channel members. Some sample ideas: motivating channel members through allowances and sales contests; driving traffic to channel members through advertising.

Marketing Spotlight: Disney Licensed Products

The Walt Disney Company is routinely recognized as having one of the strongest brands in the world. Much of its success lies in its flourishing television, movie, theme park, and other entertainment ventures. These different vehicles have created a host of well-loved characters and a reputation for quality entertainment. Disney promotes in name and its characters with Disney Consumer Products, a division comprising seven business areas that sell Disney-themed products through a variety of channels.

The Disney Store: Bringing the Disney magic to premium shopping centers in the United States and overseas

Merchandising licensing: Selectively authoring the use of Disney characters on high- quality merchandise

Publishing. Telling the Disney story in books, magazines, comics, and art

Music and audio: Playing favorite Disney songs and stories on tape and compact disc

Computer software. Programming Disney "fun" into home computers and computer game systems

Educational production: Casting the characters in award-winning films for schools and libraries

Catalog marketing: Offering Disney products via top catalogs

Disney licensed products are available at retail locations such as booksellers, music stores, newsstands, and grocery and convenience stores. Disney offers a vast range of items on its online shopping site, DisneyStore.com, and on many other e-commerce Web sites. Products can also be found at Disney Store locations and at gift shops in Disney theme parks. Numerous catalogs, for both home and education buyers, also sell Disney licensed products. The pervasiveness of the product offerings is staggering—all in all, there are over 3 billion entertainment-based impressions of Mickey Mouse received by children in total every year, equivalent to 10 million impressions a day.

Disney started licensing its characters for toys made by Mattel in the 1950s. Disney Licensing is now responsible for more than 3,000 contracts and for 16,000 products with top manufacturers worldwide. Disney licenses its standard characters (i.e., Mickey, Minnie, Donald, Goofy, and Pluto) and filmed entertainment (i.e., theatrical releases such as "Aladdin," "Lion King," and "Toy Story," and TV properties such as "Duck Tales" and "Madeline"). To capitalize on the popularity of these characters, Disney developed a family of brands for Disney licensed products. Each brand was created for a specific age group and distribution channel. Baby Mickey & Co., targeting infants, and Mickey & Co., targeting kids and adults, are sold at department and specialty gift stores. Disney Babies, targeting infants, Mickey's Stuff for Kids, targeting boys and girls, and Mickey Unlimited, targeting teens and adults, are sold through mass-market channels. Disney combined the names and characters into a specially designed logo. Each could be used in a wide range of product categories, including apparel and accessories, toys, home furnishings, social expressions and novelties, sporting goods, and gifts.

One of Disney's most successful licensed characters is Winnie the Pooh. Pooh products, which existed since Disney's 1966 animated short "Winnie the Pooh and the Honey Tree," have recently become a virtual goldmine. Between 1995 and 1998, the total licensing market for Winnie the Pooh grew from $390 million to $3.3 billion. By 2000, Pooh products generated an estimated $6 billion in sales for Disney. By comparison, Disney's other core characters—Mickey, Minnie, Goofy, Donald Duck, and Pluto—grew only 20 percent over the same period.

In 2000, retail sales for Disney licensed products totaled $13 billion, which amounted to 70 percent of revenue for Disney Consumer Products. Andrew P. Mooney, president of Disney Consumer Products, thinks this figure can eventually reach $75 billion, or 1 percent of the global retail market. A first step toward this goal was to partner with AmeriKid Foods to develop co-branded packaged goods products based on core Disney properties, rather than short-term promotions based around current movie releases. This partnership was designed to change the fact that as of 2001, Disney had no larger than a 3 percent share in any of the food and beverage categories in which it had licensed products. The addition of the AmeriKid Foods partnership gave Disney more products in the grocery and convenience channel.

Sources: Bruce Orwall. "Disney's Magic Transformation?" *Wall Street Journal*, October 4, 2000, p. B1; Stephanie Thompson. "The Mouse in the Food Aisle." *Advertising Age*, September 10, 2001, p. 71.

Questions

1. Are there any downside associations with the AmeriKids program? Is product licensing an unlimited situation? Can it be overdone?

2. Consider other products where the co-branding concept has a similar potential.

3. What marketing strategy changes should Disney consider andor make if it intends to reach the $75 billion level, given the fact that others are now moving into the arena? Is there evidence that Disney is reaching some branding and distribution limits?

Suggested Responses

1. Any brand that is well developed and controlled has to be careful that it does not overextend the brand franchise to the point that takes on a generic aura. To do so, especially in an era of fast paced competition and competitors, can be dangerous. Product licensing may be carried on indefinitely if the appeal is either universal or classic, and the image it presents keeps up with the times (Betty Crocker, Brawny, etc.). It can be overdone, however, if it spreads the name and image into products and/or services that seem to have no relationship.

2. There are many possible good answers here, but the best answers likely would emphasize products that present the highest potential in terms of carryover to and with children who can associate the value of one product with the other.

3. One meaningful strategy would be to seek out areas of activity that reinforce the current successes and bring in new demographic and psychographic targets. In addition, developing the international market, using the same proven strategies, adapted locally, would be useful.

   Since 1996, Disney failed to match its stellar growth of the 1980s and early 1990s. During 2000 and 2001 advertising revenues in its TV operations, in particular its national network ABC, were hit, theme park attendance fell off, the line-up of movie releases was passable (though none did especially well) and Disney stores and retail sales were mediocre at best.

Disney closed more than 100 of the 400-odd Disney stores, applied shorter hours to the theme parks, laid-off 4,000 employees and conducted cost cutting in movie production. A near full-on retreat from the Internet also is underway. Finally, it has been clear to many in the media and elsewhere that with Disney's almost monopoly position (brand image, not absolute economics), the goal is to dominate every market they have and charge the maximum price (according to Larry Gerbrandt, chief content officer at Kagan World Media, a media research and consulting firm, Associated Press, March 10, 2002).

Analytical Tools for Marketing Management: New Product Planning

Problems

Create a three-year payout plan based on the following information:

1. The number of cases sold in the market for year one is estimated at 8,000,000. Estimates indicate that the market will grow at a rate of 10 percent per year.

2. The average share estimated for year one is 10 percent, for year two it is estimated at 12 percent, and for year three, 20 percent.

3. The cases purchased by the pipeline are: .4 MM, .2 MM, and .1 MM for each of the three years, in that order.

4. Factory income is $10 a case, and factory cost is $5 a case.

   It is estimated that at least 50 percent of a three-year budget should be spent in year one. Year two should have 30 percent spent during that year.

6. Advertising should receive 80 percent and sales promotion should receive 20 percent of the budget in each of the three years.

Solution

New Product Planning	Year 1	2	3	Totals
1. Size of total market (in cases)	8,000,000	8,800,000	8,880,000	
2. Average market share for new brand	10%	12%	20%	
3. Cases bought by pipeline	400,000	200,000	100,000	
4. Cases bought at consumer level	1,200,000	1,300,000	1,900,000	
5. Total shipments from factory	1,600,000	1,500,000	2,000,000	
6. Factory sales (based on input price)	$12,000,000	$13,000,000	$19,000,000	
7. Less cost per case (input)	$6,000,000	$6,500,000	$9,500,000	
8. Dollars available for promotion and advertising	$6,000,000	$6,500,000	$9,500,000	$22,000,000
9. Reallocation of dollars	11,000,000	6,600,000	4,400,000	$22,000,000
10. Percent of total dollar	50.0%	30.0%	20.0%	100.0%
11. Allocation of dollars: To advertising (80%)	$8,800,000	$5,300,000	$3,500,000	$17,600,000
12. Allocation to sales promotion (15%)	$2,200,000	$1,300,000	$900,000	$4,400,000
13. Profit (or Loss)	($5,000,000)	($100,000)	$5,100,000	
14. Cumulative investment	($5,000,000)	($5,100,000)	$0	

Chapter 18—Managing Retailing, Wholesaling, and Market Logistics

Overview

Retailing and wholesaling consists of many organizations designed to bring goods and services from the point of production to the point of use. Retailing includes all the activities involved in selling goods or services directly to final consumers for their personal, nonbusiness use. Retailers can be classified in terms of store retailers, nonstore retailing, and retail organizations.

Store retailers include many types, such as specialty stores, department stores, supermarkets, convenience stores, superstores, combination stores, hypermarkets, discount stores, warehouse stores, and catalog showrooms. These store forms have had different longevities and are at different stages of the retail life cycle. Depending on the wheel-of-retailing, some will go out of existence because they cannot compete on a quality, service, or price basis.

Nonstore retailing is growing more rapidly than store retailing. It includes direct selling (door-to-door, party selling), direct marketing, automatic vending, and buying services.

Much of retailing is in the hands of large retail organizations such as corporate chains, voluntary chain and retailer cooperatives, consumer cooperatives, franchise organizations, and merchandising conglomerates. More retail chains are now sponsoring diversified retailing lines and forms instead of sticking to one form such as the department store.

Retailers, like manufacturers, must prepare marketing plans that include decisions on target markets, product assortment and services, store atmosphere, pricing, promotion, and place. Retailers are showing strong signs of improving their professional management and their productivity, in the face of such trends as shortening retail life cycles, new retail forms, increasing intertype competition, polarity of retailing, new retail technologies, and many others.

Wholesaling includes all the activities involved in selling goods or services to those who are buying for the purpose of resale or for business use. Wholesalers help manufacturers deliver their products efficiently to the many retailers and industrial users across the nation. Wholesalers perform many functions, including selling and promoting, buying and assortment-building, bulk-breaking, warehousing, transporting, financing, risk bearing, supplying market information, and providing management services and counseling.

Wholesalers fall into four groups. Merchant wholesalers take possession of the goods and include full-service wholesalers (wholesale merchants, industrial distributors) and limited-service wholesalers (cash-and-carry wholesalers, truck wholesalers, drop shippers, rack jobbers, producers' cooperatives, and mail-order wholesalers). Agents and brokers do not take possession of the goods but are paid a commission for facilitating buying and selling. Manufacturers' and retailers' branches and offices are wholesaling operations conducted by nonwholesalers to bypass the wholesalers. Miscellaneous wholesalers include agricultural assemblers, petroleum bulk plants and terminals, and auction companies.

Wholesalers also must make decisions on their target market, product assortment and services, pricing, promotion, and place. Wholesalers who fail to carry adequate assortments and inventory and provide satisfactory service are likely to be bypassed by manufacturers. Progressive wholesalers, on the other hand, adapt marketing concepts and streamline their costs of doing business.

The marketing concept calls for paying increased attention to marketing logistics, an area of potentially high cost savings and improved customer satisfaction. When order processors, warehouse planners, inventory managers, and transportation managers make decisions, they affect each other's costs and demand-creation capacity. The physical-distribution concept calls for treating all these decisions within a unified framework. The task becomes that of designing physical-distribution arrangements that minimize the total cost of providing a desired level of customer service.

Learning Objectives

After reading the chapter the student should understand:
- How retailers are classified and described
- What are fundamental retailing decisions
- Retailing trends
- How wholesalers are classified and described
- The fundamental wholesaling decisions
- The importance of marketing logistics

Chapter Outline

I.   Introduction—considering the strategies of the members of the channels, as viewed by those organizations

II.   Retailing—includes all the activities involved in selling goods and services directly to consumers for their personal, nonbusiness use

    A.   Types of retailers

        1.   Levels of service (wheel of retailing)—self-service, self-selection, full service

            a)   Major retailer types (see Table)

            b)   Nonstore retailing

            c)   Direct selling (multi-level and network)

            d)   Direct marketing

            e)   Automatic vending

            f)   Buying service

        2.   Corporate retailing—voluntary chains, retailer cooperatives, franchises, merchandising conglomerate

    B.   Marketing decisions

        1.   Target-market—until the target market is defined, the retailer cannot make consistent decisions on product assortment, store decor, advertising message and media, price levels, etc. Too many retailers have not defined their target markets

        2.   Product-assortment and procurement—breadth and depth. Several differentiation strategies are available. Growing use of direct product profitable (DPP) measurement

        3.   Services and store atmosphere—the services mix, prepurchase services, postpurchase services and ancilliary services—store differentiation

        4.   Price decision—key positioning factor related to the target market, product/service assortment mix and competition

        5.   Promotion decision—various tools used to generate traffic and support image positioning

6. Place decision—location, location, location—central business district, regional shopping center, community shopping center, shopping strip or within a larger store

C. Trends in retailing —new retail forms, growth of intertype competition, growth of giant retailers, growing investment in technology, global presence of major retailers, selling and experience, not just goods, competition between store-based and nonstore-based retailing

III. Wholesaling—includes all activities involved in selling goods or services to those who buy for resale or business use

A. Wholesalers provide: selling and promoting, buying and assortment building, bulk breaking, warehousing, transportation, financing, risk bearing, market information, management services and consulting

B. Growth and types of wholesaling—merchants, brokers and agents, manufacturers' and retailers' branches and offices, and miscellaneous

C. Wholesaler marketing decisions

1. Target-market

2. Product-assortment and services—the wholesaler's product is their assortment

3. Price decision

4. Promotion decision

5. Place decision

D. Trends in wholesaling—new level of adaptation in face of growth in direct buying. Effort to add value, reduction in operating costs, Internet

IV. Market logistics

1. The process of getting goods to customers, use of supply chain management, demand chain planning and integrated logistics systems

2. Involves planning, implementing and controlling the physical flows of materials and final goods from points of origin to points of use to meet customer requirements at a profit

B. Market-logistics objectives—getting the right goods to the right places at the right time for the least cost

C. Market-logistics decisions

1. Order processing—goal is to shorten order-to-remittance cycle

2. Warehousing—storage of finished goods. Distribution warehouses receive goods from various company plants and suppliers and move them out as soon as possible

3. Inventory—growing interest in "just in time" production to offset the costs of carrying inventory

4. Transportation—modes: rail, air, trucks, waterways, and pipelines. All have advantages and disadvantages

D. Organizational lessons about market logistics—experience with market logistics has taught executives many lessons re the value of good logistics

V. Summary

Lecture—Retailing versus E-tailing

This lecture focuses on retailing strategy in the modern marketing environment, and the role and value of understanding the history and role of retailing in the larger scheme of the overall marketing process and strategy in the United States and elsewhere. It is useful to update the examples so that students will be able to identify readily with this concept based on their general knowledge of the companies and products involved in the lecture/discussion.

Teaching Objectives

- To stimulate students to think about the important retailing issues

- Points to consider in analyzing the changes in retail pricing strategy

- Achieving a balanced position in a changing retail environment, especially in terms of the consumer, the competition and the technology driving the changes

Discussion

Introduction

The key changes in the retailing field are a result of, or a by-product of, the changes in our population, as in where and how people live work and buy. During the next decades the trends will continue, but most changes will come via the technological revolution (handling information, communication, management and in serving the needs of customers).

The major retailers must develop responses to include:

- Revive the shrinking profits by improvement of man and machine in store systems

- Take advantage of the trend to service-oriented society by offering new and more profitable services, (the boutique concept, etc.) and also store image management and creativity

- Department stores will have to face up to the increase in competition from discounters, specialty stores, food and drug chains and direct marketing (shuffling the merchandise mix)

Economic Forces

Economic forces are changing the way retailers must react. Although many retailers expect volume to grow despite the birth rate decline and the fact that the total population will not decline, there are some pros and cons to consider. Real family income is not increasing, but there are trends related to a growing demand for quality, value and specialty merchandise. Also, despite the self-service and online trends, there are indications of higher demand for increased customer service in certain retail categories.

Interestingly, most retailers are not now planning for future developments. Why? Various studies seem to indicate that there is a general view among many retailers that affluence, education and aspirations will continue to grow and accordingly will aid in the growth of their area of retailing. This viewpoint indicates the general optimism held by most retailers as sales-oriented marketers.

Social Forces

There is some optimism, a minority view, that there will be a solution to urban ghettos and a revival of the core cities. Although this has occurred, to some degree, completion of the process is still some years in the future. Mass transit is in the same category because many retail analysts feel that consumer mobility will change little in the coming years. Obviously, mobility would mean there is more demand for household-type goods to enable mobility to continue to increase (example: household cleaning products, etc.).

Employment Patterns

There is a continuing trend toward a four-day workweek, more part-timers and 365 day, 24 hour per day openings, but retailers apparently do not see the need to plan for this development. There will be more women in the labor market, more Sunday openings, more late openings and more convenience store growth. Employee turnover remains a big problem for retailers, but retailers are not ready to pursue actively a course of change. The Internet, however, is gradually forcing them to change or lose their customers.

Technological Innovations

Cable TV has had a tremendous impact on nonstore promotion and sales methods. The Internet, interactive TV, and broadband will continue to be a wave of the future. Cable opened up the arena of in-home shopping, and in-store computerized information (via scanners, etc.) brought an end to the centralization of decision-making in the large retail chains.

There has been a push to reduce transaction time, consumer anxiety and customer inconvenience. With the existence of the nationwide centralized credit and banking systems, there is an increased reduction in store and brand loyalty. The rise in the number and sales volume at the so-called wholesale clubs (Sam's Club, Price Club, and BJ's Wholesale Club) has been both a symptom and a cause in this area. The Internet is bringing the possibility of general buying facilities or cooperatives with central buying capabilities. This could become an important wave of the future.

Store Operations

There is a continuing trend toward shrinking profit margins on most primary or utilitarian retail items. This, in turn, requires tighter internal cost controls, promotion of higher margin products and services, and elimination of unprofitable items. Most retail operations have eliminated free home delivery and ended real estate ownership, leasing instead. At the same time the number of stores is coming down all the time, with the volume for the remaining operations rising.

The question is: will the changes in the future allow the same volume with 25 percent fewer stores and with a 20 percent decline in the number of items carried. For example, 10 years ago, stores with $25 million in sales averaged over 100,000 items on the shelves. Today, the number of items carried has dropped and is continuing to drop, with just-in-time (effectively 1–2 delay) inventory activities on the rise in many retail categories. Likewise, productivity levels have changed dramatically, requiring even greater flexibility in store layouts. One reason for this is the growth in the number of self-service racks, automatic vending machines and similar developments.

In the mid-1980s, approximately 50 percent of all department store volume was self-service; it is estimated that currently the number is in excess of 60 percent. This trend will continue. Much of this is due to standardized packaging units in modular form. Although this occurred originally to simplify the warehousing, handling and inventory control, the process has been equally accepted in the retail arena. Despite this, there has been no decrease in specialty and high fashion merchandise volume, only now there is more flexibility in the fashion business, especially within retail chains, both general and specialty operations. With the evolution of more scrambled merchandising and competition, and more geographical spread, suburban discounters and warehouse selling centers, the lines between budget and upscale have become increasingly blurred.

There's no doubt that retailers need to go through a shakeout before the industry can prosper again. With over 19 square feet of space for every person in the country, more than double the level of 20 years ago, there are simply too many stores. In 1974, each square foot generated an average of $175 a year in sales. Now, each square foot brings in only about $166.

Competitive Trends

With cable TV home shopping networks, catalog stores, direct mail, telemarketing, etc., it does not appear that as much merchandise activity will be in the stores. In 1984, less than one-third of all retail business was conducted outside the retail store; in 2001 it was estimated that in excess of 55 percent of retail business was conducted outside the store. This trend has continued, due to such developments as stronger warranties, a rising image of quality, and with many of the nonstores online, etc., options. There are areas, however, such as appliances and furniture, where the trend toward nonstore growth may not develop in the near future. A similar trend is occurring in the discount area, with discount retailers reaching over 27 percent of total retail volume by 2002. There appears to be an opposite reaction taking place with the department store. In addition, the one-stop shopping orientation continues in the United States and many other developed countries.

The trend to specialization and "category killers" began in the 1980s. Today, following on the precepts of the "Wheel of Retailing", the general merchandisers continue to develop boutique and specialty shop areas within department stores. Even more important is the trend toward more and more focus and size in specialty categories, ranging from pet products to sports clothing.

Future Strategies

Retailing faces some fundamental problems. This is an industry that has lost touch with its customers. The consumers who made shopping a recreational sport in the 1980s now have less time, less money, and less stomach for the whole experience. With 75 percent of women working full or part time and still shouldering most of the family chores, consumers have become precision shoppers. Over the past 15 years, they have cut down from three mall visits a month to 1.6. And instead of stopping by seven stores at a clip, they're down to just three. The consumer today is not only tightfisted but also increasingly stressed out and has lower tolerance for all the imperfections found in retailing.

In almost every category, the answer to the question of what the consumer wants is disarmingly simple: more for less. Wal-Mart and Home Depot became national powerhouses based on this simple insight. They did it by relentlessly cutting costs at every stage, from manufacturer to store shelf, and by demanding help from their suppliers who became increasingly dependent on them as they grew in size and clout. Since 1984, Wal-Mart's expenses have shrunk from 19.1 percent of sales to just above 15.5 percent. With yearly sales well over $100 billion, slated to grow to $200 billion in coming years, those savings add up fast. The contrast between the quick and near-dead in retailing is stark indeed. Bankrupt Bradlees, had an expense ratio of 29.4 percent; Caldor Corp., also bankrupt, had a 24.4 percent expense ratio. Likewise Kmart Corp. devoted 22.2 percent of its sales to expenses and went into bankruptcy during January, 2002.

There is no one formula for retailing success. Some hyper-efficient operators, such as Wal-Mart Stores Inc. and Home Depot Inc., have expanded their offerings and reduced their prices. Single-minded specialists, meanwhile, dominate narrow categories such as sunglasses or pet specialties with the deepest selections and competitive prices. Still other retailers are staking their claim to convenience, whether it's McDonald's Corp., making sure you can buy a Big Mac wherever you happen to be, or other firms that let you shop by phone or Internet for everything from a new car to a vacation. There are even signs of life among department stores, especially those with successful Internet business-to-consumer sites. It appears that for the time being they have pared down their operations and have fought to a standstill with the specialty retailers.

Some other examples include retailers who have never been considered efficient or interesting. Such formats as supermarkets, hardware stores, discount stores, travel agencies, car dealerships— are being transformed or superseded. From vast megastores to tiny one-product kiosks, new kinds of outlets are springing up that look nothing like the stores of 10 years ago. The innovative retailers are taking market share from everybody else. Not all of these new formats will succeed, but as retailers grapple with change these innovators point the way to the possible "re-storing" of America.

Even as the number of stores decline, those that remain will get bigger. The "big box" or "category killer" has already made its mark in some segments, such as home-improvement, discounting and toys. Now, the approach of offering mind-boggling assortments of a familiar product at a reasonable price is spreading to some surprising categories. Superstores devoted to single lines, from baby items to books, abound. Where does their market share come from? Their share comes out of the hides of traditional stores that have already ceded entire departments such as appliances, books, and sporting goods. The same thing will happen to other categories.

Online retailing is still impacting retailers, but because the smartest physical retailers have responded to the challenge, it is possible they will remain in the game. The number and dollar-value of products ordered online from home has continued to rise every year and is expected to continue for the indefinite future.

Note: Ask students what they would do to encourage consumers to spend more time in-store shopping.

Lecture 2—International Retailing—Business Without Borders

Introduction—Background

"I remain adamant that consumers, products and communication will always be local." That comment, made by the CEO of Nestle, may seem unusual for the leader of a global giant. But many agree with him.

From one point of view, despite the talk of globalization, there is no such thing as a global consumer. Most large companies are well aware of the necessity to adapt their products to differing regional or national tastes and needs.

Based on research conducted over the past three years by Ernst & Young with more than 10,000 consumers, however, there is also a universal desire to be treated with respect, courtesy and honesty, regardless of the product purchased or the retail channel shopped. It is clear that global retailers understand the need to provide local content in their commercial offerings while at the same time surrounding those offerings with the kind of contextual values desired by consumers.

This formula explains the global success of companies such as Wal-Mart. Consider that in less than a decade since Wal-Mart opened its first store outside the United States, the company has become the world's largest retailer, with more than 1,100 stores in nine countries in addition to its 3,200-plus units in the United States. There's little denying that retailing rapidly has become a global business.

Trends

Retailers often are the first to recognize the actual trends among billions of consumers. Wal-Mart and others are building their retail operations beyond their home base. German-based Metro AG, the fifth-largest global retailer, now operates in 20 countries through its Metro Cash & Carry subsidiary, which achieves 75 percent of its sales abroad. Similarly, Cologne-based Rewe Retail Group, No. 11 on the list of leading global retailers, operates in 11 European countries that account for 20 percent of the company's total sales.

European retail giant SPAR, operating 16,800 stores on five continents, moved into the Russian market in 2001, opening its first store in Moscow. The Home Depot, headquartered in Atlanta, bowed out of Chile and Argentina due to the lingering recession in those nations, but it expanded its operations through its acquisition of Total Home, a Mexico-based homecenter retailer.

In terms of global ranking, Wal-Mart and French hypermarket operator Carrefour are #1 and 2, followed by Kroger and Home Depot. Then there are two big European firms, followed by Kmart, Albertson's, Sears & Roebuck and Target (the top 10 in the world). Other significant international retailers include electronics retailer Best Buy, office products retailer Staples, and Swedish-based furniture chain IKEA.

Tech Support

What does it take to succeed as a global retailer? Let's start with technology. recent retail growth largely reflects the benefits from the introduction of electronic-data interchange, barcode developments, radio-frequency gun screening and improved inventory management. Such developments, together with Information Technology (IT) and, of course, the quality of management, are the keys to raising productivity.

The emergence of virtual business-to-business marketplaces, (including CPG Markets, Transora, GlobalNetXchange and the WorldWide Retail Exchange) are another major development. These e-marketplaces potentially can play a vital role in a global-retailing environment because they also give rise to the need for standards. To maximize the potential of these exchanges, we need to speak one language across our worldwide sector.

Work on such standards predates the B2B exchange. In late 1999, the Global Commerce Initiative (GCI), which consists of representatives from more than 45 retail and manufacturing companies doing business across continents or via global supply chains, was formed. The voluntary body was designed to improve the performance of the international supply chain for consumer goods through the collaborative development and endorsement of recommended standards and key business processes.

The chairman and CEO of U.K.-based Marks & Spencer pointed to the accelerated pace of change in global retailing. Today, with the rapid emergence of the Internet, exchanges and improved information technology, the pressure to develop a common language of business is more intense and more immediate than anyone imagined just a few years ago.

The search is on for a unifying force to bring manufacturers and retailers together on a worldwide parity basis to simplify global commerce and improve consumer value in the overall retail supply chain. Proponents point out that standardization will not only improve efficiency in the supply chain, but it also will decrease the waste of raw materials and consumer products, through better and faster combinations of supply and demand. These developments will turn many logistical dreams into daily reality: having the right product at the right place at the right time.

After all, should this not be the goal of any global retailer? Regardless of what technology applications retailers are investing in, the critical criterion should be on those systems that support a company's consumer-centric strategy. Too often, IT applications do not align with a company's strategic framework, resulting in misdirected investments. This becomes a critical issue as companies face increasing cost pressures in the weakening global economy.

Successful global retailers recognize the need for alignment between their strategy and their technology. Consider The Home Depot, whose business strategy focuses first on product and second on service. The home-improvement giant has staked out its competitive ground by offering a broad assortment of nearly every type of hardware, lumber and gardening product consumers might need and offering superior service. IT activity clearly is designed to support the service aspect of Home Depot's strategy. In 2001, for instance, the company introduced a new wireless scanner, called Unleashed. With it Home Depot associates scan and record the customers' purchases while they're in line. Once they get to the checkout counter, the cashier electronically retrieves the purchase record. The customer then pays and is out the door. Nobody likes waiting in line. Anything we can do to expedite this process makes customers happier.

Knowledge and Accountability

Global retailers also are beginning to recognize that their business is more knowledge-intensive than they may previously have thought. This led some operators to embark upon applied knowledge-management projects within their worldwide operations. Analysts estimate that sharing best practices throughout their far-flung organizations can contribute as much as 1 percent to 2 percent to the bottom line. The challenge comes in determining how to capture the best practices, how to share the information and how to implement it. In fact, implementation and execution remain key challenges in the retail sector, leading some global companies to consider strategic outsourcing relationships for IT knowledge-management applications, as well as other technology systems.

Global retailers also are emphasizing corporate social responsibility and environmental policies and practices. Consumers and consumer groups increasingly make their choices, positively and negatively, based on the social reputations of companies, and governments are acting to hold companies accountable for their behavior everywhere in the world. All of this translates into a need for companies to operate in a more transparent manner and to report on their social and environmental policies and practices. Many believe that retailers should take the lead in demonstrating and reporting on corporate social responsibility. Why? They are closest to consumers.

Research has indicated that executives of global companies confirm that social accountability and corporate responsibility have become increasingly important aspects of business. This is for good reason. These are issues that matter to today's consumers. Customers are looking for commercial offerings to reflect fundamental human values, such as trust, respect, dignity and fairness (i.e., the context surrounding a transaction), and not simply the products and services themselves (the content of the transaction). The results of this consumer research formed the foundation for the book "The Myth of Excellence," published in July 2001. For more information, visit www.us.cgey.com/consumerelevancy.

An example of the responsibility theme is Stop & Shop. The firm recently opened a new low-energy superstore in Foxboro, Massachusetts. The project was the result of three years of research and development aimed at reducing the energy usage of a single store by 30 percent. Energy-saving features include skylights, dimming controls, high-efficiency luminaries, state-of-the-art refrigeration systems, rooftop insulation and reflective paint, and construction materials selected for their environmental performance and recycled content. By using innovative methods to cut energy use, the company argues that it drives significant costs out of the business and at the same time demonstrates a high level of commitment on the issue. Studies indicate that their customers appreciate this.

The increasing consumer focus on value and values in commercial transactions is also one of the drivers behind the growth of the so-called organic-products business. This fact has not been lost on global retailers that have begun to devote more attention to the organic segment. As a sign of its commitment to the organic market, British retailer Tesco recently announced a new program to build its organic business to a level where it would account for at least 5 percent of all food sold at the company's stores. To reach that goal, the retailer plans to introduce hundreds of new organic products in a wide variety of categories. "Our research has highlighted a demand for change," said the Tesco CEO when he announced the new program. He went on to say, "Tesco's success is based on understanding that change and making it happen. They (customers) tell us that the main barriers preventing them from buying more are availability and affordability. We are determined to act on these concerns."

Food-safety issues also have clearly become top-of-mind in the global economy and are reflected in the planned establishment of expanded food safety controls in the United States and elsewhere. Executives from several European companies have listed food safety as the number 1 issue facing their business. In the United States, food safety was also among the leading concerns, although executives in the Asia Pacific region did not rank it quite as high on the list.

The emerging food-safety benchmarks provide standards against which existing standards can be checked and validated. The effort involves retailers representing nearly two-thirds of food retail revenue worldwide. The task force appointed by these retailers has identified four goals:

1.   To have global food-safety standards as a benchmark model everywhere in the world.

2.   To maintain an early-warning system to avoid spill-over into food-safety incidents that could impact the consumer.

3.   To develop joint food-safety initiatives with governments and organizations, ensuring that safety practices are in place, and that they are properly controlled.

4.   To inform consumers about food safety.

Key to food-safety initiatives is the growing role played by IT applications. Technology will be a primary enabler of programs that focus on tracking and traceability and early-warning systems, particularly in a global environment where the need to process food-safety information quickly and effectively is crucial. Getting IT systems up to speed to handle these kinds of applications will be of paramount importance.

The Future

Looking ahead, many global retailers anticipate continuing to expand into new international markets and to increase their global sourcing. As the marketplace evolves, one thing is certain: Change will continue to occur at a rapid pace and those retailers that respond to consumers in a fast and relevant fashion stand to succeed in the global economy.

Source: Chain Store Age Executive, December 2001

Marketing and Advertising

1.   The Mayors jewelry store ad in Figure 1 focuses on a particular type of merchandise—the diamond engagement ring—and suggests how it helps to bring luxury to the recipient.
   a.   What is the target market for this ad? How is the ad using the ad graphics and copy to appeal to this target market?
   b.   Based on this ad, what services and atmosphere would a consumer expect to find at a Mayors store? At the Mayors' Web site?
   c.   Discuss the retailer's product assortment strategy, as suggested by the item featured here.

Answer

a. The target market for this ad is women who expect to get engaged in the near future and those who are engaged and are shopping for an engagement ring. The ad uses graphics featuring happy young women and sparkling diamonds to appeal to this target market. The copy is also geared toward this market, by discussing the benefits of "never having to date again" and "packing your bags and moving out of singlehood."

b. Consumers would expect to find personal attention by knowledgeable jewelry experts at a Mayors store, along with a selection of rings and stones from which to choose; convenient shopping hours; possibly appraisal and insurance services. They would also expect a classy atmosphere consistent with the kind of expensive purchase that a diamond ring represents.

c. As a specialty store, Mayors is likely to have a narrow product line with a deep assortment, so consumers have a variety of diamond rings and other jewelry from which to choose.

2. Retailers need to plan market logistics for backward channels as well as forward channels. The ad shown in Figure 2 explains how online retailers can save time and money—and satisfy customers—by incorporating a UPS system to manage merchandise returns.

a. What flows must an online retailer consider when preparing for customer returns?

b. How would a system for managing returns be likely to affect an online retailer's decisions about warehousing and inventory?

c. What market-logistics objectives might a retailer using this UPS system set for its merchandise returns?

Answer

a. In particular, an online retailer must think about the backward flow of information and products regarding customer returns. How will the customer notify the retailer about a return? What conditions does the retailer set for accepting returns? How will the customer get the product back to the retailer? Forward flow of information, payments, and products must also be considered. For example, a customer who returns a product but wants no replacement must receive money back.

b. Online retailers need to think about having enough space in the warehouse facility to accommodate returned products being shipped in and replacements being shipped out. They also need sufficient inventory on hand to provide replacements for returned items as well as fulfill new customer orders.

c. An online retailer using this UPS return-merchandise system might set cost-control objectives, customer service objectives, timely response objectives, inventory efficiency objectives, and appropriate handling objectives (to ensure minimal damage to returned merchandise) among other types of objectives cited by students.

Online Marketing Today—W. W. Grainger

As discussed earlier, W. W. Grainger is a giant industrial wholesaler with branches throughout North America and a comprehensive Web site for online ordering at any hour. Despite competition from specialized Web marketplaces, Grainger.com draws more than one million users every month and rings up over $260 million in annual sales. After a months-long promotional campaign to attract online users, the site became so well established that Grainger was able to shift spending into advanced technology such as new search tools to help customers locate what they want even more quickly.

Browse the home page of the Grainger Web site (www.grainger.com), noting the kinds of products that are highlighted here. Then follow the "About Us" link to read about the company's history, mission and values, and special promotions. Finally, follow the "Services" link and read about the various services being offered. Who is Grainger's target market, and what is its mission? How would you describe its product assortment and services? What is this wholesaler doing to build and strengthen customer relationships by adding extra value?

Answer

Grainger's target market consists of businesses, institutions, and government agencies that want a one-stop source of many different goods and services. Its product assortment is wide and deep, covering such diverse categories as electrical products, tools, safety products, and outdoor products for industrial and institutional use. Grainger adds value in a number of ways: by offering a number of fast and convenient ordering methods; by providing information and resources related to industrial products, such as safety issues and emergency preparedness; and by showing suggested order lists for businesses in different industries to help buyers remember what they need. Students may cite other ways that Grainger adds value.

You're the Marketer—Sonic PDA Marketing Plan

Retailers and wholesalers play a critical role in marketing strategy because of their relationships with the final consumer. For this reason, manufacturers need to effectively manage their connections with these channel intermediaries.

You are responsible for channel management for Sonic's new personal digital assistant (PDA) product. Based on your previous strategic choices and your knowledge of the market, respond to the following questions in shaping your wholesaling and retailing decisions:

- What types of retailers would be most appropriate for distributing Sonic's PDA? What are the advantages and disadvantages of selling through these types of retailers?
- What role should wholesalers play in Sonic's distribution strategy? Why?
- What market-logistics issues must Sonic consider for the launch of its first PDA?
- What effect do your wholesale/retail decisions have on the other decisions you face about Sonic's marketing mix?

Now that you have examined Sonic's retail and wholesale opportunities and market logistics, summarize your ideas in a written marketing plan or type them into the Marketing Mix and Channels sections of the *Marketing Plan Pro* software.

Answer

Sonic should approach specialty retailers that serve the segments being targeted for the new PDA and that carry complementary products, have an appropriate price level in line with Sonic's pricing, and have the services to demonstrate and sell the PDA. For example, office-supply superstores such as Staples would be appropriate, as would consumer electronics stores. One benefit of selling through these retailers is spatial convenience; another is a connection with well-regarded retailers, which could enhance Sonic's reputation. One disadvantage is that Sonic PDAs would most likely be displayed near or even next to competing PDAs; another is that Sonic may have to fight for prominent shelf space and sales attention.

Because Sonic is entering an already crowded PDA market, it may need to work with wholesalers to get into the best retail chains and to reach smaller and local specialty stores. Market-logistics issues to be considered include: getting sufficient merchandise to the stores in time for the scheduled launch; transporting PDAs at an acceptable cost but with minimal damage; promptly and accurately processing orders from wholesalers and retailers; warehousing PDAs; and maintaining sufficient inventory without being overstocked. Ask students to discuss the effect of all these wholesale/retail decisions on other marketing-mix decisions, especially pricing.

Marketing Spotlight—Wal-Mart

The first Wal-Mart was opened in Rogers, Arkansas, in 1962. Founder Sam Walton envisioned a store offering high-quality products and service for low prices.

Today Wal-Mart employs more than 1.2 million employees and operates 3,118 retail locations in America, and another 1,071 overseas. These outlets range from its Wal-Mart discount stores, Sam's Club warehouse stores, Wal-Mart Supercenters combination discount and grocery stores, Neighborhood Markets mid-sized grocery stores, to ASDA grocery stores in the United Kingdom. Wal-Mart is currently the largest retailer in the United States.

A Logistics Leader

Several factors contributed to Wal-Mart's enormous success in the American retail market. Its low prices, vast selection, and superior service all keep the customers coming. One of Wal-Mart's biggest strengths—its logistics—appears only behind the scenes. As the biggest retailer in the United States, Wal-Mart's marketing logistics demands are considerable. The company must coordinate with its more than 85,000 suppliers, manage inventory in its warehouses, and bring that inventory to its 20-feet-tall retail shelves. To streamline these tasks, Wal-Mart set up a "hub-and-spoke" network of distribution centers. Centers are spaced across the country so that no store location is more than a day's drive away. Its ability to effectively manage such a vast network prompted one business writer to declare Wal-Mart "the king of store logistics."

Sam Walton was something of a visionary when it came to logistics. He had the foresight to realize, as early as the 1960s, that the company growth he was striving for required the installation of advanced information systems to manage the volumes of merchandise. In 1966 Walton hired the top graduate of an IBM school and assigned him the task of computerizing Wal-Mart's operations. As a result of this forward-looking move, Wal-Mart grew to be, in the words of another business writer, "the icon of just-in-time inventory control and sophisticated logistics—the ultimate user of information as a competitive advantage." By 1998, Wal-Mart's computer database was second only to the Pentagon's in terms of capacity.

Global Expansion

As Wal-Mart expands into global markets in South America, Asia, and Europe, it relies heavily on its logistics prowess to help it move quickly and support the rapid growth it seeks. At first, the company's system for entering foreign markets needed improvement: Wal-Mart encountered difficulty in certain markets due to the lack of historical data, inexperienced management, and the monumental task of buying and stocking 50,000 to 70,000 items for each international supercenter. When Wal-Mart opened its first supercenters in Brazil before the 1995 holiday season, managers did not anticipate sales quadruple those of comparable U.S. stores and could not keep up. By 1997, the company had made rapid progress. Wal-Mart was opening locations at 20 percent less cost, developing local distribution centers to manage the huge volumes of goods going to the stores, and tailoring the stores to meet local tastes. For example, the company added fresh pasta shops to Wal-Marts in Brazil after customer data revealed heavy pasta consumption in that market.

Wal-Mart Moves to the Internet

Wal-Mart capitalized on its logistics expertise when it took to the Internet with Walmart.com in 1996. The Web site borrowed resources like inventory, distribution, and information systems from its parent company. After Wal-Mart expanded the site in 1999, Walmart.com was widely initially criticized for its sluggishness and poor customer service. In 2000, the company partnered with a Silicon Valley venture capital firm and made Walmart.com a separate company and retooled the Web site. Among the features added was in-store returns for items purchased on the site and more reliable delivery. In June 2001, Walmart.com debuted its Internet service provider, which offer unlimited Web access for less than $10 a month.

Wal-Mart's dedication to logistics was evidenced by its promotion of H. Lee Scott, the former head of its logistics division, to CEO in 2000. Scott was famous for taking a logistics approach to Wal-Mart stores when he was took charge of merchandising for the company in 1995. He developed a system for giving current merchandise enough shelf space, limited price markdowns, and increased direct-to-store shipments from suppliers. Scott takes over the company at a time of unparalleled success. Wal-Mart's annual sales in 2000 reached $191 billion, a figure that earned the company the number two spot in the Fortune 500 ranking. The company's commitment to logistics played a major role in bringing it to that point, and will doubtless continue to be a large part of the Wal-Mart Way in years to come.

Sources: Wendy Zellner. "Someday, Lee, This May All Be Yours." *Business Week,* November 15, 1999; "Will WalMart.com Get It Right This Time?" *Business Week,* November 6, 2000; John Huey. "Discounting Dynamo: Sam Walton." *Time Magazine,* December 7, 1998; James Moore. "The Death of Competition." *Fortune,* April 15, 1999; Wendy Zellner. "Wal-Mart Spoken Here." *Business Week,* June 23, 1997; "Walmart.com to Start Internet Service." *Associated Press,* June 2, 2001; Mark Veverka. "Will Wal-Mart.com Steamroll the E-tailers." *Barron's,* October 23, 2000.

Questions

1. Wal-Mart has been highly successful in the development of logistical systems. What types of developments are critical to success in this arena?

2. As the largest retailer in the world, Wal-Mart has seen only modest success overseas. Why is this, given their vaunted marketing abilities? What changes would you make so that Wal-Mart can remain number one?

Suggested Responses

1. In addition to the raw computing power, Wal-Mart has highly sophisticated interfaces that enable not only vendor control of inventories but also the best JIT system around. This provides them with substantially higher volumes and profits per square foot. The distribution warehousing system also is and has been a major factor for them, virtually ensuring that there will be no stockouts. From a strictly logistical point of view, Wal-Mart is as good as anyone in the business, but even at Wal-Mart there is general agreement that there is still much more to be done.

Possibly the main variable is the fact that they learn from their mistakes. Although they have had many problems in implementing needed management changes, and there have been management snafus, but with their deep pockets they can keep coming back at it until they get it right. Because success in retail today demands constant improvement of the distribution and supply chain cost structure, as well as delivery times and customer service, the Wal-Mart approach is among the best.

2. In the international area Wal-Mart, largely due to a perceived need for centralization in order to maintain their strategy, often utilized a cookie-cutter approach in its stores during the first few years of overseas operation. In other countries, this often is met with virtual glee because it allows the local competition to meet them head-on and win.

Wal-Mart can get its international act together by pushing more authority into the field, working to develop a corps of top managers who speak the local language, and spreading "best practices" from the United States and elsewhere around the globe. This, along with construction of a global sourcing operation to use its huge sales volumes to command better deals, higher quality, and more innovation from both U.S. and foreign suppliers, will help them overcome the earlier problems with the international operations.

Analytical Tools for Marketing Management—Nielsen Television Audience Analysis

This exercise is only an introduction to television rating analysis. There is much more to this process, and if students are interested, they should consult a media planning textbook. Please note that although the actual current cost data for these shows is not available, we have attempted otherwise to make the problem realistic.

Questions

The Interactive Spreadsheet Data sheet shows the information for the network TV program *Friends*. We want to compare *Friends* with *Frasier* in the ability to reach women aged 25–54. The cost of a 30-second commercial on each of these programs is: $70,000 for *Friends* and $65,000 for *Frasier*.

1. Which of these two programs would be the best buy to reach the target audience of women 25–54? Show CPM proof and analysis.
2. Which of the two programs is the best for reaching women 12–24? Show CPM proof and analysis.
3. Which of the two programs is best for reaching men, aged 18–49, with incomes over $30,000 a year? Show CPM proof and analysis.

Answers

1. Which of these two programs would be the best buy to reach the target audience of women 25–54? Show CPM proof.

    a) To answer this question we need to first find the target ratings for both programs:

    i) *Frasier:* 14.8 (for women 25–54)

    ii) *Friends:* 15.1 (for women 25–54)

2. Which of the two programs is the best for reaching women 12-24? Show proof.

    a) The ratings above are multiplied by the base of all women in TV households aged 25–54 as follows:

    i) *Frasier:* 14.8 x 42,630,000 = 6,309,240

    ii) *Friends:* 15.1 x 42,630,000 = 6,437,130

    Finally, the cost per thousand should be calculated as follows:

    i) *Frasier:* ($65,000 x 1,000) / 6,309,240 = $10.30 CPM

    ii) *Friends:* ($70,000 x 1,000) / 6,437,130 = $10.87 CPM

    (a) As a result, Frasier is the better vehicle, for our purposes.

    (b) Frasier reaches almost as many targets as *Friends,* but, in terms of cost efficiency it is a better buy. Other criteria may be used in addition to the ratings and CPMs, but the information developed here probably is the most important.

    b) If we wanted to reach women aged 12–24 then *Friends* would be best because its target audience is greater and its cost-per-thousand is lower.

i)   *Frasier:* 9.8 x 25,000,000 = 2,450,000 and $65,000 x 1,000 / 2,450,000 = $26.53 CPM *

ii)   *Friends:* 17.2 x 25,000,000 = 4,300,000 and $70,000 x 1,000 / 4,300,000 = $16.28 CPM

Note: When the data contains three zeros at the end, drop the zeros from the dividend and the divisor.

2.   Which of the two programs is best for reaching men, aged 18–49, with household incomes over $30,000 a year? Show proof.

     a)   For men 18–49 with household incomes over $30,000 a year, the following data applies:

          i)   *Frasier:* 70 x 13,070,000 = 914,900 and 65,000 / 914 = $71.05 CPM

          ii)   *Friends:* 9.4 x 13,070,000 = 1,228,500 and 70,000 x 1,000 / 1,228,503 = $57.10 CPM.

Thus, although *Friends* has a lower CPM than *Frasier,* neither is a good vehicle for reaching men aged 18–49 with incomes over $30,000 because both CPMs are so high and neither reaches many such men.

Chapter 19—Managing Integrated Marketing Communications

Overview

Marketing communications is one of the four major elements of the company's marketing mix. Marketers must know how to use advertising, sales promotion, direct marketing, public relations, and personal selling to communicate the product's existence and value to the target customers.

The communication process itself consists of nine elements: sender, receiver, encoding, decoding, message, media, response, feedback, and noise. Marketers must know how to get through to the target audience in the face of the audience's tendencies toward selective attention, distortion, and recall.

Developing the promotion program involves eight steps. The communicator must first identify the target audience and its characteristics, including the image it carries of the product. Next the communicator has to define the communication objective, whether it is to create awareness, knowledge, liking, preference, conviction, or purchase. A message must be designed containing an effective content, structure, format, and source. Then communication channels both personal and nonpersonal must be selected. Next, the total promotion budget must be established. Four common methods are the affordable method, the percentage-of-sales method, the competitive-parity method, and the objective-and-task method.

The promotion budget should be divided among the main promotional tools, as affected by such factors as push-versus-pull strategy, buyer readiness stage, product life-cycle stage and company market rank. The marketer should then monitor to see how much of the market becomes aware of the product, tries it, and is satisfied in the process. Finally, all of the communications effort must be managed and coordinated for consistency, good timing, and cost effectiveness.

Learning Objectives

After reading the chapter the student should understand:

- The nine elements of the communication process
- How to identify the target audience
- How to determine the communication objectives
- How the message should be designed
- The selection of communication channels
- How the promotion budget is determined
- How the promotion mix is established
- How to evaluate and manage the communication process

Chapter Outline

I.   Introduction—the five major modes of communication (advertising, sales promotion, public relations, personal selling, and direct marketing)

II.   The communication process—communications as the management of customer buying processes over time, the nine elements of the communications model, reasons why message may not get through the receiver (selective attention, selective distortion, and selective recall)

III. Developing effective communications
- A. Identify the target audience
  1. Image analysis is a major part of audience analysis that entails assessing the audience's current image of the company, its products, and its competitors
     a) First step is to measure target audience's knowledge of the subject using a familiarity scale
     b) Second step is to determine feelings toward the product using a favorability scale
  2. Specific content of a product's image is best determined with use of semantic differential (relevant dimensions, reducing set of relevant dimensions, administering to a sample, averaging the results, checking on the image variance)
- B. Determine the communication objectives
  1. Based on seeking of a cognitive, affective, or behavioral response
  2. Assuming the buyer has high involvement with the product category and perceives high differentiation within the category, base objectives on the hierarchy-of-effects model (hierarchy: awareness, knowledge, liking, preference, conviction, purchase)
- C. Design the message (AIDA model)
  1. Message content—choosing an appeal (rational appeal to audience's self interest, emotional appeal attempt to stir up either positive or negative emotions, moral appeals are directed to the audience's sense of what is right and proper)
  2. Message structure—one-sided presentation versus two-sided argument
  3. Message format—must be strong, based on headline, copy, "sound," nonverbal clues, color, expression, dress, etc.
  4. Message source —expertise, trustworthiness and likability
- D. Select the communication channels
  1. Personal communication channels—direct (advocate, expert and social)
  2. Nonpersonal communication channels—indirect (media, atmospheres, events)
- E. Establish the total marketing communications budget
  1. Affordable method
  2. Percentage-of-sales method
  3. Competitive-parity method
  4. Objective-and-task method

IV. Deciding on the marketing communications mix
- A. Promotional tools—benefits of each tool (advertising, sales promotion, public relations and publicity, personal selling, direct marketing)
- B. Factors in setting the marketing communications mix (type of product market, buyer-readiness stage, product-life-cycle stage)
- C. Measure the communications' results

V. Managing the integrated marketing communications process
- A. A concept of marketing communications planning that recognizes the added value of a comprehensive plan
  1. Evaluates the strategic roles of a variety of communications disciplines

2.   Combines these disciplines to provide clarity, consistency and maximum communications impact through the seamless integration of discrete messages

Lecture—Marketing Communications as the Key Tool in an Uncontrollable Marketing Environment

This lecture provides focus on the increasing importance of marketing communications, as well as the concept of integrated marketing communications (IMC). Here we will look at the question of "How does interactive marketing fit with existing marketing campaigns?" Interactive marketing involves extending the reach, frequency and power of the existing communications. With current communications programs, firms likely integrate public relations, print, direct marketing, and perhaps radio, TV and Internet in some combination. Whether firms add networked media (commercial online services, the Internet and other stand-alone interactive media) to this mix, successful interactive projects work the same way as traditional vehicles: in harmony with the wider communications plan.

Teaching Objectives

- To understand how today's uncontrollable environment has led largely to the increased use of marketing communications

- To consider why integrated marketing communications is a powerful and cost-effective promotional strategy

- To present the advantages of a tool often used in an integrated marketing communications program: a company newsletter

Discussion

Integrated Marketing Communications

Not all product concepts are right for all individuals, thus bringing about the notion of market segmentation and targeting. The same holds true for marketing communications. One message does not fit all. Integrated marketing communications (IMC) focuses on discreet customer segments. With IMC, the firm learns to understand that although mass-market promotion appears cost-effective on the front end, brand/product messages are also offered to millions of people who are not interested.

Mass media no longer serves the mass audiences sought by marketers. Individual audiences for each media have decreased, thus indicating a need to ensure that whenever and wherever the prospect is exposed to the message, he/she receives a consistent one. Customers typically do not differentiate between message sources; they only remember the message they received. Considering how many messages consumers are exposed to on a regular basis, mixed messages from the same source are bound to cause confusion and, worse yet, they will be more quickly forgotten.

Although understanding the importance of marketing communications is somewhat simple, finding the best means through which to implement a marketing communications program has become increasingly difficult. The buying public has been virtually buried alive in ads. Consumers are bombarded with hundreds of ads and thousands of billboards, packages, and other logo sightings every day.

Old advertising venues are packed to the point of impenetrability as more and more sales messages are jammed in. Supermarkets carry 30,000 different packages (product packages), each of which acts as a mini-billboard, up from 17,500 a decade ago. (Source: Food Marketing Institute). Networks air 6,000 commercials a week, up 50 percent since 1983 (Source: Pretesting Co.). Prime-time TV carries up to 15 minutes of paid advertising every hour, roughly 2–4 minutes more than at the start of the 1990s. Add in the promos, and over 15 minutes of every prime-time hour are given over to ads. No wonder viewers zap so many commercials.

The IMC planning process is based on a longitudinal consumer purchase database. Ideally, this database would contain, by household, demographics, psychographics, purchase data, and perhaps some information about how the household feels about or is involved with the product category. In many cases, direct-marketing organizations already have this type of information at their disposal. An IMC program is implemented according to the needs and lifestyles of the selected target markets, thus allowing for customized, yet consistent, message strategies to sell increasingly individualized products.

Sustainable Competitive Advantage Based on IMC

It has been said integrated marketing communications will be the only sustainable competitive advantage for marketers in the near future. The other elements of the marketing mix, product development, pricing, and distribution, can be achieved at a very similar level, and in a similar way, among companies competing in a particular industry. In addition, we know the customer has taken on a completely new, powerful, role in the marketing process. Because it is largely through promotion that a company speaks most directly to its customers, it seems appropriate that a marketer's promotional strategy must change to reflect the dynamics of today's marketplace.

Some of these changes include:

- Changing technology, which has made it possible for media organizations to identify, segment, select, and attract smaller audiences for their respective vehicles

- The trend toward de-regulation that has allowed for increased competition within many industries, such as air travel, banking, and utilities

- Globalization of the marketplace, which causes promotional efforts, including advertising, sales promotion, public relations and personal selling, to be implemented throughout a worldwide market. Customization for different cultures is key to competing successfully in this arena

- Changes in the demographic and psychographic profiles of today's consumers, that have paved the way for new product category opportunities (such as health care for the aging "baby boomers" and health food/clubs for nutrition conscious consumers)

- Money-rich, time-poor consumers are seeking control of their purchases. Consumers have become adept at avoiding marketing communication, through the use of VCRs, remote controls, radio push buttons, etc. When they are listening, the message should be simply stated and easy to understand. Today's generation is also more visual than verbal, thus they rely on images, symbols and graphics more than any previous generation

It is important also to note that a marketer can communicate with customers through means other than formal marketing communications. Every element of a product's marketing mix helps to position that product in the minds of consumers. The result is that the elements of the promotional mix should all present a consistent theme. The same is true of the other "Ps" of marketing, namely product, price and place that also should support the theme:

1. Products communicate through size, shape, name, packaging, and various features/ benefits.

2. Price communicates to the consumer that the product is high quality, low quality, prestigious, common, etc.

3. Retail locations (place) where customers purchase the product will reflect upon the product's image as well. Stores are thought of as "high-class," specialty, discount, etc.

Using Newsletters for Customized Communication

One of the newest and most effective ways to stimulate and maintain positive communication with customers is through newsletters (print and online). Newsletters are useful for many reasons, but one of the best reasons is that they cross the boundary between news and advertising, providing a bit of both. Further, they bring back some much-needed credibility that has been lost with many market segments. The newsletter can be delivered physically, but more likely it will be made available via the Internet or e-mail. Newsletters not only describe, in detail, a company's philosophy, goals, and objectives but also enhance its current marketing program. In addition, newsletters can be utilized as communication tools for many other purposes.

Some of the advantages of newsletters include:
- Delivering continuous background or educational material to clients in an efficient manner
- Providing highly-targeted distribution through database utilization
- Acting as a form of personal calling, on paper, to prospects and clients
- Proving more economical than other forms of promotion
- Not obvious advertising, if done correctly
- Attention-getting
- Providing the ability to create demand
- Keeping mailing lists (or e-mail lists) accurate

Possible newsletter content may also include such as items as:
- Announcements of new products and services
- Stories of products/services in application (from either the company or its customers)
- Answers to commonly asked questions/concerns
- Information on industry trends
- Updates on new or pending legislation
- Personnel changes (but otherwise very little employee communiqué)
- Guest articles by prominent figures in the industry
- "Think" pieces—philosophy, ideas, suggestions, techniques, tactics
- Specialized news

A newsletter also provides opportunities for customer feedback:
- Brings the prospect to the marketer in the form of an inquiry
- May solicit response through use of a formal survey
- Enables experimentation with numerous formats/contents/ promotions through small sample test mailings

In addition, orienting articles to topics that are on the customer's minds will guarantee holding their interest.

Bad news should not be ignored. Any problems that are occurring, as well as actions being taken to solve these problems, need to be addressed. After all, relationships will have both ups and downs.

Most important, the primary goal of any newsletter should be to inform and educate readers; it must not become the voice of management and/or marketing alone. To that end, it must be filled with news and not exist solely to sell products/services.

Note: As a final note, you might ask the class to consider whether the newsletter approach has found additional life on the Internet. Many Web sites include elements of the newsletter approach in their operations. Ask the class to investigate some leading Web sites to prove and/or disprove this point.

Marketing and Advertising

1. The magazine ad in Figure 1 promotes UpWords, a game marketed by the manufacturer of the Scrabble word game. Although the game is portrayed in the ad, other elements are more prominent.
    a. Who is the target audience for this advertising message? What image of the game would the advertiser like to create with this ad?
    b. How do selective attention, selective distortion, and selective retention apply to this advertising message?
    c. What communication objectives might the game manufacturer set for this advertising message?

Answer
    a. The target audience is adults who like word games. The advertiser wants to create an image of UpWords as being similar to—but more challenging than—the well-known Scrabble game.
    b. To overcome selective attention by attracting attention, the ad shows a large, familiar "deer crossing" sign altered to read "deer flossing." This device also addresses selective retention, by reinforcing how the UpWords game is played (by putting letters on top of other letters). Finally, the ad addresses selective distortion by clarifying what UpWords is and how it works (through an illustration of a game in progress and a brief description in the body copy).
    c. The advertiser might set objectives for this communication such as: awareness, knowledge, liking, and preference, ultimately leading to conviction and to purchase. Challenge students to suggest how the advertiser could alter this ad to lead more directly to purchasing.

2. Sharp incorporates a clever depiction of its imaging product's key benefit—using color to reach people—to attract attention and communicate with business decision-makers in the ad shown in Figure 2.
    a. Analyze this ad in terms of the hierarchy-of-effects model.
    b. How is Sharp using message format to communicate with its target audience?
    c. How does Sharp establish source credibility in this advertisement?

Answer
    a. This Sharp ad builds awareness by coupling the brand (shown at bottom right) with a prominent illustration of the key benefit (color copying). It builds knowledge by explaining how color copying can help a business. It enhances liking and preference by explaining the benefits of Sharp's color copier. It

supports conviction and purchase by asking "So, are you ready to connect?" and by stressing affordability, efficiency, and upgradability.

b. Sharp's message format reinforces the underlying message—that color makes a difference in a business presentation—by using color to attract attention to this ad. Students may also cite other aspects of the message format.

c. Source credibility is established by alluding to Sharp's expertise in color copying and by linking Sharp to a network of authorized dealers around the country, which may already have established reputations for expertise, trustworthiness, and likability.

Online Marketing Today—VF

VF, which makes Lee jeans, has used the Internet to create a word-of-mouth tidal wave around its jeans. It started by creating Web sites for Buddy Lee, a kewpie-doll character, and Curry, a fictional race-car driver, and encouraging consumers to discover the sites on their own or e-mail their friends about the sites. Weeks later, VF ran media ads revealing that the characters were part of an elaborate online computer game. To advance to higher levels in the game, players needed to input code numbers found only on Lee jeans—which meant visiting a store and looking at Lee's products. This integrated marketing communications campaign helped push Lee's sales 20 percent higher than in the previous year.

VF continues to operate some of the sites. The Curry site is located at http://www.rubberburner.com and one of the Buddy Lee sites is at http://www.buddylee.com. Explore both sites. Also follow the "Lee Sites" link at the Buddy Lee home page and review one or two of the featured sites. How does Lee encourage consumer participation on these sites? What is the appeal of these sites? What objectives might Lee set for campaigns that rely on word-of-mouth?

Answer

Lee offers different games, contests, and other interactive activities to encourage consumer participation in its sites. These sites are witty, informal, interesting, and don't take themselves too seriously, so they're fun for consumers to visit. Ask students to be specific in commenting on at least one of the sites they visit. Lee might set a variety of word-of-mouth campaign objectives, such as striving to have the message seen/understood by a certain number of consumers and having those consumers pass the message along to a certain number of other consumers. Students may suggest other objectives, as well.

You're the Marketer—Sonic PDA Marketing Plan

Every marketing plan must include a section showing how the company will use marketing communications to connect with customers, prospects, and other stakeholders. Web-based communications must be integrated into the overall communications strategy to ensure consistency of messages.

You are responsible for planning integrated marketing communications for Sonic's introduction of its personal digital assistant (PDA). Review the data, decisions, and strategies you have previously documented in your marketing plan. Now use your knowledge of communications to answer these questions:

- What audience(s) should Sonic be targeting? What image should it seek to create for its initial PDA product?
- What objectives are appropriate for Sonic's initial communications campaign?

- What message design and communication channel(s) are likely to be most effective for the target audience?
- How should Sonic establish its marketing communications budget?
- Which promotional tools would be most effective in Sonic's promotional mix? Why?

Be sure that your marketing communications plans will support Sonic's overall marketing efforts. Now, as your instructor directs, summarize your thoughts in a written marketing plan or type them into the Marketing Mix section of the *Marketing Plan Pro* software.

Answer

Sonic should target the consumer and business segments it previously identified for the new PDA product. Students may have described these segments in detail earlier in the marketing planning process. In addition, Sonic should target channel members and other members of the trade to build enthusiasm and support. The image for the first PDA product depends on other decisions made in the marketing plan. For example, Sonic could build an image around innovation (for its voice-recognition capabilities) and value (because the PDA is priced lower than comparable models from rivals).

For the initial communications campaign, Sonic should set objectives for awareness among the targeted segments. It may also want to set objectives for knowledge, liking, preference, conviction, and purchase as time goes on. Initially, however, it must make the market aware of the brand and product. Students should use their imaginations in discussing the message design and communication channels for each target audience. They need to plan for a mix of personal and nonpersonal channels, and to build credibility. Sonic should establish its marketing communications budget using the objective-and-task method, because this ties expenditures to specific objectives that will be met. Ask students to be creative in suggesting promotional tools for Sonic's promotional mix; also ask them to discuss how their choices fit with other choices and strategies made earlier in the marketing planning process. For example, students may suggest a mix of consumer and trade advertising, sales promotion, public relations, personal selling, and online or direct marketing.

Marketing Spotlight—Mountain Dew Code Red

When Pepsi-Cola's total volume increased a mere tenth of a percent in 2000, the company quickly sought to boost sales by launching the first line extension of its popular Mountain Dew drink because Diet Mountain Dew debuted in 1988. A cross-functional team comprised of 35 people from seven Pepsi departments worked on developing the new product. The team considered several possibilities: Dew H_2O bottled water; Dew Unplugged decaf Mountain Dew; a Mountain Dew sports drink; and a new Dew flavor. The company settled on creating a new flavor, and within 10 months, instead of the usual two years it takes Pepsi to develop a new product, launched a bright red cherry-flavored beverage called Mountain Dew Code Red.

For the launch, Pepsi used radio and outdoor advertising, as well as sampling and in-store merchandising. To build buzz for Code Red, the company sent free samples to 4,000 select consumers, such as hip-hop producer Jermaine Dupri and radio DJ Funkmaster Flex. The drink was heavily sampled at marquee sporting events such as the NCAA Final Four and ESPN's 2001 winter X games. Pepsi also developed a special Website for the brand that featured an interactive game called "Mission: Code Red 2." Additionally, Pepsi marketed Code Red to urban consumers. When research revealed that urban and ethnic focus groups preferred the name Code Red to Wild Cherry Mountain Dew, Pepsi stuck with the former. The company also developed an ad campaign titled "Crack the Code" that used graffiti-art design elements and an urban setting.

Code Red attracted a rabid fanbase. According to A.C. Nielsen, Code Red tested in the top five percent of all new product concepts ever tested among teens. The drink was also popular in the high-tech community. Two programmers who discovered a computer virus named it "Code Red" after the beverage they used to maintain late hours in front of their monitors. The virus eventually infected more than 700,000 computers. Pepsi sent the pair five cases of Code Red in appreciation for the free publicity.

Within two months of its May 2000 launch, Code Red was the fifth-best-selling soft drink sold at convenience stores and gas stations (Mountain Dew is number one). This signaled tremendous success, considering that the drink came in only two single-serve sizes and the muted marketing campaign did not yet include television spots. Though the drink was launched midway through the second quarter of 2000, Pepsi credited the Code Red launch with helping to boost net sales 20 percent to $962 million that quarter. One bottler exclaimed "It's flown off the shelves for us."

Sources: www.mountaindew.com; Hillary Chura. "Pepsi-Cola's Code Red Is White Hot." *Advertising Age*, August 27, 2001, p. 1; Maureen Tkacik and Betsy McKay. "Code Red: PepsiCo's Guerilla Conquest." *Wall Street Journal*, August 17, 2001, p. B5; Abigail Klingbeil. "The Making of a Brand." Gannett News Service, June 29, 2001

Questions

1. Discuss the basis of Code Red marketing success, especially the integrated marketing implications. Evaluate the IMC concepts embodied in the overall success of the product.

2. Consider the implementation aspects of what Pepsi did with Code Red. Given the results achieved, based on the original narrow market segmentation (approximately age 17–25) that grew with the media interactivity, what can we learn about the use of IMC?

Suggested Responses

1. Most analysts would admit that there is little need for another soft drink. Pepsi did an excellent job with an IMC-based marketing strategy that was very creative, along with a rather off-beat guerrilla-oriented application of IMC. This, along with the willingness to apply superior support to the effort, did the job. This creativity worked and drew a much broader demographic than expected and thus made the campaign highly successful. Of course, they had considerable good luck related to the computer virus matter.

   Code Red demonstrates many of the IMC concepts discussed in the text. Because it already had a lot of loyal drinkers (Mountain Dew), and even though the focus of the marketing demographic was young, there were some random variables (Code Red virus) that added substantially and allowed the eventual demographic to cut across every demographic and age group. It may have started with the younger and techie segments, but the additional "news" value provided by the virus issue provided the basis for a much broader PR-oriented application.

   When combined with Pepsi's already superior integrated campaign experiences, including the Internet, Code Red and Pepsi come across somewhat like Anheuser Busch and the friendly frogs. Pepsi also successfully utilized big name celebrities online before airing on TV, and this likely created some overlap. Pepsi also provided numerous incentives for customers to register on the Website, with votes for favorite celebrity commercial.

2. During the past several years, Pepsi has crafted an effective strategy for running integrated marketing campaigns, and other marketers probably would be smart to steal a page from its playbook. Step one is to create a commercial starring a big-name celebrity who can command enough buzz to entice people to view it online before it airs on

television. Step two is to give customers an added incentive to register on your Website. For instance, Pepsi frequently will host a sweepstakes or let visitors vote for their favorite soda commercials.

Pepsi has done well with the formula. Most recently the beverage giant used this integrated marketing approach for a Britney Spears–driven promotion launched during the 2002 Super Bowl. Pepsi created three different Britney spots and invited Yahoo! visitors to view them and vote on their favorite. The commercials were viewed more than 3 million times between January 20 and February 3. More than 415,000 people voted. Add that to the 30 million that saw the Pepsi ads during the Super Bowl telecast, and you have some serious bang for the buck.

To some extent, integrated marketing is all about the data. Pepsi added over 500,000 e-mail addresses to its database during the 2002 Academy Awards effort. Having a database full of qualified leads for future promotions is as good as cold cash to a marketer; it represents a list with which to promote new products and gather active customers you can easily communicate with. According to Pepsi's head of online marketing, more than 40 percent of the e-mails Pepsi sends out actually get opened—an impressive figure.

Chapter 20—Managing Advertising, Sales Promotion, Public Relations, and Direct Marketing

Overview

Advertising—the use of paid media by a seller to communicate persuasive information about its products, services, or organization—is a potent promotional tool. Advertising takes on many forms (national, regional, local, consumer, industrial, retail, product, brand, institutional, etc.) designed to achieve a variety of objectives (awareness, interest, preference, brand recognition, brand insistence).

Advertising decision-making consists of objectives setting, budget decision, message decision, media decision, and ad effectiveness evaluation. Advertisers should establish clear goals as to whether the advertising is supposed to inform, persuade, or remind buyers. The factors to consider when setting the advertising budget are: stage in the product life cycle, market share, competition and clutter, needed frequency, and product substitutability. The advertising budget can be established based on what is affordable, as a percentage budget of sales, based on competitors' expenditures, or based on objectives and tasks, and based on more advanced decision models that are available.

The message decision calls for generating messages, evaluating and selecting between them, and executing them effectively and responsibly. The media decision calls for defining the reach, frequency, and impact goals; choosing among major media types; selecting specific media vehicles; deciding on media timing; geographical allocation of media. Finally, campaign evaluation calls for evaluating the communication and sales effects of advertising, before, during, and after the advertising.

Sales promotion and public relations are two tools of growing importance in marketing planning. Sales promotion covers a wide variety of short-term incentive tools designed to stimulate consumer markets, the trade, and the organization's own sales force. Sales promotion expenditures now exceed advertising expenditures and are growing at a faster rate. Consumer promotion tools include samples, coupons, cash refund offers, price packs, premiums, prizes, patronage rewards, free trials, product warranties, tie-in promotions, and point-of-purchase displays and demonstrations. Trade promotion tools include price-off, advertising and display allowances, free goods, push money, and specialty-advertising items. Business promotion tools include conventions, trade shows, contests, sweepstakes, and games. Sales promotion planning calls for establishing the sales promotion objectives, selecting the tools, developing, pretesting, and implementing the sales promotion program, and evaluating the results.

Marketing public relations (MPR) is another important communication/promotion tool. Traditionally, it has been the least utilized tool but is now recognized for its ability in building awareness and preference in the marketplace, repositioning products, and defending them. Broadly, MPR is those activities that support the ultimate sale of a product or service. Some of the major marketing public relations tools are news, speeches, events, public service activities, written material, audio-visual material, corporate identity, and telephone information services. MPR planning involves establishing the MPR objectives, choosing the appropriate messages and vehicles, and evaluating the MPR results.

Learning Objectives

After reading the chapter the student should understand:

- The importance of setting the advertising objectives
- How media decisions are made
- Why messages must be evaluated
- How advertising budgets are determined
- How advertising can be evaluated for effectiveness
- The purpose of sales promotion
- What sales promotion tools are available
- How sales promotion programs are developed
- The importance of evaluating sales promotion results
- The overall processes and strategies related to the use of direct marketing channels
- The issues (public and ethical) related to direct marketing
- The future of direct and on-line marketing capabilities

Chapter Outline

I. Developing and managing an advertising program

    1. Advertising is any paid form of nonpersonal presentation and promotion of ideas, goods, or services by an identified sponsor. Five major decisions involve the mission, money, message, media and measurement

    B. Setting the advertising objectives—according to whether the aim is to inform, remind, or persuade

    C. Deciding on the advertising budget—five factors to consider include stage in the product life cycle, market share and consumer base, competition and clutter, advertising frequency, and product substitutability

    D. Choosing the advertising message—creative stage

        1. Message generation—utilizing an inductive versus deductive framework

        2. Message evaluation and selection—focus on one core selling proposition and aim for desirability, exclusiveness and believability.

        3. Message execution—impact depends not only on what is said but how it is said (positioning). Creative people must also find a style, tone, and format for executing the message

        4. Social responsibility review—make sure the creative advertising does not overstep social and legal norms

II. Deciding on media and measuring effectiveness

    1. Deciding on reach (number of people exposed at least once), frequency (total number of times they are reached) and impact (qualitative value)

        - The relationship between reach, frequency and impact, specific media, media timing, geographical allocation

        a) Media selection: target audience, media habits, product, message, and cost

- Determining the most cost-effective media to deliver the desired number and type of exposures to the target audience

   2.   Choosing among major media types

      a)   Target audience media habits

      b)   Product characteristics

      c)   Message characteristics

      d)   Cost (based on cost-per-thousand exposures criterion)

   3.   New media—rethinking the options

      a)   Commercial clutter, advertorials, infomercials

      b)   Result is coming death of traditional mass media, as we know it—more direct and consumer control coming

   4.   Allocating the budget—increasingly spent attracting attention than on the product itself

   5.   Selecting specific vehicles—measures include:

      a)   Circulation, audience, effective audience, effective ad-exposed audience

      b)   CPM adjustments based on audience quality, audience-attention probability, editorial quality and ad placement policies

   6.   Deciding on the media timing

      a)   Macro-scheduling (according to seasonal or business trends)

      b)   Micro-scheduling (allocating advertising expenditures within a short period to obtain the maximum impact)

      c)   Models for media timing: Kuehn (if no carryover and habitual behavior then percent of sales justified)

   7.   Deciding on the geographical allocation

      a)   National versus international

      b)   Spot buying (ADIs and DMAs)

   8.   Evaluating advertising effectiveness

      a)   Communication-effect research—copy testing, consumer feedback, portfolio tests, laboratory tests

      b)   Sales-effect research—share of voice and share of market, historical approach, experimental design

      c)   Advertising effectiveness: a summary of current research

III.   Sales promotion

- Consists of a diverse collection of incentive tools, mostly short term, designed to stimulate quicker and/or greater purchase of particular products/services by consumers or the trade
- Rapid growth of sales promotion—result is clutter, like advertising clutter

   A.   Purpose of sales promotion

      1.   Varying purposes and results, depending on degree of brand awareness/loyalty

      2.   Farris and Quelch benefits studies—testing to lead to varied retail formats

B. Major decisions in sales promotion

1. Establishing objectives (larger sized units, trial, attract switchers, etc.)
2. Selecting the sales-promotion tools (consumer-promotion, trade-promotion, and/or business- and sales force promotion tools)
3. Selecting business and sales-force promotion tools
4. Developing the program (make decisions on the size of the incentive, conditions for participation, duration of the promotion, distribution vehicle, timing and the total sales-promotion budget)
5. Pretesting, implementing, controlling, and evaluation the program

   a) Overall, sales promotions work best when they attract competitors' customers to try a superior product and get a switch.

   b) Consumer surveys, experiments and scanner data indicate results

IV. Public relations

- Involves a variety of programs designed to promote and/or protect a company's image or its individual products. The five activities of public relations include: press relations, product publicity, corporate communications, lobbying, and counseling. Increasingly, marketing managers are turning to MPR, which seeks to support marketing objectives

A. Marketing public relations

1. Major decisions in MPR

   a) Establishing the marketing objectives (build awareness, build credibility, stimulate the sales force and dealers, and hold down promotion costs)

   (1) Differences between PR and MPR
   (2) More working together

   b) Choosing messages and vehicles

2. Implementing the plan and evaluating results

   a) Exposures, awareness/comprehension/attitude change
   b) Best: sales-and-profit impact

V. Direct marketing

A. Growth of direct marketing

1. Direct marketing is the use of consumer-direct channels to reach and deliver goods and services to customers without using marketing middlemen
2. Goal is long-term relationship building (customer relationship marketing)

B. Growth of direct marketing

1. Catalog and direct-mail sales growing at a rate of 7 percent annually, compared to retail sales growth of 3 percent
2. Electronic—Internet user population at 100+ million, and 2 million Web sites in 2001
3. Key variable is market demassification (constantly increasing number of market niches, all tied to cost of driving, traffic, parking, time, lines and lack of retail sales help)

4. Days; 1.5 million Web sites; forecast (2002) e-commerce sales of $327 billion

C. Benefits of direct marketing—benefits of focus and timing for both consumers and sellers

D. Integrated direct marketing—goal of right overall communication budget and allocation of funds to each communication tool (multiple vehicle and multiple stage campaigns)—maxi marketing

E. Major channels for direct marketing

    1. Face-to-face selling—field sales

    2. Direct mail—high target market selectivity, personalized, flexible

        a) Post office, overnight carriers, fax mail, e-mail, or voice mail

        b) Phases of direct marketing: carpet bombing, database marketing, interactive marketing, real-time personalized marketing, lifetime value marketing

    3. Constructing an effective direct-mail campaign

        a) Objectives—order-response rate is usually 2 percent

        b) Target markets and prospects

        c) Consider other elements—construct an effective offer. Five components: outside envelope, sales letter, circular, reply form, and reply envelope

        d) Offer elements

        e) Testing elements

        f) Measuring campaign's success: lifetime value

            (1) Breakeven response rate

            (2) Determining customer lifetime value (CLV)

    4. Catalog marketing—on paper, CD-ROM or online

F. Telemarketing and m-commerce

    1. Telemarketing—using the telephone to sell products/services—both inbound and outbound for telesales, telecoverage, teleprospecting and customer service and technical support

    2. Other major media for direct-response marketing (direct-response advertising, at-home shopping channels, and videotext)

G. Kiosk marketing—customer-order-placing machines

H. E-marketing—e-business includes EDI, extranets, fax and e-mail, ATMs, smart cards, the Internet and online services (marketspace)

    1. Permission marketing—letting consumers have a say in what comes to them—building trust

    2. E-marketing guidelines—giving the customer a reason to respond, personalize content of e-mail, offer something not available per direct mail, easy to "unsubscribe"

Lecture—Advertising in the New Economy

This lecture focuses on the changing nature of each of the promotional elements, particularly the decreasing use of traditional advertising and an increase in sales promotion, public relations and the interactive media.

Teaching Objectives

- To enhance the student's perspective on the important and changing role of advertising

- To give the student perspective on some of the tools not normally associated with advertising and sales promotion

- To provide specific examples and approaches for using public relations in marketing strategy

Discussion

Introduction—Where Is Advertising Headed?

The traditional use of advertising has fallen victim to new technologies and changing priorities in the marketplace. As a result, advertising agencies realize that in order to survive, they must adapt. Future success depends on the ability to understand not just advertising but all areas of promotion, and to assist clients in developing and implementing Integrated Marketing Communications programs. In this context, sales promotion, direct marketing and public relations have all gained prominence, due to the relative advantages of each tool.

It is no secret that consumers historically have been bombarded with too many advertising messages and likely cannot remember them all. This glut of promotion has led to a marketplace that is very skeptical of the traditional advertising pitch. As a result, advertisers have begun to disguise their sales messages, abandoning the familiar pitch and embedding messages subtly into popular culture. Products have begun appearing more regularly in television shows, on video and board games, and in movies.

Saturation—Are We There?

Seeking to make advertising more entertaining, popular television stars have begun portraying their characters in commercials. Research has shown that fast-paced, high movement ads are more likely to be watched, particularly when they do not highlight product attributes. This fact has led several marketers to present stories in their ads, rather than provide details on the product for sale. The result is that often it is difficult to tell the difference between an advertisement and a television program.

Brand names and logos have begun appearing on everything from bananas to bowling pins and sidewalks to ski poles. Many sports arenas are now more commonly referred to in conjunction with a major advertiser who footed the bill for needed renovation, or possibly an entirely new venue. Even infomercials, which have typically been low budget and used by relatively unknown brands, are now being employed by big brands, such as Microsoft, Ford and Eastman Kodak.

This trend toward blurring the distinction between advertising and entertainment is expected to continue for as long as traditional advertising messages represent nothing but clutter in the minds of consumers.

As has been discussed previously, the market is fragmented and harder to reach. The increased power of retailers has led to greater usage of trade-oriented promotions, new product offerings have seemed anything but innovative, and consumers clearly are less brand loyal than they once were.

As a result, there has been much more emphasis on some of the tools of promotion that once were relegated to a back seat during the height of advertising in America. It is useful to note that advertising spending as a percentage of total promotional expenditures has declined in recent years, although the Internet, sales promotion, direct marketing, telemarketing and other forms of promotion have increased.

Media advertising averaged 42 percent of company promotional budgets in 1977, but by 1999, the media advertising portion of the total budget fell to fewer than 30 percent. Much of this spending has gone to the Internet, sales promotion and direct marketing.

Seeking Benefits in Sales Promotion

Sales promotion also has become a recognized tool for reaching customers in ways not possible with other means of promotion. Although advertising focuses primarily on long-term image building, sales promotion has a short-term orientation. Because sales promotion encompasses activities ranging from coupons, samples and refund offers, it also can have a very direct and measurable impact on the consumer. In companies that continue to use a brand management structure, this is key to determining success. No other form of promotion can elicit the same speed of sales response. Those who are familiar with its benefits are also using sales promotion more strategically.

It should be pointed out, however, that sales promotion traditionally has been utilized at the point of sale so that it effects a connection only to those potential buyers already in the market for the particular product or service. This is changing, however, with at least one sales promotion tool integrated into relationship marketing strategies. Frequency marketing programs that reward a customer for multiple purchases are a widely used sales promotion tactic that encourages building long-term customer relations.

Dabbling in Direct Marketing (Including the Internet)

Direct marketing is becoming the replacement for advertising in many companies today. It is not only a logical offshoot of the one-to-one marketing trend, but it also can be significantly less expensive, if done properly. Another very important aspect of direct marketing is that it provides not only great portability and reach but also the ability to measure response. Measures of response have long been among the more important issues in advertising, and with the recent technical advances that allow pinpoint marketing, it is possible to reach virtually any customer, anywhere.

Compared with general advertising, direct marketing, whether traditional direct marketing or direct marketing via the Internet, enables a firm to sell to individual, by name, address and purchase behavior, compared to broad group demographic and psychographic identification and contact. Also, compared to general advertising, where the requirement to build image, awareness, loyalty, benefit and recall may require considerable time before a purchase action, direct marketing can motivate an immediate order or inquiry.

Another major advantage of direct marketing is the fact that there is no need for a retail channel; the channel medium now is the marketplace itself. Although this may work as a negative factor for some consumers who still want the feeling of less risk that comes from direct contact with the product, and direct recourse, the overall gain for most marketers can be substantial.

Public Relations

Another integral component in marketing strategic planning is consistent public relations activities. Public relations provide opportunities for cost-effective differentiation and is quickly becoming one of the most important elements in the marketing mix. Because it carries the impact of a respected third-party endorsement, public relations should work in tandem with other promotional tools to foster a total corporate communications package. Strategic public relations can:

- Build consumer confidence and trust

- Position companies as leaders and experts
- Introduce new products
- Cultivate new markets
- Reach secondary markets
- Extend the reach of advertising
- Make news before advertising
- Complement advertising by reinforcing messages and legitimizing claims
- Supplement advertising by communicating other product benefits
- Gain exposure for products that cannot be advertised to consumers
- Gain awareness through other than advertising media
- Tailor marketing programs to local audiences to distinguish companies and their products from the competition
- Win consumer support by identifying companies and brands with causes they care about
- Generate sales inquiries
- Motivate staff efforts

Public relations activities include: anniversaries, award programs, article writing, annual meetings, community programs and events, customer hotlines, grand openings, interviews, luncheons, newsletters, press releases, seminars and sponsorships.

Direct Marketing and Interactive Strategy

As more clients and agencies begin to understand and explore the marketing potential of the Internet, e-marketing has evolved from companies simply creating their corporate presence online, to establishment of e-commerce-enabled sites, and to the first stages of building and measuring one-to-one customer relationships. Here are several Interactive campaign competitions that had a goal to engage and create a dialogue with their respective targets. Be ready to judge each of them.

Evaluate these campaigns based on their exemplary use of the electronic media. Look for online campaigns (or components of larger, integrated campaigns) that embody innovation and creativity. How effectively does the campaign appear to achieve the marketer's objectives and goals? Do the interactive elements serve to reinforce the objective or overall strategy? Is the overall strategy creative and well geared to the online/electronic medium? Finally, does the interactive campaign push the envelope, test or experiment with new technologies, capabilities and/or formats?

Spring Fling a Winner for Cover Girl

This program involved recording a variety of kissing sounds for inclusion in the Web site. It revolved around a contest offering a chance to win $100 in free makeup, as well as a $500 shopping spree in the winner's favorite store.

The ad agency recognized that the target market—teen girls—comprise an Internet-savvy bunch who would require more motivating components than just another draw. Teen girls are very interactive, but they do not want to just be talked to, or talked at; they want to be a part of it.

Preliminary research by P&G suggested that contests, particularly those conducted online, are not memorable for teens, according to a spokesperson for Cover Girl. The Cover Girl comment: "Every teen we spoke to had entered several online contests in the past month, but not a single one could recall a sponsor from any of them."

Accordingly, the idea of the interactive campaign was to get interaction around the color palette. In other words, the "Get Color Matched Now" section of the Web site allowed browsers to select makeup hues and build a custom palette to be submitted and saved as the contest entry. The products of preference would become the foundation of the $100 Cover Girl gift pack, if the participant won. In addition, visitors also gained access to a savable/printable version of their favorite shades, for future shopping reference. This was considerably more relevant and engaging for teens to participate in than any other online contest.

An initial e-mail outlining the program was sent to 10,000 girls who had opted in to receive the Cover Girl Connections newsletter via the American Cover Girl Web site. Although there was no additional media or promotional support, the site drew more than 8,000 unique visitors during a six-week span, and more than 6,000 contest entries.

Another component that helped drive teens to the site was the refer-a-friend incentive. Kids could boost their chances at the grand prize with each successful e-mail referral at the final point of contest registration. In fact, this component drew a 34 percent response rate. Indeed, the entire campaign far surpassed the quantifiable objective of receiving a 10 percent to 15 percent response rate for the original e-mail, as the rate actually fell at 39 percent.

The ad agency determined (nothing new) that friends are the number-one influencers of teens' buying decisions. The program was successful because it creatively leveraged this consumer insight in a way that was low risk and nonintrusive—it got teens talking to their friends about Cover Girl through both the contest referral and the e-Kiss applications.

Teens could also send e-Kiss postcards, bestowing pecks to pals and boyfriends. They also were able to select the color of lips (from a range of Cover Girl shades), their shape and the sound of the kiss. A Cover Girl logo and a link were visible on the e-mail sent to gal pals, while a nonbranded version was available for boys.

In fact, teen girls seemed to embrace the smooching, as the e-Kiss cards grabbed the most attention on the Web site, recording a 70 percent response rate.

Cover Girl presented a very fun way for their target to interact with the products [and] colors, which can sometimes be a challenge. The refer-a-friend feature allowed for great pass-along and increased the database of names to market to next time. Consumers could increase their knowledge of the products with the personalized makeup palettes.

(Ask for student evaluations here.)

Suggested Response:

This is a fun and engaging campaign that provides an excellent example of the right approach matched up with the right medium and the right target audience. Teenage girls love to try out things, and the Mix & Match contest gave them this opportunity, along with a chance to win some great prizes. The e-Kiss marketing postcard was not only simple in its design, but also on target for this demographic.

Chivas Regal Stirs the Fancy of a Younger Demographic

Chivas Regal is not just for stodgy old suits, but for ambitious young suits too. This is what parent company Seagram hoped to convince the 25- to 34-year-old, university-educated crowd in just three cities, with its "When You Know" interactive campaign.

The challenge was that Chivas had an older, more established audience, and it was trying to attract younger males through a cheeky, edgy banter. Seagram hoped that the age group would recognize this label as one that relates to their lifestyle and that they would feel comfortable drinking in a public forum.

The effort was mainly about conveying the brand's sense of humor. Seagram used 22,000 no-charge, opt-in e-mail addresses from an e-marketing firm to announce the contest. When respondents visited, they were exposed to five Flash animation vignettes exhibiting the whiskey label's personality: one that is intelligent, irreverent and audacious.

In one of the scenarios, a man strains to squeeze into a pair of plaid pants. The copy reads, "When you know, it's not the clothes that make the man, but the clothes that make the man buy new clothes." Another shows an attractive woman in black lingerie holding a whip. "When you know, it's gonna hurt, but you kinda like it," it says.

The strategy, which linked back to Chivas Regal's global "When You Know" print, TV and outdoor venture, presented a targeted effort geared at upwardly mobile urbanites. The tagline neatly relates back to the brand because it implies that when you reach a certain age, you know what a good scotch is. It indicated that the campaign related to the target's sense of humor because they wanted to share it with friends.

There was, however, a risk of going overboard with the message. The question was, is this edgy enough to be relevant and impactful or is it beyond good taste?Apparently, however, it did not turn off almost 12,000 people who entered the contest, 50 percent of whom also consented to receive additional communication going forward.

Chivas also invested in a banner "run of site" campaign on Yahoo! that appeared to subscribers in the demographic range, as well as similar initiatives on Excite@Home and Hotmail.com. Advertising on Canoe.com, which included a banner leveraging relevant content such as sports, entertainment and finance, was also stirred into the mix. In total, 137,000 e-mails were sent, and more than 1.5 million impressions purchased. The average click-through rate for the entire banner ad effort was 0.44 percent, meeting the industry's overall success rate of between 0.3 percent and 0.4 percent.

Comments

The "When You Know" Chivas campaign had clean, appealing graphics with catchy, witty messaging that managed to give the product a hip and youthful spin. It did not require a high-speed connection to view. The campaign produced solid results, generating a 21.7 percent click through rate. Given that this brand was launching to a new, younger demographic, the results were good.

E*TRADE

Drawing leads for online stock trading amid a depressed economy can be a challenge. For E*TRADE this challenge called for a multimedia contest that would encourage ongoing participation.

For the contest, E*TRADE aspired to meet the total participation numbers from the previous contest, no small feat given that participation has tended to fall by as much as 46 percent in a declining market.

As well, the effort aimed to increase participation among E*TRADE's most valuable population segments: "aggressive affluent," 40-something individuals with families and capital to protect, who generally hold assets of $100,000-plus; and "get rich quick," aged 18 and up consumers who view risk as part of everyday life and tend to hold less than $50,000 in assets.

The E*COMBAT stock market game kicked off April 30 and ran to June 8. A grand prize of $15,000 and six weekly prizes of $1,000 sought to capture the target audience's attention. Boot-camp-inspired images and aggressive copy invited individuals to join in the game, which was supported by TV, radio, print and online executions from April 23 to June 1.

The game's registration process enabled E*TRADE to segment participants into three groups: those with no previous online trading experience, those who trade online with an E*TRADE competitor and those who were current E*TRADE customers. Targeted e-mail messages sent to these segments throughout the game sustained participation and encouraged conversion to account holders.

The game achieved 172 percent of the previous contest's total participation, and matched the previous contest's participation during the first three days alone. More than 5,500 trades were executed during the first 13 minutes. And the game appealed to E*TRADE's most valuable customers, with a 300 percent rise in participation among the "aggressive affluent" and a 275 percent boost among the "get rich quick."

Lecture—Marketing on the Information Superhighway: Are We There Yet?

This lecture discusses computer-based marketing. Because there is much useful information on this subject in the contemporary literature, it would be useful to update with current examples.

The discussion begins with several examples of techniques for utilizing on-line and integrated marketing to enhance the firm's market position. This leads into a discussion of the implications for the firm and the industry.

Teaching Objectives

• To stimulate students to think about the critical issues in online and integrated marketing, pro and con, for a firm

• Points to consider in proceeding into the online marketing arena, with a specific strategy

• Role of online strategies and policies in helping the firm achieve a specific strategic planning position

Discussion

Introduction—to "Net" or Not

As we all know, despite the claims to the contrary, the "Net" and the "Web" cannot be everything to everyone. They may provide a wonderful conduit for data exchange, and they offer an exciting new channel for creative communication, but for some marketers there still may be a question of the degree to which they can or will utilize the Internet on their way to a marketing "best combination" of strategy and media. The superhighway system has in many ways linked people and ideas and shortened trips to everywhere, but progress and efficiency are lost on many travelers who are far less interested in the journey than the destination.

There are many questions about what is happening in the world of marketing on the Internet. Who is doing it? Whose customers are already cruising the Web, and which customers are not even interested? What tools are being developed to make Web sites even more dynamic and inviting? Most important of all is the question of whether and how business can be conducted in cyberspace.

The goal in this discussion is to provide an answer to the traditional question asked of all parents traveling with their children: "Are we there yet?" The answer may be: "Not yet, but we're getting closer all the time."

The Data on PC/Internet Use

There are pluses and negatives for the Internet. For example a negative indicator comes from a cluster analysis that shows that although the number of Internet users in the United States and elsewhere continues to climb at substantial rates, there are many who and will remain resisters to the media and the marketing potential.

Based on information usage categories, ranging from newspaper readership to interest in home shopping, the Internet population can be divided into roughly six groups: High Brow Info Achievers, Info Strivers, Learn and Play Families, Mainstream Consumers, Information Laggards, and Low Brows.

Ideal targets for online marketers are represented by Info Achievers, Info Strivers, and to a lesser degree, Learn and Play Families. These groups, however, represent less than 30 percent of U.S. households. Stiffening levels of resistance are more likely to be encountered as the categories descend beyond mainstream families toward Information Laggards and Low Brows. Such resistance makes it clear that any penetration of PCs and PC-based technology above 70 percent will require major changes in pricing and applications.

Clusters

The following is a synopsis of cluster characteristics:

High Brow Info Achievers: This cluster includes the most educated and affluent consumers. Their intensive use of information has translated into materially successful work and lifestyles, and they tend to be managers, executives and owners. PC ownership is universal in this group. Modem and broadband (cable and DSL) penetration is also very high, as is CD- ROM use, online service and Internet penetration.

Info Strivers: This cluster comprises the second 5 percent of households. Although highly successful, and PC and modem owners, they tend to also be younger, and have not yet achieved the same degree of financial success as Info Achievers. They tend to be professionals, rather than executives and/or owners.

Learn and Play Families: The third highest cluster, Learn and Play Families are middle to upper middle class and tend to have the highest percentage of school-aged children. Subsequently, the parents of these kids are often willing to buy into technology to benefit their kids, even though they have little use for the technology themselves. PC ownership is very high in this cluster, and modem ownership and use continues to trail off but is rising. Many parents in this group remain surprisingly unaware of the benefits of online services and the Internet, and they continue to fear the potential influence of unsavory online/Internet services.

Mainstream Consumers: A broad range of occupational groups is found here. Mainstream Consumer households tend to be slightly older than both Learn and Play families and Info Strivers, and household incomes fall below $50,000 for the first time. Their relationship to technology can be summarized as: "If it is useful and not too expensive, I may be interested." Inexpensive home banking services, for instance, have begun to rope these people into expanded use. For now, however, PC penetration stands at only about 65 percent, and modem/online service penetration, although still in the area of 30 percent continues to grow every year.

Information Laggards: This group tends to consist of workers who do fairly well by earning over $40,000 per year, but who have uncomplicated information needs that are easily met by TV. A quarter of this segment holds blue-collar employment. Only about 20 percent own PCs, and modem/ nline service use remains essentially nil. Where children are found, there are positive attitudes towards use of technology to further education in the future. The modest income level of these households in the past discourages adoption, but as the prices of reasonably powerful computer systems have come down below $1,000, this argument has lost some validity. Most people/households in this category characterize PCs and the Internet as "confusing or expensive."

Low Brows: This cluster consists of several distinct types of users generally earning less than $30,000 per household that do not use information in its more complex print or media forms. For example, most retirees are found here, as are most consumers who are either without college degrees and/or are unemployed. Surprisingly, the most frequently occurring age in this cluster is 28, which sheds new light on the popular image of youth as our leading technology adopters. This group shows that many less educated or otherwise disadvantaged younger households simply don't use much information other than TV news and perhaps a newspaper or popular magazine.

They are unlikely to become computer literate because they continue to believe that computers and the Internet are "useless."

Given the lack of demonstrated interest among several substantial segments of the population, a mass-market orientation for the Internet is not yet complete. The technology continues to evolve and improve, however, and new and better applications continue to appear almost daily.

Going Online—What to Do and Not Do

For those who were under pressure a few years ago to take their company online, and were not sure about where and how to go about it, there should no longer be any question about the value of the medium. Increasingly the questions about what the Internet and other interactive media can or will do for any particular organization have been answered in the affirmative. There still remain, however, a couple of unanswered questions:

- How does the interactive media fit with the existing marketing program?

- Have the majority of targeted consumers recognized the value of the medium and use it effectively?

Fortunately, integrated marketing is not a radical departure from traditional advertising. It is about selling, a principal as old as civilization itself. To create a successful campaign, marketers have to adapt marketing conventional wisdom to fit the new media.

Marketing and Advertising

1. Absolut Vodka's ads always feature its distinctive bottle, as shown in Figure 1. For this holiday ad, the company commissioned a specially designed bottle cover to suggest that sipping Absolut is a warm holiday experience, and photographed the ad in the knit designer's New York City apartment.

    a. How would you classify this magazine ad in terms of its advertising objective?

    b. Analyze this ad in terms of message execution, style, tone, and format.

    c. What is the most striking part of the ad? Would the ad be as effective if the headline and copy were more prominent? Why?

Answer

    a. The objective of this ad appears to be to remind current customers to continue buying and drinking Absolut. It is clearly not aiming to inform or to persuade; vodka drinkers may need minimal reinforcement of their brand choice.

    b. This ad uses message execution to sell the Absolut image, not the product itself. The style is presented to reinforce and support the product's image. The format is full-color, full-page size for effective execution of the concept, with holiday colors appropriate to the season. The ad contains minimal copy to focus attention on the bottle shape and the brand name in the headline. The tone is not staid and conservative but slightly hip and stylish. Students may suggest other observations about this ad, as well.

    c. The most striking part of the ad is, of course, the bottle in a colorful knit cozy. The ad would not be as effective if the headline and copy were more prominent, because the visual representation of the bottle's shape supports and reinforces the brand image without the need for additional information provided by words.

2. The ad in Figure 2 invites advertisers to advertise on the Ask Jeeves search site, Ask.com. The message states that an ad on Ask Jeeves will reach consumers "when they are most receptive to your message."

    a. Analyze this ad in terms of the reach, frequency, and impact an advertiser might expect from using Ask Jeeves as an advertising vehicle.

    b. Discuss how a media planner might look at the four media variables of media habits, product characteristics, message characteristics, and cost when considering Ask Jeeves as an Internet advertising vehicle.

    c. What additional questions would a media planner ask when making a decision about whether to advertise on the Ask Jeeves site?

Answer

    a. An advertiser using Ask Jeeves as an advertising vehicle would be interested in knowing how many different consumers visit the Ask.com Web site during a specified period (reach) and, ideally, being sure the ad would reach as many consumers in the target market as possible. Ask Jeeves may not be the best vehicle for reaching certain targets, such as technically sophisticated consumers or business customers. In addition, the advertiser would expect to get multiple exposures for its ad, building frequency as needed to convey its message and allow the target market to comprehend the meaning. Finally, the advertiser would expect a powerful impact from linking its ad to a popular, well-known search engine—more impact than if the advertiser used a different online vehicle.

    b. When considering media habits, a media planner would want to know the composition of the Ask Jeeves audience, described by demographics, behavior, and other characteristics. This information would allow the media planner to be sure that the audience matches the target market for the product being advertised. Next, the media planner would look at product characteristics to be sure that the good or service being advertised could be adequately described or displayed in a banner ad or other link on the Ask Jeeves Web site. Also, the media planner would consider message characteristics to be sure that the amount of information in the Ask Jeeves message and the timing of the message are appropriate for the product being promoted. Then the media planner would have to look at the cost of reaching each Ask Jeeves visitor in terms of the overall advertising budget.

    c. Students may suggest a number of questions that a media planner would ask when making a decision about advertising on the Ask Jeeves site. These might include (but not be limited to): the experiences of other advertisers in achieving reach and frequency goals; the lead time for preparing new online ads; limitations in size, color, and other message characteristics; and the ability to target specific consumer segments based on questions asked or other behavior.

3. ****BONUS AD--See Companion Web site!** As this ad shows, Reckitt Benckiser used coupons to introduce a new product, Old English Furniture Wipes. The ad also reinforced the new product's key benefit ("cleans and shines without residue build-up").

    a. What type of objective is Reckitt Benckiser likely to have set for this sales promotion? Why are coupons especially appropriate for this objective, rather than other sales promotion tools?

    b. What implementation issues did Reckitt Benckiser have to consider when planning this sales promotion?

c. How might the company evaluate the results of this sales promotion?

Answer

a. Reckitt Benckiser probably set a consumer trial objective for this coupon promotion, because the product is new. It may also have set a repurchase objective to encourage consumers to buy again after they have tried the new product for the first time. Coupons are especially appropriate for both these objectives. A coupon lowers the price and therefore makes the product seem less risky to first-time buyers; it also rewards repeat purchasers by lowering the price on a subsequent purchase.

b. The company had to consider a number of implementation issues, such as: how far in advance the coupons had to be created, printed, and provided to the media vehicle for distribution; how much stock was in place in retail stores, ready for consumer purchase, when the coupons were distributed; and how retailers would be compensated for accepting this coupon. Students may identify additional issues as well.

c. Reckitt Benckiser can count the number of coupons redeemed and compare that to the program's objectives as a way to evaluate the outcome of this promotion. The company may also want to determine whether this sales promotion affected other objectives, such as brand-name awareness.

4. ****BONUS AD--See Companion Web site!** This Toyota magazine ad is based on one of the company's social responsibility initiatives, specifically its efforts to create environmentally friendly vehicles.

a. Does this ad use a rational or emotional positioning? Why is the positioning appropriate for this message?

b. At which stage(s) in the hierarchy of effects model might this ad be most effective in influencing the targeted consumer segments?

c. Why do you think Toyota made the graphics more prominent than the headline and copy in this ad?

Answer

a. This ad uses rational positioning by providing specific information about how Toyota is working toward more environmentally friendly vehicles. This is an appropriate positioning because it provides hard evidence of Toyota's commitment and progress, in keeping with the copy, which states that "we've done more than just talk."

b. This ad might be most effective in targeting car buyers in the knowledge, liking, preference, and conviction stages of the hierarchy of effects, because it provides specific evidence of Toyota's commitment to and progress toward vehicles that are environmentally-friendly—information that would be viewed in a positive light by consumers who hold strong beliefs about the need to protect the environment.

c. The graphics seem designed to attract attention by stimulating curiosity. Once readers notice the leaf-like car and read the headline, they are more likely to continue reading and find out why the other cars are following this single green car. In addition, this approach lightens the tone of the ad so it does not come across as too sanctimonious or preachy but rather seems friendly and upbeat.

Online Marketing Today—Start Sampling

More manufacturers are working with Web-based companies to mount targeted consumer sales promotions on the Internet. StartSampling, for example, helped Golden Books Publishing distribute samples of a new book to mothers of young children. In exchange for receiving a free sample, the mothers filled out a brief online survey. The results far exceeded the company's expectations: although Golden Books projected a 25 percent response rate from this online sampling program, it actually achieved a 67 percent response rate—and it obtained valuable marketing research at the same time.

To see how StartSampling operates, visit its home page (www.startsampling.com). What benefits does this site emphasize for participants? How does it encourage consumers to continue returning for additional samples? How can manufacturers become involved with this site? Why would a manufacturer choose to offer samples through StartSampling rather than through another method (such as in-store sampling, for example)?

Answer

The StartSampling site stresses that participants will be able to try new things (a major benefit for consumers who crave variety or want to be the first to have a new product). It also emphasizes that companies need and want consumer feedback. Students may cite other benefits that appear on the home page or other pages. To keep consumers returning to the site, StartSampling offers contests and frequency marketing points, rotates its offers, and other techniques. Manufacturers can learn how to get their samples distributed through StartSampling by clicking on a link on the home page and following the instructions—a process purposely made as easy as possible to encourage more companies to participate. StartSampling says its sampling methods are not only cost-effective, but companies can obtain a significant amount of research data because consumers must answer survey questions to qualify for samples.

You're the Marketer—Sonic PDA Marketing Plan

Advertising, sales promotion, public relations, and direct marketing—both online and off—are among the most visible outcomes of any marketing plan. Marketers plan these programs with special care because of the support they provide for the product, pricing, and distribution strategies described in the marketing plan.

At Sonic, you are starting to plan the promotional support for launching the new personal digital assistant (PDA) product next year. After reviewing your earlier marketing-mix decisions and thinking about the current situation (especially your competitive circumstances), respond to the following questions as you decide on your promotion strategy:

- Based on the overall promotion decisions you made in the previous chapter, should Sonic use advertising to support the PDA introduction? If so, what advertising goals will you set, and how will you measure your results?
- What message(s) do you want to communicate to your target audience? What media are most appropriate, and why?
- Should you use consumer or trade promotion or both? Which promotion tools would be most appropriate for your new product introduction?
- Should you use public relations to promote Sonic and its products? If so, what objectives will you set, and which tools will you plan to use?
- How can you use integrated direct marketing to support your new product introduction?
- Which of the direct marketing channels are most appropriate for reaching PDA buyers?
- What role should e-marketing plan in your new product launch?

Consider how the promotion programs you are planning will fit with the other decisions you have made and with Sonic's goals and objectives. As your instructor directs, summarize your programs in a written marketing plan or type them into the Marketing Mix section of the *Marketing Plan Pro* software.

Answer

Advertising is likely to be needed to support Sonic's sales and profit goals and to create a brand image within the target market. Students may suggest advertising objectives related to (1) informing consumers and business buyers about the new product's features and benefits, (2) making them aware of the brand and build positive attitudes and preferences, and (3) stimulating trial. To measure results, Sonic would compare actual sales during and after the ad campaign with the sales projections that were set prior to the campaign. Sonic will also want to commission research to measure awareness, attitudes, and preferences among the target audience.

Students may suggest various messages and media. Their answers should relate to Sonic's overall goals, mission, and strategy, including establishing the brand image and helping the company compete in an increasingly crowded market. (Ask them to look back at their answers to the questions in the previous chapter.) Messages and media must also be appropriate for the target market. Similarly, students' suggestions about the use of sales promotion, public relations, and direct marketing must be consistent with Sonic's strategy, audience, and other marketing-mix decisions. Thus, Sonic will want to offer a product warranty and perhaps a point-of-purchase display as well as sales contests, but coupons, prizes, sampling, and free goods are probably not appropriate for introducing a high-tech product. Public relations should be an important part of Sonic's marketing plan, including news releases, product publicity, and corporate communication. Integrated direct marketing would help Sonic coordinate all its messages in all media for a multiple vehicle, multi-stage campaign that ultimately results in product sales. Students should use their creativity in suggesting suitable direct marketing and e-marketing approaches for the Sonic PDA.

Marketing Spotlight—Volkswagen

Volkswagen, the fifth-largest automaker in the world, was founded in 1937. The first prototype was actually built in 1935 by Ferdinand Porsche, founder of the car company bearing his name, who had been commissioned by Hitler to build a "Peoples Car." Volkswagen began selling its Beetles in North America in 1949, a year in which only two of the vehicles sold in the United States for $995 each. By 1955, the company had sold one million vehicles worldwide. Today, Volkswagen manufactures a number of other car brands, including Audi, Lamborghini, Bugatti, Bentley, Rolls-Royce, Skoda, and Seat.

Growth Years

With the help of creative and effective marketing, Volkswagen became a household name in America during the 1960s. The company's marketing program in the United States during this decade was designed to make the brand's underdog status an advantage. This was accomplished with self-deprecating advertising that made light of the Beetle's shortcomings. Some memorable slogans for the Bug include "Think Small," "It's Ugly But It Gets There," and "Nobody's Perfect." These self-effacing slogans ran counter to the advertising tradition of U.S. automakers, which usually involved lofty descriptions of a car's style, power, grace, and superior design. The classic Beetle rapidly became a cult favorite, then a popular favorite, and eventually was to become the number-one selling car in history with over 22 million units sold. Volkswagen was not afraid to use the occasional hard sell. One particularly persuasive print ad paired a Volkswagen with a snowplow and a heavy blanket of snow on the ground and asked, "What do you think the snowplow driver drives to work?" Volkswagen also developed a stylish automobile called the Karmann Ghia, which was humorously advertised as the car "for people who can't stand the sight of a Volkswagen."

Decline and Recovery

After sales of VW cars in America peaked at 569,000 units in 1970, cutthroat competition among compacts, especially from Japanese manufacturers, hurt Volkswagen's sales. The company also made an unfortunate marketing move that compounded its problems. It "Americanized" its image, by advertising the opening of an VW assembly line in Pennsylvania—the first U.S. assembly line set up by a foreign auto maker—at a time when imports were become popular. The 1980s were not much better for the company, as sales continued to decline.

By 1990, Volkswagen was looking for ways to revitalize its business in the United States. Sales had slipped to a mere 1.3 percent of the American market from a high of 7 percent in 1970. The company developed an advertising campaign that centered on the word Fahrvergnugen, German for "driving pleasure." This strategy was considered a risk at the time because many assumed Americans would not adopt a German word as a slogan. The hard-to-pronounce word nevertheless became an instant pop-culture buzzword, but U.S. sales continued to drop to under 50,000 units. The company clarified its brand message under the umbrella of the "Drivers Wanted" slogan in 1995, and U.S. sales rose 18 percent to 135,907 cars in 1996.

Classic Influences Tempt Consumers

In 1998, Volkswagen released a modernized version of its iconic Beetle to a car-buying public nostalgic for the vintage style. Ads for the New Beetle echoed the irreverent humor of the ads from the 1960s, with one ad reading "If you sold your soul in the '80s, here's your chance to buy it back." Another ad emphasized the difference between the modern engine and notoriously underpowered traditional Beetle with the slogan "Less Flower, More Power." American buyers leapt at the chance to buy the classically influenced—but clearly modern—cars, often at well above sticker price. Waiting lists for the new cars, which sold more than 55,000 units in 1998, were common. The company also experimented with the Internet as a marketing and sales medium, holding a special Web-only launch of 2,000 New Beetles in two previously unavailable colors, Reflex Yellow and Vapor Blue. Volkswagen sold out its inventory immediately. By drawing consumers into Volkswagen showrooms, the New Beetle helped the company achieve 50 percent growth in sales volume between 1998 and 1999.

In 2001, the company unveiled its latest retro offering—the Microbus—as a concept car. The car, not expected to be available to the American public until 2003, will likely set off another wave of nostalgia and help the company achieve further sales growth. Other new models slated for introduction include a sport utility vehicle and a luxury V-8 Passat sedan designed to compete with BMW and Mercedes. Volkswagen's history of brilliant marketing will likely lead to success for these new models.

Sources: Al Beeber, "Volkswagen Sets Stage for New Microbus." Lethbridge Herald, June 14, 2001; Rupert Spiegelberg, "If You Love Bug, Rejoice." Houston Chronicle, June 29, 1997; David Kiley, "VW Goes More Off Beat With 'Wanted' Ads." Brandweek, April 28, 1997; David Welch. "VW: Now That's How to Rebuild a Brand." Business Week, June 19, 2000; Keith Naughton. "Can You Say Fahrvergnugen?" The Detroit News, February 2, 1990; Randall Rothenberg. "The Advertising Century." Advertising Age, March 29, 1999; "Volkswagen Sales Fall with Beetle's Demise." Reuters News Agency, October 15, 1982

Questions

1. What are some of the ways in which Volkswagen epitomizes the meaning and value of the marketing concepts in the text?

2. Suggest creative extensions of VW's marketing tactics and strategies in applications of advertising, promotion, public relations and other promotional techniques?

Suggested Responses

1. VW is an excellent example in the resourceful application of many different marketing forms and media. With few resources available to draw buyers, VW has conducted seemingly offbeat and nonmass advertising campaigns. Maybe part of the success is due to the nature of the VW as the people's car. Where most cars are similar to every other, VW defies the traditional approach in both vehicles and advertising. VW's success may be due to many factors, but it draws a generally higher demographic and also those who wish to be different and unique versus "move with the herd." In addition, the demographic tends toward younger people (or aspire to younger), single men and women, those oriented toward German quality, and those who expect and demand high value and mechanical quality versus high style. VW marketing appears to fit the uniqueness of the car and the people who own and drive it.

2. The VW tendency toward "self-effacing" to draw attention indicates that a logical extension could be sports marketing connections because many in the VW demographic appear to be fitness and sport-minded, including both men and women. They also could consider utilizing marketing connections with other marketers that appeal to the same type(s) of customer. Accordingly, the Internet and other interactive media could be a logical and effective extension for VW. This application could fit well with VW's national buys, augmenting and enhancing existing advertising and brand images. There is possible synergy between the qualities of the newer interactive media and the VW demographic. Because VW products are perceived to be innovative and cutting edge, they should have considerable appeal to potential customers who also utilize some of the more innovative interactive media such as digital cable and the Internet.

   On a Web site such as Sports.com, with content such as fan forums, games, and celebrity chat interviews, VW could promote a sporty model such as the Golf to an international audience. In addition, this would be an appropriate setting to run pop-up questions related to car-buying habits and user tendencies that could provide information useful for future interactive media placements. Because VW produces and sells well in many developing countries, especially in Mexico and South America, the sports connection has considerable value related to the passion for soccer.

   Another application could be a Web site promotion with a major department store and/or with an AOL or MSN lifestyle site. The VW Polo might be an appropriate model to utilize in a lifestyle site because the Polo appeals to younger women who have in the past been a major factor in the worldwide VW demographic.

Analytical Tools for Marketing Management—Advertising Weight Decisions

Note the concept of and process for calculating BDIs and CDIs explained in an earlier Analytical Tools exercise. If students have forgotten this concept and calculation process, they should be urged to reread that exercise.

Questions

1. Based on the data provided in the Student Guide, calculate the BDIs and CDIs for the ten markets.

2. Determine which are problem and/or opportunity markets (See Student Guide for discussion).

3. Assume that the brand spends $10,000,000 a year for national advertising. How many dollars should he added to each problem or opportunity market, based on the decision rules discussed previously? Show work.

4. If another factor is added to this problem, specifically, the "responsiveness to advertising," would this improve the method of weighting markets? Explain.

Answers

1. BDIs and CDIs for the ten markets.

		BDI	CDI
1.	Indianapolis	93	99
2.	Houston	105	110
3.	Hartford	91	91
4.	Atlanta	113	105
5.	Buffalo	96	100
6.	Cincinnati	87	105
7.	Miami	198	170
8.	Milwaukee	88	95
9.	Memphis	133	151
10.	Kansas City	121	117

Sample calculation—for Indianapolis: BDI .98 / 1.05 = 93

$$\frac{.98}{1.05} x100 = 93 \qquad\qquad \frac{1.04}{1.05} x100 = 99$$

CDI 1.04 / 1.05 = 99

2.   Calculations for Problem and Opportunity Markets:

Problem Markets are:	Opportunity Markets are:
a. Indianapolis	a. Houston
b. Buffalo	b. Cincinnati
c. Milwaukee	c. Memphis

3. Adding extra dollars to the problem and opportunity markets is done as follows:

Problem Markets	Budget ($)	Add 5% of total	Add 20% to problem markets	Bring opportunity markets to CDI levels	Totals
Indianapolis	$9,800	$967	$1,960		$12,727
Buffalo	8,200	967	10,000		10,807
Boston	8,000	8,333	20,000		10,567
Opportunity Markets					
Houston	$13,500	$967		$648	$15,115
Cincinnati	8,100	967		1,677	10,744
Memphis	10,000	967		1,020	11,987

- Note that the sum of advertising budgets for the 10 markets was $116,000. Five percent of the $116,000 divided by six markets was $967.
- Remind students that all markets likely would receive the benefit of national advertising such as network TV or national magazines. This technique is, in reality, a local/regional add-on type of budgeting activity.

Responsiveness to advertising is difficult to prove, but a weighting technique might be a step in the right direction. Still, the tough part is determining how many sales were directly related to or as a result of advertising because there are so many marketing mix variables operating in the marketplace. How can one be sure of the role of advertising versus a price reduction, an increase in distribution, or a new package design?

Chapter 21—Managing the Sales Force

Overview

Most companies use sales representatives, and many companies assign them the pivotal role in the marketing mix. Salespeople are very effective in achieving certain marketing objectives. At the same time they are very costly. Management must give careful thought to designing and managing its personal-selling resources.

Sales force design calls for decisions on objectives, strategy, structure, size, and compensation. Sales force objectives include prospecting, communicating, selling, and servicing, information gathering, and allocating. Sales force strategy is a question of what types and mix and selling approaches are most effective (solo selling, team selling, and so on). Sales force structure is a choice between organizing by territory, product, customer, or a hybrid combination, and developing the right territory size and shape. Sales force size involves estimating the total workload and how many sales hours—and hence salespeople—would be needed. Sales force compensation involves determining pay level and components such as salary, commission, bonus, expenses, and fringe benefits.

Managing the sales force involves recruiting and selecting sales representatives and training, directing, motivating, and evaluating them. Sales representatives must be recruited and selected carefully to hold down the high costs of hiring the wrong persons. Sales-training programs familiarize new salespeople with the company's history, its products and policies, the characteristics of the market and competitors, and the art of selling. Salespeople need direction on such matters as developing customer and prospect targets and call norms and using their time efficiency through computer-aided information, planning and selling systems, and inside support salespeople. Salespeople also need encouragement through economic and personal rewards and recognition because they must make tough decisions and are subject to many frustrations. The key idea is that appropriate sales force motivation will lead to more effort, better performance, higher rewards, higher satisfaction, and therefore still more motivation. The last management step calls for periodically evaluating each salesperson's performance to help him or her do a better job.

The purpose of the sales force is to produce sales, and this involves the art of personal selling. One aspect is salesmanship, which involves a seven-step process: prospecting and qualifying, preapproach, approach, presentation and demonstration, overcoming objections, closing, and follow-up and maintenance. Another aspect is negotiation, the art of arriving at transaction terms that satisfy both parties. The third aspect is relationship management, the art of creating a closer working relationship and interdependence between the people in two organizations.

In summary, the primary variables for the sales force/management effort includes the following: (1) Setting objectives—objectives can be general rules for guiding salespeople or more specific expectations for behavior. Regardless, the sales objectives should address the relationship between sales, customer satisfaction, and company profit; (2) Designing strategy—strategy requires decisions on sales force structure, size, and compensation. Variations in this mixture are appropriate for differing industries, markets, and sales objectives; (3) Recruiting and selecting—knowing in advance what characteristics will always produce good salespeople is very difficult. Selection procedures should attempt to screen candidates for both ability and retention-related issues; (4) Training salespeople—issues in training center on skills such as order taking and order getting, seeing customers as people who require problem solutions; (5) Supervising salespeople—supervision addresses problems in directing and coordinating salespeople's organization, time management, motivation, and customer relationships; and (6) Evaluating salespeople—evaluation requires both qualitative and quantitative measures of sales force performance.

Learning Objectives

After reading the chapter the student should understand
- The key factors in designing a sales force
- How one manages a sales force successfully
- The fundamental principles of personal selling

Chapter Outline

I.   Introduction—various classifications of sales positions ranging from least to most creative types of selling (deliverer, order taker, missionary, technician, demand creator, solution vendor)

II.   Designing the sales force
    A.   Sales force objectives and strategy
        1.   Objectives (tasks to perform include: prospecting, targeting, communicating, selling, servicing, information gathering, and allocating)
        2.   Strategy—approach can be: sales rep to buyer, sales rep to buyer group, sales team to buyer group, conference selling, or seminar selling. A company can utilize a direct (company) or contractual (outside) sales force.
    B.   Sales force structure (territorial, product, market, complex)
    C.   Sales-force size
        1.   Based on number of customers to reach
        2.   Workload approach: customer volume size classes, call frequencies, total workload, average number of calls, number of sales reps needed
    D.   Sales—force compensation—level and appropriate combination of components (fixed, variable, expense allowances, and benefits)

III. Managing the sales force
    A.   Recruiting and selecting sales reps
        1.   What makes a good sales representative?
        2.   Recruitment procedures
        3.   Applicant-rating procedures
    B.   Training sales reps
        1.   Goals: to know and identify with the company, to know the company's products, to know the customers' and competitors' characteristics
        2.   Other goals: to know how to make effective sales presentations, and to understand field procedures and responsibilities
    C.   Supervising sales reps
        1.   Norms for customer calls
        2.   Norms for prospect calls
        3.   Using sales time efficiently
            a)   Time and duty analysis/improving productivity
            b)   Inside sales force
                (1)   Due to rising cost of outside sales force
                (2)   Rising automation (for inside and outside sales forces)
    D.   Motivating sales reps—the higher the salesperson's motivation, the greater his or her effort

1. Sales quotas
2. Supplementary motivators (meetings, contests, etc.)
E. Evaluating sales representatives
   1. Sources of information—sales reports including activity plans and write-ups of activity reports
   2. Formal evaluation (current-to-past sales comparisons, customer-satisfaction evaluation, qualitative evaluation)

IV. Principles of personal selling
A. Professionalism—major steps involved in any sales presentation
B. Prospecting and qualifying—identify and screen out leads
   1. Preapproach—learning about the prospect
   2. Approach—greeting the prospect
   3. Presentation and demonstration—tell the product "story"
   4. Overcoming objections—psychological and logical resistance
   5. Closing—asking for the sale
   6. Follow-up and maintenance—ensure satisfaction
C. Negotiation
   1. Negotiation defined—in negotiated exchange, price and other terms are set via bargaining behavior, in which two or more parties negotiate long-term binding agreements
   2. When to negotiate—appropriate whenever a zone of agreement exists
   3. Formulating a negotiation strategy—note classic bargaining tactics
D. Relationship marketing—based on the premise that important accounts need focused and continuous attention. Main steps in establishing a relationship marketing program include:
   1. Identify the key customers meriting relationship marketing
   2. Assign a skilled relationship manager to each key customer
   3. Develop a clear job description for relationship managers
   4. Appoint an overall manager to supervise the relationship managers
   5. Have relationship managers develop long-range goals and annual customer-relationship plans

Lecture—the Death and Rebirth of the Salesperson

This lecture focuses on the process of and changes in this important area of marketing. We also consider the role and value of effective sales force policy and strategy in the overall marketing process for the organization. It is useful to update the examples so that students will be able to identify readily with this concept based on their general knowledge of the companies and products involved in the lecture/discussion.

The discussion begins by considering past sales force strategy variables. This leads into a discussion of the implications for the introduction of new strategies for the future, given the substantial technological and other changes sales professionals and firms will encounter in the medium and long run environment.

Teaching Objectives

- To stimulate students to think about the critical sales force and policy issues
- Recognize some of the directional variables in sales force policy

Discussion

Introduction — Is the Customer Your Partner?

Today's customers want solutions, and companies are remaking their sales forces to satisfy them. Nevertheless, total quality goals and sales quotas still clash. This is the primary theme related to the new enlightened sales force of the future. In the past, sales people would brag that their primary purpose in life was to push metal (IBM) or slam boxes (Xerox). Today, the sales force gauges success as much by customer satisfaction as the units sold. The former is generally a much more rigorous yardstick than the latter. As companies today are finding that if you anticipate what your customers need and then deliver it beyond their expectations, order flow takes care of itself.

As more managers awake to the challenge, old stereotypes are fading faster than Willy Loman's smile and shoeshine. Forget the mythical lone-wolf salesman; today's trend-setting salespeople tend to work in teams. The traditional sample case is more likely to hold spreadsheets than widgets. Today's best salespeople see themselves as problem solvers, not vendors. They gauge success not just by sales volume but also by customer satisfaction. They do not "sell"; they "partner" with the customer.

Companies that dismiss the new, more collaborative sales methods as a fad are likely to slip behind. Today's demanding buyers are running out of patience with mere product pushers, whether at the new-car showroom, on the floor of a department store, or in the corporate conference room. They will tell you that do not want to deal with anyone selling anything unless they can tell the firm exactly how it will help their business.

Developing a New Attitude in Selling

If ever there was a business that cried out for a new way of selling, it is that of moving cars from the showroom floor to the driveways of America. The familiar but widely despised old approach is known among automotive historians as the Hull-Dobbs method, named after Memphis dealers Horace Hull and James Dobbs, who reputedly created it following World War II. In the old Hull-Dobbs drill, customers exist to be manipulated, first by the salesman, who negotiates the ostensibly final price, then by the sales manager and finance manager, who each in succession try to bump you to a higher price.

Car buyers are fed up. A recent survey by J. D. Power & Associates found that only 35 percent felt well treated by their dealers, down from 40 percent a decade ago. In 1983, 26 percent of buyers rated the integrity of their dealers excellent or very good; by 2001, that figure had dropped to fewer than 20 percent. "People feel beaten up by the process," says the owner of 13 import and domestic franchises in the suburbs of Washington, D.C. "You think you got a good deal until you walk out the door. The salesmen are inside doing high fives, and the customer is lying out on the street."

This is where Saturn came into the car game a few years back and presented its original, no-dicker sticker system. The price you pay for a Saturn is the one on the sticker (between $9,995 and $18,675, depending on model and features). That is, however, only part of the package. Buy a Saturn and you buy the company's commitment to your satisfaction. Their contact with and to the customer may appear corny, but last year Saturn scored third in a J. D. Power customer satisfaction study, just behind Lexus and Infiniti, which cost up to five times as much. Maybe it is corny, but it works. The philosophy of the new breed car dealer, like those at Saturn, is to exceed customer expectations.

Saturn reformed their sales methods to exploit an obvious market opportunity; the same is true for the reformed IBM sales force, which is only half the size it was in 1990. Those who survived are part of a new operation that is a cross between a consulting business and a conventional sales operation. Big Blue now encourages buyers to shop for salesmen before they shop for products.

Consultants obviously need a more sophisticated set of skills than metal pushers, and in their new role as purveyors of solutions rather than products, IBM's sales teams do not always recommend Big Blue's merchandise. About a third of the equipment IBM installs are made by DEC and other competitors.

One aspect of managing a sales team has not changed much: how you motivate flesh-and-blood salespeople. It remains the same idiosyncratic bleed of financial incentive, inspiration, and cajolery. As the sales pros will say: "There is nothing magical about sales. You want to be truthful and present a credible story so people will want to do business with you now and in the future. To sell effectively, you need to present the facts, list your supporting arguments, and learn all the nonverbal cues your customer gives while you're making your presentation."

With one element of sales motivation, how they pay their salespeople, many companies believe they can improve on tradition. IBM, for example, is following a growing trend to base compensation partly on customer satisfaction. For some of the new wave salespeople, 45 percent of the variable component of a paycheck depends on how customers rate the salesperson. In addition, usually this depends on how well the salesperson has done in helping the customer meet their business objectives. Result: the salesperson can make a lot more or a lot less.

We're All Salespeople—Officially or Unofficially

What does it take to be a truly outstanding salesperson? As is always the case, there are no simple answers. Moreover, achieving excellence in one type of sales endeavor, say selling personal insurance, undoubtedly requires somewhat different aptitudes and skills than achieving excellence when selling sophisticated information systems to corporate buyers.

High-performing salespeople generally differ from other salespeople in terms of some general attitudes they have about the job and the manner in which they conduct their business. High-performing salespeople:

- Represent the interests of their companies and their clients simultaneously to achieve two-way advocacy

- Exemplify professionalism in the way they perform the sales job

- Are committed to selling and the sales process because they believe the sales process is in the customer's best interest

- Actively plan and develop strategies that will lead to programs benefiting the customer

Marketing and Advertising

1. Saab uses ads such as the one in Figure 1, which appeared in a national business magazine, to bring prospects into its dealers' showrooms. Note that Sweden-based Saab, owned by General Motors, is promoting GM's OnStar navigation system as a standard feature in this convertible.

   a. What kind of training do you think Saab's dealers' sales reps need to successfully sell to consumers?

   b. How can Saab dealers qualify prospects for this convertible?

   c. Why are good follow-up and maintenance skills important for dealers' sales reps?

Answer

a. Saab's dealers' reps need training in the features and benefits of each vehicle, as well as training in customers' and competitors' characteristics, effective sales presentation methods, and appropriate field procedures.

b. Saab dealers might qualify prospects by asking about their preferences (to see whether they match with this Saab model or another), their schedule for buying, and their price requirements.

c. Good follow-up and maintenance skills are important because these keep customers returning for service at the dealership and encourage customers to buy the next vehicle from the same dealer.

2. The Anthro direct-response ad shown in Figure 2 is geared toward businesses that need office furniture for their employees. The headline refers to follow-up calls placed by Anthro reps to check on customer satisfaction, and the fine print invites business buyers to call to discuss needs or request a product catalog.

   a. Which of the six types of sales representatives are prospects likely to speak with when they call Anthro's toll-free phone number?

   b. Which of the specific sales tasks is this sales rep likely to perform?

   c. Why would Anthro's advertising put so much emphasis on its follow-up call policy?

Answer

a. Because Anthro does business primarily by phone and on the Internet, prospects who call will probably speak with a solution vendor who can help them solve their problems by designing a furniture system to meet their needs.

b. This sales rep is likely to communicate information about Anthro's offerings, sell the offerings, provide service, and possibly gather information. Students may say that these reps will also perform allocation tasks if products are in short supply.

c. Follow-up and maintenance ensure customer satisfaction, so Anthro wants prospects to know that the sale does not end when products are ordered and delivered.

3. ****BONUS AD--See Companion Web site!** Dassault Falcon uses print ads like this reach business decision-makers who may be considering the purchase of a larger or faster corporate jet. Note the mention of technical features as well as general benefits.

   a. What situation and problem questions might a Dassault Falcon salesperson raise with prospects who contact the company after seeing this ad?

   b. How does Dassault Falcon benefit by employing a direct sales force to sell its jets?

   c. On the basis of this ad, how does Dassault Falcon appear to be structuring its sales force? Why is this structure appropriate for the company?

Answer

a. Students can be creative in answering this question. One possible situation question: "What kind of jet do you use now and how do you use it?" One possible problem question: "What kinds of problems have you experienced with your current corporate jet?"

b.　Dassault Falcon benefits by being able to hire, train, and motivate salespeople to sell its aircraft the way the company wants them sold. These salespeople sell only Dassault Falcon jets, so they get to know the products very well and can consult with customers on solutions to problems involving corporate aircraft. The salespeople also project the image that the company wants to create.

c.　Dassault Falcon appears to be structuring its sales force by geographic territory, because the ad indicates one individual in the United States and one in France.

4.　**BONUS AD--See Companion Web site!** As this ad indicates, Ericsson customizes information network systems that can be expanded to keep up with a company's growing and changing technology needs.

a.　How does naming satisfied clients in this ad support Ericsson's personal selling process?

b.　Given the opportunity for personal sales discussions about network needs and capabilities, why would this ad include only a Web address, not a telephone number or other contact information?

c.　Do you think Ericsson uses major account management? Why or why not?

Answer

a.　Including the name of satisfied clients enhances Ericsson's credibility and paves the way for its salespeople to make claims about the company's offerings.

b.　Ericsson seems to be using this ad for image-building and to pave the way for personal sales contact, rather than to generate leads for its sales force.

c.　Ericsson very likely uses major account management because it has many large corporate accounts that require the attention of cross-functional teams. Using major account management also allows Ericsson to assign people to certain very important accounts, as needed.

Online Marketing Today—Siebel Systems

As noted earlier in this chapter, Siebel Systems uses its own sales-management software to monitor its sales reps' activities, manage the sales process, and assess customer satisfaction. In the past, Siebel worked with 20 resellers who sold the company's software as well as with 760 other "Siebel Partners" who provide support in the form of installation, customization, upgrading, and other services. Now, however, the company has eliminated indirect sales in favor of its direct sales force. "When we analyzed customer feedback from the reseller channel, the results were not living up to the standards that we expected," explains Siebel's vice president and general manager for alliances. "The customers were effectively telling us that they would rather have Siebel involved in the sale." Partners still have an opportunity to build sales and profits because customers spend at least $7 in implementation, training, hardware, and other items for every $1 spent on Siebel software.

Go to Siebel's Web site (www.siebel.com) and review the products, events, and customized views available on the home page. Then follow the link to information for sales professional (or, if this is unavailable, locate the information about Siebel's sales management software). What benefits does Siebel highlight for its sales management offerings? Why are these benefits important for business customers? How do both Siebel and its prospects gain from the company's online product demonstrations? From attendance at the company's product seminars?

Answer

Some of the benefits highlighted on the Siebel site include the ability to: monitor sales activities to grow sales and profits predictably; improve sales forecasting; align sales compensation with sales goals; improve sales productivity; and better manage sales territories. These benefits are valuable for business customers because they help the companies better manage their resources, control sales activities, and analyze and reward sales efforts. Siebel's online product demonstrations reduce the amount of time a Siebel salesperson must offer demonstrations to prospects; at the same time, they allow prospects to experience and evaluate Siebel products without obligation and on their schedule. Prospects gain from attending Siebel product seminars because they learn how to get the most of Siebel products and they can ask questions and share experiences with others. Siebel gains from the opportunity to reach many prospects at once and generate qualified leads based on interest expressed through attendance and inquiries.

You're the Marketer—Sonic PDA Marketing Plan

Many marketers have to consider sales force management in their marketing plans. Because of the high cost of maintaining a direct sales force, however, some companies are substituting online, mail, and telephone sales for some of their personal sales calls.

In your marketing role at Sonic, you are planning sales strategy for the company's new personal digital assistant (PDA). After reviewing the data you previously gathered and the decisions you made about other marketing-mix activities, answer these questions about Sonic's use of personal selling:

- Does Sonic need a direct sales force or can it sell through agents and other outside representatives?

- Toward whom should Sonic's sales activities be geared? How can the company's sales activities support the rest of the marketing plan and the goals that have been set?

- What kind of sales objectives should Sonic set for its sales personnel?

- What kind of training will sales representatives need to sell the new Sonic PDA?

Once you have answered these questions and looked at how your sales management ideas will work with Sonic's goals and objectives, either summarize your programs in a written marketing plan or type them into the Marketing Mix, Marketing Organization, and Sales Forecast sections of the *Marketing Plan Pro* software.

Answer:

Students who say Sonic needs a direct sales force may argue that this helps the company hire, train, and motivate the right kind of reps to sell only the Sonic PDA to major business accounts and to intermediaries. Those who argue against a direct sales force may say that as a start-up, Sonic should not invest in a direct sales force but should rely on agents and other outside representatives until the first product has been established.

Sonic's sales activities should be geared toward (1) channel members and, to a lesser extent, (2) major business accounts. These sales activities will help Sonic get the channel representation it needs for its first PDA and encourage businesses to buy in bulk for corporate use. In turn, such sales will help Sonic reach its sales goals. Sales personnel should go after sales objectives related to volume levels needed to achieve market penetration by territory or according to another appropriate measure. To do this, the reps need training about Sonic as a company and its goals; the first PDA product and the features and benefits; customers and competitors' characteristics; sales presentation methods; and sales procedures and responsibilities.

Marketing Spotlight: Oracle

Larry Ellison, along with three partners, founded the database management software company System Development Laboratories in 1977. In 1982, the company changed its name to Oracle, after the name of its first product. By 1988, Oracle had a 36 percent share of the U.S. government's PC database market. The company began offering consulting services to its customers in 1989.

Oracle's adjustment to this rapid growth was not seamless, however. The company developed a reputation as a leader in "vaporware," or products that are announced publicly but are still under development and therefore unavailable. Its software often contained numerous bugs or lacked promised features. The company found itself embroiled in an accounting scandal in 1990, a result of a widespread practice among the sales representatives of recording sales a quarter early in order to boost earnings during slow quarters. Oracle was forced to restate earnings, pay a fine to the SEC, and spend millions of dollars settling shareholder lawsuits. The company's stock plummeted as a result of these developments.

Beginning in 1991, Ellison enacted a plan that rescued Oracle from the brink. He secured $80 million in financing from Nippon Steel, installed experienced Booz Allen manager Ray Lane as COO and president, reduced headcount by 10 percent, and imposed stricter policies governing its sales force. Ellison took a hands-on approach to establishing sales protocol for his company. He rewrote sales contracts himself and initiated a standard pricing policy that eliminated haggling. He also altered the compensation scheme so that managers were rewarded for meeting profit-margin targets rather than for reaching sales volume quotas regardless of cost.

These moves, along with the launch of the next-generation Oracle 7 database in 1993, allowed the company to complete a turnaround. By 1994, the company was the number-one database management software maker in the world, with sales exceeding $2 billion that year. Oracle's revenues tripled between 1995 and 1999, yet the company's sales force doubled during the same period. In 1998, the company split its sales force into two teams. One team concentrated on the company's core products—database software—although the other team was charged with selling Oracle's data-processing applications. More than anything else, however, Oracle's sales reps were able to handle the heavy workload because the company embraced the Internet. In 1999, 25 percent of the company's software sales were accomplished online.

As business continued to flood the company, Oracle sought to take more of its business to the Web. It invested in a new e-commerce site called OracleSalesOnline.com—later renamed Sales.Oracle.com—that enables customers to place orders directly online. The site also lets customers purchase upgrades and add users to its license. Oracle also developed another site that sales reps use to demonstrate software during phone calls with customers, who are then directed to order online. Additionally, it required sales reps to enter detailed customer data into a central system that other salespeople or executives can access. In 2001, the company integrated online customer service and support features with the Sales.Oracle.com service, calling this new site Support.Oracle.com. The company also licensed its sales and support applications to more than 10,000 companies around the world.

Oracle's network of information and its powerful software helped trim costs considerably. The company claimed in an aggressive ad campaign that it saved $1 billion in 2000 by running its own e-business software. In a specific instance, a manager noticed one day that U.S. sales forecasts dropped $3.5 million. Using the network, the manager identified which company had changed its purchase and contacted the sales rep working with the account who renegotiated the deal in less than 24 hours. In another example of cost-cutting, the company moved its sales and training meetings with customers from hotels and conference centers to the Web. These Web-conferences reduced costs from $325 per person to $2 a head.

Competitors are quick to criticize Oracle's aggressive sales tactics. An executive from IBM criticized Oracle's strategy of overpromising: "They take the P.T. Barnum approach to business: There's a sucker born every minute." Oracle's 85 percent customer-retention rate, which is higher than either Microsoft's or IBM's, proves that many customers are satisfied with the company's products and service.

Sources: Steve Hamm. "Oracle: Why It's Cool Again." *Business Week*, May 8, 2000; Michael Moeller. "Oracle: Practicing What It Preaches." *Business Week*, August 16, 1999; Steve Hamm. "Is Oracle Finally Seeing Clearly?" *Business Week*, August 3, 1998; Mitch Wagner, "Oracle's Savings Don't Add Up." *InternetWeek*, March 12, 2001

Questions

1. Aggressive sales and marketing, along with sales force automation based on the Internet, have helped Oracle become the largest application server company in the world. Oracle, however, faces some complex marketing issues for the future. Develop some of these issues, based on information from the text and case materials.

2. Oracle's turnaround was rapid and dramatic, but was their marketing success the cause or the effect of other important changes? Discuss.

3. If Oracle continues to apply aggressive sales tactics, despite the high rate of customer retention, what can we assume about its customers and the future of the business sector?

4. What changes would you make to Oracle's marketing strategy to avoid the problems they appear to face?

Suggested Responses

1. Oracle had to be extremely competitive in this environment, and clearly heavy early use of the Internet was a big variable in helping the firm succeed in the face of enormous pressure and competition. One of the biggest variables in their favor was the fact that they provided the entire enterprise package to customers, something that no other firm did during the 1990s and early twenty-first century. In addition, Oracle had a substantial headstart on the later competition that also was effectively forced to utilize Oracle to complete the application process. The number of competitors upset with Oracle's often overly aggressive sales efforts and over-promising have begun to organize to grab some of the substantial hold that Oracle holds over several of the market sectors in the enterprise server business.

2. Oracle overcame many obstacles, but it appears that most were sales and marketing oriented, the result of an aggressive marketing and sales organization that also was organized to take advantage of the overall lack of competition against Oracle. Unfortunately, aggressive sales can also lead to sales force attitudes that eventually breed contempt for the leader.

3. We can assume that because most of its customers are organizational and business buyers, Oracle's products and services provided the desired results. Some of the criticism of Oracle is that it charged aggressively to lock in customers so that they could not easily break off part of their enterprise business and move to a lower priced competitor for that part of the business. The result is that Oracle effectively made monopoly profits during its growth years. Such market control and high margins, however, inevitably bring competition, lower prices, lower margins, relatively less aggressive sales tactics, and faster industry maturity. Thus, although there is early pain in such situations, in the end society gains, at the expense of the early winner.

The best strategy for Oracle might be to move toward more openness in dealing with the situation so that competition will enter less swiftly. It may be also that the only strategic direction Oracle can take now is a continuing pursuit of control over user systems. Because Oracle relied heavily on the Internet and their own server software, it is likely that they will continue to enhance their online access capabilities, migrating increasing levels of activity from onsite uses to centralized Oracle-run sites that run many businesses from one or a small number of platforms, using the Internet to service the business(es) online.

Chapter 22—Managing the Total Marketing Effort

Overview

This chapter examines how the marketing function is organized and how it relates to other company functions and how marketing plans must be implemented in order to succeed in the marketplace.

The modern marketing department evolved through several stages. It started as a sales department, and later took on ancillary functions, such as advertising and marketing research. As the ancillary functions grew in importance, many companies created a separate marketing department to manage them. Sales and marketing people generally worked well together. Eventually, the two departments were merged into a modern marketing department headed by a marketing vice-president. A modern marketing department, however, does not automatically create an effective marketing company unless the other departments accept and practice customer orientation. When a company refocuses its organizational structure on key process, rather than departments, it becomes a process-outcome-based company.

Modern marketing departments are organized in a number of ways. A functional marketing organization is where separate managers head marketing functions, reporting to the marketing vice-president. A geographical marketing organization allocates its sales organization resources along geographic lines, nationally, regionally, or locally. A product management organization assigns products to product managers who work with functional specialists to develop and achieve product plans. A market management organization assigns major markets to market managers who in turn work with functional specialists to develop and implement their plans. Some large companies use a product and market management organization called a matrix organization. Finally, multi-division companies usually operate with a corporate marketing department and divisional marketing departments.

Marketing must work harmoniously with other functional areas. In its pursuit of the customer's interests, marketing may come into conflict with R&D, engineering, purchasing, manufacturing, operations, finance, accounting, credit, and other functions. These conflicts can be reduced when the company president commits the firm to a customer orientation and when the marketing vice-president learns to work effectively with the other executives. Acquiring a modern marketing orientation requires top executive support, a marketing task force, outside marketing consulting help, in-house marketing training, acquisition of strong marketing talent, a customer-oriented system, and other related steps.

Those responsible for the marketing function must not only develop effective marketing plans but also implement them successfully. Marketing implementation is the process of turning plans into action exercises describing who does what, when, and how. Effective implementation requires skills in allocating, monitoring, organizing, and interacting at all levels of the marketing effort. Evaluations and control include annual-plan control, profitability control, efficiency control, and strategy control. The capstone effort in this process is the marketing audit.

Learning Objectives

After reading the chapter the student should understand:

- The need for organization
- Organization of the marketing and sales functions

- How marketing relates to other key business functions
- How to develop a stronger market-focused organization and orientation
- The skills needed for effective implementation
- How a company may improve its marketing implementation skills

Chapter Outline

I. Trends in company organization

    A. Companies must reorganize in response to globalization, deregulation, advances in computer technology and telecommunications, market fragmentation, and other developments

    B. Responses: reengineering, outsourcing, benchmarking, supplier partnering, customer partnering, merging, globalizing, flattening, focusing, empowering

II. Marketing organization

    A. Evolution of the marketing department

        1. Simple sales department—sales vice president, selling orientation, occasional outside support

        2. Sales department with ancillary marketing functions

        3. Separate marketing department—still with a focus on sales

        4. Modern marketing department/effective marketing company—beginning of customer orientation

            a) Sales and marketing relatively equal

            b) Planning from marketing

            c) Implementation by sales

            d) Key is that *all* employees must realize that their jobs are to create, serve, and satisfy customers.

        5. Process- and outcome-based company—focus of structure on key processes (new-product development, customer acquisition, etc.) versus departments

    B. Organizing the marketing department

        1. Functional organization

        2. Geographic organization

        3. Product- or brand-management organization

            a) Advantages and disadvantages

            b) Alternative to product managers is product teams

        4. Market-management/customer management organization

            a) For firms that sell their products to many different markets

            b) Or those that deal with individual customers versus the mass-market or even market segments

        5. Product-management/market-management organization

            a) Known also as a matrix organization

            b) Focus on meeting their market's needs versus selling a particular product

6. Corporate/divisional organization—from no corporate marketing staff to a strong corporate marketing staff

C. Relations with other departments
   1. R & D
   2. Engineering and purchasing
   3. Manufacturing and operations
   4. Finance
   5. Accounting and credit

D. Building a company wide marketing orientation—main steps:
   1. Convince the senior management of the need to become customer focused
   2. Appoint a senior marketing officer and a marketing task force
   3. Get outside help and guidance
   4. Change the reward structures in the company
   5. Hire strong marketing talent
   6. Develop strong in-house marketing training programs
   7. Install a modern marketing planning system
   8. Establish an annual marketing excellence recognition program
   9. Shift from a department focus to a process/outcome focus
   10. Empower the employees

E. Injecting more creativity into the organization
   1. Key question—whether marketers give too much allegiance to the marketing concept
   2. Point—marketers should not emphasize satisfying customers at the expense of imaginative strategies

III. Marketing implementation

A. Process that turns marketing plans into action assignments and ensures that such assignments are executed in a manner that accomplishes the plan's stated objectives

B. Strategy: what and why of marketing activities; implement the who, where, when, and how

C. Skills related to effective implementation
   a) Diagnostic skills
   b) Identification of company level
   c) Implementation skills
   d) Evaluation skills

IV. Evaluation and control—types of control

A. Annual-plan control
   1. Sales analysis
   2. Market share analysis
   3. Marketing expense-to-sales analysis
   4. Financial analysis

5.   Market-based scorecard analysis

    B.   Profitability control

         1.   Marketing-profitability analysis (identifying the functional expenses, assigning the functional expenses to the marketing entities, and preparing a profit-and-loss statement for each marketing entity)

         2.   Determining corrective action

         3.   Direct versus full costing (direct costs, traceable common costs, and nontraceable common costs)

    C.   Efficiency control

         1.   Sales force efficiency

         2.   Advertising efficiency

         3.   Sales-promotion efficiency

         4.   Distribution efficiency

    D.   Strategic control

         1.   Marketing-effectiveness review

         2.   Marketing audit

         3.   Marketing excellence review

         4.   Ethical and social responsibility review

Lecture—Reorganizing Marketing Management—Media Neutrality

Introduction

There is a new direction emerging in marketing management and planning. It begins with clients and agencies using new ways to connect with consumers. Accordingly, marketing plans for some new products call for adoption of nonconventional patterns of advertising support. For, example, Volvo launched its new S60 via the Web last year, while Kellogg created demand for its Real Fruit Winders using a mix of public relations and online activity.

Advertisers also have begun signing deals direct with media owners who provide access to a wide range of media options. Perhaps the most high-profile of these moves was Unilever's decision to sign a multiyear, multimillion dollar deal to advertise brands, such as Ragu and Dove, in AOL Time Warner's new media and print outlets.

Such examples may currently be the exception rather than the rule, but they also provide signs that "media- neutral" planning is starting to mean more than "let's use posters as well as TV."

Spoiled for Choice

The rise of different media channels has created a new range of options for clients. Not only is there more Internet, combined with other media, but there is also a growth in sponsorship opportunities and the arrival of a new type of media owner. The non-TV media have begun to claim success in persuading clients that media spending should not go just to television ad spots. In addition, respected research companies now can provide case studies that prove that hitting the consumer across a range of different media can boost impact well beyond that provided solely in the traditional broadcast and print media.

Despite this, the actual pattern of total media spending has not yet changed significantly. In recent years, TV's percentage of total ad expenditure has been squeezed slightly, radio has gained a larger share and direct marketing has moved itself up a few percentage points. In broad terms, however, spending patterns have not changed radically.

Some media analysts believe that marketers are aware that they probably should be doing things differently. Some of them are nearer than others, but none are taking bold steps yet. There are a number of problems with the adoption of a potentially beneficial media-neutral approach.

First, there is considerable cultural resistance against changing a formula that has worked in the past and from which revenue patterns have been established.

Another factor is the need for brand clients to ensure that they are giving out the right message in all their marketing efforts. On the one hand, they claim they want integrated planning, but on the other hand most have not updated their audit measures to account for changes in the way consumers receive and process messages.

Last, the pressure for financial accountability works against a new approach because it encourages agencies to stick with the media they know best and those that best suit their budgets and plans.

Media Neutral or Not?

The gradual movement from commission to fee-based systems encourages marketing planners and advertising agencies to be bolder and broader in their media schedules. The view is that as the process becomes more fee-based, marketing and media decisions also will be more impartial.

There will be organizational and structural issues, however, because the client advertising managers dominate the current system. If the budget moves to a more integrated marketing approach, these folks may be left behind, and they will not be happy. Also, there will be an increasing need to train media planners who can cross the artificial line that divides traditional from integrated media, with the integrated media perceived as less glamorous.

Direct marketing is in long-term growth, but integration with traditional advertising campaigns is sadly a rarity. Public relations campaigns frequently operate in total isolation from paid-for media communications. It seems that although media-neutral planning may be a no-brainer in principle, actually putting it into practice is proving much more challenging. One solution may be to simplify the agency relationship, so that client and agencies can work closer together.

A number of forward looking marketing-oriented companies, such as Canon, have moved their business onto a more global basis and revamped their planning and ad agency structures. Canon appointed one agency to handle its media, another to do consumer creative, another to do business-to-business creative, another to do direct mail and another to handle PR.

In the Canon structure, the agencies sit down with company executives on Canon's brand continuity group to ensure that everyone takes part in the early discussions. In this manner, they determine that if the consumer business is doing X, it is shared with the B2B people, and the creative agencies work with the media agency before the brief is even formulated.

The bottom line is that Canon gets more bang for the buck by integrating the marketing and media program, not just in terms of visual identity, but also in terms of tone.

New Coordination?

Integration may improve coordination of campaigns, but the key question is whether it encourages a change in marketing planning and in media spending? It appears that over time an entirely new budget model will evolve. There is no question that the efforts to get the right mix will take time, and firms continually will evaluate the spending balance, trying to determine the right balance between the traditional and newer approaches and media.

The Hands-On Client

Another development is the emerging concept of the "brand custodian". Although most marketing analysts agree that the client has to be the custodian of the brand, there also is agreement that there are too many firms that have abrogated the responsibility to their agencies. They can use partners to help with the problem, but the owner of the brand has to maintain the ultimate identity of what the brand should be and the sorts of media channels to utilize in the brand development and maintenance effort.

It is important to have expertise in-house because it is dangerous to rely on an external resource for all marketing strategic development. The circumstances of the early twenty-first century make it clear that there must be more two-way knowledge to maintain direction once there is agreement on the objectives and strategy.

Agencies and partners need and appreciate quality of thought within the client company so that they can bounce ideas off those who best understand the brand. The agencies need such expertise in order to be able to judge their performance and that of their media choices. Lastly, the media planning organization should be able to provide content rather than just advertise. The point is that if all they do is advertise at people then they are not engaging with them.

It is becoming more and more clear that great marketing firms tend to allow communication strategy to lead the actual creative strategy because they must put emphasis on who they are communicating to and by what sort of channel. Further, the goal for marketers and creative agencies should be to become better at understanding their consumers and as a result become more confident about reaching them directly. Instead of looking at rate cards every day, they should instead think about the right media channel for a communication effort to the right target market. They should ask: "What's the audience here and can we reach them better?"

Low Budget Neutrality

Another trend is the movement for smaller and medium-size firms also to engage in such planning and control versus only the large and deep-pocket firms. To assist in this process, there are marketing firms that can "parachute" into a company to provide marketing expertise on a short-term basis, effectively representing the client and to be neutral on the marketing integration issue. There have been creative independents and media independents in the past, but now we have account management independents.

There will be more of that sort of agency down the road to overcome the lack of strategic focus in media planning, to make sure that it is aligned with brand objectives. Three major issues need to be resolved, however, before true consumer-centric media-neutral planning is possible are the following:

1. First, there is a question of money. Accountability criteria should move away from efficiency toward effectiveness. This is something that payment by results or sales would encourage.

2. Second, there is a need for agencies to understand how all the media channels fit together, including direct marketing and PR.

3. Third, we need an environment that encourages change, creates new ways of doing business and provides incentives to move in a media-neutral manner.

Although ad agencies can currently offer media-neutral thinking in "pockets," they lack consistency. Most big agencies, in pockets, are good at it, but the challenge is to be consistent across the board.

In addition, the media are ideally positioned to take advantage of client needs, but they still do not have the right skill sets. It is an open goal for the media agencies but they have to up their skills.

They have to find a way of managing the dichotomy between the economics of the business and serving the client.

PR and the Web drive well-organized marketing efforts to maximum capacity within two to three months, and in some recent examples the brands have not utilized TV until six months after launch. In any case, marketers should be aware that future budgets for new launches or for brand extensions might not allow the use of traditional strategies.

Given the level of competition, shorter product life cycles, consumer awareness, and changing channels of distribution, budgets just may not be there anymore, and marketing firms will have to come up with different solutions. This will lead, sooner than later, to media neutrality in the implementation of marketing plans and strategies.

Source: *Media Week*, March 1, 2002.

Marketing and Advertising

1. When Bumble Bee introduced the new vacuum-sealed pouch highlighted in the ad in Figure 1, it had to coordinate the work of the marketing department with the work of many other departments within the company.

   a. How would the marketing department have needed to interact with purchasing in the course of developing and launching this new product package?

   b. In creating this new product, what kinds of interactions would the product manager have had with his or her counterparts in the manufacturing department?

   c. Outline how Bumble Bee's marketing managers would have interacted with employees in finance, accounting, and credit as they planned and implemented the marketing of this product.

Answer

   a. The marketing department at Bumble Bee would have needed to check with purchasing before placing orders for new packaging materials. Marketers would also have had to discuss costs and anticipated volumes so purchasing could plan for these needs.

   b. The product manager would have needed to discuss various timing and production issues with people in the manufacturing department. In particular, manufacturing would have to plan for the right amount of supplies at the right time, ensure that the proper equipment and materials were in place to handle the new packaging, train manufacturing employees to make the new packaging, and plan for any new handling procedures related to bringing in the raw materials and shipping out finished products.

   c. The marketing people would have needed to talk with the credit department to arrange for credit with the companies from whom materials and equipment would be purchased and to alert the credit people that distributors would be placing orders for this new product. Marketing would also have to talk with finance about the financial resources available to support planning, testing, and implementation of the new product plans and to discuss potential returns on this financial investment. Finally, marketers would have to work with accounting to plan for new bills and payment discounts related to payments for planning, creating, and executing the new packaging, and the advertising to support the new product.

2. The ad in Figure 2 uses a first-person story to show how Iomega's Zip technology can help a company move more quickly—and make the employee look good, as well.

   a. What measurements could Iomega use to determine the efficiency of its print advertising campaign?

   b. What implementation issues would Iomega's marketers need to consider when planning this advertisement?

   c. What questions should Iomega marketers ask in determining whether corrective action is needed if this advertising campaign does not meet expectations?

Answer

   a. Iomega might look at sales trends in relation to the cost and frequency of the print advertising campaign. It also might examine the advertising cost per thousand target buyers reached by this ad, the percentage of the audience who were exposed to the ad, attitude measures based on the ad, and consumer reactions to the ad.

   b. Students may suggest several issues. Two examples: (1) externally, are distributors ready for this campaign and stocked with sufficient inventory to handle the expected sales volume; and (2) internally, are all departments within Iomega alerted to the timing and content of the ad so they can support implementation.

   c. Students will have different ideas, but here are some sample lines of inquiry: did the ad appear in the right publications, and did the proper target audience see it? Did the ad appear on time and in the right position within the magazines? Was the timing appropriate for the selling cycle?

3. ****BONUS AD--See Companion Web site!** ConAgra used this mouth-watering ad to inform consumers about the health benefits of its Egg Beaters products.

   a. Using the ConAgra figure, identify the interactions that the product manager of Egg Beaters would need to plan and implement this ad.

   b. What elements in the customer-performance scorecard would be most useful for identifying market response to the Egg Beaters product? Why?

   c. What other stakeholders should ConAgra consider when planning ads for Egg Beaters? Explain.

Answer

   a. Students will identify numerous interactions that the Egg Beaters product manager would need to plan and implement for this ad, including interaction with the ad agency, the media, promotion services, purchasing, market research, and legal people (among others).

   b. Elements in the customer-performance scorecard that would help identify market response to this ad include: (1) percentage of customers falling into very dissatisfied, dissatisfied, neutral, satisfied, and very satisfied categories; (2) percentage of customers who say they would repurchase the product; (3) percentage of customers who say they would recommend the product to others; (4) percentage of target market customers who have brand awareness or recall; (5) percentage of customers who say that the company's product is the most preferred in its category; (6) percentage of customers who correctly identify the brand's intended positioning and differentiation; and (7) the average perception of company's product quality relative to chief competitor.

c.   ConAgra should also consider competitors when planning its ads (to be sure it has differentiated its products from those of competitors); legal and regulatory experts (to comply with all guidelines); the media (to ensure consistency with other public relations initiatives); and employees (so they are aware of what the company is doing and can serve as ambassadors to the market). Students may identify other stakeholders to be considered, as well.

Online Marketing Today—BrightHouse

BrightHouse, as noted earlier, specializes in helping companies generate innovative marketing ideas. By hiring outside experts to jump-start the innovation process, management can gain valuable insights and identify new ways of exploiting market opportunities. For example, BrightHouse helped Coty create "ghost myst" perfume—a product that became the best-selling perfume in the market during its first year. BrightHouse uses a four-step process to come up with innovative ideas, starting with investigation (to learn more about the situation) and incubation (to allow time for different thoughts to surface), then continuing with illumination and illustration (the steps in which the ideas are elaborated and brought to life with detail).

Learn more about BrightHouse by visiting its Web site (www.brighthouse.com). Review the home page and then follow the "bright profile" link to read about how this company approaches its assignments. Also, look at the glossary at the bottom of the page. How do BrightHouse's techniques help a company innovate on a more systematic basis? What are the pros and cons of hiring an outside firm to help with innovation?

Answer

BrightHouse helps companies innovate by providing a structured process for identifying innovations, using specialists from various fields to help expand and clarify ideas, and effectively communicating the idea so employees can shape it into a marketable offering. Pros of hiring an outside firm: new ideas and new methods for innovation; professional help in developing a structured process that the company can use in-house; and expertise of outsiders who can bring their knowledge and experience with a range of problems and products. Cons of hiring an outside firm: employees may feel less ownership of the resulting ideas; employees may not learn or adopt the process after the outsiders leave; and outsiders may not understand the company or the market sufficiently thoroughly to develop appropriate innovations.

You're the Marketer—Sonic PDA Marketing Plan

No marketing plan is complete without provisions for organizing, implementing, evaluating, and controlling the total marketing effort. In addition to measuring progress toward financial targets and other objectives, marketers need to plan how to audit and improve their marketing activities.

Sonic has asked you to plan the management of the marketing effort for the launch of the company's new personal digital assistant (PDA) product. Look back over the parts of the marketing plan that you have already developed, especially the goals, strategies, and programs. Now answer these questions about managing Sonic's marketing activities:

- What is the most appropriate organization for Sonic's marketing and sales departments?

- What can Sonic do to create a more market- and customer-focused organization?

- What control measures should Sonic incorporate into its marketing plan?

- What can Sonic do to evaluate its marketing?

- How can Sonic evaluate its level of ethical and socially responsible marketing?

After you have answered these questions, summarize your recommendations in a written marketing plan or type them into the Marketing Organization and Implementation sections of the *Marketing Plan Pro* software. To complete your marketing plan, write the Executive Summary of the plan's highlights.

Answer

Student answers will vary, depending on the choices and recommendations made earlier in the marketing planning process. A functional organization structure could help keep employees focused on their areas of expertise, which would be helpful in launching a new product. On the other hand, because Sonic is planning more than one new product later, a geographical, product-management, or market-management organization might be more effective. Sonic can create a more market-focused organization by top management emphasis on customer needs and satisfaction; rewarding employees for building relations with channel partners and customers; investing more heavily in marketing talent, programs, and planning systems; and shifting to a process/outcome focus.

Among the control measures Sonic should build into its marketing plan are: annual-plan controls such as sales analysis and market-share analysis; profitability controls measured by product, segment, trade channel, and so on; efficiency controls to improve productivity of the sales force, advertising, and other marketing elements; and strategic control through market audits and other methods that reveal whether is fully exploiting the best marketing opportunities and applying its marketing resources properly. To evaluate its ethics and social responsibility initiatives, Sonic can perform a regular, perhaps annual social audit of its performance in those areas.

Marketing Spotlight—Socially Conscious Marketers

Cause Related Marketing (CRM) can be defined as a strategic positioning and marketing tool which links a company or brand to a relevant social cause or issue, for mutual benefit. Companies can choose to partner with a charity or volunteer organization and donate money and resources, or they can work to remedy a problem directly. The cause benefits from the resources, money, and attention added by the company's involvement, and the company benefits from improved consumer perceptions and increased purchasing. According to Dominic Cadbury, the chairman of Cadbury Schweppes, "CRM is an effective way of enhancing corporate image, differentiating products, and increasing both sales and loyalty." For these reasons, cause related marketing is currently very much in vogue among corporations. Here we highlight three companies with long-standing commitments to CRM:

Avon—Breast Cancer Awareness Crusade

Avon's Breast Cancer Awareness Crusade, started in 1993, is a cause marketing campaign committed to funding care for victims of breast cancer and finding a cure. The company relies heavily on its direct sales force of more than 550,000 U.S. representatives, who forego sales commissions on Avon Crusade products. The net proceeds from sales of all Avon Crusades products, totaling more than $45 million since 1993, are donated to the cause. Other fundraising efforts include the Avon Breast Cancer 3-Days, which are three-day endurance walks held in nine major cities across the country, and through sales of other products like the collectible Breast Cancer Crusade Bear. Since they began in 1998, the three-day walks have raised a total of $63 million for the Crusade. Avon is the largest corporate sponsor of the breast cancer cause, with more than $110 million raised in the United States since the program was started. The money is donated to national cancer centers, medical centers, service organizations, and nonprofit health programs nationwide. Some of Avon's partner organizations include the YWCA, the National Alliance of Breast Cancer Organizations, and the National Cancer Institute.

British Airways—Change for Good

British Airways partnered with UNICEF and developed a cause marketing campaign called Change for Good. Travelers on British Airways flights are encouraged to donate leftover foreign currency from their travels. Because coins in particular are difficult to exchange at banks and currency exchanges, the program targets loose change. The scheme is simple: passengers deposit their surplus currency in envelopes provided by British Airways, which collects the deposits and donates them directly to UNICEF. British Airways advertises its program during an in-flight video, on the backs of seat cards, and with in-flight announcements. The company also developed a television advertisement that featured a child thanking British Airways for its contribution to UNICEF. Because Change for Good can be directly targeted to passengers and can produce immediate results, it does not require extensive advertising or promotion and therefore is one of the most cost-efficient cause marketing campaigns.

Tesco—Computers for Schools

British supermarket chain Tesco's Computers for Schools program, started in 1992, is the best-known cause related marketing campaign in the United Kingdom, with awareness levels near 50 percent. Customers receive vouchers from Tesco for every £10 spent, which they can donate to the school of their choosing. The chosen school exchanges the vouchers for new computer equipment. Parent/teacher associations and school governors joined to maximize voucher collection, which further enhances the community involvement in the program. To strengthen the connection between the Computers for Schools program and the Tesco brand, the company integrated the program into advertising for its in-store "Every little bit helps" campaign, which sought to enhance the customer experience with such improvements as wider aisles, baby changing facilities, and shorter checkout lines. Tesco capitalized on the link between its brand and the Computers for Schools program in 1998, when the company began selling computer hardware. Since the program began, Tesco Computers for Schools has delivered almost $90 million worth of computer equipment to schools in the United Kingdom.

Sources: www.avoncrusade.com; Hamish Pringle and Marjorie Thompson. *Brand Spirit.* John Wiley, New York: 1999; "The Prime Minister Launches the 10th Tesco Computers for Schools Scheme." *M2 Presswire,* January 26, 2001.

Questions

1. Do you believe that Cause Related Marketing (CRM) is a valid marketing management tool for the firms in this Spotlight? Why? Are there downside issues as well as upside benefits to CRM activities?

2. Would you assume that there is as much CRM in the United States as in Europe? What is the basis for your belief? What are your views?

Suggested Responses

1. CRM provides significant public relations and marketing as well as general business value to these companies, especially when the CRM activity presents a connection to the business of the firm. For the firms here (Avon, BA and Tesco), it is clear that each has gained considerable corporate, product and brand image awareness, and overall business

value. For Avon, because the majority of its sales force and customers are women, the campaign is logical. For British Airways, in the travel business, it also makes good sense. For Tesco, the connection may be a bit more complicated, but when you look at the community connection Tesco stores have, computers for kids make a great deal of sense.

Despite the well-known advantages, there are downside considerations when a firm that participates in these activities subsequently is found to be involved in a questionable operational activity. An example of this would be Nike; despite the firm's activities related to environmental responsibility, the exploitation of labor, child and adult, in plants that manufactured Nike shoes in developing countries, created a substantial backlash.

2.   Firms in Europe generally have been more involved in such programs because there is a substantial degree of social consciousness in Europe, with high expectations for social responsibility placed on European firms. Whether this is due to Europe's longer and varied history or because of the continuing focus on community is debatable, but what is not debatable is the fact that European nations generally expect and demand more of their companies in their interactions with society. Accordingly, European firms tend to be more committed to CRM due to genuine concerns for their society as much as a marketing activity.

Note: For background information on this latter point, note the text chapter on international marketing and suggested lecture 2 for the retailing chapter.